The SundayTribune

Guide to Politics
2003

Published by Tribune Publications Ltd
15 Lower Baggot Street, Dublin 2

© November 2002

Designed and produced by Gerard Siggins

Cover design by Belknap&Co
Cover photographs by Photocall Ireland!

Printed by Colour Books Ltd

ISBN 0 - 9526035 - 6 - X

THE SUNDAY TRIBUNE

GUIDE

TO POLITICS

2003

EDITED BY MICHAEL MARSH

The**Sunday Tribune**

CONTENTS

*All photographs in The Sunday Tribune Guide
to Politics were taken by Photocall Ireland!
except where stated*

Jim Farrelly
Managing Director
The Sunday Tribune

THE last few years have been a defining time for politics and politicians on this island. While the Celtic Tiger roared, the people demanded accountability, transparency and, above all, performance from their politicians on both parts of the island. Intolerance of humbug, secrecy, disingenuity, red tape and unacceptable practices by our political leaders grew exponentially as more and more citizens began to flourish financially and see that their dreams could be fulfilled. And the citizenry itself had to grow up and answer fundamental questions about the kind of island it desired, the kind of leaders it wanted, the kind of institutions it expected and the way it wanted the State managed socially and monetarily. Above all it had to twice address the question: to be European or xenophobic. And it had to confront new phenomena like globalisation, privatisation, the eco agenda and the once unthinkable proposition: immigration as opposed to emigration.... and immigration involving non-Irish ethnic groupings into the bargain.

During this fast-forward maturation of the Irish political psyche, *The Sunday Tribune* has been a vital touchstone. It has served up, and continues to serve up an indispensable diet of penetrating investigations, reports, comment, analysis and opinion on a rapidly moving political landscape. Thus the paper has built up a huge following for its political and public affairs coverage each Sunday in the marketplace.

And it is to service this loyal, literate, and hungry constituency of *Sunday Tribune* readers we are publishing this, the second in *The Sunday Tribune's Guide to Politics* series. It brings together the unrivalled expertise of *The Sunday Tribune's* own journalists with that of top-flight academics to give you the story of the elections of 2002, to assess the political process and to reflect on the significance of the changes which the voting has brought about.

Our electoral process, which is rich in personalities and in the detail of the voting record, is one that has always attracted enormous interest. The ordinary voter, the political activist and the dedicated researcher all value the details of the constituency-by-constituency, count-by-count record which is provided here in sufficient detail to satisfy the most dedicated of political 'anoraks'.

This *Guide*, however, goes beyond the details of the vote to reflect much more widely on the political environment in which that vote took place. In significant reviews of the Economy and the Tribunals, Matt Cooper and Michael Clifford provide a broader perspective on politics before and after the election.

Michael Marsh and Michael Laver examine the election itself. Michael Marsh examines the background to the election, and explores the mechanics of some of the most important results: in particular, how did Fine Gael lose so many seats and how did Fianna Fáil do so well with such a rel-

atively small vote? Michael Laver looks at some evidence on what sort of people voted for the different parties and suggests there are signs of a trend that could have considerable significance for Irish politics in the 21st Century. Stephen Collins takes up the story of the only two parties who had a bad election, Fine Gael and Labour, both of whom subsequently changed their leaders. Why did they fail to convince the voters that they had more to offer than the Fianna Fáil-PD coalition, or the alternative opposition of Greens, Sinn Féin and independents? Joe Lee, *Tribune* columnist as well as an outstanding historian, then looks at the leader for whom the election was a triumph, Bertie Ahern. What is his secret and where does he fit into the pantheon of Fianna Fáil's leaders?

A major item on the agenda of the new government has been the unfinished business of the Nice Treaty, which was put before the people again last month. Michael Marsh looks at the voting figures and explains which part of the word 'no' the government did not understand and why the voters, when asked again, said 'yes'. Brigid Laffan provides the viewpoint of both an academic and an activist on the process and considers what lies ahead.

Shane Coleman provides a comprehensive review of the past five years that tells us exactly when and in what order the major political milestones in the life of the last government appeared.

Finally, at the heart of the book, are profiles and details about the elected representatives on this island: their record, their interests, their personal details and, in particular, how they can be contacted.

On behalf of *The Sunday Tribune* I must thank Professor Michael Marsh of Trinity College for bringing all this together. I have worked personally with Michael before. I have always marvelled at his understated brilliance, wisdom and profundity. I was delighted that he was willing to join us in this enterprise.

Both Michael and his team of researchers, Kathryn Marsh and Bríd Ingoldsby, have done a wonderful job in assembling all the material so quickly and so completely. Finally, I must thank Gerard Siggins, *The Sunday Tribune's* Assistant Editor, who put the whole thing together and who turned the thousands of computer files into an attractive book.

Jim Farrelly
Managing Director,
The Sunday Tribune.
November 2002.

After the landslide, it all went horribly wrong for Bertie

Just a few short months ago the Taoiseach was in heaven, and an overall majority looked on the cards.
Matt Cooper analyses where it all went wrong

FOR A few hours last May it seemed that Bertie Ahern was on the verge of the most remarkable achievement in modern Irish political history, a return to power with an overall majority. His Fianna Fáil/Progressive Democrats government had entered the 2002 general election campaign in confident mood, encouraged by the opinion polls and the failure of the opposition to launch sustained attacks or outline a credible alternative. Fianna Fáil was almost returned to power on its own but at the end of the count it fell just two seats short, mainly due to the extraordinary achievements of independents, many of whom came from the FF 'gene pool'. It was still success.

Once whatever disappointment was felt had passed there were those who argued that Ahern had got lucky again. Some considered it was better for Ahern that he was compelled to share office with the PDs. As Jack Lynch found to his cost, having a big overall majority only ferments dissent among those on the backbenches for whom there is no room at the top. Having the PDs on board also meant that blame could be shared if anything went wrong.

Nobody expected things to go wrong as quickly as they did. Within months Ahern's position was so badly damaged that there is now widespread speculation that he will not be able to lead Fianna Fáil into the next election. Many expect him to step down prior to that date, if he is not forced out, leaving Brian Cowen in position to succeed. Micheál Martin may have other ideas of course and Cowen may have reason to fear the public embrace he has received from Ahern in recent months. Cowen was the man who brought in the Nice Treaty referendum result for Ahern and having overcome that hurdle Ahern immediately announced that he and Cowen would be making the North their priority in the months running up to Christmas. Any more of this and Cowen will be seen by the public, perhaps damningly, as Ahern's most important ally.

There is little doubt that Ahern's position has suddenly and unexpectedly weakened in other areas too. The economy turned long before the election – 15 months before in fact – but the full impact has only been felt since. *The Sunday Tribune* revealed some of the health cuts that were pending just before the election although this was largely unnoticed by the electorate, despite the efforts of the opposition. A range of controversial cuts in other areas, mainly focused on the weak and disadvantaged who did not have a strong enough voice to complain, raised some controversy. These were not cuts, of course, they were readjustments of spending that had been planned for the rest of the year but which now would not take place. The axing of funding for the National Stadium, Ahern's one expensive piece of vision was the only real cut conceded.

Such spinning would not hold its credibility for long. The revelation in *The Sunday Tribune*

Mary Harney and Bertie Ahern at Government Buildings where they launched details of their new programme for government

PHOTOCALL IRELAND

sideshow, something that did not capture the imagination of the public and most certainly would not influence their voting intentions. But the language of Mr Justice Flood, who called corruption when he saw it, was riveting. Chief among his targets was Ray Burke and suddenly Ahern's decision to appoint Burke to cabinet five years previously – when a cloud of suspicion hovered over him – became a major liability.

It was not enough to bring Ahern down immediately – and nobody realistically expected that it would be – but he has reason to fear forthcoming sessions of the Flood tribunal. There will be public probing of the political (and associated) fund-raising actions of his close friend Des Richardson when Ahern was in charge of party finances. The Taoiseach's hope may be that this will not happen soon.

Even so, 'ordinary' political considerations could do for him. Surprisingly, for a former chief whip so steeped in the modern history of Fianna Fáil, Ahern is in danger of alienating his grass roots, particularly by his almost total reliance on unelected officials for advice, to the chagrin of elected deputies. Having held out the promise of promotion to the parliamentary party his cabinet choices were, in the main, highly conservative and his handling of the junior ministries created unnecessary resentment too.

Already, TDs are worried about their seats and the flak they are getting for cutbacks has led to stern criticism of Ahern and McCreevy at parliamentary party meetings. They know that things are going to worse before they get better. The government will still be looking to curtail public services even after a return to borrowing next year. A new national pay deal will be extraordinarily difficult to achieve. The cost of benchmarking for the public service – at over 1.1bn each year – would necessitate a 3% rise in the top rate of income tax according to the ESRI, and that in turn would result in private sector job losses. It may not have mattered in the run-up to the election but from here on "it's the economy stupid" with corruption from the tribunals adding volatility to the political mix.

The local and European elections, before the mid-point of the life of this Dáil, will be telling for Ahern. If the party suffers heavy losses his TDs may think that only a change in leadership – along with the windfall from the SSIAs that are due to mature in 2006 and 2007 – will be enough to save them, especially if Fine Gael and Labour both show signs of getting their act together under new leadership. Even if they don't Sinn Féin may continue its rise, although that depends on improvements in the situation in the North, and the Greens may also prosper, as long as they don't become too associated with the Shinners in the minds of middle class potential voters. Whatever happens, it's all far from those hours when an overall majority seemed likely.

in September of a confidential government memorandum outlining a series of further savage cuts in the "existing level of service" for 2002 – amounting to 900m – as preparation for further major cutbacks focused attention on the actions of finance minister Charlie McCreevy prior to the election. It was not possible that the detailed cuts outlined by the minister in the memo for the first cabinet meeting of the new government could have been drawn up in the short period of time since the election. It was clear that McCreevy knew the full extent of the problems from the start of the year and had been unable to prevent his government colleagues overspending at a time when tax revenues were well below expectations.

But the real blow came with the publication of the second interim report of the Flood tribunal. Many politicians had, wrongly, come to see the tribunals as nothing more than an irritating

For a former chief whip, Ahern is in danger of alienating his grass roots, particularly by his almost total reliance on unelected officials for advice, to the chagrin of elected deputies

Michael Noonan and Bertie Ahern chat with RTE presenter Miriam O'Callaghan before their live debate on PrimeTime   PHOTOCALL IRELAND

Ahern leads FF to victory from the front

A presidential-style campaign by Bertie Ahern, allied to misplaced optimism about the economy meant it was the main opposition parties that were rejected by the voters as FF came within a whisker of an overall majority in the first election since 1973 that didn't change the government.
Michael Marsh analyses General Election 2002

THE general election of 2002 was a long time coming. When Fianna Fáil and the PDs agreed to form a government in 1997 with the support of four independents, few commentators expected that it would last the full term. Either the independents would break ranks, or the PDs would make a demand that could not be met. Fianna Fáil's record as a coalition partner was not good; the first coalition with the PDs lasted only two years and the Fianna Fáil-Labour coalition did little better. The independents too seemed a motley crew. Add to that the fall out from the McCracken Inquiry into links between Ben Dunne and the former Fianna Fáil Taoiseach, Charles Haughey, and it appeared that the coalition would be subjected to stresses that it would not be tough enough to endure.

Certainly there were strains, starting with Ray Burke, who eventually resigned both his position as Minister for Foreign Affairs and his seat in the Dáil only a few months into the life of the government. This followed revelations concerning large donations given to Burke by businessmen. Many other current and past members of Fianna Fáil also found their names linked with real or alleged misdeeds as the various investigative committees and tribunals of inquiry steadily uncovered what appeared to be evidence of widespread corruption, and several members of the Fianna Fáil parliamentary party were forced to resign the whip. (Michael Clifford details this sad record in greater detail on Page 225.)

There were other problems, most notably the O'Flaherty affair, concerning the appointment of a former judge to a plum European job only months after he had been forced to step down from the High Court when news broke that he had behaved improperly when investigating, on behalf of a friend, the progress of a criminal case.

But there were also triumphs. The signing of the Belfast Agreement on Good Friday 1999 was the highlight, but the continued health of the economy was even more important. Growth was rapid, unemployment fell to unheard of levels and taxes were cut in accordance with the promises made by the government parties during the 1997 election. This all helped to maintain the government. In particular, it made it much easier to keep the independents onside. Given the sort of access to government that Fianna Fáil backbenchers could only envy, the 'gang of four' were able to see all sort of pet projects implemented, and were informed enough to be able to claim the credit for whatever goodies were being handed out to their constituents. Although they had to wait until 2002 for it, they even got a referendum that sought yet again to roll back the judgement of the Supreme Court in the 'X' case.

THE NEW DÁIL

The new Dáil looks very different to the old one in some respects. There was a turnover of 31%, a relatively high figure: 47 deputies arrived for the first time ever, while a further five renewed old acquaintance. But the TDs themselves look rather like those of the 28th Dáil. The overwhelming majority are male, they are middle aged, and most come from a middle class background. There are only 22 women, a figure that has not changed significantly since 1992. Only 25 TDs are under 40, and six under 30. Only 13 are over 60. Most TDs now describe themselves as 'professional politicians'. And the vast majority of new TDs now have university degrees.

Of course there was a downside to the government's record. While growth was substantial, the fruits of that growth were not distributed equally. Personal income inequalities had grown, and perceptions of inequalities between different regions were significant. It was also clear that the public services were falling well short of what might be expected in a now rich First World country. The health services, with long waiting lists for those not in private schemes, and moves towards the centralisation of many facilities, provoked much anger. Inadequate transport infrastructures and woeful public transport services also seemed out of place now Ireland was an economic star. Hence John Bruton's ill-fated 'Celtic snail' campaign in 2000 in preparation for a 2001 election, which was intended to highlight how the government had mismanaged the boom. The mirth this campaign provoked was one of factors that led to Bruton's downfall, as Stephen Collins' contribution to this book explains on Page 216.

Going in to the election the government was in good shape. Polls in March indicated that satisfaction with the government was extremely high, showing a surplus of 24% of those satisfied over those dissatisfied. The Taoiseach was even more popular, and the Tánaiste more popular than any opposition politician. Fianna Fáil was also riding high in the polls, IMS putting the party at around 50% in all its recent polls (although MRBI's new adjusted estimate for the Fianna Fáil vote was much lower, at around 41-42%). Moreover, the main pillars of any alternative government were shaky. Fine Gael's vote had been in the low 20s at best for some time. Michael Noonan's popularity was lower even than that of his predecessor, John Bruton, who had been replaced because he was seen to be unpopular with the electorate. Labour had amalgamated with Democratic Left to create a stronger left, but the whole was less than the sum of its parts and its support was little more than 10% in recent polls. Moreover Labour had opted out of Fine Gael's proposed 'Rainbow Coalition' alternative, which would have included Fine Gael, Labour and the Greens, keeping all of its options open in the event of the PDs proving inadequate to the task of sustaining a Fianna Fáil administration – even if Fine Gael was the Labour Party's preferred option.

Fianna Fáil dominated the campaign. The party accepted the fact that there were problems in areas like the health services and transport but nonetheless claimed that its record was a good one. It took responsibility for the strong economy over the last few years and promised to continue its work to improve the public services: "A lot done. More to do" was the slogan. Then the leader was sent on a tour of the country, pressing flesh rather than speaking to reporters, while the Fianna Fáil media centre coordinated a high-

Attorney General Michael McDowell bins a copy of *Magill* magazine with party leader Mary Harney looking on during a PD conference on waste management   PHOTOCALL

was 'All over – bar the voting'. The only question to be answered was who, if anyone, would form the next government with Fianna Fáil? 'One-Party Government? NO Thanks' said the PD's Michael McDowell, and energised his party's campaign, warning of the dangers of one-party rule and, in typically colourful language, attacking the integrity of the very people his party had been in government with since 1997. Even so, from a near impossibility before the campaign started, a one-party government became the strongest probability with the bookies as poll followed poll and Fianna Fáil's vote showed no signs of falling.

The introduction of electronic voting machines in three constituencies ensured that some results would be known, if not before midnight on election day, at least soon after, providing a hint as to the possible outcome many hours before the usual harbinger, the 'early tallies'. When the results for Meath, Dublin North and Dublin West were declared the possibility of an overall majority remained open: Fianna Fáil's vote was up, but not hugely. One thing was certain, however: the count would be a long, bad day for Fine Gael and so it turned out. If this was to be the last of the hand counted elections, 2002 gave us much to remember with several counts going on past the weekend and the final result in Cork North Central and Wicklow delayed for several days.

Fianna Fáil eventually finished just short of an overall majority, but Fine Gael collapsed to its worst seat total for half a century and Labour stood still while Greens, Sinn Féin and independents, as well as the PDs, all saw their stock rise handsomely. The government was reconstructed, this time with an overall majority, ending a run of government-changing elections dating back to 1973. As Charlie McCreevy pointed out, it was an election in which the opposition was voted out of office. Fine Gael and Labour between them held 75 seats going into the election, but emerged with only 52.

Fianna Fáil won 41.5% of the vote and 81 seats. This was an increase of only just over 2% on 1997 but it brought rich rewards. The vote was actually up in 28 of the 41 constituencies (Dublin Mid West is a new one) and was down in 13. More votes sometimes won more seats, as in Donegal South West and Limerick West, but the party also won where its vote did not increase to any significant extent, as in Cork South West. The last three elections have given the party its three lowest votes since 1932 and this probably indicates that the days of Fianna Fáil winning the 45% plus it has averaged since the foundation of the State are now over. However, the fact that it is able to come so close to an overall majority with such a relatively small vote indicates that the judgement of those who decided that the party could never again win an overall majority was

ly professional operation, modelled on New Labour's in the UK, which provided space-filling food for the ever greedy media and 'pre-butted' adverse messages. Fine Gael and Labour chose to contest the election on Fianna Fáil's ground, highlighting what needed to be done but doing little to refute Fianna Fáil's claims to effective economic management. Most voters saw Fianna Fáil as simply more capable. Fine Gael also made the mistake of promising something to everyone, a tactic that may have worked for Fianna Fáil in the past but sat uneasily with Fine Gael's reputation for honesty and financial probity and probably served to weaken the party's already strained credibility with voters.

The initial polls then removed whatever relevance Fine Gael might have had for the outcome, all of them putting Fianna Fáil at least in touching distance of an overall majority, and IMS in particular giving grounds for thinking, in the words of the *Irish Independent*'s headline, that it

> **It was an election in which the opposition was voted out of office. Fine Gael and Labour between them held 76 seats going in to the election, but emerged with only 52**

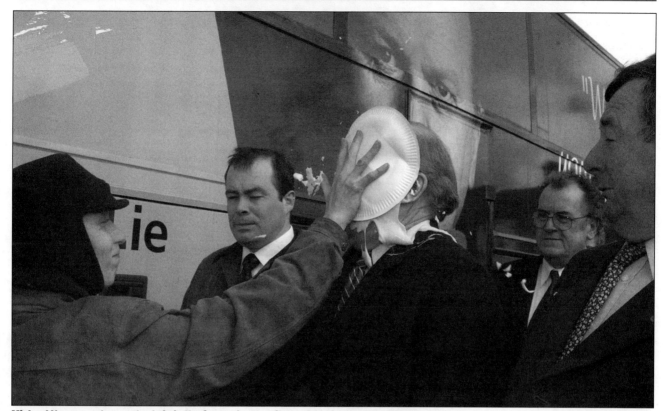

Michael Noonan gets a custard pie in the face, minutes after arriving in Boyle, Co Roscommon   JAMES CONNOLLY / PICSELL8

premature. The party won 81 seats in February 1982 and did the same again in 1987, although with a significantly larger vote. 44% this time would have given the party a landslide win.

Fine Gael dropped 5% of the vote, which if not quite the electoral 'meltdown' implied in some polls, was a disaster in terms of seats. The party lost 23 seats, falling to only 31. It was the Fine Gael's worst performance since 1948 by any measure, and this time there was not the compensation of winning office. Still, in ten constituencies the party's vote did go up, if only marginally in most cases. Mostly it was down, in 22 constituencies by more than 5%. It was there that the seats tended to be lost: Carlow-Kilkenny, Cavan-Monaghan, Cork North Central, Cork South West, Cork South Central, Dublin South East, Dublin South, Dublin North, Dun Laoghaire, Kildare South, Longford-Roscommon, Laois-Offaly, Mayo, Sligo-Leitrim, and Wexford. Only in Meath, Dublin North Central and Dublin South Central (which had become a five-seater) did the party hang on. Other losses were sustained in marginal seats, such as Galway East, and where re-organisation made things difficult, such as Dublin South West, even when losses were small. Nowhere did its vote go up

enough to win a seat, although it came close in Tipperary North. Ironically the party's best performance was in Limerick West, where it rose by more than 4% but a seat was lost to Fianna Fáil whose vote was up by 21%! The collapse was particularly marked in Dublin. Its highest vote share there was the 20% in Dublin South; outside Dublin it topped 40% in only two constituencies and 30% in three others. Labour is now the second largest party in terms of votes in Dublin; when it comes to seats Fine Gael lags behind all of the other parties apart from Sinn Féin.

Labour's result was a deeply disappointing one. It hoped the merger with Democratic Left would provide the basis for a move back to the heights of the 30+ seats won in 1992 but its campaign never took off and the eventual total of 21 seats was no better than that won by Labour and Democratic Left separately in 1997. Overall, its vote was down 2% on the combined total of Labour and DL in 1997. While it was up in 13 constituencies, it was up by 5% or more in only one and it fell by more than 5% in eight. Moreover, its extra seats all came at the expense of Fine Gael, its most likely coalition partner, while it lost some of its own seats to Sinn Féin and left-wing independents.

Labour hoped the merger with Democratic Left would provide the basis for a move back to the heights of the 30+ seats won in 1992 but its campaign never took off

The PDs had a triumphant election that brought the party double the number of seats held at dissolution. All the gains came from Fine Gael. A concentrated campaign, that saw the party focussing on seats rather than votes, helped to do the trick. The party ran only 20 candidates in 18 constituencies, compared to 26 in 26 last time so the fact that its vote was down by 0.6% may be discounted. Where it had no TD but won significantly more votes it picked up a seat (apart from in Kildare North) and where it held a seat the vote stayed firm, or rose. Only in Limerick East did it fall, and there the seat was retained anyway.

For the Greens and Sinn Féin this was the election in which they each crossed a threshold, if not to formal parliamentary group status (which requires eight deputies) then at least to a state where a meeting of their parliamentary party is not a joke. The Green Party increased its vote from 2.6% to 3.8%, fielding five more candidates than in 1997, and gained four seats, all at the expense of Fine Gael. In only nine constituencies did its vote fall; in 25 it rose, by between 1% and 5%. But only in three constituencies did the party top 10% (the PDs did so in eight) so its hold on this new status is precarious, and its chance of significant increase would require a lot more votes.

Sinn Féin appear stronger than the Greens in most respects, despite winning one seat fewer. Up to 6.5% from only 2.4%, its vote rose everywhere but Cavan-Monaghan, and exceeded 10% in ten constituencies. It ran 37 candidates as against 15 in 1997, a tactic that boosted the overall vote and increased the spending allowed to the party nationally. Its gains generally came from Labour, not from Fianna Fáil as has been the traditional expectation.

Independent and minor party candidates also proved more popular this time, winning a few more votes (10.9%: + 0.6%) and seven more seats, all but one of them from Fine Gael. This group of independents is the largest since 1951. The substitution of signatures for a deposit did not lead to a plethora of candidates this time: there were only 138, which was 21 less than in 1997. Their share of the vote rose in 21 constituencies and fell in 20 so there was no clear national trend. It shows perhaps that the electorate almost everywhere is receptive where there is a good candidate. They were very diverse of course. Several independents were disaffected Fianna Fáil members who had been denied a nomination at some point. Jackie Healy-Rae in Kerry South is the best-known example but in Galway East, Clare, and Cork South West there were others, some successful, other not. There are also independent left candidates such as Tony Gregory and Finian McGrath in Dublin. Discontent with the health services underlay some of these campaigns, and formed the major plank in the campaigns of others such as Dr Jerry Cowley (Mayo) and Dr Liam Twomey (Wexford) with no previous party pedigree. The ability of independents to win concessions from the outgoing government obviously made a vote for such a candidate a more credible option in 2002, particularly given the absence of any alternative to a Fianna Fáil led government. It will be interesting to see whether this changes before the next election.

Many observers were taken aback by the extent of seat changes. They were amazed that Fianna Fáil could come so close to an overall majority with such a relatively small share of the vote, that Fine Gael could lose so many seats with just a 5% drop in its vote, and that independents could do so much better with virtually the same vote as in 1997. Fianna Fáil's 'bonus' of 12 seats equalled its haul in 1997 and exceeded the nine seats in won in 1969 and 1977; Fine Gael's shortfall of six was its worst ever.

Two features of our PR–STV electoral system make this possible: the small size of the multi-member constituencies means the strict proportional allocation of seat shares to first preference votes is problematic, and the importance of second, third and minor preferences mean that, to some degree, the comparison of seats with first preference votes is inappropriate. Even so, these features are not new but they do make possible the sort of results we have seen in 2002.

Fine Gael lost so many seats because the margin by which it had won many seats in 1997 was so small. It won seats last time with a lot less than a full quota in a particular constituency. The fall in votes, which was generally more than 5% where seats were lost, dropped the party well below the quota. Transfers also explain differences between seats won and first preferences obtained. Obviously a party that does well out of lower preferences effectively tops up its first preference votes and wins more seats. The Greens did much better in terms of later votes than Sinn Féin, which is how Greens were able to win more seats with fewer first preference votes. Independents also did very well out of transfer votes in some places but the persistent

	votes	vote %	candidates	seats	seat %	vote/seat difference
FF	770,748	41.5	106	81	48.8	7.3
FG	417,619	22.5	85	31	18.7	−3.8
Labour	200,130	10.8	46	21	12.7	1.9
PDs	73,628	4.0	20	8	4.8	0.8
Green	71,470	3.8	31	6	3.6	−0.2
SF	121,020	6.5	37	5	3.0	−3.5
Others	203,287	10.9	138	14	8.4	−2.5
TOTAL	1,857,902	100	463	166	100	0

Many observers were taken aback by the extent of seat changes. They were amazed that Fianna Fáil could come so close to an overall majority with such a relatively small share of the vote

shortfall in seats for such candidates is because independents do not transfer consistently to one another. Transfers also explain some of the Fianna Fáil seat bonus. In the past the party obtained very few transfers from other parties. Now it has decided to look for lower preferences it reaps the benefit that we would expect to accrue to a large party simply because it has the candidates in the frame to get transfers. Add to that the weakness of the Fine Gael-Labour link in 2002 and there is nothing at all surprising in Fianna Fáil's seat return. Over 50% of terminal transfers from Fine Gael and Labour went to one another; in 2002 it was only a little over 30%. Previous failures by Fine Gael to win 'bonus' seats typically also coincided with weak transfers from Labour, and in was in those years that Fianna Fáil's bonus was greatest. Many years ago Fianna Fáil (and Fine Gael) were able to keep the vast majority of their vote within the family. Intra-party transfer rates have now declined, with less than two-thirds of votes staying within the fold when that is possible. But the effectiveness of Fianna Fáil in picking up votes from elsewhere more than makes up for that.

But what accounts for the voters' choices in 2002? Elections are decided by a number of factors: long-term predisposition of people to vote for a particular party, the appeal of individual politicians, both leaders and candidates, and the issues of the day. The basic stability of Irish politics – most votes are won by Fianna Fáil, Fine Gael and Labour, and in that order, stems from long-term predispositions. Leaders and candidates change – and small parties in particular may owe much to the quality of local candidates – but the main things which change from election to election are the issues of the day: what concerns voters, and how the government has performed. On this count, the incumbent government did well. Economic growth undoubtedly produced a feel-good factor that concerns about public services could not dispel. This is clear in the RTE/Lansdowne exit poll (discussed at length by Michael Laver in his contribution on Page 235). This reported a clear majority of voters as saying their standard of living and quality of life had got better since 1997. There were complaints, but voters did not have much confidence that the established opposition parties would address those complaints. Health was said by most voters to be an important issue, but neither Fine Gael nor Labour could convince the electorate that they could do better than Fianna Fáil. Only selected independents were able to do that, tapping effectively into local discontent with the availability of services. The failure of Fine Gael and Labour to do so is less easily explained but the polls suggest that this lack of confidence is of long standing and not simply a failure of the election campaign. This lack of credibility opens a gap, and the independents, Greens and Sinn

A voter casts her electronic vote in the polling station in St Cronan's Primary School, Brackenstown, Co Dublin

PHOTOCALL IRELAND

Féin moved into the space. The fact that the election seemed 'all over – bar the voting' helped the smaller parties by removing the major government alternative from the equation. As in a European Parliament election voters could perhaps express themselves rather than concern themselves with who would govern.

The new Dáil promises some interesting politics over the next few years with competition within the opposition as fierce as that between the opposition and the government. The declining economy and the tribunals (revitalised by Flood's preliminary report) promise rich pickings for opposition scavengers. However, since 1989, when Fianna Fáil abandoned its so-called 'core value' of rejecting coalition, that party has been well placed to cope with whatever any opponents might throw at it. Barring a massive increase in the strength of Fine Gael it remains hard to see any alternative to a Fianna Fáil led coalition, and barring a similar improvement in Labour's fortunes it is also hard to see how a government led by even a resurgent Fine Gael could form. Like Italy's Christian Democrats for so many years, and Sweden's Social Democrats, Fianna Fáil's strength, allied to its centrist position and a fragmented opposition, make it indispensable. Of course the graveyards of politics are full of those who were indispensable, as the Italian Christian Democrats found out when the party system was completely reformed in the wake of scandals that make our own look like children's mischief. Barring such a catastrophe, however, the outlook is good for our largest party.

The new Dáil promises some interesting politics over the next few years... The declining economy and the tribunals promise rich pickings for opposition scavengers

MINISTERS

TAOISEACH
Bertie Ahern

TÁNAISTE AND MINISTER FOR ENTERPRISE, TRADE AND EMPLOYMENT
Mary Harney

MINISTER FOR DEFENCE
Michael Smith

MINISTER FOR AGRICULTURE AND FOOD
Joe Walsh

MINISTER FOR FINANCE
Charlie McCreevy

MINISTER FOR FOREIGN AFFAIRS
Brian Cowen

MINISTER FOR EDUCATION AND SCIENCE
Noel Dempsey

MINISTER FOR COMMUNICATIONS, MARINE AND NATURAL RESOURCES
Dermot Ahern

MINISTER FOR ARTS, SPORT AND TOURISM
John O'Donoghue

MINISTER FOR HEALTH AND CHILDREN
Micheál Martin

MINISTER FOR TRANSPORT
Séamus Brennan

MINISTER FOR JUSTICE, EQUALITY AND LAW REFORM
Michael McDowell

MINISTER FOR THE ENVIRONMENT AND LOCAL GOVERNMENT
Martin Cullen

MINISTER FOR COMMUNITY, RURAL AND GAELTACHT AFFAIRS
Éamon Ó Cuív

MINISTER FOR SOCIAL AND FAMILY AFFAIRS
Mary Coughlan

MINISTERS OF STATE

Mary Hanafin
Minister of State at the Department of the Taoiseach with special responsibility as Government Chief Whip, and for the Information Society, and at the Department of Defence

Dick Roche
Minister of State at the Department of the Taoiseach and at the Department of Foreign Affairs with responsibility for European Affairs

Síle de Valera
Minister of State at the Department of Education & Science with special responsibility for adult education, youth affairs and educational disadvantage

James McDaid
Minister of State at the Department of Transport with special responsibility for road traffic including road haulage

Frank Fahey
Minister of State at the Department of Enterprise, Trade and Employment with special responsibility for labour affairs including training

Noel Treacy
Minister of State at the Department of Agriculture and Food with special responsibility for food and horticulture

Willie O'Dea
Minister of State at the Department of Justice, Equality & Law Reform with special responsibility for equality issues including disability Issues

Tom Kitt
Minister of State at the Department of Foreign Affairs with special responsibility for overseas development and human rights

Pat the Cope Gallagher
Minister of State at the Department of the Environment and Local Government

Liam Aylward
Minister of State at the Department of Agriculture and Food, with special responsibility for animal health and welfare and customer service

John Browne
Minister of State at the Department of Communications, Marine & Natural Resources

The new cabinet lines up after receiving their seals of office from President McAleese: (BACK ROW) Mary Hanafin, Eamon Ó Cuív, Michael McDowell, Martin Cullen, Séamus Brennan, Noel Dempsey, Dermot Ahern, John O'Donoghue, Mícheál Martin, Mary Coughlan, Joe Walsh, (FRONT ROW) Charlie McCreevy, Michael Smith, Bertie Ahern, Mary McAleese, Mary Harney, Dick Roche and Brian Cowen

Michael Ahern
Minister of State at the Department of Enterprise, Trade and Employment, with special responsibility for trade and commerce

Ivor Callely
Minister of State at the Department of Health & Children, with special responsibility for services for older people

Noel Ahern
Minister of State at the Department of the Environment and Local Government, with special responsibility for housing and urban renewal, and at the Department of Community, Rural and Gaeltacht Affairs, with special responsibility for drugs strategy and community affairs

Brian Lenihan
Minister of State at the Department of Health & Children, at the Department of Justice, Equality & Law Reform and at the Department of Education & Science, with special responsibility for children

Tim O'Malley
Minister of State at the Department of Health & Children, with special responsibility for disability and mental health services and food safety

Tom Parlon
Minister of State at the Department of Finance, with special responsibility for the Office of Public Works

ATTORNEY GENERAL
Rory Brady SC

The Taoiseach and ministers were appointed on 6 June 2002. Ministers of State appointed on 6 June and 19 June.

AHERN, BERTIE - FF
Dublin Central

AHERN, DERMOT - FF
Louth

AHERN, MICHAEL - FF
Cork East

AHERN, NOEL - FF
Dublin North West

ALLEN, BERNARD - FG
Cork North Central

ANDREWS, BARRY - FF
Dun Laoghaire

ARDAGH, SEÁN - FF
Dublin South Central

AYLWARD, LIAM - FF
Carlow-Kilkenny

BLANEY, NIALL - IND FF
Donegal North East

BOYLE, DAN - GP
Cork South Central

BRADY, JOHNNY - FF
Meath

BRADY, MARTIN - FF
Dublin North East

BREEN, JAMES - IND
Clare

BREEN, PAT - FG
Clare

BRENNAN, SÉAMUS - FF
Dublin South

BROUGHAN, TOMMY - LAB
Dublin North East

BROWNE, JOHN - FF
Carlow-Kilkenny

BRUTON, JOHN - FG
Meath

BRUTON, RICHARD - FG
Dublin North Central

BURTON, JOAN - LAB
Dublin West

CALLANAN, JOE - FF
Galway East

CALLELY, IVOR - FF
Dublin North Central

CAREY, PAT - FF
Dublin North West

CARTY, JOHN - FF
Mayo

CASSIDY, DONIE - FF
Westmeath

COLLINS, MICHAEL - FF
Limerick West

CONNAUGHTON, PAUL - FG
Galway East

CONNOLLY, PAUDGE - IND
Cavan-Monaghan

COOPER-FLYNN, BEVERLEY - FF
Mayo

COSTELLO, JOE - LAB
Dublin Central

COUGHLAN, MARY - FF
Donegal South West

COVENEY, SIMON - FG
Cork South Central

COWEN, BRIAN - FF
Laois-Offaly

COWLEY, JERRY - IND
Mayo

CRAWFORD, SEYMOUR - FG
Cavan-Monaghan

CREGAN, JOHN - FF
Limerick West

CROWE, SEÁN - SF
Dublin South West

CUFFE, CIARÁN - GP
Dun Laoghaire

CULLEN, MARTIN - FF
Waterford

CURRAN, JOHN - FF
Dublin Mid-West

DAVERN, NOEL - FF
Tipperary South

DE VALERA, SÍLE - FF
Clare

DEASY, JOHN - FG
Waterford

DEENIHAN, JIMMY - FG
Kerry North

DEMPSEY, NOEL - FF
Meath

DEMPSEY, TONY - FF
Wexford

DENNEHY, JOHN - FF
Cork South Central

DEVINS, JIMMY - FF
Sligo-Leitrim

DURKAN, BERNARD - FG
Kildare North

ELLIS, JOHN - FF
Sligo-Leitrim

ENGLISH, DAMIEN - FG
Meath

ENRIGHT, OLWYN - FG
Laois-Offaly

FAHEY, FRANK - FF
Galway West

FERRIS, MARTIN - SF
Kerry North

FINNERAN, MICHAEL - FF
Longford-Roscommon

FITZPATRICK, DERMOT - FF
Dublin Central

FLEMING, SEÁN - FF
Laois-Offaly

FOX, MILDRED - IND
Wicklow

GALLAGHER, PAT THE COPE - FF
Donegal South West

GILMORE, EAMON - LAB
Dun Laoghaire

GLENNON, JIM - FF
Dublin North

GOGARTY, PAUL - GP
Dublin Mid-West

GORMLEY, JOHN - GP
Dublin South East

GREALISH, NOEL - PD
Galway West

GREGORY, TONY - IND
Dublin Central

HANAFIN, MARY - FF
Dun Laoghaire

HARKIN, MARIAN - IND
Sligo-Leitrim

HARNEY, MARY - PD
Dublin Mid-West

HAUGHEY, SEÁN - FF
Dublin North Central

HAYES, TOM - FG
Tipperary South

HEALY, SÉAMUS - IND
Tipperary South

HEALY-RAE, JACKIE - IND
Kerry South

HIGGINS, JOE - SOC
Dublin West

HIGGINS, MICHAEL D - LAB
Galway West

HOCTOR, MÁIRE - FF
Tipperary North

HOGAN, PHIL - FG
Carlow-Kilkenny

HOWLIN, BRENDAN - LAB
Wexford

JACOB, JOE - FF
Wicklow

KEAVENEY, CECILIA - FF
Donegal North East

KEHOE, PAUL - FG
Wexford

KELLEHER, BILLY - FF
Cork North Central

KELLY, PETER - FF
Longford-Roscommon

KENNY, ENDA - FG
Mayo

KILLEEN, TONY - FF
Clare

KIRK, SEAMUS - FF
Louth

KITT, TOM - FF
Dublin South

LENIHAN, BRIAN - FF
Dublin West

LENIHAN, CONOR - FF
Dublin South West

LOWRY, MICHAEL - IND
Tipperary North

LYNCH, KATHLEEN - LAB
Cork North Central

MARTIN, MICHEÁL - FF
Cork South Central

McCORMACK, PADRAIC - FG
Galway West

McCREEVY, CHARLIE - FF
Kildare North

McDAID, JAMES - FF
Donegal North East

McDOWELL, MICHAEL - PD
Dublin South East

McELLISTRIM, THOMAS - FF
Kerry North

McGINLEY, DINNY - FG
Donegal South West

McGRATH, FINIAN - IND
Dublin North Central

McGRATH, PAUL - FG
Westmeath

McGUINNESS, JOHN - FF
Carlow-Kilkenny

MCHUGH, PADDY - IND
Galway East

MCMANUS, LIZ - LAB
Wicklow

MITCHELL, GAY - FG
Dublin South Central

MITCHELL, OLIVIA - FG
Dublin South

MOLONEY, JOHN - FF
Laois-Offaly

MORGAN, ARTHUR - SF
Louth

MOYNIHAN, DONAL - FF
Cork North West

MOYNIHAN, MICHAEL - FF
Cork North West

MOYNIHAN CRONIN, BREEDA - LAB
Kerry South

MULCAHY, MICHAEL - FF
Dublin South Central

MURPHY, GERARD - FG
Cork North West

NAUGHTEN, DENIS - FG
Longford-Roscommon

NEVILLE, DAN - FG
Limerick West

NOLAN, M J - FF
Carlow-Kilkenny

NOONAN, MICHAEL - FG
Limerick West

Ó CAOLÁIN, CAOIMHGHÍN - SF
Cavan-Monaghan

O'CONNOR, CHARLIE - FF
Dublin South West

Ó CUÍV, ÉAMON - FF
Galway West

O'DEA, WILLIE - FF
Limerick East

O'DONNELL, LIZ - PD
Dublin South

O'DONOGHUE, JOHN - FF
Kerry South

O'DONOVAN, DENIS - FF
Cork South West

O'DOWD, FERGUS - FG
Louth

Ó FEARGHAÍL, SEÁN - FF
Kildare South

O'FLYNN, NOEL - FF
Cork North Central

O'HANLON, RORY - FF
Cavan-Monaghan

O'KEEFFE, BATT - FF
Cork South Central

O'KEEFFE, JIM - FG
Cork South West

O'KEEFFE, NED - FF
Cork East

O'MALLEY, FIONA - PD
Dun Laoghaire

O'MALLEY, TIM - PD
Limerick East

O'SHEA, BRIAN - LAB
Waterford

Ó SNODAIGH, AENGUS - SF
Dublin South Central

O'SULLIVAN, JAN - LAB
Limerick East

PARLON, TOM - PD
Laois Offaly

PATTISON, SÉAMUS - LAB
Carlow Kilkenny

Fianna Fáil TD Michael Moynihan engages in a spot of set dancing with Brenda O'Sullivan before attending the new Dáil in June   PHOTOCALL

PENROSE, WILLIE - LAB
Westmeath

PERRY, JOHN - FG
Sligo-Leitrim

POWER, PETER - FF
Limerick East

POWER, SEÁN - FF
Kildare South

QUINN, RUAIRI - LAB
Dublin South East

RABBITTE, PAT - LAB
Dublin South West

RING, MICHAEL - FG
Mayo

ROCHE, DICK - FF
Wicklow

RYAN, EAMON - GP
Dublin South

RYAN, EOIN - FF
Dublin South East

RYAN, SEÁN - LAB
Dublin North

SARGENT, TREVOR - GP
Dublin North

SEXTON, MAE - PD
Longford-Roscommon

SHERLOCK, JOE - LAB
Cork East

SHORTALL, RÓISÍN - LAB
Dublin North West

SMITH, BRENDAN - FF
Cavan-Monaghan

SMITH, MICHAEL - FF
Tipperary North

STAGG, EMMET - LAB
Kildare North

STANTON, DAVID - FG
Cork East

TIMMINS, BILLY - FG
Wicklow

TREACY, NOEL - FF
Galway East

TWOMEY, LIAM - IND
Wexford

UPTON, MARY - LAB
Dublin South Central

WALL, JACK - LAB
Kildare South

WALLACE, DAN - FF
Dublin North Central

WALLACE, MARY - FF
Meath

WALSH, JOE - FF
Cork South West

WILKINSON, OLLIE - FF
Waterford

WOODS, MICHAEL - FF
Dublin North East

WRIGHT, G V - FF
Dublin North

5 SEATS

3 Fianna Fáil
1 Fine Gael
1 Labour

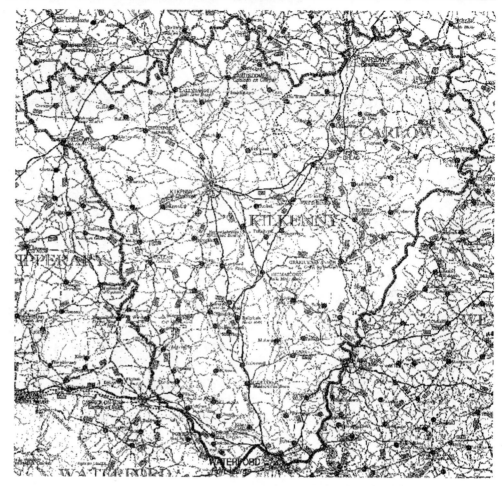

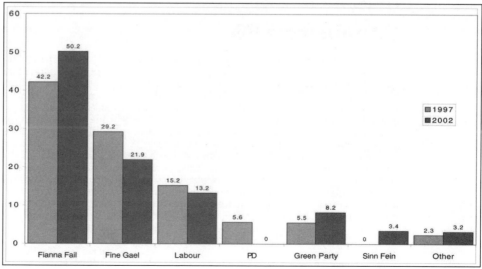

5 SEATS

ELECTORATE
97,071

TOTAL POLL
61,688

SPOILED
844

VALID POLL
60,844

QUOTA
12,169

* DENOTES
OUTGOING TD

NEWLY
ELECTED TDS
IN CAPITALS

		1	2 Votes of B Nolan	3 Votes of C'ns-Hughes	4 Votes of Kiernan	5 Votes of O'Brien	6 Votes of Browne	7 Aylward surplus	8 Votes of White
*S PATTISON	Lab	√ Re-elected unopposed as Ceann Comhairle							
*L AYLWARD	FF	12489 √							
			+28	+286	+428	+442	+127	+224	+1233
*J McGUINNESS	FF	9343	9371	9657	10085	10527	10654	10878	12111 √
			+61	+115	+253	+64	+628	+63	+1114
MJ NOLAN	FF	8711	8772	8887	9140	9204	9832	9895	11009 √
			+11	+222	+165	+664	+3335		
*P HOGAN	FG	7841	7852	8074	8239	8903	12238 √		
			+62	+140	+92	+132			
F Browne	FG	5468	5530	5670	5762	5894	eliminated		
			+42	+398	+654	+641	+633	+26	
M White	GP	4961	5003	5401	6055	6696	7329	7355	elim'td
			+58	+85	+153	+2057	+1021	+7	+2962
J Townsend	Lab	4272	4330	4415	4568	6625	7646	7653	10615
			+7	+207	+274				
M O'Brien	Lab	3732	3739	3946	4220	eliminated			
			+20	+118					
T Kiernan	SF	2078	2098	2216	eliminated				
			+30						
E Collins-Hughes	Ind	1614	1644	eliminated					
B Nolan	Ind	335	eliminated						
Non transferable			16	73	197	220	150	0	2046

FF gain from FG

SÉAMUS Pattison's was elected unopposed as outgoing Ceann Comhairle so this effectively became a four-seater. If the 1997 party division of the vote had been repeated this would have meant the last seat would have gone either to Labour or to Fine Gael, with Labour very much the favourite.

However, there was a lot of change in voting preferences. Fianna Fáil had one of its best performances here (up 8%). Fine Gael did poorly (down 7.3%). The party was shocked late in the day by the decision of outgoing TD John Browne to retire. He was succeeded by his son Fergal who actually did as good a job retaining his father's votes as his running mate Phil Hogan did retaining his own. Labour also failed to hold its 1997 vote in the absence of Pattison. Fine Gael had no chance of two seats but who would get the seat Fine Gael won last time?

The Green vote for the party's deputy leader Mary

White was up by 2.7%, so she too was in the hunt along with Labour and Fianna Fáil.

A potentially complicating factor in all this was the county divide in the constituency. MJ Nolan, the Carlow based former FF deputy who lost out last time to running mate John McGuinness from Kilkenny, raised the unlikely spectre his county being without a deputy. He was joined by the *Carlow Nationalist* ('Nightmare for Carlow') which cited a poll suggesting Labour's Kilkenny-based candidate, O'Brien, would take the last seat, and called for Carlow people to vote for the Carlow candidates. But in reality all three possibilities, White, Nolan and Labour's Jim Townsend, were Carlow-based.

Nolan eventually just got home by 394 votes from Townsend. White's transfers went 40% to Townsend and 32% to FF, 15% of them to Nolan. Townsend needed more like 44%. Had a few more votes from Browne gone to White rather than Townsend, it would have been

The bas: Bertie Ahern meets Kilkenny hurling star DJ Carey while canvassing in the constituency in May   PHOTOCALL IRELAND!/LEON FARRELL

White pushing Nolan for the last seat and perhaps she would have done better from Townsend's transfers than he did from hers but it was not to be. Fianna Fáil gained an unlikely seat, winning three here for the first time since 1977, Labour missed a good opportunity, and the Green party had to settle for an all-male parliamentary party.

Eddie Collins-Hughes ran here to publicise the plight of carers and took over 2% of the vote. Sinn Féin's first appearance here collected 3% for the party.

LIAM AYLWARD
FIANNA FÁIL

Topping the poll once again in the constituency he has represented since 1977, Aylward has now served as a junior minister under Taoisigh Haughey, Reynolds and Ahern with his appointment as Minister of State for Agriculture and Food with responsibility for Animal Health and Welfare and Customer Services.

OCCUPATION
Full-time public representative, former laboratory technician

ADDRESS
Aghaviller, Hugginstown, Co Kilkenny

PHONE
Home
(056) 776 8703
Fax (056)776 8229

Constituency
Fax (056) 68 229

Office
(01) 662 9211

Leinster House
(01) 618 3489
Fax (01) 662 2170

EMAIL
liam.aylward@agriculture.gov.ie

BORN
Knockmoylon, Mullinavat, Co Kilkenny, September 1952

EDUCATION
St Kieran's College, Kilkenny (Diploma in Building and Construction)

MARITAL STATUS
Married to Kathleen Noonan. Two sons, two daughters

PHIL HOGAN
FINE GAEL

Since he was first elected to the Dáil in 1989 Phil Hogan has held a wide range of posts as Minister of State or Front Bench spokesman and was Chairman of the Parliamentary Party and Director of Organisation from 1995-2001, continuing in the latter post until June 2002. Defeated by Enda Kenny in the leadership election, Deputy Hogan was appointed spokesperson on Enterprise, Trade and Employment in June 2002.

OCCUPATION
Full-time public representative, former insurance broker and auctioneer

CONSTITUENCY OFFICE
1 High Street, Kilkenny

PHONE
Constituency
(056) 777 1490
Fax (056) 777 1491

Leinster House
(01) 618 4096
Fax (01) 618 4603

EMAIL
philip.hogan@oireachtas.ie

BORN
Kilkenny, July 1960

EDUCATION
St Joseph's College, Freshford; St Kieran's College, Kilkenny; University College, Cork (BA, HDipEd)

MARITAL STATUS
Married to Kathleen Murphy. One son

JOHN MCGUINNESS

FIANNA FÁIL

McGuinness claims to have been "Ireland's first TD in cyberspace". Whether it was his presence in cyberspace or his family's three generations of service on Kilkenny Corporation, he managed to double his personal vote since he was first elected in 1997. He is vice-chairman of Public Accounts commitee.

OCCUPATION
Full-time public representative, former transport company director

ADDRESS
Brooklawn, Ballyfoyle Road, Kilkenny

CONSTITUENCY OFFICE
O'Loughlin Road, Kilkenny

PHONE
Constituency
(056) 777 0672/3
Fax (056) 777 0674
Mobile (087) 285 5834

Leinster House
(01) 618 3137
Fax (01) 618 4539

EMAIL
johnmcg@eircom.net

WEBSITE
www.johnmcguinness.com

BORN
Kilkenny, March 1955

EDUCATION
Christian Brothers, Kilkenny; Carlow RTC (Diploma in Business Management)

MARITAL STATUS
Married to Margaret Redmond. Three sons, one daughter

MJ NOLAN

FIANNA FÁIL

Nolan, who narrowly lost his seat to Fianna Fáil colleague John McGuinness in 1997, came back from the Seanad to give his party representation in both halves of the constituency again.

OCCUPATION
Full-time public representative, former special adviser to the Minister for Defence

ADDRESS
Shandon House, Strawhall, Carlow

CONSTITUENCY OFFICE
Lismard House, Tullow Street, Carlow

PHONE
Constituency
(059) 914 2691
(0503) 914 2691 (also Fax)

Leinster House
(01) 618 3252
Fax (01) 618 4556

EMAIL
mjnolan@oceanfree.net

BORN
Bagenalstown, Co Carlow, January 1951

EDUCATION
De La Salle School, Bagenalstown, Co Carlow;
Cistercian College, Roscrea, Co Tipperary

MARITAL STATUS
Married to Mary.
Four children

SÉAMUS PATTISON

LABOUR (UNOPPOSED)

Ceann Comhairle of the 28th Dáil and now Leas-Cheann Comhairle, Séamus Pattison was Father of the Dáil before his unanimous election to the Chair, having first been elected to his father's former seat in 1961. His early trade union experience has been brought to bear at all levels from the local to the European, although he resigned from the European Parliament upon his appointment as Minister of State in the Department of Social Welfare in 1983.

OCCUPATION
Full-time public representative

CONSTITUENCY OFFICE
6 Upper New Street, Kilkenny

PHONE
Constituency
(056) 772 1295
Fax (056) 775 2533

Leinster House
(01) 618 3444
Fax (01) 618 4111

EMAIL
LeasCC@Oireachtas.ie

BORN
Kilkenny, April 1936

EDUCATION
St John of God NS, Kilkenny;
St Patrick's De La Salle NS, Kilkenny;
St Kieran's College, Kilkenny;
University College Dublin (Extra Mural Hons Diploma in Social and Economic Science)

MARITAL STATUS
Single

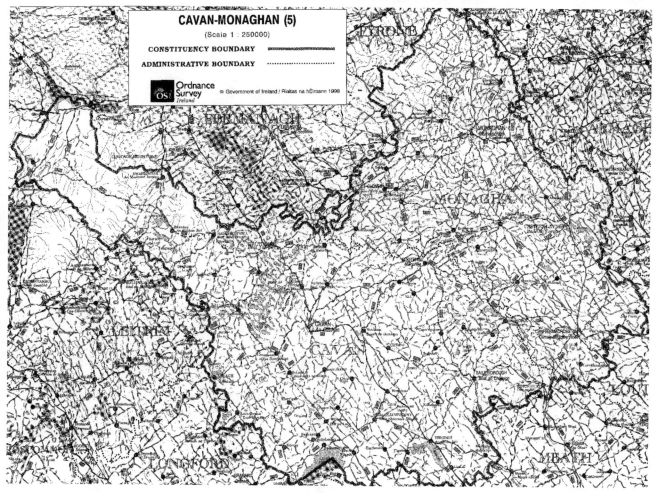

5 SEATS

1 Sinn Féin
1 Independent
2 Fianna Fáil
1 Fine Gael

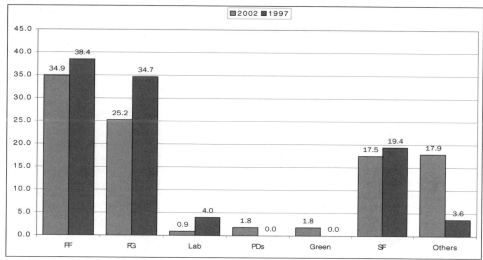

	2002	1997
FF	34.9	38.4
FG	25.2	34.7
Lab	0.9	4.0
PDs	1.8	0.0
Green	1.8	0.0
SF	17.5	19.4
Others	17.9	3.6

Candidate	Party	1	2 Ó Caoláin's surplus	3 B Smith's surplus	4 Votes of Cullen and T Smith	5 Votes of Brennan	6 Votes of McCaughey	7 Votes of McCabe	8 Votes of Martin
*C Ó CAOLÁIN	SF	10832 √							
*B SMITH	FF	10679 √							
P CONNOLLY	Ind	7722	+145 7867	+4 7871	+75 7946	+429 8375	+239 8614	+359 8973	+705 9678
*R O'HANLON	FF	7204	+91 7295	+184 7479	+62 7541	+107 7648	+159 7807	+136 7943	+719 8662
*S CRAWFORD	FG	6113	+23 6136	+3 6139	+39 6178	+108 6286	+111 6397	+112 6509	+294 6803
*A Boylan	FG	4819	+36 4855	+34 4889	+172 5061	+23 5084	+127 5211	+163 5374	+142 5516
P O'Reilly	FG	4639	+28 4667	+31 4698	+119 4817	+19 4836	+119 4955	+153 5108	+212 5320
R Gallagher	FF	3731	+58 3789	+85 3874	+47 3921	+83 4004	+193 4197	+122 4319	+216 4535
V Martin	Ind	1943	+49 1992	+5 1997	+90 2087	+178 2265	+106 2371	+275 2646	elim'td
G McCaughey	PD	1131	+13 1144	+10 1154	+65 1219	+42 1261	eliminated		
M McCabe	GP	1100	+38 1138	+5 1143	+158 1301	+84 1385	+128 1513	eliminated	
J Brennan	Ind	1026	+20 1046	+1 1047	+67 1114	eliminated			
D Cullen	Lab	550	+16 566	+6 572	eliminated				
T Smith	CSP	358	+7 365	+3 368	eliminated				
Non transferable			0	0	46	41	79	193	358

5 SEATS

ELECTORATE
87,087

TOTAL POLL
62,710

SPOILED VOTES
863

VALID POLL
61,847

QUOTA
10,308

* DENOTES OUTGOING TD

NEWLY ELECTED TDS IN CAPITALS

Ind gain from FG

FOLLOWING Caoimghín O Caoláin's historic win in 1997, many expected no change this time but an impressive performance from Paudge Connolly, campaigning to protect Monaghan Hospital, provided a real upset. He appears to have taken first preference votes from all parties, and certainly picked up the lion's share of transfers, to be elected on the 9th count. Ironically, he displaced a Cavan candidate, Fine Gael's Andrew Boylan, who had represented the constituency since 1987. The decision by Fine Gael to build on its strength and run two candidates from Cavan and only one from Monaghan always meant Boylan would run behind Seymour Crawford and on the last count, despite getting more than two thirds of O'Reilly's transfers, he was still 121 votes short.

Fianna Fáil and Fine Gael won almost 86% of the votes here in 1989 with the former topping 50%; this time together they secured only 60%.

Labour, with a change of personnel, PDs and Greens all ran candidates (the PDs and Greens for the first time) but they proved almost invisible to the voters, winning only 4.5% between them.

Curiously, four of the five TDs are now based in Monaghan although that county actually has a smaller electorate than Cavan.

9	10	11	12
Votes of Gallagher	O'Hanlon's surplus	Connolly's surplus	O'Reilly's votes
+1192			
10870 ✓			
+2370			
11032 ✓			
+275	+314	+310	+1463
7078	**7392**	**7702**	**9165** ✓
+117	+211	+61	+3139
5633	**5844**	**5905**	**9044**
+109	+199	+82	
5429	**5628**	**5710**	**elim'td**

eliminated

472	*0*	*109*	*1108*

Fianna Fáil strategist PJ Mara at an election press conference

PHOTOCALL IRELAND

PAUDGE CONNOLLY

INDEPENDENT

Paudge Connolly took votes from all the established candidates to be elected with Rory O'Hanlon at the ninth count. His long career in nursing and representation of both psychiatric nurses and other Monaghan nurses on the North East Health Board led him to believe that the healthcare aspirations of nurses and the people of Monaghan could only be achieved by taking the crusade to Leinster House.

OCCUPATION
Full-time public representative, former nurse

ADDRESS
Tallylush, Silverstream, Monaghan

PHONE
Home
(047) 82 386
Fax (047) 83 268

Leinster House
(01) 618 3247
Fax (01) 618 4778

EMAIL
paudge.connolly@oireachtas.ie

BORN
Monaghan, September 1953

EDUCATION
St Macartan's College, Monaghan;
St Davnet's School of Nursing, Monaghan

MARITAL STATUS
Married to Winnie, four sons

SEYMOUR CRAWFORD

FINE GAEL

First elected in 1992 and a key representative of the meat and livestock sector at national and international levels throughout his career, Seymour Crawford, who is a member of the Presbyterian Church and a strict adherent to Sabbath observance, was appointed deputy spokesman on Community, Rural and Gaeltacht Affairs in June 2002.

OCCUPATION
Public representative, dairy farmer

ADDRESS
Drumkeen, Aghabog, Monaghan, Co Monaghan

PHONE
Constituency
(047) 71911
Fax (047) 71912

Leinster House
(01) 618 3408
Fax (01) 618 4647

BORN
Monaghan, June 1944

EDUCATION
Clones High School, Monaghan

MARITAL STATUS
Single

CAOIMHGHÍN Ó CAOLÁIN

SINN FÉIN

Despite losing votes to independent health services candidate Paudge Connolly, Ó Caoláin once again topped the poll by a substantial margin. Regarded as a hard-working constituency TD, his election to the last Dáil was the first for Sinn Féin since 1953, and he was the first to take his seat since the Civil War. He has now been joined by four party colleagues.

OCCUPATION
Full-time public representative, former bank official

ADDRESS
Mallaghdun, Monaghan

PHONE
Constituency
(047) 82917
Fax (047) 71849

Leinster House
(01) 618 3005
Fax (01) 618 3188

EMAIL
ocaolain@oireachtas.ie

BORN
Monaghan, September 1953

EDUCATION
St Mary's CBS, Monaghan

MARITAL STATUS
Married, four daughters, one son

RORY O'HANLON

FIANNA FÁIL

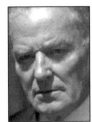

The new Ceann Comhairle has been a member of Dáil Éireann since 1977. He was Fianna Fáil spokesman on Health 1983-1987, Minister for Health from 1987 to 1991, and Minister for the Environment from 1991-92. Since 1995 he has been Chairman of the Parliamentary Party.

OCCUPATION
Full-time public representative, former Leas-Cheann Comhairle, former medical practitioner

ADDRESS
Mullinary, Carrickmacross, Co Monaghan

PHONE
Home
(042) 966 1530
Fax (042) 966 3220

Leinster House
(01) 618 3457
Fax (01) 618 4100

EMAIL
Ceann.Comhairle@oireachtas.ie/
Rory.Ohanlon@oireachtas.ie

WEBSITE
www.roryohanlon.com

BORN
Dublin, February 1934

EDUCATION
St Mary's College, Dundalk; Blackrock College, Dublin; UCD (MB, Bch, BAO, Dch, LM)

MARITAL STATUS
Married to Teresa Ward. Four sons, two daughters

BRENDAN SMITH

FIANNA FÁIL

He was elected to Dáil Éireann in 1992, the first time he ran for public office at any level, after a long political apprenticeship as adviser to former Tánaiste John Wilson. Chair, British-Irish Parliamentary Body

OCCUPATION
Full-time public representative, former political adviser to John Wilson

ADDRESS
3 Carrickfern, Keadue, Co Cavan

PHONE
Home
(049) 436 2366
Fax (049) 436 2367

Leinster House
(01) 618 3376
Fax (01) 618 4550

EMAIL
brendan.smith@oireachtas.ie

BORN
Cavan, June 1956

EDUCATION
St Camillus College, Killucan; University College Dublin (BA Politics and Economics)

MARITAL STATUS
Married to Anne McGarry

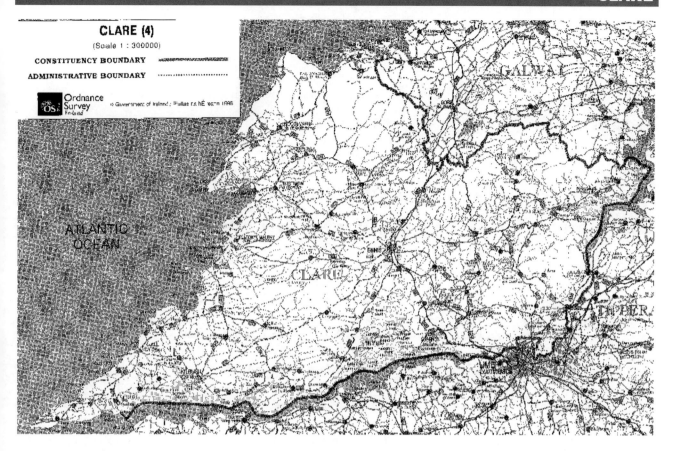

4 SEATS

1 Independent
1 Fine Gael
2 Fianna Fáil

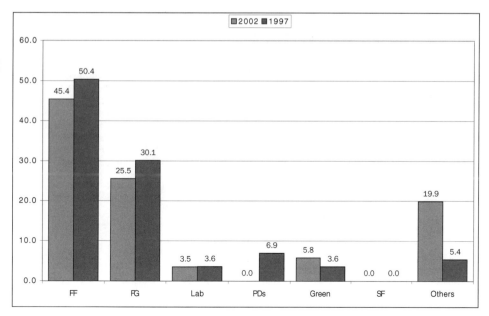

■2002 ■1997

	FF	FG	Lab	PDs	Green	SF	Others
2002	45.4	25.5	3.5	0.0	5.8	0.0	19.9
1997	50.4	30.1	3.6	6.9	3.6	0.0	5.4

4 SEATS

ELECTORATE
80,412

TOTAL VOTE
50,341

SPOILED
539

VALID VOTE
49,802

QUOTA
9,961

* DENOTES
OUTGOING TD

NEWLY
ELECTED TDS
IN CAPITALS

			1	2 Votes of Corley and Whelan	3 Votes of Meaney	4 Votes of Carey	5 Votes of Taylor-Quinn
J BREEN	Ind		9,721	+333 10,054 √			
*T KILLEEN	FF		8,130	+122 8,252	+388 8,640	+424 9,064	+418 9,482 √
*S DE VALERA	FF		7,755	+111 7,866	+598 8,464	+355 8,819	+551 9,370 √
*B Daly	FF		6,717	+69 6,786	+128 6,914	+172 7,086	+597 7,683
P BREEN	FG		4,541	+160 4,701	+564 5,265	+1,669 6,934	+4,462 11,396 √
M Taylor-Quinn	FG		4,124	+225 4,349	+685 5,034	+1,692 6,726	eliminated
*D Carey	FG		4,015	+212 4,227	+364 4,591	eliminated	
B Meaney	GP		2,903	+605 3,508	eliminated		
M Corley	Lab		1,720	eliminated			
D Whelan	CSP		176	eliminated			
Non transferable				59	781	279	698

Ind gain from FF

TWO new faces here, both called Breen! Fine Gael once hoped to win back the seat lost to Fianna Fáil in 1997 but it was the Ennis based one-time Fianna Fáil local councillor, James Breen, who upset Fianna Fáil's apple cart, topping the poll and pushing out another Ennis man, the long serving TD and former Minister of Defence, Brendan Daly.

Breen campaigned on a platform of improving local health services and protecting Shannon Airport and won on the second count, although he had only announced his candidacy in January. He was the first independent elected for Clare since 1948 and only the second ever. Fianna Fáil's share of the vote here fell under 50% for the first time since 1943 and was at its lowest since 1927.

Another long serving deputy, Fine Gael's Donal Carey, also lost his seat, in this instance to a running mate, Kilrush local councillor Pat Breen. Pat Breen outpolled the incumbent Carey and the former TD, Senator Madeleine Taylor-Quinn (as he did in the local elections).

Carey's transfers left Breen just 208 votes ahead of Taylor-Quinn on the 4th count, and Breen was then elected on her transfers. Brian Meaney's Green support, up more than 1,200 votes on 1997, was one of the better performances by the party outside Dublin.

Labour, who won a seat here with Moosajee Bhamjee in 1992, never looked like winning it back as Michael Corley secured only 36 votes more than Brídín Twist had done last time.

JAMES BREEN

INDEPENDENT

James Breen was a Fianna Fáil representative on Clare County Council for 16 years, first in Miltown Malbay and then, after the redrawing of boundaries, in Ennis. He worked in De Beers Industrial Diamonds in Shannon and was a shop steward. He finally broke with the party in late 2001 because he felt local health issues were being neglected.

OCCUPATION
Full-time public representative, part time farmer

ADDRESS
Ballyknock, Kilnamona, Co Clare

PHONE
Constituency
(065) 682 8180

Leinster House
(01) 618 3916
Fax (01) 618 4301

EMAIL
james.breen@oireachtas.ie

BORN
Co Clare, May 1945

EDUCATION
Kilnamona NS;
Ennis Vocational School

MARITAL STATUS
Married to Eileen.
Four children

PAT BREEN

FINE GAEL

Elected to the 29th Dáil in 2002, popular local councillor Pat Breen defeated party colleague Donal Carey who had held the seat for 20 years. He is Fine Gael deputy spokesman on Defence.

OCCUPATION
Full-time public representative

ADDRESS
Home
Lisduff, Ballynacally, Co.Clare

Constituency
Park View House, Lower Market Street Car Park, Ennis, Co Clare

PHONE
(065) 686 8466
Fax (065) 686 8486

Leinster House
(01) 618 4224
Fax (01) 618 4383

EMAIL
pat.breen@oireachtas.ie

BORN
Co Clare, March 1957

EDUCATION
St Flannan's College, Ennis;
Limerick LIT

MARITAL STATUS
Married.
Two children

SÍLE DE VALERA

FIANNA FÁIL

Minister for Arts, Heritage, Gaeltacht and the Islands in the last administration, Síle de Valera is a granddaughter of Éamon de Valera and was the youngest member of the Dáil when she was elected for Dublin Mid-County in 1977. She is now Minister of State at the Department of Education and Science (with special responsibility for Adult Education, Youth Affairs and Educational Disadvantage).

OCCUPATION
Full-time public representative

ADDRESS
9 Chapel Lane, Ennis, Co Clare

PHONE
Constituency
(065) 682 1100
Fax (065) 684 0695

Leinster House
(01) 889 2302
Fax (01) 618 3614
(01) 889 6495

EMAIL
webmaster@education.gov.ie

BORN
Dublin, December 1954

EDUCATION
Loreto Convent, Foxrock, Co Dublin;
UCD (BA, HDipED, Dip Career Guidance, D Psych Sci)

MARITAL STATUS
Single

TONY KILLEEN

FIANNA FÁIL

First elected in 1992, Tony Killeen was pushed from his former poll-topping position by Independent James Breen. Despite resigning the whip over the Shannon stopover in 1993 he is now Chair of the Oireachtas Committee on Education and Science and National Chairman of Fianna Fáil Councillors Association.

OCCUPATION
Full-time public representative, former national school teacher

ADDRESS
Kilnaboy, Corofin, Co Clare

PHONE
Constituency
(065) 684 1500
Fax (065) 684 1514

Leinster House
(01) 618 3560
Fax (01) 618 4543

EMAIL
t.killeen@oireachtas.ie

BORN
Corofin, Co Clare, June 1952

EDUCATION
St Flannan's College, Ennis;
Mary Immaculate College of Education, Limerick

MARITAL STATUS
Married to Lily O'Keeffe.
Five sons

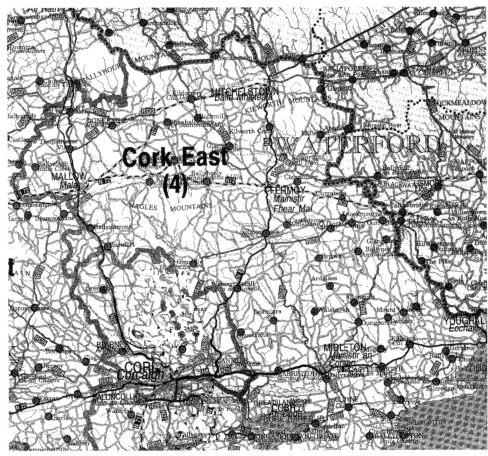

4 SEATS

2 Fianna Fáil
1 Labour
1 Fine Gael

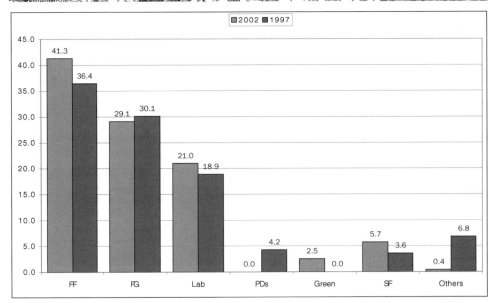

	2002	1997
FF	41.3	36.4
FG	29.1	30.1
Lab	21.0	18.9
PDs	0.0	4.2
Green	2.5	0.0
SF	5.7	3.6
Others	0.4	6.8

The only person that counts: the days of manual counting are numbered with the introduction of electronic voting, which was experimented with in three constituencies during the 2002 general election

Tough times ahead: Bertie Ahern led the first government not to be rejected at a general election since 1973, but he may have handed himself a poisoned chalice

The SundayTribune

THE BEST FOR
Politics

A COMPLETE OVERVIEW FROM IRELAND'S ESSENTIAL NEWSPAPER

Noonan quits in FF rout

● Fine Gael wiped out in Dublin ● Labour fail to capitalise on FG collapse ● Surprise rise in seats for PDs

OUT OUT OUT OUT OUT OUT OUT OUT

ELECTION COMMENT
Opposition must now realign

THE foundations of Irish politics are shift-...

Ahern clings to power in secret Cowen deal

Ahern agrees to back Cowen for party leadership in return for support now

STEPHEN COLLINS and LIAM REID

BERTIE Ahern and Brian Cowen have struck a secret deal about the succession to the leadership of Fianna Fáil, The Sunday Tribune has learned. Cowen will continue to back Ahern through the troubled political times that lie ahead, and the Taoiseach, when the time comes for him to quit, will support deputy leader...

intention of leading a heave against the leader now or in the future. While that has not stopped all mutterings on the back benches, it has helped to keep the lid on simmering discontent.

The Taoiseach faces a number of challenges in the weeks ahead. The most immediate are the continuing controversy over his...

mental file on the sale of passports to the Mahfouz family. Recontroversy over the Mahfouz passports that led to Burke's resignation in October 1997.

Ahern was shown the file on the instructions of Albert Reynolds in 1994 but has said there was nothing...

Exclusive: secret memos reveal McCreevy's deceit

● €900m spending cuts next year
● 27% spending increase before election
● No tax cuts in budget; big excise rises
● S...   ...€1.25bn more than planned
● ...   ...employment

The SundayTribune

€1.65 (£1.30stg) • Vol 22 No34 • 29 September 2002

INCLUDING IRELAND'S BEST BUSINESS SECTION

REVEALED: THE SINN FEIN LEADER'S CAREER IN THE IRA. SEE pages 12-15

Gerry Adams: the shocking truth about the 'disappeared'

THE MENU

NEWS
Dublin hospital charged for free drugs
St Vincent's Hospital in Dublin charged pa...

See no evil, hear no evil

Ahern was warned a decade ago that Burke was corrupt; Ahern also asked for file on or...

MATT COOPER

STEPHEN COLLINS

SHANE COLEMAN

MICHAEL CLIFFORD

DIARMUID DOYLE

ANN MARIE HOURIHANE

HARRY McGEE

SUSAN McKAY

BRENDA POWER

LIAM REID

SAM SMYTH

MARTIN WALL

			1	**2** N O'Keeffe's surplus	**3** Votes of Murphy, M O'Keeffe, Manning	**4** Votes of Mulvihill
*N O'KEEFFE	FF		10,574 √			
				+864		
*M AHERN	FF		8,340	9,204 √		
				+171	+494	+513
*P Bradford	FG		7,053	7,224	7,718	8,231
				+55	+654	+1,460
*D STANTON	FG		6,269	6,324	6,978	8,438 √
				+25	+721	
J Mulvihill	Lab		4,813	4,838	5,559	eliminated
				+223	+1,177	+2,468
J SHERLOCK	Lab		4,792	5,015	6,192	8,660 √
				+61		
J Murphy	SF		2,624	2,685	eliminated	
				+15		
M O'Keeffe	GP		1,136	1,151	eliminated	
				+2		
P Manning	CSP		187	189	eliminated	
Non transferable				0	979	1,118

4 SEATS

ELECTORATE
72,702

TOTAL VOTE
46,334

SPOILED
546

VALID POLL
45,788

QUOTA
9,158

* DENOTES
OUTGOING TD

NEWLY
ELECTED TDS
IN CAPITALS

A disenfranchised canine at the polls

Lab gain from FG

FINE Gael's best result in 1997 was its two seats out of four here on the back of only 30% of the vote and it was always going to be hard to match that, particularly with Joe Sherlock, the former Democratic Left deputy, looking for a seat on behalf of Labour. Fine Gael's vote held up well, dropping by only 1%, but the Mallow based Sherlock pushed the Labour/DL vote up by over 2% and that was sufficient to nudge out a Fine Gael deputy.

In the event it was the younger if more experienced man, Paul Bradford, who lost out as David Stanton hung on by only 207 votes to the seat he first won in 1997. The key to his win was geography. When Labour's former TD, John Mulvihill from Cobh, was eliminated, 1,460 transfers went to Stanton in nearby Midleton and only 513 to Bradford from far-off Mallow. Chief Whip under Michael Noonan and not yet 40, Bradford has time on his side. Only 44% of Mulvihill's final votes transferred to Sherlock. This might suggest the DL/Labour merger is not yet seamless, but in 1997 the transfer was only 32%, which accounted for Sherlock's failure to win the seat on that occasion.

Both incumbents were returned for Fianna Fáil with Ned O'Keeffe shrugging off the loss of his junior ministry to top the poll again with a significantly increased vote.

Fianna Fáil's support was its highest since the days of Jack Lynch. Labour's 21% of the vote was its best since 1937, although Democratic Left and Labour separately won almost 27% in 1992 and the Workers' Party and Labour won over 21% in 1989. The PDs opted out here, running no candidate this time, but the Greens tested the waters for the first time (they were too cold) while Sinn Féin saw its support up by over 1,000 votes.

MICHAEL AHERN

FIANNA FÁIL

The son of Senator, later Deputy, Liam Ahern, and from a family with a long political tradition, Michael Ahern was first elected in 1982. In the last Dáil he was Minister of State at the Department of the Environment and he has now been appointed Minister of State at the Department of Enterprise, Trade and Employment.

OCCUPATION
Public representative, accountant

ADDRESS
Libermann, Barryscourt, Carrigtwohill, Co Cork

PHONE
Home
(021) 488 3592
Fax (021) 488 3436

Leinster House
(01) 631 2241
Fax (01) 631 2808

EMAIL
michael-ahern@entemp.ie

BORN
Dungourney, Co Cork, January 1949

EDUCATION
Rockwell College, Cashel, Co Tipperary;
University College, Dublin (BA);
Kimmage Manor, Dublin

MARITAL STATUS
Married to Margaret Monahan.
Three daughters

NED O'KEEFFE

FIANNA FÁIL

Minister of State at the Department of Agriculture and Food (with special responsibility for Food), July 1997 to February 2001.

He resigned when questions were asked in the Dáil about a swill feeding licence for a family farm although he no longer owned it or was involved in its management.

OCCUPATION
Full-time public representative, former company director and farmer

ADDRESS
Ballylough, Mitchelstown, Co Cork

PHONE
Constituency
(022) 25 285
Fax (022) 25 495

Leinster House
(01) 618 3304
Fax (01) 618 4645

BORN
Mitchelstown, Co Cork, August 1942

EDUCATION
Darra College, Clonakilty, Co Cork;
University College, Cork (Diploma in Social and Rural Science)

MARITAL STATUS
Married to Ann Buckley.
Three sons, two daughters

JOE SHERLOCK

LABOUR

Labour Party Spokesperson on Defence. Joe Sherlock was elected to Dáil Éireann for the Workers Party on three occasions since 1981 and was a member of the Seanad from 1993 to 1997.

OCCUPATION
Full-time public representative

ADDRESS
20 Blackwater Drive, Mallow, Co Cork

PHONE
Constituency
(022) 21 053
Fax (022) 21 053
Mobile (086) 813 5828

EMAIL
sherlockjoe@yahoo.com

BORN
Kildorrery, Co Cork, 1935

EDUCATION
Graigue National School

MARITAL STATUS
Married.
Three children

DAVID STANTON

FINE GAEL

A surprise winner in 1997, when he took a lot of votes from Labour, David Stanton pipped party colleague Paul Bradford for the final seat this time around. He is deputy spokesperson on Education and Science with special responsibility for the Information Society.

OCCUPATION
Full-time public representative, former teacher and guidance counsellor

ADDRESS
Coppingerstown, Midleton, Co Cork

PHONE
Constituency
(021) 463 2867
Fax (021) 462 1133

Leinster House
(01) 618 3181
Fax (01) 618 4575

EMAIL
david.stanton@oireachtas.ie

WEBSITE
www.stanton.ie

BORN
Cork, February 1957

EDUCATION
St Colman's Vocational School, Midleton;
University College, Cork (BA, Dip Career Guidance, Dip Ed Admin, M Ed)

MARITAL STATUS
Married to Mary Lehane.
Four sons

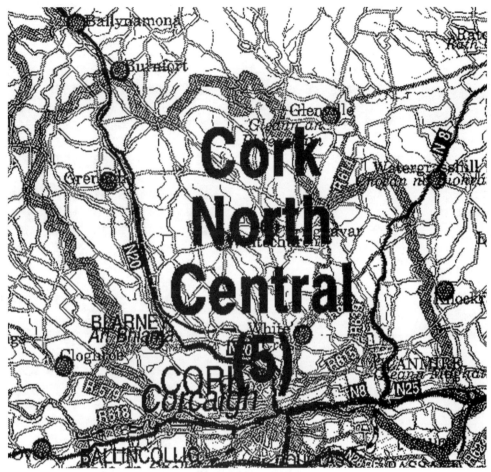

5 SEATS

3 Fianna Fáil
1 Labour
1 Fine Gael

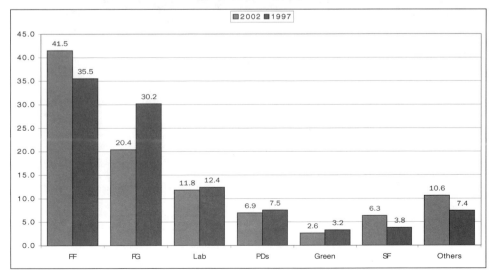

	2002	1997
FF	41.5	35.5
FG	20.4	30.2
Lab	11.8	12.4
PDs	6.9	7.5
Green	2.6	3.2
SF	6.3	3.8
Others	10.6	7.4

			1	2 Votes of Tynan, Duffy	3 Votes of Barry	4 Votes of McMurray	5 Votes of Minihan	6 Votes of O'Brien	7 Votes of O'Callaghan
*N O'FLYNN	FF		7387	+54 7441	+54 7495	+30 7525	√		
*B KELLEHER	FF		5801	+48 5849	+36 5885	+55 5940	+690 6630	+339 6969	+487 7456 √
*D WALLACE	FF		5537	+71 5608	+24 5632	+43 5675	+560 6235	+342 6577	+610 7187 √
*B ALLEN	FG		5458	+45 5503	+94 5597	+75 5672	+512 6184	+417 6601	+1049 7650 √
K LYNCH	Lab		5313	+89 5402	+226 5628	+514 6142	+541 6683	+813 7496	+922 8418 √
G Kelly	FG		3744	+23 3767	+51 3818	+93 3911	+493 4404	+164 4568	+369 4937
J O'Callaghan	Ind		3154	+68 3222	+97 3319	+138 3457	+248 3705	+760 4465	eliminated
J Minihan	PD		3126	+26 3152	+21 3173	+113 3286	eliminated		
J O'Brien	SF		2860	+105 2965	+258 3223	+182 3405	+78 3483	eliminated	
N McMurray	GP		1155	+41 1196	+133 1329	eliminated			
M Barry	SP		936	+90 1026	eliminated				
T Tynan	WP		458	eliminated					
G Duffy	CSP		215	eliminated					
Non transferable				13	32	86	164	648	1028

5 SEATS

ELECTORATE
73,300

TOTAL POLL
45,692

SPOILED
548

VALID POLL
45,144

QUOTA
7,525

* DENOTES
OUTGOING TD

NEWLY
ELECTED TDS
IN CAPITALS

Lab gain from FG

FIANNA Fáil triumphed here in 1997 by winning three out of the five seats with under 36% of the vote while Labour failed to get the seat it usually secures. Hence, there was some expectation of change. Fianna Fáil's vote increased by 6%, securing the seats of the party's three incumbent deputies, but the Fine Gael vote collapsed, falling by almost 10% as it did in so many urban constituencies. So by simply maintaining its vote around the 1997 level Labour won a seat from Fine Gael.

Kathleen Lynch, the new Labour TD, is a former Democratic Left TD who won a by-election in the constituency in 1994 but lost her seat in 1997.

The big increase in the Fianna Fáil vote was due largely to Noel O'Flynn, whose vote rose from just under 5,000 to 7,387, almost a full quota. O'Flynn achieved national prominence with his criticisms of asylum seekers but his electorate was less critical of his views than were the national media, and his party leader. An independent candidate, Joe O'Callaghan, who expressed similar views and was expelled from the Labour party in consequence, also did well, winning over 3,000 votes. Judging by the pattern of his transfers these came from all the established parties.

The PDs held a seat here for ten years but party chairman John Minihan was unable to win it back; his vote fell just below that won by Máirín Quill last time. 50% of his transfers went to Fianna Fáil.

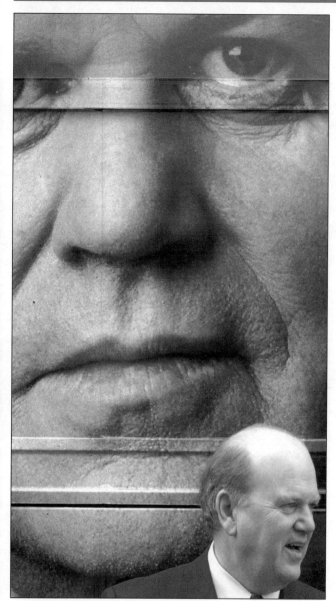

Fine Gael leader Michael Noonan canvassing in Navan   PHOTOCALL

BERNARD ALLEN

FINE GAEL

Bernard Allen was first elected to the Dáil in 1981. Between 1994 and 1997 he was Minister of State at the Departments of Education and Environment with special responsibility for Youth and Sport and he was Fine Gael's Front Bench Spokesperson on Tourism, Sport and Recreation from February 2001 – June 2002, fitting posts for a man who is a member of the Pitch and Putt Union of Ireland, Ból Chumann na hÉireann, the Golfing Union of Ireland, the GAA and the FAI. Deputy Allen was appointed spokesperson on Environment & Local Government in June 2002.

OCCUPATION
Full-time public representative

ADDRESS
7 Mount Prospect, Shanakiel, Cork

PHONE
Constituency
(021) 430 3068
Fax (021) 430 4188

Leinster House
(01) 618 3371
Fax (01) 618 4521

EMAIL
bernard.allen@oireachtas.ie

BORN
Cork, September 1944

EDUCATION
North Monastery CBS, Cork; University College, Cork (Diploma in Chemical Technology)

MARITAL STATUS
Married, two daughters

BILLY KELLEHER

FIANNA FÁIL

Billy Kelleher was first elected to the Dáil in 1997 having been appointed to the Seanad, where he was Fianna Fáil spokesman on Social Welfare, in 1993. His first outing was in 1992 when he lost by only 25 votes to his Fine Gael uncle Liam Burke. On his second attempt he lost to Kathleen Lynch in the 1994 by-election. Member of Joint Committees on Agriculture, Food and the Marine; Environment and Local Government; Tourism, Sport and Recreation. He is also Deputy Government Whip.

OCCUPATION
Public representative, farmer

ADDRESS
28A Ballyhooley Road, Dillon's Cross, Cork

PHONE
Constituency
(021) 450 2289
Fax (021) 450 2356

Leinster House
(01) 618 3219
Fax (01) 618 4547

EMAIL
billykelleher@eircom.net

BORN
Cork, January 1968

EDUCATION
Sacred Heart College, Carrignavar, Co Cork

MARITAL STATUS
Single

KATHLEEN LYNCH

LABOUR

First elected to Dáil Éireann for Democratic Left in a by-election in 1994, Kathleen Lynch lost her seat in 1997 for the same party. In 2002 she successfully held on to both the Democratic Left and Labour votes of that year to win the seat for the Labour Party on the seventh count.

OCCUPATION
Full-time public representative

ADDRESS
Farrancleary House,
5 Assumption Road, Blackpool,
Cork

PHONE
Constituency
(021) 439 9930
Fax (021) 430 4358

Leinster House
(01) 618 4034

EMAIL
kathleen.lynch@oireachtas.ie

WEBSITE
www.labour.ie

BORN
Cork, July 1953

EDUCATION
Blackpool, Cork

MARITAL STATUS
Married to Bernard Lynch.
Four children

NOEL O'FLYNN

FIANNA FÁIL

From new boy in 1997 Noel O'Flynn has risen to be poll-topper in 2002. He has attracted considerable publicity for his criticism of immigrants, which he was asked to explain to the Taoiseach. He is Chair of the Committee on Communications, Marine and Natural Resources

OCCUPATION
Public representative, managing director

ADDRESS
Unit 3A, NOS Commercial Centre,
Kilnap, Mallow Road, Cork

PHONE
Constituency
(021) 421 1200
Fax (021) 421 1110

Leinster House
(01) 618 3286
Fax (01) 618 4326

EMAIL
noflynn@eircom.net

BORN
December 1951

EDUCATION
Regional Technical College, Cork

MARITAL STATUS
Married to Frances O'Keeffe.
Three sons

DAN WALLACE

FIANNA FÁIL

Dan Wallace is a hard-working TD who, without ever achieving a high national profile in the Dáil, has kept his constituents happy enough to have elected him every time since 1982. In 2002 he was elected along with party colleague Billy Kelleher without reaching the quota.

OCCUPATION
Full-time public representative, former clerical officer with Henry Ford Ltd.

ADDRESS
60 Thomas Davis Street,
Blackpool, Cork

PHONE
Constituency
(021) 439 3111
Fax (021) 421 2236

Leinster House
(01) 618 4426
Fax (01) 618 4458

BORN
Cork, June 1942

EDUCATION
North Monastery CBS, Cork;
School of Commerce, Cork

MARITAL STATUS
Married to Ethel Sutton.
Two sons, three daughters

3 SEATS

2 Fianna Fáil
1 Fine Gael

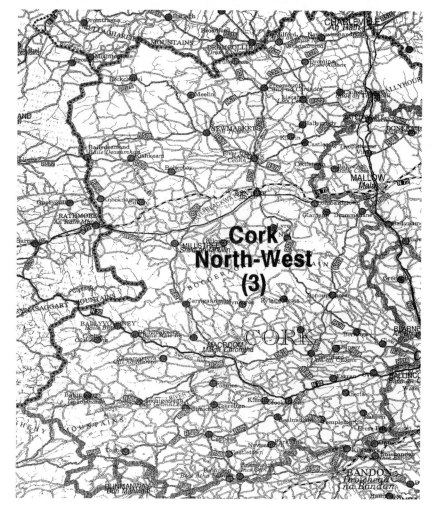

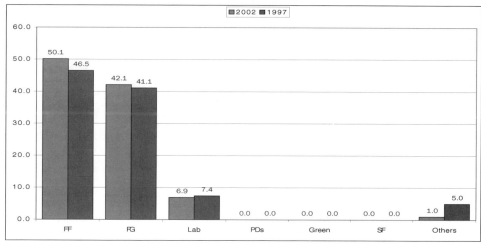

	2002	1997
FF	50.1	46.5
FG	42.1	41.1
Lab	6.9	7.4
PDs	0.0	0.0
Green	0.0	0.0
SF	0.0	0.0
Others	1.0	5.0

			1	2	3	4
				M Moynihan's surplus	Votes of Coughlan and Duffy	D Moynihan's surplus
*M MOYNIHAN	FF		10,540 √			
*D MOYNIHAN	FF		8,893	+592 9,485	+669 10,154 √	
G MURPHY	FG		8,548	+181 8,729	+688 9,417	90 9,507 √
*M Creed	FG		7,787	+30 7,817	+1,340 9,157	303 9,460
M Coughlan	Lab		2,668	+26 2,694 eliminated		
G Duffy	CSP		383	+6 389 eliminated		
Non transferable				0	386	56

3 SEATS

ELECTORATE
53,699

TOTAL POLL
39,393

SPOILED
574

VALID POLL
38,819

QUOTA
9,705

* DENOTES
OUTGOING TD

NEWLY
ELECTED TDS
IN CAPITALS

No change

AS IN 1997, Cork North west returned two Fianna Fáil deputies and one from Fine Gael. Fine Gael's vote share here was its largest anywhere in the country, and actually went up by 1% over 1997, but Fianna Fáil's vote rose by almost 4% to just over 50%, in one of the party's best performances of 2002. With over 90% of the vote between the two civil war parties, Cork North West shows us politics as it used to be!

There was one significant change. A newcomer, County Councillor Gerard Murphy, edged out Macroom-based Michael Creed. Creed had held the seat for Fine Gael since 1989, and his father had held it earlier. Murphy won enough first preference votes to stay ahead of Creed as the transfer votes from Macroom UDC member Martin Coughlan (Lab) favoured Murphy's better located running mate.

Remarkably, both successful Fianna Fáil candidates share the name of Moynihan. Michael pulled further ahead of his senior running mate Donal, extending his 1997 lead of 442 votes to 1,647 votes on this occasion.

DONAL MOYNIHAN

FIANNA FÁIL

First elected November 1982, the famously gentlemanly Donal Moynihan lost his seat in 1989 but returned to the Dáil in 1992 and was elected on the third count in 2002. Donal's father was a member of Cork County Council from 1928 to 1970. Donal was co-opted in 1970 and is now the longest serving Fianna Fáil member of the County Council.

OCCUPATION
Public representative, farmer

ADDRESS
Gortnascorty, Ballymakeera, Co Cork

PHONE
Home
(026) 45019

Constituency
(026) 43 937
Fax (026) 43 938

Leinster House
(01) 618 4085

EMAIL
donalmoynihanccc@eircom.net

BORN
Ballymakeera, Co Cork,
October 1941

EDUCATION
Ballyvourney Vocational School,
Co Cork

MARITAL STATUS
Married to Catherine Twomey.
Four sons, five daughters

MICHAEL MOYNIHAN

FIANNA FÁIL

Unusually Michael Moynihan, who has topped the poll on both his outings, had never held any public office before being first elected to Dáil Éireann in 1997, although he has a strong Fianna Fáil family background. A dairy farmer, he is a member of the ICMSA and is a member of the Joint Committees on Agriculture, Food and the Marine, and Heritage and the Irish Language.

OCCUPATION
Public representative, dairy farmer

ADDRESS
Means, Kiskearn, Mallow, Co Cork

CONSTITUENCY OFFICE
Percival Street, Kanturk, Co Cork

PHONE
Constituency
(029) 51299
Fax (029) 51300

Leinster House
(01) 618 3595

EMAIL
michael@michaelmoynihan.ie

BORN
Cork, January 1968

EDUCATION
Boherbue Comprehensive School,
Mallow, Co Cork

MARITAL STATUS
Single

GERARD MURPHY

FINE GAEL

Serving his second term on Cork County Council and Leader of the Fine Gael Group there. Gerard Murphy displaced party colleague Michael Creed to be returned to the Dáil for the first time. He has been appointed deputy spokesperson on Enterprise, Trade & Employment.

OCCUPATION
Full-time public representative

ADDRESS
New Street, Newmarket, Co Cork

PHONE
Constituency
(029) 51922
Fax (029) 20928

Leinster House
(01) 618 4208
Fax (01) 618 44323

EMAIL
gerard.murphy@oireachtas.ie

BORN
March 1951

EDUCATION
Cistercian College,
Mount St Joseph, Roscrea,
Co Tipperary

MARITAL STATUS
Married.
Two children

5 SEATS

3 Fianna Fáil
1 Fine Gael
1 Green

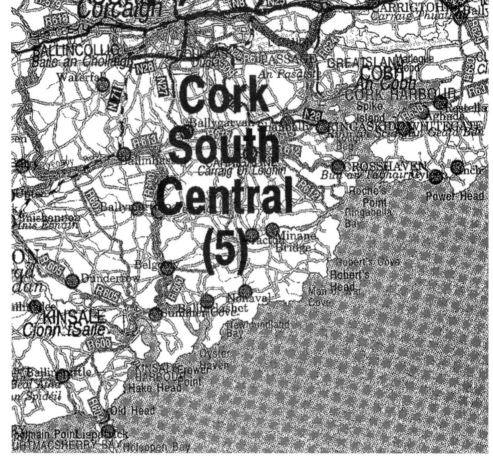

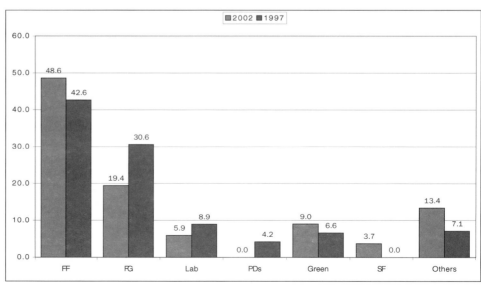

DAN BOYLE

GREEN

Dan Boyle was first elected to Cork Corporation in 1991 and is now in his tenth year as a Green Party Cork city councillor. With a background in youth and community work, he has served as Vice-President of the National Youth Council of Ireland, is a member of the National Economic and Social Council (NESC) and the Public Transport Partnership Forum. He is currently Party Chief Whip, spokesperson on Finance, Social and Family Affairs, Community, Rural Development and the Islands.

OCCUPATION
Public representative, former youth and community worker and political researcher

ADDRESS
45 Capwell Avenue, Turner's Cross, Cork

PHONE
Constituency
(021) 470 4238
(021) 470 4239

Leinster House
(01) 618 4227

EMAIL
dboyle@oireachtas.ie

WEBSITE
www.iol.ie/~dboyl

BORN
Chicago, USA, 1962

EDUCATION
Colaiste Chríost Rí, Cork; Cork Institute of Technology

MARITAL STATUS
Married to Bláithín Hurley. One daughter

SIMON COVENEY

FINE GAEL

Simon Coveney was still in the process of taking over the family farm and business interests when the untimely death of his father, the very popular TD Hugh Coveney, in 1998 thrust him into the Dáil at the subsequent by-election. His youth made him a natural for the post of spokesperson on Drugs and Youth Issues upon entry and he is now spokesperson on Communications, Marine and Natural Resources.

OCCUPATION
Full-time public representative

ADDRESS
Abbottswood, Rochestown, Cork

CONSTITUENCY OFFICE
6a Anglesea Street, Cork

PHONE
Constituency
(021) 431 3100
Fax (021) 431 6696

Leinster House
(01) 618 3753
Fax (01) 618 4506

EMAIL
simon.coveney@oireachtas.ie

WEBSITE
www.simoncoveney.ie

BORN
Cork, June 1972

EDUCATION
Clongowes Wood College, Kildare; University College Cork; Gurteen Agricultural College; Royal Agriculture College, Gloucestershire

MARITAL STATUS
Single

JOHN DENNEHY

FIANNA FÁIL

First elected in 1987, but lost his seat in 1992 and returned to the Dáil in 1997 after unsuccessfully contesting the 1994 by-election. An active local politician, he just squeezed ahead of independent Kathy Sinnott on the final recount. He is a member of the Joint Committees on Finance and the Public Service and on Health and Children, and Chair of the Oireachtas Joint Services Committee.

OCCUPATION
Full-time public representative, former engineering supervisor, Irish Steel Ltd.

ADDRESS
Avondale, 13 Westside Estate, Togher, Co Cork

PHONE
Constituency
(021) 496 2908
Fax (021) 432 0799

Leinster House
(01) 618 4431

EMAIL
johndennehytd@eircom.net

BORN
Togher, Cork, March 1940

EDUCATION
Sharman Crawford Technical Institute; Cork College of Commerce

MARITAL STATUS
Married to Philomena Martin. Five sons and two daughters

MICHEÁL MARTIN

FIANNA FÁIL

Following his success as Minister for Education from 1997-2000 the charismatic Martin was handed what many perceive to be the poisoned chalice of the Health and Children portfolio in January 2000. Recent financial constraints seem to have led to a lower profile. His local popularity is such that he had a surplus of 5,540 votes at the first count. Micheál Martin is the son of Paddy Martin, former international boxer.

OCCUPATION
Full-time public representative, former secondary school teacher

ADDRESS
Lios Laoi, 16 Silver Manor, Ballinlough, Cork

PHONE
Constituency
(021) 432 0088
Fax (021) 432 0089

Leinster House
(01) 671 1026
Fax (01) 671 4508

EMAIL
minister@doh.irlgov.ie

BORN
Cork, August 1960

EDUCATION
Coláiste Chríost Rí, Cork; University College, Cork (BA, HDipED, MA)

MARITAL STATUS
Married to Mary O'Shea. One son, one daughter

		1	2 Martin's surplus	3 Votes of Neville and O'Sullivan	4 Votes of O'Connell	5 Votes of Hanlon	6 Votes of Ryan	7 Votes of Clune	8 Coveney's surplus
*M MARTIN	FF	14742 √							
			+1668	+55	+114	+301	+203	+213	+219
*B O'KEEFFE	FF	6556	8224	8279	8393	8694	8897	9112	9331 √
			+312	+38	+96	+93	+518		
*D Clune	FG	5535	5848	5886	5982	6075	6593	eliminated	
			+1723	+39	+402	+364	+220	+199	+204
*J DENNEHY	FF	5533	7256	7295	7697	8061	8281	8480	8684
			+574	+36	+113	+132	+596	+4939	
*S COVENEY	FG	5183	5757	5793	5906	6038	6634	11573 √	
			+409	+98	+418	+541	+765	+509	+930
K Sinnott	Ind	4984	5393	5491	5909	6450	7215	7724	8654
			+442	+112	+260	+568	+1427	+543	+1013
D BOYLE	GP	4952	5394	5506	5766	6334	7761	8304	9317 √
			+179	+48	+234	+223			
B Ryan	Lab	3282	3461	3509	3743	3966	eliminated		
			+113	+78	+226				
T Hanlon	SF	2063	2176	2254	2480	eliminated			
			+93	+90					
C O'Connell	Ind	1821	1914	2004	eliminated				
			+11						
T Neville	Ind	371	383	eliminated					
			+10						
M O'Sullivan	SWP	218	228	eliminated					
Non transferable			0	16	141	258	237	188	0

5 SEATS

ELECTORATE
90,399

TOTAL POLL
55,785

SPOILED
446

VALID POLL
55,338

QUOTA
9,224

* DENOTES
OUTGOING TD

NEWLY
ELECTED TDS
IN CAPITALS

Green gain from FG

AFTER what may be the last of the long, long counts if electronic voting is extended to the whole country at the general election, John Dennehy held on to Fianna Fáil's third seat by just six votes from the independent candidate Kathy Sinnott. This is just the sort of experience that electronic voting is designed to avoid; nerve wracking for the participants and inconvenient for those who are planning the next government, but the sort of experience that makes the count so exciting for us, the spectators. Of course had not Micheál Martin walked off with almost 15,000 of his party's 27,000 votes the count might have been over rather more quickly. Martin's was the best personal vote of any candidate in the country; this was not one of the party's vote management triumphs.

For Fine Gael, the election followed the same pattern as it did in several middle class Dublin constituencies:

a sharp decline in the vote, and a seat loss to the Greens. Their vote was down by more than 11%, although the 1997 vote was higher than at any time since 1982. Dan Boyle, running for the Greens in his third general election, increased his vote to 9%; just enough to keep him in the long count and so pick up generous transfers to get ahead of FG's Deirdre Clune. Clune and Coveney were only 54 votes apart when she was eliminated. He owes his seat to Brendan Ryan's Labour transfers which just nosed him ahead of her after the sixth count.

Kathy Sinnott gained a high public profile after winning a court case against the State on the issue of education for her autistic son, and targeted the constituency of the Minister for Health to advance her campaign for the fair treatment of such children. She was later narrowly defeated for a Seanad seat.

9	**10**
O'Keeffe's surplus	Boyle's surplus
+82	+23
8766	**8789** √
+42	+87
8696	**8783**
0	*0*

In his cup: Ruairí Quinn during the election campaign

BATT O'KEEFFE

FIANNA FÁIL

First elected in 1987, the popular local politician and GAA star lost his seat in 1989, but was re-elected in 1992 after three years in the Seanad. Appointed Chairman of the Joint Committee on Health and Children in December 1997, he returns to that post in the 29th Dáil.

OCCUPATION
Full-time public representative, former lecturer in Regional Technical College, Cork

ADDRESS
8 Westcliffe, Ballincollig, Co Cork

PHONE
Constituency
(021) 487 1393
Fax (021) 487 1393

Leinster House
(01) 618 3348

EMAIL
batt.okeeffe@oireachtas.ie

BORN
Mallow, Co Cork, April 1945

EDUCATION
St Brendan's Killarney, Co Kerry; University College, Cork (BA, HDipED)

MARITAL STATUS
Married to Mary Murphy. One son, three daughters

3 SEATS

2 Fianna Fáil

1 Fine Gael

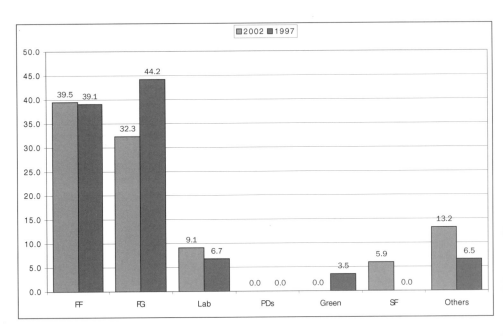

3 SEATS

ELECTORATE
54,274

TOTAL POLL
38,132

SPOILED
434

VALID POLL
37,698

QUOTA
9,425

* DENOTES
OUTGOING TD

NEWLY
ELECTED TDS
IN CAPITALS

		1	2 Votes of Butler	3 Votes of Heaney	4 Votes of Ó Súill'bháin and O'Leary	5 Votes of McCarthy	6 Votes of O'Sullivan	7 O'Donovan's surplus
D O'DONOVAN	FF	7,695	+79 / 7,774	+88 / 7,862	+415 / 8,277	+586 / 8,863	+1,316 / 10,179 √	
*J WALSH	FF	7,187	+84 / 7,271	+124 / 7,395	311 / 7,706	413 / 8,119	+878 / 8,997	+390 / 9,387 √
*J O'KEEFFE	FG	6,358	+118 / 6,476	+146 / 6,622	+213 / 6,835	+889 / 7,724	+772 / 8,496	+95 / 8,591 √
*PJ Sheehan	FG	5,831	+33 / 5,864	+68 / 5,932	+224 / 6,156	+831 / 6,987	+1,300 / 8,287	+269 / 8,556
C O'Sullivan	Ind	3,609	+75 / 3,684	+165 / 3,849	+454 / 4,303	+841 / 5,144	eliminated	
M McCarthy	Lab	3,442	+63 / 3,505	+131 / 3,636	+394 / 4,030	eliminated		
C Ó Súilleabháin	SF	1,308	+21 / 1,329	+43 / 1,372	eliminated			
A O'Leary	SF	899	+9 / 908	+37 / 945	eliminated			
T Heaney	Ind	748	+116 / 864	eliminated				
E Butler	Ind	621	eliminated					
Non transferable			23	62	306	470	878	0

FF gain from FG

THERE were not many constituencies where Fine Gael took more seats than Fianna Fáil in 1997; in 2002 there were none. FG surrendered the 2:1 advantage it had held since 1981 and FF won two seats in this three seater for the first time despite local predictions.

PJ Sheehan, from the far west of the constituency and one of the truly colourful members of the last Dáil, lost his seat to Bantry-based Denis O'Donovan. At least his wife will be spared the drive to Dublin.

The margin between Sheehan and O'Keeffe was only 35 votes on the final count. The immediate cause of the change was the collapse of the Fine Gael vote, which fell by almost 12%, one of the worst results for the party anywhere. Sheehan lost over 2,000 votes and O'Keeffe more than 1,000. Most damage was done by an independent candidate, Christy O'Sullivan, running to highlight the neglect of the area by all governments. O'Sullivan is a former Fianna Fáil member (and brother of a former candidate) who ran as an independent in the 1999 local election with considerable success. The new FF TD's personal vote was up by 1,700 votes on 1997, following on from an impressive performance in the local elections, and he actually polled better than the high-profile Minister for Agriculture Joe Walsh.

Agriculture minister Joe Walsh: missed out on topping poll to colleague Denis O'Donovan

DENIS O'DONOVAN

FIANNA FÁIL

The son of a founder member of the Kilcrohane Fianna Fáil Cumann, Denis O'Donovan has been an active public representative at local level since 1985 and at national level since he was nominated to Seanad Éireann by the Taoiseach in 1989. His achievement in topping the poll in a strong field is a reflection of his work for local communities and particularly of his willingness to help local organisations with his legal advice. He is Chair of the All-party Committee on the Constitution.

OCCUPATION
Public representative, solicitor

ADDRESS
Montrose House, Slip, Bantry, Co Cork

PHONE
Constituency
(027) 53 840
Fax (027) 53 834

Leinster House
(01) 618 3079
Fax (01) 618 4562

BORN
Bantry, Co Cork; July 1955

EDUCATION
Coláiste an Spioraid Naoimh, Bantry, Co Cork;
Coláiste an Chroí Ró-Naofa, Carrignavar, Co Cork;
Incorporated Law Society of Ireland, Dublin (BCL Hons)

MARITAL STATUS
Married to Mary G Murphy.
Three sons, one daughter

JIM O'KEEFFE

FINE GAEL

First elected to the Dáil in 1977, Jim O'Keeffe held his seat after a recount demanded by popular party colleague PJ Sheehan. During his time in the Dáil he has held Front Bench responsibility for a range of portfolios and is currently deputy spokesperson on Justice, Equality and Law Reform.

OCCUPATION
Full-time public representative, former solicitor and notary public

ADDRESS
Oldchapel, Bandon, Co Cork

PHONE
Constituency
(023) 41 399
Fax (023) 41 421

Leinster House
(01) 618 3196
Fax (01) 618 3583

EMAIL
jim.okeeffe@oireachtas.ie

BORN
Skibbereen, Co Cork, March 1941

EDUCATION
St Fachtna's High School, Skibbereen; University College Cork; University College Dublin; School of the Incorporated Law Society of Ireland

MARITAL STATUS
Married to Maeve O'Sullivan.
Seven daughters, one son

JOE WALSH

FIANNA FÁIL

Re-appointed to the ministry he has held or shadowed since 1992, Walsh ran second to party colleague O'Donovan this time around. First elected in 1977, he lost his seat in 1981 but was re-elected in February 1982 and at each subsequent election. He is regarded as a skilful negotiator.

OCCUPATION
Government Minister, former dairy manager

ADDRESS
5 Emmett Sq, Clonakilty, Co Cork

PHONE
Constituency
(023) 33 575
Fax: (023) 34 267

Leinster House
(01) 676 4223
Fax: (01) 618 3707

EMAIL
joe.walsh@daff.irlgov.ie

BORN
Ballineen, Co Cork, May 1943

EDUCATION
St Finbarr's College, Farranferris, Cork;
University College, Cork
(Dairy Science)

MARITAL STATUS
Married to Marie Donegan.
Three sons, two daughters

3 SEATS

2 Fianna Fáil

1 Independent

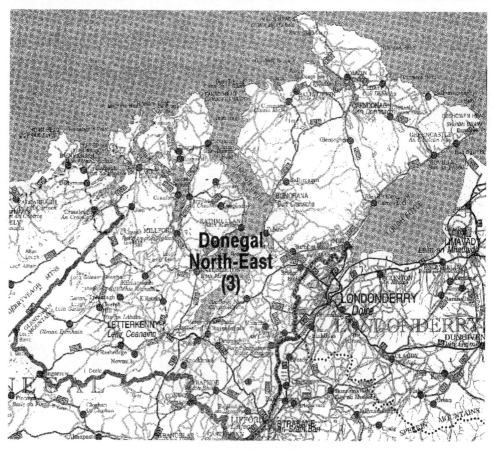

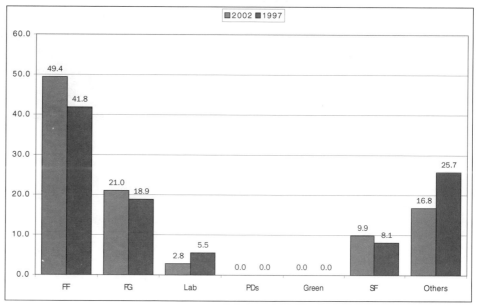

		1	2 Votes of McNair	3 McDaid's surplus	4 Votes of MacLochlainn	5 Keaveney's surplus	6 Votes of McGuinness
3 SEATS							
*J McDAID	FF	9,614 √					
			+123	+249	+1,012		
*C KEAVENEY	FF	8,340	8,463	8,712	9,724 √		
			+137	+131	+1,275	+364	+758
N BLANEY	Ind FF	6,124	6,261	6,392	7,667	8,031	8,789 √
			+187	+10	+265	+175	
B McGuinness	FG	3,914	4,101	4,111	4,376	4,551	eliminated
			+358	+100	+446	+53	+2,752
S Maloney	FG	3,723	4,081	4,181	4,627	4,680	7,432
			+103	+37			
P Mac Lochlainn	SF	3,611	3,714	3,751	eliminated		
J McNair	Lab	1,021	eliminated				
Non transferable			113	0	753	45	1,041

ELECTORATE
58,208

TOTAL POLL
36,896

SPOILED
549

VALID POLL
36,347

QUOTA
9,087

* DENOTES
OUTGOING TD

NEWLY
ELECTED TDS
IN CAPITALS

No change

DONEGAL North east again returned two Fianna Fáil deputies and one from independent Fianna Fáil. Fianna Fáil's vote was up by almost 8%, and despite a 2% increase in its vote Fine Gael is unrepresented in this constituency for the second time. Jim McDaid's success in obtaining benefits for his area paid off with over 3,000 additional votes for the outgoing minister. Fine Gael's best hope was to displace Niall Blaney, the new independent Fianna Fáil candidate. Blaney did not match his uncle's vote winning power but did enough to maintain his family's well-established Dáil presence of behalf of the constituency.

Fine Gael chose the 1997 Labour candidate, Seán Moloney as one of its two candidates. Moloney out-polled McGuinness and took 60% of his running mate's transfers – and almost 80% of his transferable votes – but it was not enough to push him ahead of Blaney who remained 1,367 votes again on the last count. Blaney benefited from Sinn Féin transfers, winning twice as many of them as did his two Fine Gael rivals combined. The new Labour party candidate polled poorly, but did transfer 35% of his votes to the old Labour party candidate, Moloney.

Happy man: Jim McDaid celebrates his re-election

NIALL BLANEY

INDEPENDENT FIANNA FÁIL

Son of Harry Blaney, grandson of Neal, and nephew of Neil T, Niall Blaney takes over the family Dáil seat, held first for Fianna Fáil since 1927 and for Independent Fianna Fáil since they broke away from the main party in 1973 after the Arms Crisis, except for the period after the 1996 by-election which followed his uncle's death.

OCCUPATION
Public representative, former civil engineer

ADDRESS
Rossnakill, Letterkenny, Co Donegal

PHONE
Constituency Office
(074) 912 7754
Fax (074) 912 7783

Home
(074) 59 014
Fax (074) 59 700

Leinster House
(01) 618 4047
Fax (01) 618 4583

EMAIL
n_blaney@hotmail.com

WEBSITE
www.independentfiannafail.com

BORN
Letterkenny, Co Donegal, January 1974

EDUCATION
Mulroy College, Milford;
Letterkenny Institute of Technology

MARITAL STATUS
Married to Rosaleen Shovelin

CECILIA KEAVENEY

FIANNA FÁIL

Daughter of Paddy Keaveney (Ind FF) TD 1976-1977, Cecilia Keaveney replaced her late father on Donegal County Council in 1995, and was first elected to the Dáil at the by-election in April 1996 which followed the death of Neil Blaney. She has strong cross-border interests and is Chair of the Oireachtas Committee on Arts, Sports and Tourism.

OCCUPATION
Full-time public representative, former music teacher

ADDRESS
Loreto, Moville, Co Donegal

PHONE
Constituency
(074) 938 2177
Fax (074) 938 2832

Leinster House
(01) 618 3552
Fax (01) 618 3569

EMAIL
cecilia.keaveney@oireachtas.ie

BORN
Derry City, November 1968

EDUCATION
Carndonagh Community School;
University of Ulster, Jordanstown
(BMus, MPhil Research Masters,
PGCE Music)

MARITAL STATUS
Single

JIM McDAID

FIANNA FÁIL

The former Minister for Tourism, Sport and Recreation, who was forced to refuse the Defence portfolio in 1991 when his picture appeared in the press with a convicted IRA member, was first elected in 1989. He is now Minister of State at the Department of Transport. He maintains a particular interest in the hospice movement.

OCCUPATION
Government Minister, medical doctor

ADDRESS
Pearse Road, Letterkenny, Co Donegal

PHONE
Constituency
(074) 912 5132
Fax (074) 912 6637

Leinster House
(01) 676 2550
Fax (01) 604 1320

BORN
Termon, Co Donegal, October 1949

EDUCATION
St Eunan's College, Letterkenny, Co Donegal;
University College Galway

MARITAL STATUS
Separated.
Three sons and one daughter

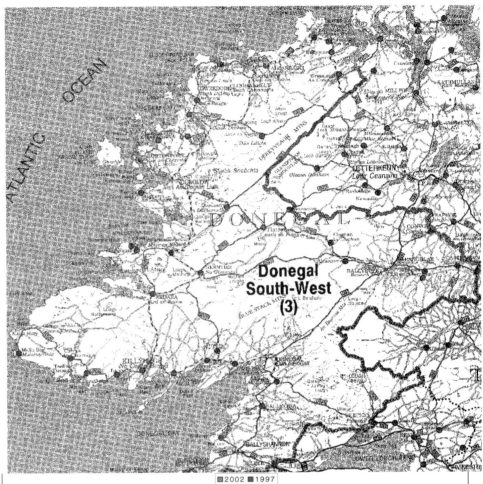

3 SEATS

2 Fianna Fáil
1 Fine Gael

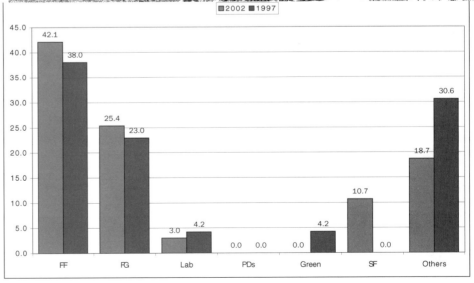

			1	**2** Votes of Breslin	**3** Votes of Dignam	**4** Votes of Rodgers	**5** Votes of Pringle	**6** Votes of Kelly	**7** Gallagher's surplus	**8** Votes of Doherty
3 SEATS	P the C GALLAGHER	FF	7,740	+103 7,843	+117 7,960	+242 8,202	+300 8,502	+779 9,281	√	
	*M COUGHLAN	FF	7,257	+123 7,380	+85 7,465	+82 7,547	+788 8,335	+422 8,757	+175 8,932	√
	J White	FG	4,680	+40 4,720	+20 4,740	+82 4,822	+339 5,161	+224 5,385	+17 5,402	+528 5,930
	*D McGINLEY	FG	4,378	+106 4,484	+28 4,512	+285 4,797	+419 5,216	+705 5,921	+81 6,002	+1,368 7,370 √
	J Kelly	Ind	3,091	+83 3,174	+45 3,219	+110 3,329	+467 3,796	eliminated		
	P Doherty	SF	2,696	+75 2,771	+800 3,571	+149 3,720	+446 4,166	+1,004 5,170	+99 5,269	elimt'd
	T Pringle	Ind	2,630	+257 2,887	+21 2,908	+170 3,078	eliminated			
	T Dignam	SF	1,133	+15 1,148	eliminated					
	S Rodgers	Lab	1,079	+120 1,199	+6 1,205	eliminated				
	G Breslin	Ind	951	eliminated						
	Non transferable			29	26	85	319	662	0	3,373

ELECTORATE
54,789

TOTAL POLL
36,135

SPOILED
500

VALID POLL
35,635

QUOTA
8,909

* DENOTES OUTGOING TD

NEWLY ELECTED TDS IN CAPITALS

FF gain from Ind

THIS is the only instance of an independent TD failing to retain his seat. Tom Gildea, one of the surprises of the 1997 election when he was elected on the basis of a campaign to secure cheap access to British television, did not even try to defend it. An IMS/*Independent* poll in February suggested seats would go as they did even if Gildea were to have stood. His place went to Pat 'the Cope' Gallagher, recalled from a stint in Brussels as an MEP to gain a seat for his party, although Gildea had voted for Bertie Ahern as Taoiseach and proved to be a loyal supporter of the coalition government.

Both major parties increased their vote here by 4% (Fianna Fáil) and 2% (Fine Gael) with Gildea out of the picture but both are still well down on what they won in 1992. The main contest was for the FG seat. Jim White, a former Fine Gael TD who retired in 1982, was back on the ticket along with the incumbent Dinny McGinley. White won more first preferences but, just as in 1992, McGinley's ability to pick up more transfers, not least from his constituency neighbour, Sinn Féin's Pearse Doherty, saw him comfortably home. SF's 11% of the vote was one of its best performances not to be rewarded by a seat.

Independent FF man Joe Kelly polled well if not quite up to the level of his colleague, Niall Blaney, in Donegal North east, and independent local councillor, Thomas Pringle from Killybegs, running on a general jobs, health and infrastructure platform also recorded a healthy vote. Gwen Breslin, Gildea's successor was also quite well supported but this time there were simply not enough votes for independents to repeat Gildea's 1997 success.

MARY COUGHLAN

FIANNA FÁIL

The Minister for Social and Family Affairs, who was first elected to the Dáil in 1987, is a daughter of the late Cathal Coughlan, Dáil Deputy 1983-1986, and niece of the late Clement Coughlan, TD 1980-83. Before the 2002 election she was Minister of State at the Department of Arts, Heritage, Gaeltacht and the Islands.

OCCUPATION
Full-time public representative, former social worker

ADDRESS
Cranny Inver, Co Donegal

PHONE
Constituency
(074) 973 6002/973 6535
Fax (074) 973 6333

Leinster House
(01) 704 3662
Fax (01) 704 3869

BORN
Donegal Town, May 1965

EDUCATION
Ursuline Convent, Sligo;
University College Dublin (BSocSc)

MARITAL STATUS
Married to David Charlton.
One son and one daughter

PAT 'THE COPE' GALLAGHER

FIANNA FÁIL

The nickname descends from his grandfather Paddy 'the Cope', a pioneer of the Irish Cooperative movement. He has particular interests in fisheries and the Irish language. MEP for Connacht/Ulster) since 1994, he returned to top the poll and be rewarded with the position of Minister of State at the Department of Environment and Local Government.

OCCUPATION
Full-time public representative

ADDRESS
Dungloe, Co Donegal

PHONE
Constituency
(074) 952 1276
(074) 952 1133

Leinster House
(01) 888 2570
(01) 618 3261
Fax (01) 878 8642

EMAIL
patthecopeg@eircom.net

WEBSITE
www.patthecope.com

BORN
Burtonport, Co Donegal,
March 1948

EDUCATION
St Enda's College, Galway;
University College Galway

MARITAL STATUS
Married to Ann Gillespie

DINNY McGINLEY

FINE GAEL

First elected to the Dáil in 1982, Dinny McGinley has held a range of front bench positions. In February 2001 he was appointed Fine Gael spokesperson on Arts, Heritage, Gaeltacht and the Islands. Deputy McGinley was appointed spokesperson on Defence in June 2002, a change from his usual concentration on Gaeltacht issues.

OCCUPATION
Full-time public representative, former national school teacher

ADDRESS
Magheralosk, Bunbeg,
Co Donegal

PHONE
Constituency
(074) 953 1719
Fax/Phone (074) 953 1025

Leinster House
(01) 618 3452
Fax (01) 618 4177
LoCall 1890 337 889

EMAIL
dinny.mcginley@oireachtas.ie

BORN
Gweedore, Co Donegal, 1945

EDUCATION
St Patrick's Teacher Training College, Dublin;
University College Dublin (BA, HDipEd);
Coláiste Íosagáin, Ballyvourney, Co Cork

MARITAL STATUS
Single

4 SEATS

2 Fianna Fáil

1 Independent

1 Labour

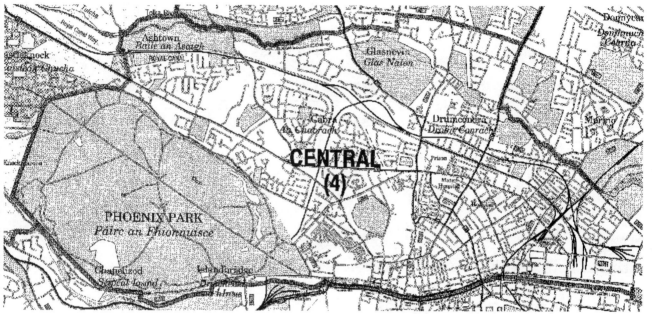

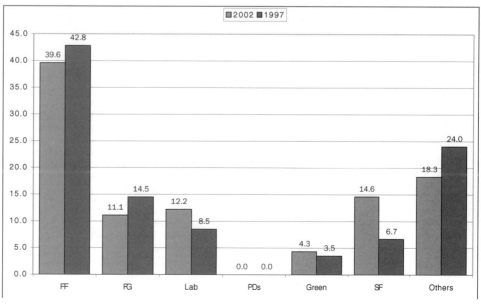

		1	2	3	4	5	6	7
			Ahern's surplus	Votes of O'Loughlin, Prendeville O'Donnell	Votes of Simpson	Votes of Mitchell	Costello's surplus	Gregory's surplus
4 SEATS								
*B AHERN	FF	10882 √						
			+813	+148	+617			
*T GREGORY	Ind	5664	6477	6637	7242	√		
			+328	+43	+144	+331	+359	+162
N Kehoe	SF	4979	5300	5343	5487	5818	6177	6339
			+363	+40	+507	+2824		
J COSTELLO	Lab	4136	4499	4539	5046	7870	√	
			+207	+87	+205			
*J Mitchell	FG	3769	3976	4063	4268	eliminated		
			+2265	+113	+75	+517	+704	+154
D FITZPATRICK	FF	2590	4855	4968	5043	5560	6264	6418 √
			+76	+107				
T Simpson	GP	1469	1545	1652	eliminated			
			+11					
P O'Loughlin	CSP	366	377	eliminated				
			+6					
T Prendeville	Ind	97	103	eliminated				
			+6					
P O'Donnell	Ind	89	95	eliminated				
Non transferable			0	37	104	596	0	119

ELECTORATE
62,180

TOTAL POLL
34,517

SPOILED
483

VALID POLL
34,034

QUOTA
6,807

* DENOTES
OUTGOING TD

NEWLY
ELECTED TDS
IN CAPITALS

Lab gain from FG

IT WAS certain that Bertie Ahern would top the poll and that veteran independent Tony Gregory would retain his seat but after that it was a case of musical chairs with four candidates chasing two places. Labour's Joe Costello edged out Fine Gael's deputy leader Jim Mitchell, and Fianna Fáil Senator Dermot Fitzpatrick just saw off the challenge from Nicky Kehoe on behalf of Sinn Féin. City councillor Kehoe replaced Christy Burke, the standard bearer in 1992 and 1997, while the former TD Fitzpatrick won the race to be the Taoiseach's running mate only on the eve of the election. Marian McGennis, who stood successfully last time, moved to South Central following boundary changes.

The vote shares of the established parties did not change a lot, but the changes were crucial for Jim Mitchell. His vote dropped by 3.4% and Costello's was up 3.7%, a net shift between the two that saw Mitchell eliminated on the fourth count, some 800 votes short of Costello and Fitzpatrick. Mitchell's transfers easily elected Costello, who received two-thirds of them. Mitchell had argued strongly for an electoral alliance with Labour and his supporters followed his lead.

The Fianna Fáil vote was down 3% but a better spread of votes between Ahern and Fitzpatrick would have eased the latter's agonies, as would a transfer rate of more than 55% (lower than Mitchell to Costello and lower than in 1997 when it was 59%). Fitzpatrick was eventually successful with the lowest first preference vote of any elected candidate. The contest between Kehoe and Fitzpatrick was very tight with only 74 votes in it at the last count. Sinn Féin support was up almost 8% to 14%, more votes than either Fine Gael or Labour. Mitchell's transfers favoured Fitzpatrick and Gregory's surplus split pretty evenly but Kehoe did pick up 1,041 votes in lower preferences after Ahern's surplus was distributed as against Fitzpatrick's 1,567.

BERTIE AHERN

FIANNA FÁIL

Former Taoiseach Charlie Haughey is said to have called Bertie Ahern "the most ruthless, the most devious, the most cunning of them all". He was elected Taoiseach on Thursday 26 June 1997 having been leader of the Fianna Fáil party since 11 November 1994. Despite tribunals, myopia among the trees of North Dublin and the waning of the tiger economy, Bertie Ahern's political astuteness, personal charm and phenomenal appetite for hard work continue to make him popular with both party and people, especially in his home constituency.

OCCUPATION
Full-time public representative

ADDRESS
St Luke's, 161 Lower Drumcondra Road, Dublin 9

PHONE
Constituency
(01) 837 4129
Fax (01) 836 8877

Leinster House
(01) 619 4020
Fax (01) 676 4048

EMAIL
taoiseach@taoiseach.ie

WEBSITE
www.ie/taoiseach/

BORN
Dublin, September 1951

EDUCATION
St Aidan's CBS, Whitehall;
Rathmines College of Commerce

MARITAL STATUS
Separated, two daughters

JOE COSTELLO

LABOUR

Joe Costello has been a member of the Oireachtas since 1989, was deputy for Dublin Central 1992-1997 and party leader in the Seanad 1997-2002. Spokesperson on Education & Science. A teacher, trade unionist (former president of ASTI) and human rights activist, Joe is also a Councillor on Dublin City Council.

OCCUPATION
Full-time public representative, former secondary school teacher

ADDRESS
66 Aughrim Street, Dublin 7

PHONE
Leinster House
(01) 618 3896
Fax (01) 618 4596

EMAIL
joe_costello@oireachtas.ie

BORN
Sligo, July 1945

EDUCATION
Summerhill College, Sligo;
Maynooth College;
University College Dublin

MARITAL STATUS
Engaged to Emer Malone

DERMOT FITZPATRICK

FIANNA FÁIL

One of the eleven appointed to the Seanad by the Taoiseach in 1997, Dr Fitzpatrick was selected on the eve of the election to run in Dublin Central. He won a seat here in 1987 but lost it in the 'Spring tide' of 1992. He has been a member of Dublin Corporation since 1985, elected in the Cabra-Glasnevin area where he has a general practice. Nicky Kehoe, who ran him close for the final seat on this occasion, is from the same area.

OCCUPATION
Public representative,
family doctor

ADDRESS
80 Navan Road, Dublin 7

PHONE
Constituency
(01) 838 7515

Leinster House
(01) 662 9255

BORN
Dublin, April 1940

EDUCATION
Coláiste Mhuire, Dublin;
University College Dublin
(BDS, MB, BCh, BAO)

MARITAL STATUS
Married to Mary Wallace.
One son, three daughters

TONY GREGORY

INDEPENDENT

The Sinn Féin grass roots campaign may have damaged other candidates in Dublin Central but Tony Gregory has perfected grass roots politics, and the initiative and activity that brought the IFSC and docklands development to Dublin Central mean that the tie-less TD, who was first elected in February 1982, increased his vote again.

OCCUPATION
Full-time public representative, former secondary school teacher

HOME ADDRESS
5 Sackville Gardens, Ballybough, Dublin 3

PHONE
Constituency
(01) 872 9910

Leinster House
(01) 618 3488
Fax (01) 618 4195

Mobile
(087) 812 6348

EMAIL
tony.gregory@oireachtas.ie

BORN
Dublin, December 1947

EDUCATION
O'Connell's School, Dublin;
University College Dublin
(BA, HDipEd)

MARITAL STATUS
Single

3 SEATS

1 Fianna Fáil

1 PD

1 Green

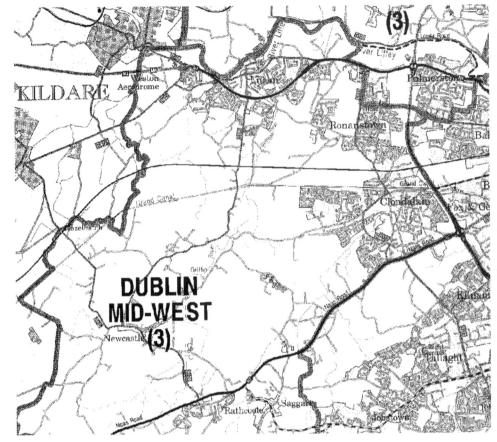

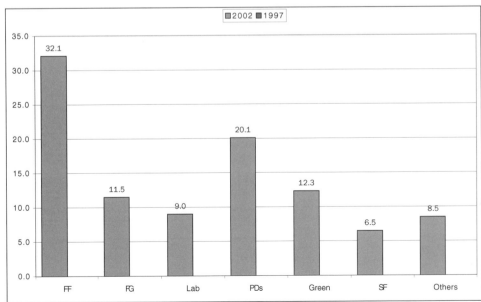

JOHN CURRAN

FIANNA FÁIL

First elected public representative in the June 1999 local elections, Curran is a keen sportsman and local fundraiser.

OCCUPATION
Public representative, businessman

ADDRESS
15 Knockmeenagh Road, Clondalkin, Dublin 22

PHONE
Constituency
(01) 457 9913
Fax (01) 462 6465

Leinster House
(01) 618 3792
Fax (01) 618 4786

EMAIL
jcurran@sdublincoco.ie

BORN
June 1960

EDUCATION
University College Dublin (BComm)

MARITAL STATUS
Married.
Three children

PAUL GOGARTY

GREEN

While those from outside the constituency may have been surprised at Paul Gogarty's success, those who had noticed that the Lucan-based journalist topped the polls in the 1999 local elections were less so. His successful track record on his main platform of proper infrastructure for the sprawling West Dublin suburbs was bound to be a crowd pleaser.

OCCUPATION
Full-time public representative, occasional journalist

PHONE
Leinster House
(01) 618 3022
Fax (01) 618 4784

EMAIL
pgogarty@sdublincoco.ie

BORN
Co Westmeath, December 1968

EDUCATION
CBS, Lucan Co Dublin;
DIT, Rathmines, Dublin (journalism)

MARITAL STATUS
Single

MARY HARNEY

PROGRESSIVE DEMOCRATS

One of the few people so convinced that the PDs would double their representation in the Dáil that she put her money on it, the Tánaiste has been a groundbreaker throughout her career, from first Lady Auditor of the College Historical Society in Trinity College, through youngest ever member of the Oireachtas in 1977, to first woman leader of a political party in Ireland.

OCCUPATION
Tánaiste and Government Minister, former research worker

ADDRESS
11 Serpentine Terrace, Ballsbridge, Dublin 4

PHONE
Constituency
(01) 667 5543
(01) 631 2172
Fax (01) 631 2815

Leinster House
(01) 676 1071
Fax (01) 631 2814

EMAIL
tanaiste@entemp.ie

WEBSITE
www.entemp.ie

BORN
Ballinasloe, Co Galway,
March 1953

EDUCATION
Convent of Mercy, Inchicore, Dublin; Presentation Convent, Clondalkin, Co Dublin; Trinity College, Dublin (BA(Mod))

MARITAL STATUS
Married to Brian Geoghegan

3 SEATS

ELECTORATE
55,184

TOTAL POLL
28,693

SPOILED
237

VALID POLL
28,456

QUOTA
7,115

* DENOTES
OUTGOING TD

NEWLY
ELECTED TDS
IN CAPITALS

			1	2 Votes of Callanan	3 Votes of O'Mara	4 Votes of McGrath, McGuinness	5 Votes of Green	6 Votes of Ridge	7 Votes of Flannery	8 Votes of Currie
J CURRAN	FF		5904	+24 5928	+51 5979	+133 6112	+180 6292	+216 6508	+401 6909	+177 7086
*M HARNEY	PD		5706	+13 5719	+13 5732	+80 5812	+141 5953	+243 6196	+152 6348	+576 6924
P GOGARTY	GP		3508	+15 3523	+18 3541	+86 3627	+243 3870	+77 3947	+647 4594	+666 5260
D Kelly	FF		3218	+14 3232	+5 3237	+53 3290	+91 3381	+53 3434	+191 3625	+112 3737
J Tuffy	Lab		2563	+3 2566	+36 2602	+142 2744	+147 2891	+308 3199	+395 3594	+901 4495
*A Currie	FG		2008	+9 2017	+6 2023	+28 2051	+49 2100	+473 2573	+114 2687	elim'td
T Flannery	SF		1855	+6 1861	+51 1912	+119 2031	+213 2244	+82 2326	eliminated	
T Ridge	FG		1268	+3 1271	+43 1314	+105 1419	+117 1536	eliminated		
D Green	Ind		1078	+14 1092	+78 1170	+143 1313	eliminated			
C McGrath	Ind		487	+1 488	+33 521	eliminated				
A McGuinness	WP		393	+0 393	+14 407	eliminated				
M O'Mara	Ind		361	+1 362	eliminated					
C Callanan	CSP		107	eliminated						
Non transferable				*4*	*14*	*39*	*132*	*84*	*426*	*255*

New constituency: 1 FF, 1 PD, 1 Green

ESSENTIALLY we can see the result as a Fine Gael loss to the Greens. However, this is a new three-seater constituency carved out of the old Dublin West and South West constituencies. Three incumbent TDs were directly affected by the change. Liam Lawlor's old base was moved into Dublin Mid West, but he decided not to stand again; Austin Currie and Mary Harney also found their traditional territories had been moved and so moved themselves, but only Harney did so with success.

Without a clear 1997 baseline there was much uncertainty about what would happen but Mary Harney was widely expected to be re-elected, and Fianna Fáil would surely win a seat, probably with John Curran, a good

vote winner in the local elections in Clondalkin. This was reinforced by a *Star*/Lansdowne poll published in January. The big question was who would win the third seat.

Given the first preferences, with the Greens winning 12.3%, Fine Gael 11.5%, Labour 9% we might have expected the seat to go to Labour or Fine Gael but Paul Gogarty, South Dublin council member for Lucan, got home by 1,000 votes. His was the second lowest first preference vote in the country for an elected TD. Obviously the transfers were crucial. The internal Fine Gael transfer rate from Therese Ridge to Austin Currie was a woeful 31%, and then Currie's transfer to Labour's Joanna Tuffy – another Lucan based candidate – was

9	10
Votes of Kelly	Curran's surplus

+2264	
9350 √	
+600	
7524 √	
+385	+700
5645	**6345** √
eliminated	
+313	+563
4808	**5371**

175	*972*

PD leader Mary Harney canvassing with her husband Brian Geoghegan at the Temple Bar Food Market in Dublin
PHOTOCALL IRELAND

only 34%, with Gogarty getting 25%.

Sinn Féin polled quite well here, winning almost 2000 votes, and an independent, David Green, running on a young drivers motor insurance platform won a creditable 1,078 votes.

The second Fianna Fáil candidate, Des Kelly, raised his profile during the campaign by taking a court case against the State for not including the secretarial and postal privileges allowed to Dáil deputies to be treated as part of their election expenditure; while he won in court, he fared less well with the voters.

4 SEATS
1 Green
1 Labour
2 Fianna Fáil

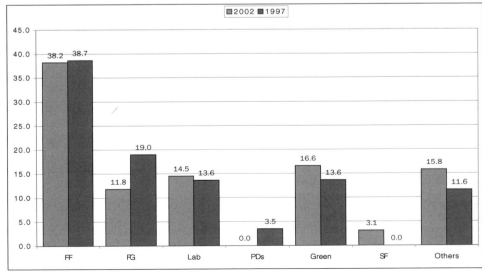

	2002	1997
FF	38.2	38.7
FG	11.8	19.0
Lab	14.5	13.6
PDs	0.0	3.5
Green	16.6	13.6
SF	3.1	0.0
Others	15.8	11.6

4 SEATS

ELECTORATE
72,908

TOTAL POLL
43,942

SPOILED
0

VALID POLL
43,942

QUOTA
8,789

* DENOTES
OUTGOING TD

NEWLY
ELECTED TDS
IN CAPITALS

		1	2 Votes of Quinn, Walshe	3 Votes of Goulding	4 Votes of Boland	5 Votes of Davis	6 Votes of Owen	7 Sargent's surplus	8 Votes of Kennedy
*T SARGENT	GP	7294	+86 7380	+298 7678	+140 7818	+300 8118	+1667 9785 √		
*S RYAN	Lab	6359	+48 6407	+128 6535	+130 6665	+182 6847	+1731 8578	+550 9128 √	
J GLENNON	FF	5892	+53 5945	+83 6028	+124 6152	+142 6294	+217 6511	+85 6596	+2044 8640 √
*GV WRIGHT	FF	5658	+49 5707	+32 5739	+38 5777	+91 5868	+271 6139	+110 6249	+2368 8617 √
C Daly	SP	5501	+50 5551	+179 5730	+66 5796	+448 6244	+346 6590	+182 6772	+751 7523
M Kennedy	FF	5253	+56 5309	+59 5368	+54 5422	+110 5532	+200 5732	+69 5801	elimt'd
*N Owen	FG	4012	+18 4030	+102 4132	+588 4720	+43 4763	eliminated		
M Davis	SF	1350	+32 1382	+42 1424	+16 1440	eliminated			
C Boland	FG	1177	+12 1189	+27 1216	eliminated				
C Goulding	Ind	914	+95 1009	eliminated					
E Quinn	Ind	285	eliminated						
D Walshe	CSP	247	eliminated						
Non transferable			33	59	60	124	331	0	638

Lab gain from FG

LABOUR'S gain is relative to the 1997 election. Labour's Seán Ryan won a seat at the expense of Fianna Fáil in the by-election held here in 1998 after Ray Burke's resignation from the Dáil, so we might also see this as a Fianna Fáil gain, but Fine Gael's loss is unambiguous.

Nora Owen, Justice Minister in the last Fine Gael led government and deputy leader under John Bruton, was one of the party's many high profile casualties. Perhaps the writing was on the wall when she failed to get elected to Fingal County Council in 1999. Her running mate, Skerries based councillor Cathal Boland, who ran foul of the party's internal inquiry into donations made to candidates, polled poorly and so provided her with little help.

The major uncertainty here was whether Fianna Fáil would win back Burke's seat and, if so, at whose expense? Fianna Fáil's vote dropped 0.5% but Fine Gael's dropped by over 7% with the new Green Party leader Trevor Sargent, who topped the poll, Mick Davis

for Sinn Féin and Clare Daly for the Socialist Party all showing a significant increase. Sargent, as is appropriate for the party leader, won the highest Green vote in the country. Aer Lingus shop steward Clare Daly led both of the eventually successful Fianna Fáil candidates going in to the penultimate count having secured good transfers from eliminated candidates.

This was one of three constituencies singled out for the experiment in electronic voting so the count provoked no excitement although there were few surprises. Good vote management saw all three Fianna Fáil candidates within 700 votes of one another on the first count but the first preference order, and the gap between the candidates, was unaffected by the various counts and Swords county councillor Michael Kennedy was still almost 450 votes behind incumbent GV Wright when he was eliminated.

JIM GLENNON

FIANNA FÁIL

Jim Glennon is from a politically active family. His father was a County Councillor in the 1960s. Although he served in the Seanad during the last Dáil, his profile in the world of rugby has probably been higher than that in the world of politics until now.

OCCUPATION
Full-time public representative

ADDRESS
Skerries, Co Dublin

PHONE
Constituency
(01) 849 1577
Fax (01) 849 2856

Leinster House
(01) 618 3910
Fax (01) 618 4648

EMAIL
jglennon@oireachtas.ie

WEBSITE
www.jimglennon.com

BORN
Skerries, Co Dublin, 1953

EDUCATION
Cistercian College, Roscrea

MARITAL STATUS
Married.
Three children

SEÁN RYAN

LABOUR

Seán Ryan has had a roller-coaster ride in Dublin North, from poll-topper in 1992 to a lost seat in 1997, and back again to the top in the by-election following the departure from politics of Ray Burke. A County Councillor since 1983, he is perceived in the Dáil as a man who is always highly vocal on local issues.

OCCUPATION
Full-time public representative, former production controller and work study supervisor with CIÉ and Iarnród Éireann

ADDRESS
1 Burrow Road, Portrane, Co Dublin

PHONE
Constituency
(01) 843 6254
Fax (01) 843 6254

Leinster House
(01) 618 3421
Fax (01) 618 4584

EMAIL
sean.ryan@oireachtas.ie

WEBSITE
www.labour.ie

BORN
Dublin, 1943

EDUCATION
North Strand Vocational School;
College of Technology, Bolton Street;
College of Industrial Relations;
School of Management, Rathmines

MARITAL STATUS
Married to Patricia Brehony

TREVOR SARGENT

GREEN

Elected to Fingal County Council in 1991, he became the sole Green TD in 1992. As party leader he now sees five fellow Green TDs. Dedicated constituency work, and the perception that he practises what he preaches, have seen him work his way from outsider to poll-topper position, despite mysterious rumours that he is about to move to a more fashionable area that circulate in Balbriggan every election time.

OCCUPATION
Full-time public representative, former national school principal

ADDRESS
Home: 37 Tara Cove, Balbriggan, Co Dublin
Constituency: 35 Main St, Sord Cholm Chille, Fingal, Contae BAC

PHONE
Home: (01) 841 2371 also fax
Mobile: (087) 254 7836
Constituency: (01) 890 0360
Fax (01) 890 0361
Leinster House
(01) 618 3465/618 4088
LoCall 1890 337 889
Fax (01) 618 4524

EMAIL
trevor.sargent@oireachtas.ie

WEBSITE
www.greenparty.ie

BORN
Dublin, May 1960

EDUCATION
High School; Coláiste Oideachais Eaglais na hÉireann, Rath Maonais; Coláiste na Trionóide, BAC.

MARITAL STATUS
Married to Heidi Bedell

GV WRIGHT

FIANNA FÁIL

Fianna Fáil is well served with sportsmen in the Dublin North constituency where GV Wright supplements Glennon's rugby status with his own football and international basketball. Many in the constituency expected his political association with Burke to damage his vote but in the event the constituency's north-south divide meant that he came in comfortably ahead of party colleague Michael Kennedy.

OCCUPATION
Public representative, former fishmonger

ADDRESS
58 The Moorings, Malahide, Co Dublin

PHONE
Constituency
(01) 845 0710
Fax (01) 845 5545

Leinster House
(01) 618 3549
Fax (01) 618 4549

EMAIL
gv.wright@oireachtas.ie

WEBSITE
www.fiannafail.ie/

BORN
Dublin, August 1947

EDUCATION
Chanel College, Coolock

MARITAL STATUS
Married to Monica Kane.
Two sons, one daughter

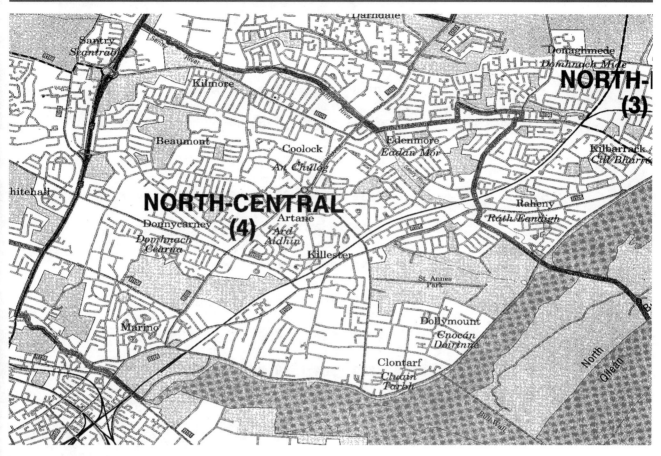

4 SEATS

2 Fianna Fáil
1 Fine Gael
1 Independent

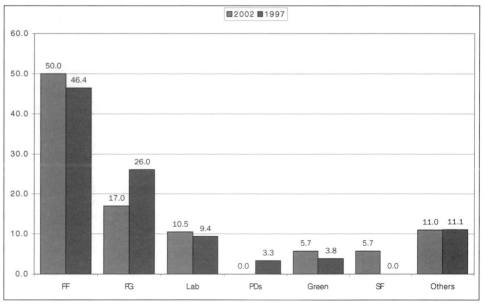

	2002	1997
FF	50.0	46.4
FG	17.0	26.0
Lab	10.5	9.4
PDs	0.0	3.3
Green	5.7	3.8
SF	5.7	0.0
Others	11.0	11.1

		1	2	3	4	5	6
			Votes of Browne	Votes of Breen	Votes of McCole	Votes of Maher	Votes of McDowell
*S HAUGHEY	FF		+41	+63	+310		
		7614	7655	7718	8028	√	
*I CALLELY	FF		+41	+98	+178	+225	+395
		6896	6937	7035	7213	7438	7833 √
D Heney	FF		+31	+63	+175	+299	+426
		5533	5564	5627	5802	6101	6527
*R BRUTON	FG		+36	+1052	+115	+388	+2295
		5159	5195	6247	6362	6750	9045 √
*D McDowell	Lab		+82	+146	+288	+829	
		4203	4285	4431	4719	5548	eliminated
F McGRATH	Ind		+112	+128	+677	+1058	+1882
		3781	3893	4021	4698	5756	7638 √
F McCole	SF		+146	+14			
		2299	2445	2459	eliminated		
B Maher	GP		+128	+83	+572		
		2275	2403	2486	3058	eliminated	
G Breen	FG		+11				
		1650	1661	eliminated			
R Browne	SWP	638	eliminated				
Non transferable			10	14	144	259	550

4 SEATS

ELECTORATE
65,583

TOTAL POLL
40,475

SPOILED
427

VALID POLL
40,048

QUOTA
8,010

* DENOTES
OUTGOING TD

NEWLY
ELECTED TDS
IN CAPITALS

Ind gain from Lab

FINIAN McGrath, Dublin City Council member for Clontarf and a well-established left-wing voice in the area, displaced Labour's Finance spokesman Derek McDowell. Seán Haughey, whose posters showed his first name rather more clearly than his second one, topped the poll by holding his 1997 vote while his running-mate Ivor Callely's vote was down by over 4,000 votes on his 1997 figure.

Richard Bruton's success was the only one for Fine Gael in Dublin north of the river Liffey although his party's vote fell by 9% here relative to 1997. This was a result owing much to transfers, with both Deirdre Heney for Fianna Fáil and Derek McDowell defeated by those winning fewer first preferences than them. McDowell actually won a larger share of the vote than he did in 1997, when he was elected despite winning less than half a quota. Newly elected local councillor Heney was added to the ticket to supplement the party's two incumbent TDs and Seán Haughey complained loudly, and perhaps to good effect, that the party was pushing her rather than himself. The party came close to winning three seats here, pushing its vote up to 50% but was still almost 1,000 votes short in the end.

McGrath went one better than did the veteran independent campaigner Seán Dublin Bay Loftus in 1997

Victory roar: Finian McGrath celebrates his election

when he was runner-up while McGrath won only a small vote. Starting over 400 votes behind McDowell, he took more transfers than McDowell from the Socialist Workers Party (+30), Sinn Féin (+389) and the Greens (+229) to finish over 200 ahead of him after the 5th count. McDowell's transfers then took McGrath ahead of Heney. Of his 5,548 votes, only 8% went to Fianna Fáil and 34% to the independent with Fine Gael getting the biggest share – 42% – to see Bruton comfortably home.

RICHARD BRUTON

FINE GAEL

The brother of former Taoiseach John Bruton, Richard Bruton was Fine Gael Director of Policy from February 2001 to June 2002. Although he has always had a lower profile than his brother he is seen as having a keen analytical mind and performed well as Minister for Enterprise and Employment. He lost to Enda Kenny in the recent leadership election and is Deputy Leader and Finance spokesman.

OCCUPATION
Full-time public representative, former economist

ADDRESS
210 Griffith Avenue, Drumcondra, Dublin 9

PHONE
Leinster House
(01) 618 4063
Fax (01) 618 4501

EMAIL
richard.bruton@oireachtas.ie

WEBSITE
www.richardbruton.net

BORN
Dublin, March 1953

EDUCATION
Belvedere College, Dublin;
Clongowes Wood College;
University College Dublin;
Nuffield College, Oxford
(BA, MA Mphil (Oxon) Economics)

MARITAL STATUS
Married to Susan Meehan.
Two sons, two daughters

IVOR CALLELY

FIANNA FÁIL

1997 poll-topper Ivor Callely came second to Seán Haughey this time but nonetheless moves another rung up the political ladder with his appointment as Minister of State at the Department of Health and Children with special responsibility for Services for Older People – a post in which he will be closely watched by an ageing constituency population.

OCCUPATION
Full-time public representative, former representative for pharmaceutical firm

ADDRESS
7 St Lawrence Road, Clontarf, Dublin 3

PHONE
Constituency
(01) 833 4331
Fax (01) 833 4332

Leinster House
(01) 618 3333
Fax (01) 671 4904

EMAIL
ivor.callely@oireachtas.ie

BORN
Dublin, May 1958

EDUCATION
St Paul's College, Raheny;
College of Marketing, Dublin
(Diploma in Business Studies and Accountancy, Sales and Marketing)

MARITAL STATUS
Married to Jennifer Foley.
Two sons, one daughter

SEÁN HAUGHEY

FIANNA FÁIL

The son and grandson of Taoisigh, Seán Haughey is possibly the only candidate whose surname is regularly given low visibility on his election posters. Despite the scandals clinging to the family name in recent years his hard constituency work brought him to the top of the poll this time round.

OCCUPATION
Full-time public representative

ADDRESS
Home
Chapelfield Lodge, Baskin Lane, Dublin 17
Constituency Office
5 Mornington Park, Malahide Road, Artane, Dublin 5

PHONE
(01) 845 0111
Fax (01) 845 1444

Leinster House
(01) 618 3000

EMAIL
sean_haughey@oireachtas.ie

BORN
Dublin, November 1961

EDUCATION
St Paul's College, Raheny;
Trinity College Dublin
(BA, Economics and Politics)

MARITAL STATUS
Married to Orla O'Brien.
Two sons, one daughter

FINIAN McGRATH

INDEPENDENT

Finian McGrath's personal experience with the poor provision of state disability services for his child led him to stand as an Independent campaigning on the health and disability platform, despite Sinn Féin hopes that this experienced Councillor, who was for a long time active in Tony Gregory's Dublin Central machine, would stand on their ticket.

OCCUPATION
Public representative, former full-time voluntary community worker with the Simon Community, former national school teacher

ADDRESS
342 Charlemont, Griffith Avenue, Dublin 9

PHONE
Constituency
(01) 837 8028
Mobile
(087) 673 8041

Leinster House
(01) 618 3942
Fax (01) 618 4993

EMAIL
cllr_finian.mcgrath@dublincity.ie

BORN
Tuam, Co Galway, April 1953

EDUCATION
Tuam CBS;
St Patrick's College, Drumcondra

MARITAL STATUS
Married to Anne.
Two children

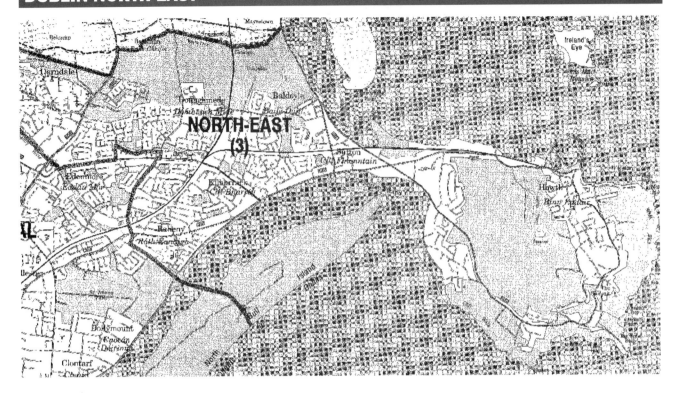

4 SEATS

2 Fianna Fáil
1 Labour
1 Fine Gael

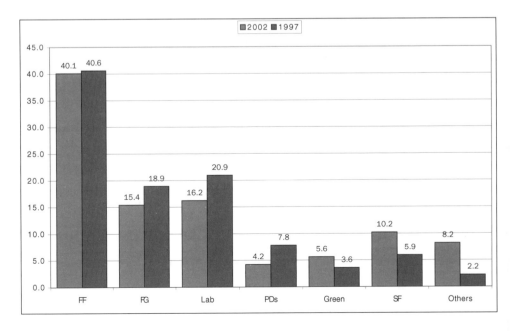

	2002	1997
FF	40.1	40.6
FG	15.4	18.9
Lab	16.2	20.9
PDs	4.2	7.8
Green	5.6	3.6
SF	10.2	5.9
Others	8.2	2.2

3 SEATS

ELECTORATE
52,105

TOTAL POLL
29,634

SPOILED
316

VALID POLL
29,318

QUOTA
7,330

* DENOTES
OUTGOING TD

NEWLY
ELECTED TDS
IN CAPITALS

			1	2 Votes of Jenkinson, Kelly	3 Votes of Healy	4 Votes of Cosgrave	5 Votes of Harold	6 Votes of O'Toole	
*M WOODS	FF		6457	+285 6742	+169 6911	+227 7138	+414 7552	√	
*M BRADY	FF		5304	+227 5531	+126 5657	+119 5776	+279 6055	+854 6909	√
*T BROUGHAN	Lab		4758	+173 4931	+495 5426	+450 5876	+949 6825	+1601 8426	√
L O'Toole	SF		3003	+80 3083	+203 3286	+87 3373	+347 3720	eliminated	
*M J Cosgrave	FG		2349	+105 2454	+92 2546	eliminated			
G Doyle	FG		2155	+218 2373	+202 2575	+1510 4085	+563 4648	+289 4937	
M Harrold	Ind		2116	+205 2321	+485 2806	+106 2912	eliminated		
D Healy	GP		1656	+200 1856	eliminated				
N Ryan	PD		1219	eliminated					
T Jenkinson	Ind		301	eliminated					
Non transferable				27	84	47	360	976	

FG loss

MORE musical chairs here as this was reduced from a four to a three seat constituency and four TDs scrambled for the three places. The Fianna Fáil vote held up, Fine Gael dropped 3.5% and Labour 4.7%, but Labour still had the edge, and had only one candidate, so it was a Labour bottom that finished up on the last seat.

Fianna Fáil's Michael Woods, outgoing Education minister and one of the most experienced TDs, topped the poll with Michael Brady, first elected in 1997, close behind. While the party won only a little over 1.6 quotas, the extreme fragmentation of the opposition ensured their two seats were quite safe.

Fine Gael's vote was divided between veteran TD Michael Joe Cosgrave and newcomer Gavin Doyle. Cosgrave was eliminated first, and while his transfer to Doyle was almost 60%, just a little below the national average for the party, it was nowhere near enough. Even 100% would have left Doyle behind Tommy Broughan.

Sinn Féin polled well here; Larry O'Toole, an experienced candidate for the area, took over 10% of the vote, an increase of 4% on 1997 and fourth place in first preferences. On his elimination 43% of his vote went to Labour, 23% to FF and 8% to FG. Last time Fianna Fáil got the lion's share. David Healy for the Greens took almost 6% and Noelle Ryan, a late declaring PD candidate, 4%.

Labour candidate Tommy Broughan retained his seat on the final count
PHOTOCALL

MARTIN BRADY

FIANNA FÁIL

First elected in 1997, it was probably Deputy Brady's observations of life in the Donaghmede electoral area he represents on Dublin City Council that made him suggest advertising restrictions to prevent the promotion of junk food during children's television programming.

OCCUPATION
Full-time public representative, former executive officer in Telecom Éireann

ADDRESS
37 Grangemore Drive, Dublin 13

PHONE
Constituency
(01) 848 4509

Leinster House
(01) 618 3368
Fax (01) 618 4557

EMAIL
martin.brady@oireachtas.ie

BORN
Virginia, Co Cavan, May 1947

EDUCATION
Franciscan Brothers College, Clara, Co Offaly

MARITAL STATUS
Married to Veronica.
Three daughters

TOMMY BROUGHAN

LABOUR

A busy councillor who was first elected to the Dáil in 1992 and is heavily involved in local business development schemes – as well as anything involving football, whether GAA or soccer.

OCCUPATION
Full-time public representative, former teacher

ADDRESS
23 Riverside Road, Coolock, Dublin 17

PHONE
Constituency
(01) 847 7634
Fax (01) 847 7634

Leinster House
(01) 618 3557
Fax (01) 618 4545

EMAIL
thomas.p.broughan@oireachtas.ie

BORN
Dublin, August 1947

EDUCATION
Moyle Park, Clondalkin;
University College Dublin;
London University
(BA, BSc, MSc (Econ), HDipEd)

MARITAL STATUS
Married to Carmel Healy

MICHAEL WOODS

FIANNA FÁIL

First elected to the Dáil in 1977, Michael Woods was on the front bench most of the time since 1979, and filled a very wide range of posts including the Ministries of Social Welfare, Agriculture, the Marine and Natural Resources and Education. He was spokesperson on Justice when in opposition. He is now Chair of the Oireachtas Foreign Affairs Committee.

OCCUPATION
Full-time public representative, former horticultural scientist

ADDRESS
13 Kilbarrack Grove, Raheny, Dublin 5

PHONE
Constituency
(01) 832 3357
Fax (01) 832 5222

Leinster House
(01) 618 3000

EMAIL
compass@indigo.ie

BORN
Bray, Co Wicklow, December 1935

EDUCATION
Synge Street CBS, Dublin;
University College Dublin
(B Agr Sc, PhD, DSc);
Institute of Public Administration, Dublin;
Harvard Business School

MARITAL STATUS
Married to Margaret Maher.
Three sons, two daughters

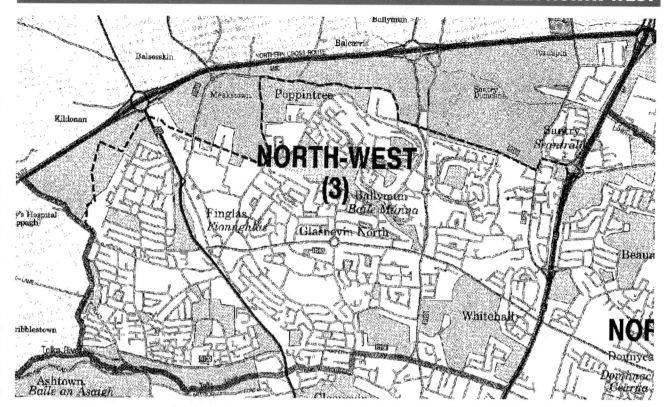

3 SEATS

2 Fianna Fáil
1 Labour

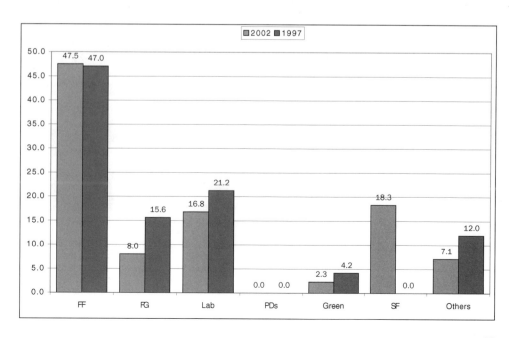

			1	2	3	4	5	6
				Votes of Larkin	Ahern's surplus	Votes of Ó Cionnaith	Votes of O'Brien	Votes of Brady and Tormey
*N AHERN	FF		6912	√				
				+42	+262	+79	+62	+631
*P CAREY	FF		5523	5565	5827	5906	5968	6599 √
				+18	+26	+168	+105	+504
D Ellis	SF		4781	4799	4825	4993	5098	5602
				+9	+43	+186	+286	+2017
*R SHORTALL	Lab		4391	4400	4443	4629	4915	6932 √
				+18	+20	+25	+58	
B Brady	FG		2082	2100	2120	2145	2203	eliminated
				+28	+9	+68	+146	
B Tormey	Ind		1100	1128	1137	1205	1351	eliminated
				+6	+6			
S Ó Cionnaith	WP		608	614	620	eliminated		
				+22	+6	+69		
E O'Brien	GP		607	629	635	704	eliminated	
M Larkin	CSP		154	eliminated				
Non transferable				11	0	25	47	402

3 SEATS

ELECTORATE
47,641

TOTAL POLL
26,543

SPOILED
385

VALID POLL
26,158

QUOTA
6,540

* DENOTES
OUTGOING TD

NEWLY
ELECTED TDS
IN CAPITALS

Lab loss

THIS was reduced from a four to a three seat constituency and with former DL leader and now Labour Party president Proinsias De Rossa now in the European Parliament only three TDs were looking for the three seats. The main challenge came from Sinn Féin's Dessie Ellis who was running for the first time. Ellis did well in the local elections and he polled exceptionally well on this occasion, winning 18% of first preferences, the third best performance in the country by a Sinn Féin candidate. This was more than Caoimghín Ó Caoláin, Arthur Morgan and Aengus Ó Snodaigh, all of whom were elected. However, in a three seater the party will have to do even better if it is to win a seat, or else it will have to improve in the transfer market. Roisín Shortall, who held the seat for Labour in 1997, started 390 voted behind Ellis but by the 6th count had pulled 1330 votes ahead of him. The decisive transfers were from Brendan Brady (FG) and Dr Bill Tormey (Ind), one time Labour member and independent Labour candidate running on a health services platform, who were both eliminated after the 5th count. Shortall took 2017 of their votes as against 504 going to Ellis, changing a deficit into a comfortable surplus.

Fine Gael held a seat here consistently until 1997, and held two seats in 1981, but can have little hope of recovering even one seat in the foreseeable future. Their vote was cut in half this time, down to only 8%, their lowest support in the country.

Martin McGuinness and Dessie Ellis canvassing in Finglas

Noel Ahern and Pat Carey, a Dublin City Council member maintained the Fianna Fáil vote here with Ahern, the brother of the Taoiseach, elected on the first count. The division of the vote between them was closer than in 1997 but again, 70% of Ahern's surplus went to Carey, who finished with a cushion of almost 1000 votes over Ellis.

NOEL AHERN

FIANNA FÁIL

The Taoiseach's big brother has been appointed Minister of State at the Department of the Environment and Local Government and at the Department of Community, Rural and Gaeltacht Affairs. Housing, urban renewal and drugs strategy are no sinecures though. Like his brother he is a committed constituency worker.

OCCUPATION
Full-time public representative, former senior clerical officer with Iarnród Éireann

ADDRESS
25 Church Avenue, Drumcondra, Dublin 9

PHONE
Constituency
(01) 888 2581
Fax (01) 888 2062

Leinster House
(01) 888 2591
Fax (01) 878 6676

EMAIL
mos@environ.irlgov.ie

BORN
Dublin, December 1944

EDUCATION
O'Connell's School, Dublin; University College Dublin; College of Commerce, Rathmines (DPA, MCIT)

MARITAL STATUS
Married to Helen Marnane. Two sons, one daughter

PAT CAREY

FIANNA FÁIL

This Kerryman has long since successfully transplanted himself to Dublin, having been a Councillor since 1985. He keeps his interest in the development of the Irish language and combines it with active work for educational opportunities.

OCCUPATION
Full-time public representative, former teacher

ADDRESS
69 Bourne View, Ashbourne, Co Meath

PHONE
Home
(01) 835 0544
Fax (01) 835 0430

Constituency
(01) 864 4118
Fax (01) 864 4119

Leinster House
(01) 618 3377
Fax (01) 618 3638

EMAIL
pat.carey@oireachtas.ie

WEBSITE
www.fiannafail.ie

BORN
Castlemaine, Co Kerry, November 1947

EDUCATION
Presentation Brothers, Milltown, Co Kerry; St Patrick's Teacher Training College, Drumcondra; University College Dublin (BA); Trinity College Dublin (HDipEd)

MARITAL STATUS
Single

RÓISÍN SHORTALL

LABOUR

Róisín Shortall's family background in Fianna Fáil has never hindered her determined attacks on the present government, particularly in relation to the attitude of some of its members to asylumseekers. Her problems with her own party during the merger with Democratic Left, which at one time seemed to threaten her long-term future, were placed firmly in the past when Proinsias de Rossa departed for Europe. Unsuccessful candidate in the leadership contest won by Pat Rabbitte.

OCCUPATION
Full-time public representative, former teacher of the deaf

ADDRESS
12 Iveragh Road, Whitehall, Dublin 9

PHONE
Constituency
(01) 837 0563

Leinster House
(01) 618 3593
Fax (01) 618 4380

EMAIL
roisin.shortall@oireachtas.ie

WEBSITE
www.labour.ie

BORN
Drumcondra, Dublin, April 1954

EDUCATION
Dominican College, Eccles Street; University College Dublin

MARITAL STATUS
Married.
Three children

5 SEATS

2 Fianna Fáil
1 PD
1 Fine Gael
1 Green

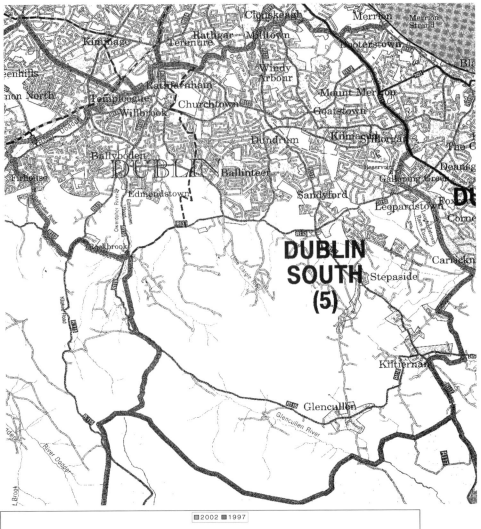

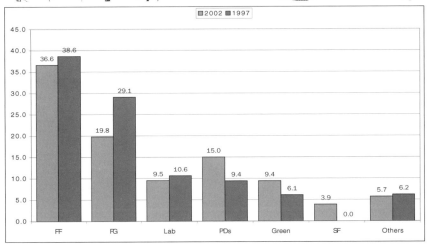

SÉAMUS BRENNAN

FIANNA FÁIL

The Minister for Transport was first elected in 1981. Government Chief Whip in the last Dáil, his communication and strategy skills have always made him a key player in Fianna Fáil. Other ministries he has held include Education, Commerce and Technology, and Tourism.

OCCUPATION
Minister, former accountant and management consultant

ADDRESS
31 Finsbury Park, Churchtown, Dublin 14

PHONE
Constituency
(01) 295 7171
Fax (01) 604 1604

Leinster House
(01) 604 1074
Fax (01) 604 1183

EMAIL
minister@transport.irlgov.ie

WEBSITE
www.transport.ie

BORN
Galway, February 1948

EDUCATION
St Joseph's, Galway;
University College Galway;
(BComm, BA (Econ));
University College Dublin
(MComm)

MARITAL STATUS
Married to Ann O'Shaughnessy.
Two sons, four daughters

TOM KITT

FIANNA FÁIL

The son of Michael F Kitt TD and brother of Senator Michael P Kitt, former TD for Galway East. Tom Kitt has held his seat since 1987. It has often been suggested that Kitt, with his strong record on human rights, is likely front bench material but once again he falls just short as Minister of State at the Department of Foreign Affairs with special responsibility for Overseas Development and Human Rights.

OCCUPATION
Minister of State, former teacher

ADDRESS
4 Ashgrove Terrace, Dundrum, Dublin 16

PHONE
Constituency
(01) 298 2304
Fax (01) 298 2460

Leinster House
(01) 408 2031
Fax (01) 408 2024

EMAIL
tomkitt@iveagh.irlgov.ie

WEBSITE
www.tomkitttd.ie

BORN
Galway, July 1952

EDUCATION
St Jarlath's College, Tuam, Co Galway;
St Patrick's Teacher Training College, Drumcondra, Dublin

MARITAL STATUS
Married to Jacinta Burke-Walshe.
Three sons, one daughter

OLIVIA MITCHELL

FINE GAEL

Ever since her election to Dáil Éireann at her third attempt in 1997, when she was Cathaoirleach of Dún Laoghaire Rathdown Council, Deputy Mitchell has occupied a prominent position on the Fine Gael benches. Olivia Mitchell was appointed spokesperson on Health and Children, June 2002.

OCCUPATION
Full-time public representative, former teacher

ADDRESS
8 Ballawley Court, Sandyford Road, Dundrum, Dublin 16

PHONE
Constituency
(01) 295 3033

Leinster House
(01) 618 3088
Fax (01) 618 4579

EMAIL
olivia.mitchell@oireachtas.ie

BORN
Birr, Co Offaly, 1947

EDUCATION
Trinity College Dublin
(BA Economics & Politics, HDipEd)

MARITAL STATUS
Married,
Two sons, one daughter

LIZ O'DONNELL

PROGRESSIVE DEMOCRATS

A junior minister in the previous government, she stepped down from office in the 29th Dáil despite a massive increase in her personal vote, but O'Donnell is sure to remain a high-profile figure and maintains her interest in all justice issues, particularly those involving the rights of women and children.

OCCUPATION
Full-time public representative, former lawyer

ADDRESS
23 Temple Gardens, Rathmines, Dublin 6

PHONE
Constituency
(01) 618 4684
Fax (01) 475 1462

Leinster House
(01) 618 3469
Fax (01) 618 4307

EMAIL
liz.odonnell@oireachtas.ie

WEBSITE
www.lizodonnell.ie

BORN
Dublin, July 1956

EDUCATION
Salesian College, Limerick;
Trinity College Dublin

MARITAL STATUS
Married to Michael Carson SC.
Two children

	1	2 Votes of Maher	3 Brennan's surplus	4 Votes of Canning	5 Votes of Whelan	6 Votes of Corrigan	7 Kitt's surplus	8 Votes of Shatter
5 SEATS								
*S BRENNAN FF	**9326** √							
		+56	+12	+291	+169	+499		
*L O'DONNELL PD	**8288**	**8344**	**8356**	**8647**	**8816**	**9315** √		
		+113	+60	+200	+379	+2430		
*T KITT FF	**7744**	**7857**	**7917**	**8117**	**8496**	**10926** √		
		+61	+4	+211	+84	+214	+398	+4508
*O MITCHELL FG	**5568**	**5629**	**5633**	**5844**	**5928**	**6142**	**6540**	**11048** √
		+47	+3	+155	+85	+40	+140	
*A Shatter FG	**5363**	**5410**	**5413**	**5568**	**5653**	**5693**	**5833**	**eliminate**
		+153	+4	+319	+354	+155	+251	+625
E Fitzgerald Lab	**5247**	**5400**	**5404**	**5723**	**6077**	**6232**	**6483**	**7108**
		+260	+3	+676	+963	+195	+700	+527
E RYAN GP	**5222**	**5482**	**5485**	**6161**	**7124**	**7319**	**8019**	**8546**
		+40	+25	+173	+230			
M Corrigan FF	**3180**	**3220**	**3245**	**3418**	**3648**	**eliminated**		
		+173	+2	+127				
D Whelan SF	**2172**	**2345**	**2347**	**2474**	**eliminated**			
		+117	+2					
K Canning Ind	**2090**	**2207**	**2209**	**eliminated**				
L Maher SP	**1063**	**eliminated**						
Non transferable		*43*	*0*	*57*	*210*	*115*	*226*	*173*

ELECTORATE
92,645

TOTAL POLL
55,690

SPOILED
427

VALID POLL
55,263

QUOTA
9,211

* DENOTES
OUTGOING TD

NEWLY
ELECTED TDS
IN CAPITALS

Green gain from FG

NOTORIOUSLY fickle in their political attachments, the voters of Dublin South dismissed an incumbent TD and changed the balance of party power in the area for the fifth successive time. On this occasion, Green candidate Éamon Ryan displaced Fine Gael's Alan Shatter, giving the constituency a Green TD for the first time since 1992.

The changes in first preferences tell the story well enough. Fine Gael dropped almost 10% to fall below 20% in a constituency where the party won over 50% twice in 1982 while the Greens were up over 3% to 9%, more than the vote of Roger Garland, the first ever Green TD in 1987. Labour hoped to win back a seat with Eithne Fitzgerald, poll topper in 1992 and subsequently a junior minister, but the party's vote dropped to just over 9%, only 25 votes ahead of Ryan. The extent of Fine Gael's collapse probably sealed her fate. All would depend on lower preferences. Ryan won by collecting more votes from every party except Fine Gael. By the time Fitzgerald collected Fine Gael transfers Ryan was 1,500 votes ahead, a gap Mitchell's surplus could not bridge, even though that favoured Labour by a ratio of almost 2:1.

Despite the fact that these two candidates attracted the highest Fine Gael share of the vote in the Dublin area it was still only 20%, enough votes for one seat. One of the two front bench spokespersons had to go. Local councillor Olivia Mitchell, who had adopted a high profile by being critical of travellers in the area, edged out Alan Shatter. Shatter was first elected here in 1981 but Mitchell won more first preferences and attracted more transfers than her running mate.

Top of the poll and elected on the first count was Séamus Brennan, chief whip in the outgoing administration. Tom Kitt, a junior minister dropped to third place after heading the poll in 1997. New candidate Maria Corrigan, elected to the county council in 1999, was well down the poll but transferred two thirds of her votes to the party.

Liz O'Donnell's 15% of the vote, up almost 6% on 1997 and the best PD return here since the heady days of 1987, was a surprise to those who thought her party's support for the abortion referendum in this particularly liberal constituency might have damaged her. She needed Fianna Fáil transfers in 1997 but not this time.

9

Mitchell's
surplus

+1155
8263
+682
9228 √

0

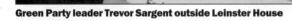

Green Party leader Trevor Sargent outside Leinster House   PHOTOCALL IRELAND

ÉAMON RYAN

GREEN

Éamon Ryan, who was co-opted to Dublin Corporation in 1998 when John Gormley resigned his seat to avoid a dual mandate, has been Chairman of the Dublin Cycling Campaign since 1995 and became Chair of Dublin Corporation's Strategic Policy Committee on traffic and transport in 1998. He has successfully carried his commitment to green transport into his commercial life as managing director of Irish Cycling Safaris.

OCCUPATION
Public representative, managing director of Irish Cycling Safaris

PHONE
Leinster House
(01) 618 3273
Fax (01) 618 4363

EMAIL
eamon.ryan@oireachtas.ie

BORN
Dublin, July 1964

MARITAL STATUS
Married to journalist Victoria White. Three children

One woman and her dog voting at Scoil Mhuire polling station in Sandymount, Dublin   PHOTOCALL IRELAND

5 SEATS

1 Fine Gael
2 Fianna Fáil
1 Sinn Féin
1 Labour

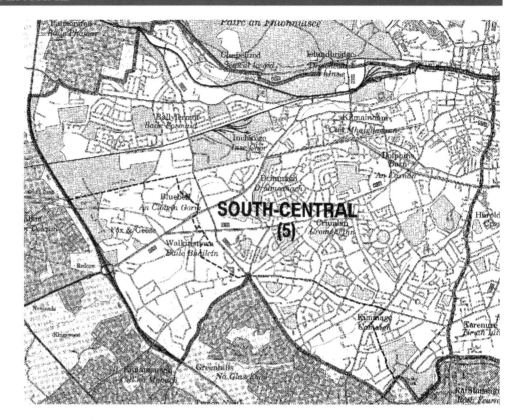

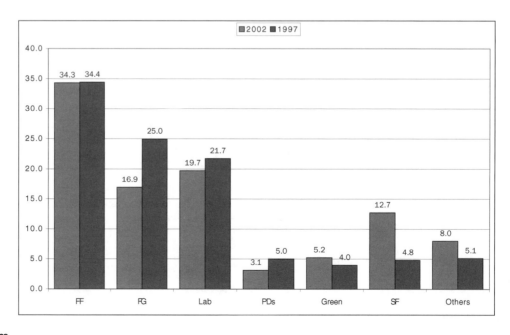

SEÁN ARDAGH

FIANNA FÁIL

Seán Ardagh was first elected to the Dáil in 1997 and has been a County Councillor since 1985. Outspoken on matters of financial probity, he is Chairman of the Joint Committee on Justice, Equality and Women's Rights.

OCCUPATION
Public representative, chartered accountant

ADDRESS
168 Walkinstown Road, Dublin 12

PHONE
Constituency
(01) 456 8736
Fax (01) 408 0436

Leinster House
(01) 618 3597
Fax (01) 618 4193

EMAIL
sean@ardagh.org

WEBSITE
www.ardagh.org

BORN
Dublin, November 1947

EDUCATION
Marian College, Ballsbridge; University College Dublin (BSc, Physics and Mathematics); University of Toronto (CA)

MARITAL STATUS
Married to Máire Bhreathnach. Two sons, one daughter

GAY MITCHELL

FINE GAEL

First elected to the Dáil in 1981, Gay Mitchell was appointed Fine Gael spokesperson on Foreign Affairs in June 2002 and has been on the front bench since 1989. In February 2000, he unveiled the Fine Gael policy document "Beyond Neutrality", which called for Irish participation in a European defence organisation on a non-obligatory basis.

OCCUPATION
Full-time public representative, former accountant

ADDRESS
192 Upper Rathmines Road, Dublin 6

PHONE
Constituency
(01) 490 3744

Leinster House
(01) 618 3727
Fax (01) 618 4512

EMAIL
gay.mitchell@oireachtas.ie

BORN
Inchicore, Dublin, 1951

EDUCATION
Emmet Road Vocational School, Dublin; St Michael's Christian Brothers School, Inchicore; College of Commerce, (Accountancy and Business); Queen's University, Belfast (MSc Politics); Associate of Institute of Taxation in Ireland; Fellow: Irish Institute of Secretaries and Administrators

MARITAL STATUS
Married to Norma O'Connor. One son, three daughters

MICHAEL MULCAHY

FIANNA FÁIL

The former Fianna Fáil spokesperson on Justice in the Seanad and Vice-President of the Council of European National Youth Committees contested general elections in Dublin South Central in 1992 and 1997, and by-elections in 1994 and 1999. He is a former Lord Mayor of Dublin.

OCCUPATION
Public representative, practising barrister at the Dublin Bar, member of the Eastern Circuit

ADDRESS
171 Drimnagh Road, Dublin 12

PHONE
Constituency
(01) 676 1319
Fax (01) 465 2595

Leinster House
(01) 618 4271
Fax (01) 618 4779

EMAIL
info@michaelmulcahy.ie

WEBSITE
www.michaelmulcahy.ie

BORN
Dublin, June 1960

EDUCATION
St Conleth's College, Dublin; Trinity College Dublin (Degree in Mental and Moral Science, Degree in Legal Science); King's Inns, Dublin (Barrister-at-Law)

MARITAL STATUS
Married to Veronica Gates

AENGUS Ó SNODAIGH

SINN FÉIN

The former worker with Bord na Gaelige, teacher, and journalist has been active in politics since the Wood Quay rallies his teens. Party spokesperson on Justice and Equality; Cultúr, Gaeilge and Gaeltachts; and International Affairs and Defence he is member of the Ard Chomhairle and Sinn Féin representative to the National Forum on Europe.

OCCUPATION
Former community worker, shop steward

ADDRESS
75 The Coombe, Dublin 8

PHONE
Constituency
Phone and Fax (01) 454 1868

Leinster House
(01) 618 4084
Fax (01) 618 4324

EMAIL
aosnodaigh@oireachtas.ie

BORN
Dublin, August 1964

EDUCATION
Scoil Lorcan, Monkstown; Colaiste Eoin, Booterstown; UCD (BA, HdipEd)

MARITAL STATUS
Married to Aisling, Two children

			1	2 Votes of Kelly	3 Votes of Smith	4 Votes of Kavanagh	5 Votes of Ní Chonaill	6 Votes of Jackson	7 Votes of Quinn	8 Votes of Byrne
*S ARDAGH	FF		6031	+2 6033	+14 6047	+19 6066	+65 6131	+71 6202	+197 6399	+73 6472
A Ó SNODAIGH	SF		5591	+28 5619	+140 5759	+120 5879	+220 6099	+277 6376	+55 6431	+91 6522
*G MITCHELL	FG		5444	+12 5456	+13 5469	+38 5507	+105 5612	+96 5708	+233 5941	+1339 7280
M MULCAHY	FF		4990	+4 4994	+13 5007	+17 5024	+78 5102	+63 5165	+177 5342	+49 5391
*M UPTON	Lab		4520	+9 4529	+64 4593	+84 4677	+72 4749	+114 4863	+247 5110	+222 5332
E Byrne	Lab		4159	+29 4188	+77 4265	+100 4365	+71 4436	+132 4568	+91 4659	+180 4839
*M McGennis	FF		4085	+0 4085	+25 4110	+50 4160	+39 4199	+224 4423	+158 4581	+95 4676
K McElroy	GP		2299	+12 2311	+89 2400	+91 2491	+84 2575	+196 2771	+203 2974	+141 3115
C Byrne	FG		2012	+3 2015	+10 2025	+34 2059	+32 2091	+55 2146	+113 2259	elim'td
B Quinn	PD		1377	+4 1381	+14 1395	+10 1405	+67 1472	+62 1534	eliminated	
V 'B' Jackson	Ind		1142	+5 1147	+56 1203	+120 1323	+88 1411	eliminated		
Á Ní Chonaill	Ind		926	+4 930	+19 949	+17 966	eliminated			
B Smith	SWP		617	+16 633	eliminated					
L Kavanagh	WP		553	+139 692	+90 782	eliminated				
S Kelly	WP		270	eliminated						
Non transferable				3	9	82	45	121	60	69

5 SEATS

ELECTORATE
86,161

TOTAL POLL
44,768

SPOILED
752

VALID POLL
44,106

QUOTA
7,337

* DENOTES
OUTGOING TD

NEWLY
ELECTED TDS
IN CAPITALS

SF gain

THIS constituency became a five seater in 2002 having been a four seater before so there was an empty seat up for grabs. Labour, Fianna Fáil and Sinn Féin all hoped to take it. Labour ran incumbent deputy Mary Upton, who had won the 1999 by election following the death of her brother Pat Upton, and former DL TD Eric Byrne. Byrne won a seat for the Workers' Party in 1989 and DL in 1995 and lost out by only 200 votes to Pat Upton last time. Fianna Fáil ran Seán Ardagh, the incumbent, Marian McGennis, elected for Dublin Central in 1997 but affected by boundary changes, and Michael Mulcahy, who ran well here before. The Sinn Féin candidate was Aengus Ó Snodaigh, who had represented the party in the by-election.

Labour's vote was almost 20%, 2% down on the combined Labour/DL vote in 1997, and Fianna Fáil's vote was stable; Sinn Féin was up 8% and Fine Gael down more than 8%. Fianna Fáil could not win three seats; Mulcahy started and finished well ahead of McGennis for the second seat behind Ardagh, who topped the poll.

9	**10**	**11**
Votes of McElroy	Votes of McGennis	Ardagh's surplus
+123	+1612	
6595	**8207** √	
+370	+390	+241
6892	**7282**	**7523** √
+429		
7709 √		
+106	+1867	
5497	**7364** √	
+954	+389	+288
6286	**6675**	**6963** √
+599	+220	+186
5438	**5658**	**5844**
+151		
4827	**eliminated**	
eliminated		

Gay Mitchell and his wife Norma celebrate his re-election   PHOTOCALL

383   *349*   *228*

Michael Mulcahy with supporters at the RDS   PHOTOCALL

DR MARY UPTON

LABOUR

Dr Mary Upton was elected to the Dáil in the October 1999 by-election caused by the death of her brother, Dr Pat Upton.

OCCUPATION
Public representative, university lecturer

ADDRESS
Leinster House, Dublin 2

PHONE
Leinster House
(01) 618 3756
Fax (01) 618 4637

EMAIL
maryupton@eircom.net

WEBSITE
www.labour.ie

BORN
Co Clare, May 1946

EDUCATION
Coláiste Mhuire, Ennis, Co Clare;
University College Galway;
University College Dublin

MARITAL STATUS
Single

Ó Snodaigh was within 1,500 votes of a quota and picked up significant bundles from all eliminated candidates (including the largest share of those from the Workers' Party, Áine Ní Chonaill, of the Immigration Control Platform, and Vincent Ballyfermot Jackson, another independent).

Mary Upton and Eric Byrne were only 361 votes apart on the first count. That narrowed to 295 after six counts but Upton increased that lead once transfers came from the PDs, Greens, Fine Gael and Fianna Fáil, all of which favoured old Labour over old DL.

Gay Mitchell, a strong supporter of the deposed party leader, John Bruton, topped the poll last time and held on to one of only three seats that fell to his party in Dublin without too much trouble but even with the larger electorate his vote was down by almost 3,500 votes. His running mate, Councillor Catherine Byrne actually performed better than her predecessor Ruairí McGinley.

4 SEATS

1 Green
1 PD
1 Fianna Fáil
1 Labour

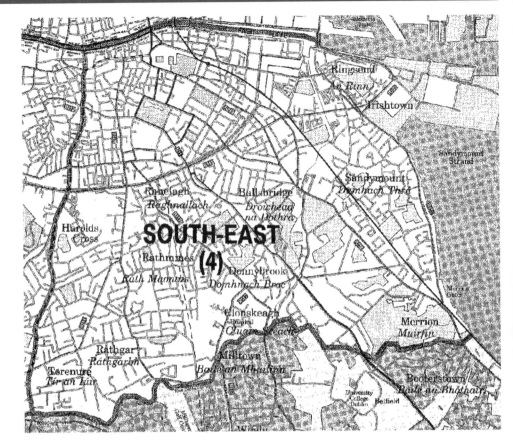

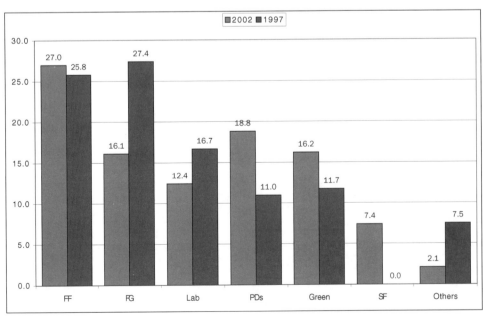

	FF	FG	Lab	PDs	Green	SF	Others
2002	27.0	16.1	12.4	18.8	16.2	7.4	2.1
1997	25.8	27.4	16.7	11.0	11.7	0.0	7.5

			1	2	3	4	5	6
				Votes of Ryan, Gray Crilly	Votes of Mac Eochaidh	Votes of Doolan	Votes of Andrews	Ryan's surplus
4 SEATS	M McDOWELL	PD	6093	+28 6121	+297 6418	+91 6509	√	
	*E RYAN	FF	5318	+54 5372	+36 5408	+415 5823	+2819 8642	√
	*J GORMLEY	GP	5264	+219 5483	+310 5793	+1051 6844	√	
	*R QUINN	Lab	4032	+95 4127	+191 4318	+356 4674	+477 5151	+709 5860 √
	C Andrews	FF	3449	+24 3473	+27 3500	+324 3824	eliminated	
	*F Fitzgerald	FG	3337	+21 3358	+1013 4371	+72 4443	+225 4668	+587 5255
	D Doolan	SF	2398	+157 2555	+23 2578	eliminated		
	C Mac Eochaidh	FG	1873	+32 1905	eliminated			
	S Ryan	SWP	286	eliminated				
	T Crilly	WP	284	eliminated				
	N Gray	Ind	99	eliminated				
	Non transferable			39	8	269	303	859

ELECTORATE
59,896

TOTAL POLL
32,720

SPOILED
287

VALID POLL
32,433

QUOTA
6,487

* DENOTES
OUTGOING TD

NEWLY
ELECTED TDS
IN CAPITALS

PD gain from FG

ATTORNEY General, and PD president Michael McDowell turned things upside down in this constituency with his late entry into the fray. He topped the poll and displaced Fine Gael, who as late as 1989 secured two of the seats in this four seat constituency. Ruairi Quinn, Labour Party leader, limped home to win the last seat. Both Labour and Fine Gael saw their vote drop, the latter by over 11%, which was the biggest drop in support anywhere after Dun Laoghaire. In 1997 McDowell and the Green's John Gormley endured a week-long wait that ended with Gormley's election by a mere 27 votes. This time both of them enjoyed a much more comfortable count and both were elected on the 4th count

A pre-election poll, just after McDowell's candidacy was declared, suggested Fianna Fáil might win a second seat, but with only 1.4 quotas the party was never in the hunt. There was an excellent transfer rate of 74% from popular local councillor Chris Andrews, son of former TD and MEP Niall Andrews, to junior minister Eoin Ryan but the party still recorded its second lowest vote ever here and had no chance of two seats.

Frances Fitzgerald, the defeated Fine Gael incumbent, saw her support down by over 2,000 votes; her new running mate, the barrister and environmental campaigner

Rock musician Shay Ryan: got 286 votes for the SWP

Colm Mac Eochaidh, was almost 3,000 votes down on the total won by veteran Joe Doyle in 1997. His transfer rate was poor, only 53%, but it would have taken something like 85% to get Fitzgerald above Quinn. It was hoped that MacEochaidh would take votes from Gormley but only 310 of his 1,905 votes transferred to the Greens, so it is doubtful if the strategy worked to any significant extent.

Daithí Doolan's 7.4% was a strong showing in what is one of the more well-heeled constituencies. In one of the curiosities of PR, Doolan saw his transfers elect McDowell.

JOHN GORMLEY

GREEN

Gormley, who became active in the Greens in Germany as a student, was elected to Dublin City Council in 1991 and became Lord Mayor in 1994. He was elected to the Dáiil in 1997 after a cliff-hanger count with Michael McDowell.

OCCUPATION
Full-time public representative, former director of Academy of European Languages

ADDRESS
119 Ringsend Park, Ringsend, Dublin 4

PHONE
Home
(01) 281 5134

Leinster House
(01) 618 4247
Fax (01) 618 4597

EMAIL
johngormley@eircom.net

WEBSITE
www.JohnGormley.com

BORN
Dublin, August 1959

EDUCATION
St Munchin's College, Limerick; University College Dublin; Freiburg University, Germany

MARITAL STATUS
Married to Penny Stuart. One daughter, one son

MICHAEL McDOWELL

PROGRESSIVE DEMOCRATS

When he was defeated by Green Party TD John Gormley in the 1997 General Election, many speculated that this time Michael McDowell really would give up politics and return permanently to his legal practice. McDowell confounded them again, becoming Attorney General and President of the Progressive Democrats in 2002. Now Minister for Justice, Equality and Law Reform.

OCCUPATION
Public representative, practised as barrister since 1974 and senior counsel since 1987

ADDRESS
5 Triangle, Ranelagh, Dublin 6

PHONE
Constituency
(01) 498 8084
Fax (01) 498 8087

Leinster House
(01) 602 8321
Fax (01) 676 7797

EMAIL
info@justice.irlgov.ie

WEBSITE
www.michaelmcdowell.ie

BORN
Dublin, May 1951

EDUCATION
Pembroke School; Gonzaga College; University College Dublin (Economics and Politics)

MARITAL STATUS
Married to Niamh Brennan. Three sons

RUAIRÍ QUINN

LABOUR

Ruairí Quinn first entered the Dáil in 1977 and has been a TD continuously since February 1982. Leader of the Labour Party from 1997 to 2002, and deputy leader from 1990 to 1997. Some members of the party undoubtedly felt that his pragmatism lacked inspiration and were distrustful of his willingness to deal with Fianna Fáil.

OCCUPATION
Full-time public representative, former architect

ADDRESS
23 Strand Road, Sandymount, Dublin 4

PHONE
Leinster House
(01) 618 3434
Fax (01) 618 4153

EMAIL
ruairi.quinn@oireachtas.ie

BORN
Dublin, April 1946

EDUCATION
St Michael's Primary School Dublin; Blackrock College; School of Architecture, University College Dublin; Graduate Research Student, Athens School of Ekistics, Doxiadis Centre, Athens

MARITAL STATUS
One son, one daughter by previous marriage to Nicola Underwood. Remarried July 1990 to Liz Allman, one son

EOIN RYAN

FIANNA FÁIL

The former Minister of State at the Department of Local Government, grandson of Dr Jim Ryan, who served as a Minister in every Fianna Fáil government for over 30 years. Was expected to reach the front bench quickly when he was first elected to Dáil Éireann in 1992, but is still waiting. Chair of the Oireachtas Committe on Transport.

OCCUPATION
Full-time public representative, former restaurateur

ADDRESS
19 Vavasour Square, Sandymount, Dublin 4

PHONE
Leinster House
(01) 618 4375
Fax (01) 618 4464

BORN
Dublin, February 1953

EDUCATION
Willow Park; St Mary's College, Rathmines; College of Commerce, Rathmines; Kildalton Horticulture College, Co Kilkenny

MARITAL STATUS
Married to Sheila McKeever. One son, two daughters

4 SEATS

1 Sinn Féin
2 Fianna Fáil
1 Labour

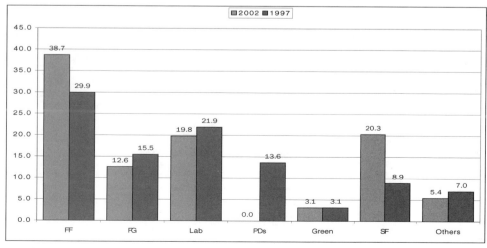

4 SEATS

ELECTORATE
67,947

TOTAL POLL
37,216

SPOILED
414

VALID POLL
36,802

QUOTA
7,361

* DENOTES
OUTGOING TD

NEWLY
ELECTED TDS
IN CAPITALS

		1	2 Votes of Kelly	3 Votes of O'Reilly	4 Crowe's surplus	5 Votes of Walsh	6 Votes of Murphy
S CROWE	SF	7466 √					
			+34	+153	+19		
C O'CONNOR	FF	7155	7189	7342	7361 √		
			+36	+116	+18	+111	
*C LENIHAN	FF	7080	7116	7232	7250	7361 √	
			+50	+135	+24	+667	+458
*P RABBITTE	Lab	6314	6364	6499	6523	7190	7648 √
			+27	+122	+12	+95	+174
*B Hayes	FG	4654	4681	4803	4815	4910	5084
			+57	+120	+14	+60	+279
P Quinn	GP	1157	1214	1334	1348	1408	1687
			+13	+20	+4		
E Walsh	Lab	971	984	1004	1008	eliminated	
			+40	+61	+14	+35	
M Murphy	SP	954	994	1055	1069	1104	eliminated
			+19				
D O'Reilly	CSP	760	779	eliminated			
R Kelly	Ind	291	eliminated				
Non transferable			15	52	0	40	193

SF gain from FG; PD loss

THERE was a major boundary change here which reduced South west from five to four seats. Mary Harney, the Progressive Democratic leader opted to stand in the new Dublin Mid West constituency. There was a widespread expectation that Sinn Féin was going to win a seat in Dublin it would do so here. Seán Crowe polled well in 1997 and since then Crowe in particular and the party in general had mobilised a big vote in the local election, and Crowe had also won almost 20,000 votes as the candidate for Dublin in the European Parliament elections. But whose seat would fall? Chris Flood, one of the two incumbent Fianna Fáil TDs, retired, which left the party somewhat vulnerable; the 30% of the vote won in 1997 would hardly be enough for two seats in a four-seater. Conor Lenihan was standing again, alongside Charlie O'Connor, a new Dáil candidate but with an impressive local pedigree. Brian Hayes topped the poll last time, but Fine Gael won only 16% here in 1997 and could not afford to see that drop. The safest seat should have been that of Pat Rabbitte, the former DL deputy. Labour and DL won a combined 22% in 1997, but it remained to be seen whether the merged party could repeat the feat. The former Labour TD, Eamon Walsh, joined Rabbitte on the ticket.

The first count ended most of the speculation. Crowe

Eyeball to eyeball: Conor Lenihan (FF) and Seán Crowe (SF)

topped the poll, winning more than a quota, and Fianna Fáil increased its vote by 9% to almost 39%; Hayes' vote was down to 13% while Labour's was down only 1% on the combined 1997 vote with Rabbitte getting 87% of the Labour vote. O'Connor actually outpolled Lenihan and took the second seat. Lenihan took the third and Rabbitte comfortably took the fourth, and probably would not have needed the 67% transfer from Walsh.

Darragh O'Reilly won 760 votes for the Christian Solidarity party here, that party's best performance of 2002.

SEÁN CROWE

SINN FÉIN

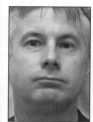

A community activist, Seán Crowe was elected to South Dublin County Council in 1999. He is party spokesman on Education, Transport, Social and Family Affairs and Communications, and sits on the Dáil Committee on Education. He has been involved in Sinn Féin since the Hunger Strikes.

OCCUPATION
Printing industry

ADDRESS
16 Raheen Green, Tallaght, Dublin 24

PHONE/FAX
Constituency
(01) 414 9063

Leinster House
(01) 618 3805
Fax (01) 618 4787

EMAIL
sean.crowe@oireachtas.ie

BORN
Dublin, March 1957

EDUCATION
De La Salle Churchtown;
Dundrum Technical School

MARITAL STATUS
Married to Pamela.

CONOR LENIHAN

FIANNA FÁIL

Son of the late Brian Lenihan, and brother of Brian, TD for Dublin West, Conor Lenihan was first elected in 1997.

OCCUPATION
Full-time public representative, former political correspondent and programme manager with Esat Digifone

ADDRESS
44 Templeogue Village, Dublin 6W

PHONE
Constituency
(01) 459 6285
Fax (01) 244 3363

Constituency
(01) 618 3060
Fax (01) 618 4169

EMAIL
conor.lenihan@oireachtas.ie

BORN
Dublin, March 1963

EDUCATION
Belvedere College;
University College Dublin (BA [Hons] Econ, History and Politics); Dublin City University (Post-Graduate Diploma in Journalism)

MARITAL STATUS
Married to Denise Russell.
One son

CHARLIE O'CONNOR

FIANNA FÁIL

First elected to the Dáil in 2002, Charlie O'Connor was a member of the former Dublin County Council from 1991-1994 and Chair of South Dublin County Council 1999–2000. He has been particularly active in the areas of healthcare and education in the more deprived parts of South west Dublin.

OCCUPATION
Full-time public representative

ADDRESS
County Hall, Tallaght, Dublin 24

PHONE
Home
(01) 414 9050
Fax (01) 414 9111

Constituency
(01) 461 0715
Fax (01) 461 0721

Leinster House
(01) 618 4080
Fax (01) 618 4187

EMAIL
coconnor@southdublincoco.ie
charlie.oconnor@oireachtas.ie

BORN
Dublin, April 1946

EDUCATION
Synge Street CBS;
Drimnagh Castle CBS;
Irish Management Institute,
Industrial Relations Institute

MARITAL STATUS
Separated.
Three sons

PAT RABBITTE

LABOUR

The new leader of the Labour Party, Pat Rabbitte is a former Democratic Left TD, first elected to the Dáil in 1989. He was appointed Minister of State with responsibility for Commerce, Science and Technology in the Rainbow Coalition, the only Minister of State to attend cabinet meetings. An entertaining speaker, with a knack for producing a memorable phrase, Pat is a former National Secretary of the Irish Transport and General Workers Union and former President of the Union of Students in Ireland.

OCCUPATION
Full-time public representative, former trade union official

ADDRESS
56 Monastery Drive, Clondalkin, Dublin 22

PHONE
Constituency
(01) 459 3191

Leinster House
(01) 618 3980
Fax (01) 618 4032

EMAIL
pat.rabbitte@oireachtas.ie

WEBSITE
www.labour.ie

BORN
Mayo, May 1949

EDUCATION
St Colman's College, Claremorris;
University College Galway

MARITAL STATUS
Married to Derry

DUBLIN WEST

3 SEATS

1 Fianna Fáil
1 Socialist
1 Labour

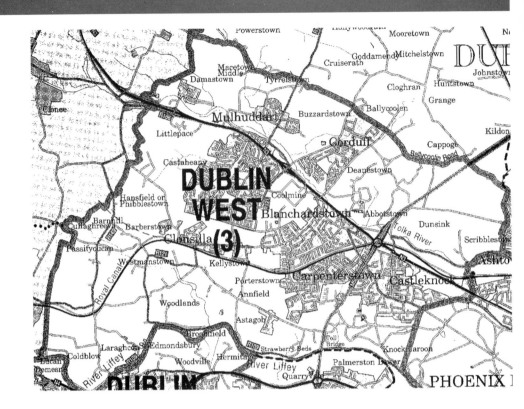

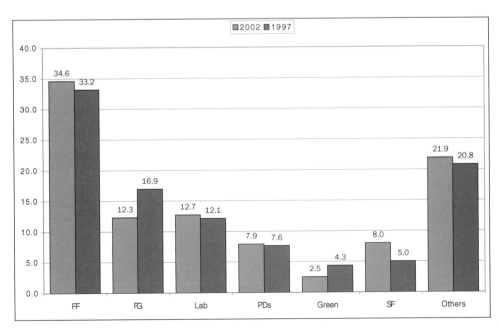

		1	2 Votes of Bonnie and Smyth	3 Lenihan's surplus	4 Votes of McDonald	5 Votes of Morrissey	6 Votes of Doherty
3 SEATS							
*B LENIHAN	FF	8086 √					
			+218	+71	+1122		
*J HIGGINS	SP	6442	6660	6731	7853 √		
			+210	+59	+296	+750	+1175
J BURTON	Lab	3810	4020	4079	4375	5125	6300 √
			+89	+46	+153	+881	+806
S Terry	FG	3694	3783	3829	3982	4863	5669
			+94	+26			
M-L McDonald	SF	2404	2498	2524	eliminated		
			+110	+74	+108		
T Morrissey	PD	2370	2480	2554	2662	eliminated	
			+86	+312	+358	+672	
D Doherty Ryan	FF	2300	2386	2698	3056	3728	eliminated
R Bonnie	GP	748	eliminated				
J Smyth	CSP	134	eliminated				
Non transferable			75	0	487	359	1747

ELECTORATE 52,676

TOTAL POLL 29,988

SPOILED 0

VALID POLL 29,988

QUOTA 7,498

* DENOTES OUTGOING TD

NEWLY ELECTED TDS IN CAPITALS

Lab gain. FG and FF loss

FORMERLY a four seater, this is now a three seat constituency. As a four seater it elected two Fianna Fáil, one independent (Socialist Party) and one Fine Gael. Incumbent Fine Gael deputy Austin Currie moved to Dublin Mid-West and Liam Lawlor, elected for Fianna Fáil in 1997, did not stand in either place. With Joe Higgins expected to retain his seat, and Fianna Fáil unlikely to win two in a three seater, the contest was essentially between Labour and Fine Gael for the last seat. The Labour candidate was Joan Burton, one of the several Labour members of the rainbow government to suffer defeat in 1997. Fine Gael fielded Sheila Terry, a former PD local councillor and Dáil candidate who topped the poll as an independent in 1999 for the Castleknock area in the County Council elections. Sinn Féin ran Mary-Lou McDonald, one of few women candidates in a party that is supported disproportionately by men.

Lenihan topped the poll and was elected on the first count. Higgins also ran well, increasing his vote share by 5% and was elected on the 3rd count with the help of a 44% transfer from Sinn Féin, one of many illustrations of the fact that Sinn Féin's urban support is leftist rather than nationalist. The Fine Gael vote dropped by 3.6% and Labour's rose by 0.6%, just enough to give Burton a lead over Terry of 116 votes on the first count. This extended to 162 after five counts. The elimination of Ryan Doherty, the second Fianna Fáil candidate,

Joan Burton is congratulated on her return to the Dáil

sealed Burton's victory as she took 1,175 votes from Doherty to Terry's 806. Only the PD transfers favoured Terry, and that only marginally. However, far more of these went to Labour and Fine Gael than to Fianna Fáil, who took only 25% of them.

JOAN BURTON

LABOUR

On her first election to Dáil Eireann in 1992 Joan Burton was immediately appointed Minister of State for Social Welfare, where she was responsible for the Combat Poverty Programmes, later increasing Ireland's Overseas Aid budget as Minister of State for Development Co-operation, but this did not help her when the 'Spring Tide' ebbed in 1997 and she lost her seat.

OCCUPATION
Full-time public representative, former chartered accountant and senior lecturer in accountancy

ADDRESS
81 Old Cabra Road, Dublin 7

PHONE
Constituency
(01) 838 8711

Leinster House
(01) 618 4006
Fax (01) 618 4175

EMAIL
joan@joanburton.ie

WEBSITE
www.joanburton.ie

BORN
Dublin, February 1949

EDUCATION
Sisters of Charity, Stanhope Street Secondary School;
University College Dublin (Commerce);
Fellow of the Institute of Chartered Accountants

MARITAL STATUS
Married to Pat Carroll.
One daughter

JOE HIGGINS

SOCIALIST

Joe Higgins is once again the Socialist Party's sole TD. He takes only an average industrial wage from his Dáil salary and donates the rest to the Socialist Party and various charities. His campaigns against water and rubbish collection charges, first on Dublin and then on Fingal County Councils, ensure him a large measure of popular support.

OCCUPATION
Full-time public representative, former second-level teacher

ADDRESS
155 Briarwood Close,
Mulhuddart, Dublin 15

PHONE
Constituency
(01) 820 1753

Leinster House
(01) 618 3038
Fax (01) 618 4158

EMAIL
joe.higgins@oireachtas.ie

WEBSITE
www.socialistparty.net

BORN
Kerry, May 1949

EDUCATION
Dingle CBS;
University College Dublin

MARITAL STATUS
Single

BRIAN LENIHAN

FIANNA FÁIL

First elected at the by-election in 1996 caused by death of his father, the former Tánaiste and Minister. He is a brother of Conor Lenihan TD and nephew of Senator Mary O'Rourke. He was Chairman of the All-Party Oireachtas Committee on the Constitution in the last Dáil and is now Minister of State at the Departments of Health and Children, Justice, Equality and Law Reform, and Education and Science with special responsibility for children.

OCCUPATION
Full-time public representative, former lecturer in law

ADDRESS
Longwood, Somerton Road,
Strawberry Beds, Dublin 20

PHONE
Constituency
(01) 822 0970
Fax (01) 822 0972

Leinster House
(01) 671 8142
Fax (01) 671 8985

EMAIL
brian.lenihan@oireachtas.ie

BORN
Dublin, May 1959

EDUCATION
Belvedere College;
Trinity College Dublin (BA (Mod) Legal Science);
Cambridge University (LLB);
King's Inns

MARITAL STATUS
Married to Patricia Ryan.
One son, one daughter

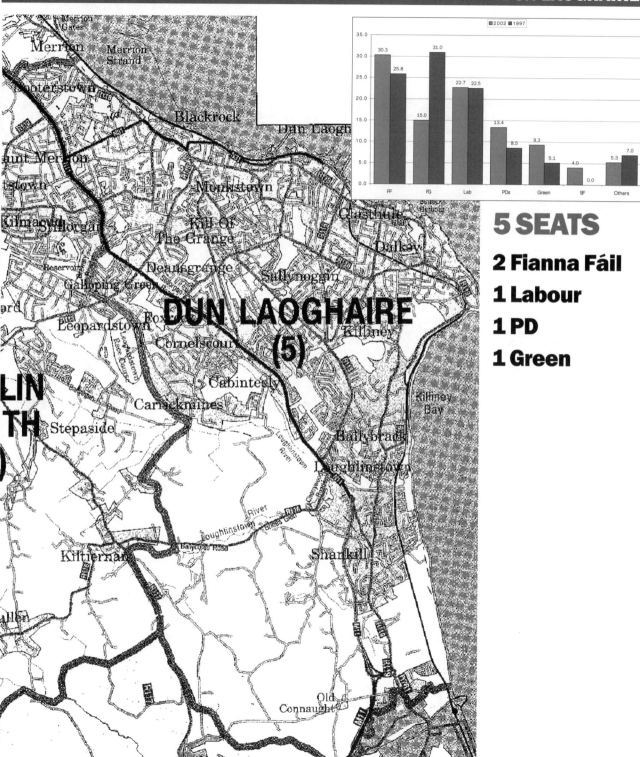

■2002 ■1997

5 SEATS

2 Fianna Fáil

1 Labour

1 PD

1 Green

5 SEATS

ELECTORATE
91,522

TOTAL POLL
54,071

SPOILED
438

VALID POLL
53,633

QUOTA
8,939

* DENOTES
OUTGOING TD

NEWLY
ELECTED TDS
IN CAPITALS

		1	2 Votes of Hyland	3 Votes of Redmond	4 Votes of Williams	5 Votes of O Buachalla	6 Votes of MacDowell	7 Votes of Boyd Barrett, and O'Keeffe	8 Votes of Bailey
*M HANAFIN	FF		+9	+93	+30				
		8818	8827	8920	8950 √				
*E GILMORE	Lab		+13	+13	+46	+32	+39	+348	+180
		8271	8284	8297	8343	8375	8414	8762	8942 √
B ANDREWS	FF		+6	+18	+10	+24	+36	+157	+66
		7425	7431	7449	7459	7483	7519	7676	7742
F O'MALLEY	PD		+5	+17	+29	+43	+49	+189	+79
		7166	7171	7188	7217	7260	7309	7498	7577
C CUFFE	GP		+10	+21	+75	+69	+129	+389	+104
		5002	5012	5033	5108	5177	5306	5695	5799
N Bhreathnach	Lab		+6	+1	+35	+35	+32	+100	+145
		3893	3899	3900	3935	3970	4002	4102	4247
H Keogh	FG		+1	+3	+19	+20	+16	+54	+527
		3229	3230	3233	3252	3272	3288	3342	3869
L Cosgrave	FG		+2	+16	+14	+14	+24	+67	+639
		3135	3137	3153	3167	3181	3205	3272	3911
M O'Brien	SF		+1	+13	+3	+16	+13	+200	+16
		2159	2160	2173	2176	2192	2205	2405	2421
J Bailey	FG		+1	+6	+8	+15	+10	+50	
		1705	1706	1712	1720	1735	1745	1795	elimt'd
R Boyd Barrett	SWP		+2	+2	+10	+26	+16		
		876	878	880	890	916	932	eliminated	
P O'Keefe	Ind		+3	+18	+14	+56	+40		
		593	596	614	628	684	724	eliminated	
D O'Buachalla	Ind		+7	+8	+19				
		346	353	361	380	eliminated			
V MacDowell	Ind		+9	+15	+25	+24			
		345	354	369	394	418	eliminated		
H E Williams	Ind		+4	+15					
		319	323	338	eliminated				
M Redmond	CSP		+2						
		265	267	eliminated					
B Hyland	Ind	86	eliminated						
Non transferable			5	8	1	6	14	102	39

PD gain from FG; GP gain from FG

9	10	11
Votes of O'Brien	Votes of Keogh	Votes of Bhreathnach
+547	+78	+551
8289	8367	8918 √
+130	+552	+1005
7707	8259	9264 √
+800	+319	+1752
6599	6918	8670 √
+303	+540	
4550	5090	eliminated
+47		
3916	eliminated	
+85	+2330	+1204
3996	6326	7530
eliminated		
509	97	578

TO LOSE one is unfortunate, to lose two smacks of carelessness. Fine Gael will plead misfortune, as both Seán Barrett and Monica Barnes, their incumbent TDs, retired, but the party failed miserably in their efforts to recruit strong candidates to replace them. Various names were touted but in the end the party could only field Senator Helen Keogh, a recent blow-in from the PDs, and Senator Liam Cosgrave, a former TD who is the son of one former taoiseach and grandson of another, but who had been refused a nomination under John Bruton and was last elected in 1982. At the last minute a local GAA figure John Bailey was added to the ticket. Labour always hoped to pick up a Fine Gael seat here, with former DL incumbent TD Eamon Gilmore and former TD and Labour Minister for Education Niamh Bhreathnach on their ticket. The PDs nominated Fiona O'Malley, daughter of the party's founder and a newly elected local councillor. Fianna Fáil fielded their incumbent TD, Mary Hanafin, daughter of former senator Des, and Barry Andrews, the son of David Andrews the former Minister for Foreign Affairs and long serving TD for the area. Ciaran Cuffe was nominated by the Greens for the first time in this constituency and, surprisingly, is unrelated to any former Oireachtas member.

All the Fine Gael nightmares came true as their vote dropped by 16% to only 19%, the largest drop it experienced across the 42 constituencies. Even that might have been enough in a five seater in some circumstances. The transfers were reasonable but not good enough: 65% from Bailey to Keogh/Cosgrave and then 60% from Keogh to Cosgrave.

Fiona O'Malley's success was generally unexpected but she must have looked to some Fine Gael voters like the sort of candidate they hoped their party might have provided for them to support. She increased the PD vote to over 13%, well up on Helen Keogh's 8% in 1997 and was finally elected on the distribution of Fine Gael transfers.

Bhreathnach's attempt at a comeback required a bigger Labour vote if it were to succeed but there was no increase. Worse still, the Green vote was well up and Cuffe took transfers that might otherwise have gone to Labour. She was eliminated after the 9th count and her transfers then elected Cuffe. Fine Gael would have hoped for more than 24% of those transfers. O'Malley got 20%, but Cuffe won 34%, extending his lead over Cosgrave.

Mary Hanafin, a junior minister in the previous government who was regularly wheeled out by the party as spokeswoman, topped the poll but was deeply disappointed to be rewarded by inheriting Séamus Brennan's bed of nails in the whip's office.

Richard Boyd Barrett's 876 votes for the Socialist Workers' Party was his party's best haul in 2002 – ironically perhaps, given this constituency's strong middle class profile.

BARRY ANDREWS

FIANNA FÁIL

Son of David Andrews, who represented the constituency from 1965, and nephew of Niall, Barry Andrews was first elected to Dún Laoghaire Rathdown County Council in June 1999. Already on his third career (he is a former teacher and barrister) he is a member of the Oireachtas Committee on European Affairs.

OCCUPATION
Public representative, former secondary teacher and barrister

ADDRESS
43 Temple Road, Blackrock, Co Dublin

PHONE
Constituency
(01) 288 0099

Leinster House
(01) 618 3856
Fax (01) 618 4599

EMAIL
barryandrews@ireland.com
bandrews@oireachtas.ie

BORN
Dublin, May 1967

EDUCATION
Blackrock College;
University College Dublin;
King's Inns

CIARÁN CUFFE

GREEN

Ciarán Cuffe has used his expertise in architecture and urban planning in a number of campaigns for improvements to transport and development in Dublin and its environs. Many might see his most spectacular personal achievement as being his coast-to-coast cycle ride across the USA.

OCCUPATION
Public representative, lecturer in urban planning

ADDRESS
Carrig Golligan, Quarry Road, Shankill, Co Dublin

PHONE
Leinster House
(01) 618 3082
Fax (01) 618 4341

EMAIL
ciaran@ciarancuffe.com

WEBSITE
www.ciarancuffe.com

BORN
Shankill, Co Dublin, April 1963

EDUCATION
University College Dublin (Architecture and Planning)

MARITAL STATUS
Single
Two children

ÉAMON GILMORE

LABOUR

Intelligent and articulate, Éamon Gilmore was first elected as a Worker's Party deputy in 1989 and has held the seat ever since, first for DL and this time for Labour and was junior minister with special responsibility for the Marine in the Rainbow coalition. He is also a member of Dun Laoghaire-Rathdown County Council. He stood unsuccessfully for the leadership when Ruairi Quinn stood down but finished third, behind Rabbitte and Howlin.

OCCUPATION
Trade Union official

ADDRESS
1 Corbawn Close, Shankill, Co Dublin

PHONE
Constituency

Leinster House
(01) 618 4037
Fax (01) 618 4574

EMAIL
eamon.gilmore@oireachtas.ie

BORN
Caltra, Galway, April 1955

EDUCATION
Gorbally College, Ballinasloe; University College Galway

MARITAL STATUS
Married.
Three children

MARY HANAFIN

FIANNA FÁIL

The Minister of State at the Department of the Taoiseach (with special responsibility as Government Chief Whip and for Minister of State at the Department of Defence is the daughter of pro-life campaigner Senator Des Hanafin. She has been a member of the Fianna Fáil National Executive since 1980.

OCCUPATION
Government minister, former teacher

ADDRESS
7 Oaklands Drive, Rathgar, Dublin 6

PHONE
Leinster House
(01) 619 4080
Fax (01) 676 5757

EMAIL
minister.hanafin@taoiseach.gov.ie

BORN
Thurles, Co Tipperary, June 1959

EDUCATION
Presentation Convent, Thurles; St Patrick's College, Maynooth (BA, HDipED); Dublin Institute of Technology (Diploma in Legal Studies)

MARITAL STATUS
Married to Éamon Leahy SC

FIONA O'MALLEY

PROGRESSIVE DEMOCRATS

Daughter of PD founder Dessie O'Malley and cousin of Tim, his successor in Limerick, Fiona O'Malley has served on Dún Laoghaire-Rathdown Council as Chairperson of the Housing Special Policy Committee and as a member of the Transport Committee and the County Development Board.

OCCUPATION
Full-time public representative, former arts administrator

ADDRESS
Dáil Eireann, Leinster House, Dublin 2

PHONE
Leinster House
(01) 618 3373
Fax (01) 618 4344

EMAIL
fomalley@oireachtas.ie

WEBSITE
www.fionaomalley.ie

BORN
Limerick, January 1968

EDUCATION
Laurel Hill, Limerick; Trinity College, Dublin (History of Art and French); City University, London (MA)

MARITAL STATUS
Single

4 SEATS

1 Fine Gael
2 Fianna Fáil
1 Independent

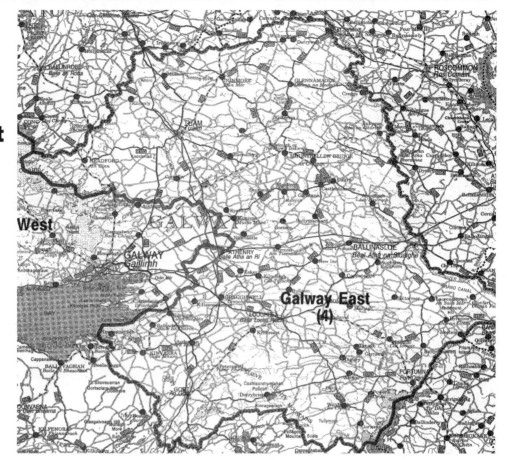

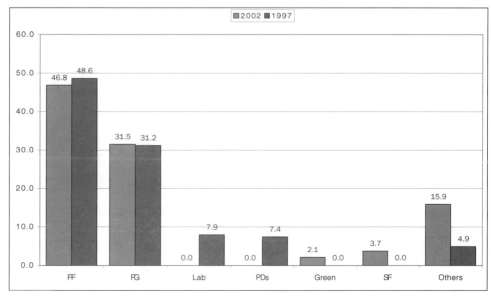

4 SEATS

ELECTORATE
73,659

TOTAL POLL
49,874

SPOILED
452

VALID POLL
49,422

QUOTA
9,885

* DENOTES
OUTGOING TD

NEWLY
ELECTED TDS
IN CAPITALS

			1	2 Votes of Ní Bhroin, Mac M'main	3 Votes of Mac an Bhaird	4 Votes of Burke	5 Connaughton's surplus
*P CONNAUGHTON	FG		8,635	+131 8,766	+218 8,984	+4,987 13,971 √	
J CALLANAN	FF		7,898	+65 7,963	+352 8,315	+1,099 9,414	+952 10,366 √
P McHUGH	Ind		7,786	+256 8,042	+539 8,581	+244 8,825	+1,056 9,881 √
*N TREACY	FF		7,765	+82 7,847	+244 8,091	+635 8,726	+527 9,253 √
*M Kitt	FF		7,454	+59 7,513	+198 7,711	+239 7,950	+293 8,243
*U Burke	FG		6,941	+211 7,152	+293 7,445	eliminated	
D Mac an Bhaird	SF		1,828	+240 2,068	eliminated		
Ú Ní Bhroin	GP		1,022	eliminated			
M Mac Meanmain	CSP		93	eliminated			
Non transferable				*71*	*224*	*241*	*1258*

Ind gain from FG

FIANNA Fáil had hopes of a third seat in both Galway constituencies but succeeded in neither of them. Here, Fine Gael lost the seat Ulick Burke won so narrowly with the aid of superb vote management in 1997, but it was the disaffected former Fianna Fáil councillor Paddy McHugh, running as an independent, who collected the seat. Labour and the PDs both opted out here, which helps explain why the Fine Gael vote held up so well.

A better division of the vote between their two candidates would probably not have helped Fine Gael unless Kitt's voters had favoured Burke over McHugh and there is no reason to think they would.

Paul Connaughton ensured his 20 year stint in the Dáil would continue by topping the poll. All three Fianna Fáil candidates were closely grouped after the first count, only 334 votes apart. However, this order did not change. Joe Callanan, who came close in 1997, winning the highest share of the vote of any losing Fianna Fáil candidate, thus won a seat from sitting TD Michael Kitt, who was first elected in 1975. Callanan simply won more transfers than Kitt, particularly from Ulick Burke, who like Callanan is from south of the railway line that divides the constituency, while Kitt, like Tuam-based McHugh, is from the north side.

JOE CALLANAN

FIANNA FÁIL

Joe Callanan, who narrowly missed election in 1997, has been a member of Galway County Council for the past 20 years and a member of the Western Health Board for the past 18 years.

OCCUPATION
Public representative;
full time farmer

ADDRESS
Calla, Kilconnell, Ballinasloe,
Co Galway

PHONE
Constituency
(091) 870 642
or (090) 968 6695
Fax (091) 870 643

Leinster House
(01) 618 4410
Fax (01) 618 4797

EMAIL
jcallanan@iolfree.ie

BORN
Galway, January 1949

EDUCATION
St Killian's Vocational School,
New Inn

MARITAL STATUS
Married to Noreen.
Six children

PAUL CONNAUGHTON

FINE GAEL

Paul Connaughton has been appointed Fine Gael spokesperson on Regional Development. He was first elected to the Dáil in 1981 and has served as Minister of State or spokesperson on a range of portfolios including the Marine, Natural Resources and Energy, Agriculture, Social Welfare, Regional Development, Defence and Tourism throughout his career.

OCCUPATION
Full-time public representative,
farmer

ADDRESS
Mountbellew, Ballinasloe,
Co Galway

PHONE
Constituency
(090) 967 9249

Leinster House
(01) 618 3779
Fax (01) 618 4508
LoCall 1890 337 889

EMAIL
paul.connaughton@oireachtas.ie

BORN
Mountbellew, Galway, 1944

EDUCATION
St Mary's Secondary School,
Ballygar, Co Galway;
St Jarlath's Vocational School,
Mountbellew;
Mountbellew Agricultural College;
Irish Management Institute

MARITAL STATUS
Married.
Two sons, five daughters

PADDY McHUGH

INDEPENDENT

First elected to Galway County Council in 1985 on the Fianna Fáil ticket, Paddy McHugh failed to get the party nomination and stood as an Independent. He was Chairman of Galway County Council 1999-2000 and is a former Chairman of County Galway VEC. He has campaigned strongly for the reopening of the Bon Secours Hospital in Tuam.

OCCUPATION
Architect

HOME ADDRESS
Shop Street, Tuam, Co Galway

PHONE
Constituency
(093) 26455
Fax (093) 28419

Leinster House
(01) 618 3903
Fax (01) 618 4435

EMAIL
paddy.mchugh@oireachtas.ie

BORN
Galway, January 1953

EDUCATION
Tuam Vocational School;
Waterford Institute of Technology

MARITAL STATUS
Married to Teresa.
Two daughters, one son.

NOEL TREACY

FIANNA FÁIL

Noel Treacy, who was first elected to the Dáil in May 1982, has once again been appointed Minister of State, this time at the Department of Agriculture and Food. Whilst he has never been a cabinet minister there can be few with a wider experience of government departments. He maintains his memberships of the IAVI and Irish Livestock Auctioneers Association.

OCCUPATION
Minister of State,
former auctioneer and financial services manager

ADDRESS
Gurteen, Ballinasloe, Co Galway

PHONE
Constituency
(091) 844 360
or (090) 967 7094
Fax (090) 967 7955

Leinster House
(01) 607 2000
Fax (01) 676 3947

BORN
Ballinasloe, Co Galway,
December 1952

EDUCATION
St Joseph's College, Garbally,
Ballinasloe, Co Galway

MARITAL STATUS
Married to Mary Cloonan.
Four daughters

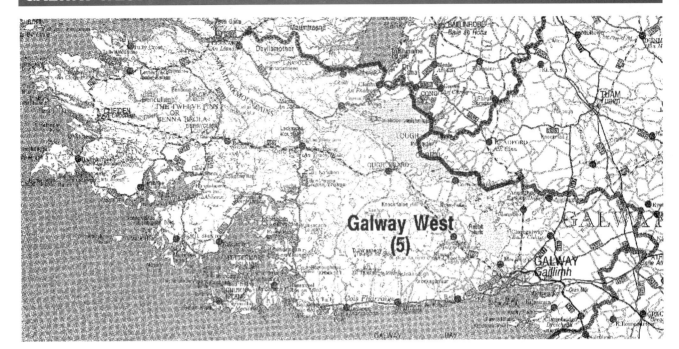

5 SEATS

3 Fianna Fáil
1 Fine Gael
1 Labour
1 PD

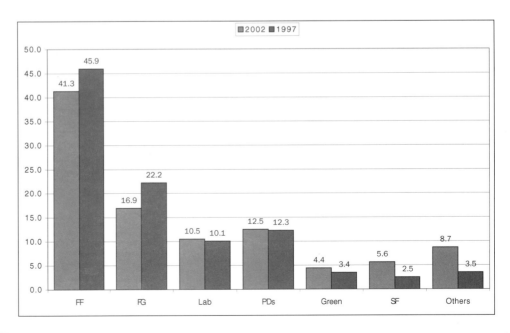

FRANK FAHEY

FIANNA FÁIL

The Minister of State at the Department of Enterprise, Trade and Employment with special responsibility for Labour Affairs is a former member of Galway County Council. First elected in February 1982, he lost his seat and moved to the Seanad in 1992. In 1997 he returned to the Dáil and became Minister of State at the Department of Health, with special responsibility for Children.

OCCUPATION
Minister of State, former secondary school teacher

ADDRESS
Constituency office Ballybane Industrial Estate, Galway

PHONE
Constituency
(091) 771 020
Fax (091) 771 040

Leinster House
(01) 631 3221
Fax (01) 631 3265

EMAIL
frank_fahey@entemp.ie

BORN
Dublin, June 1951

EDUCATION
St. Mary's College, Galway; Our Lady's, Gort, Co Galway; University College Galway (BA, HDipEd)

MARITAL STATUS
Married to Ethelle Griffin. Two sons, one daughter

NOEL GREALISH

PROGRESSIVE DEMOCRATS

A PD member of Galway County Council for the Oranmore area in 1999, Noel Grealish was one of three candidates selected from all corners of the constituency to replace Bobby Molloy when he stood down at the last minute. The surprise victor is said to have asked Molloy the way to the Dáil. Carnmore Hurling Club and his other Carnmore friends gave him 400 votes in the local box to speed him on his way

OCCUPATION
Director of the Glass Centre, Galway

ADDRESS
Carnmore, Oranmore, Co Galway

PHONE
Constituency
(091) 764 807
Fax (091)

EMAIL
noel.grealish@oireachtas.ie

BORN
Galway, December 1965

EDUCATION
St Mary's College Galway

MARITAL STATUS
Single

MICHAEL D HIGGINS

LABOUR

First elected in 1981 and re-elected in 1987 after 5 years in the Seanad, he was Minister for Arts, Culture and the Gaeltacht in January 1993–1997, being well qualified for the post as an author and poet. He was first recipient of the Seán MacBride Peace Prize of the International Peace Bureau in Helsinki in 1992 in recognition of his work for peace with justice in many parts of the world.

OCCUPATION
Public representative, former university lecturer

ADDRESS
Letteragh, Circular Road, Raheen, Galway

PHONE
Constituency
(091) 524 513
Fax (091) 528 501

Leinster House
(01) 618 3268
Fax (01) 618 4586

EMAIL
michael.d.higgins@oireachtas.ie

WEBSITE
www.michaeldhiggins.ie

BORN
Limerick, April 1941

EDUCATION
Ballycar NS, Co Clare; St Flannan's College, Ennis, Co Clare; University College Galway; Indiana University; Manchester University

MARITAL STATUS
Married to Sabina Coyne. One daughter, three sons

PÁDRAIC McCORMACK

FINE GAEL

Chairman of the Fine Gael Parliamentary Party, Pádraic McCormack was elected to the Dáil in 1989. He is a former member of Galway County Council, and is currently a member of Galway City Council. He was Mayor of Galway from 1992-1993.

OCCUPATION
Full-time public representative

ADDRESS
3 Renmore Park, Galway Constituency Office
114 Bohermore, Galway

PHONE
Constituency
(091) 753 992
or (091) 568 688
Fax (091) 569 204

Leinster House
(01) 618 3767
Fax (01) 618 4513

EMAIL
padraic.mccormack@oireachtas.ie

BORN
Longford, 1942

EDUCATION
Ballymahon Secondary School, Longford; Multyfarnham Agricultural College, Co Westmeath

MARITAL STATUS
Married, four children

5 SEATS

ELECTORATE
82,213

TOTAL POLL
50,146

SPOILED
680

VALID POLL
49,466

QUOTA
8,245

* DENOTES
OUTGOING TD

NEWLY
ELECTED TDS
IN CAPITALS

		1	2 Ó Cuív's surplus	3 Votes of Manning and Nulty	4 Votes of Healy-Eames	5 Votes of Ac Cois'Ibha	6 Votes of McDonnell	7 Votes of Scallon	8 Votes of Callanan
*E Ó CUÍV	FF	9947	√						
*F FAHEY	FF	7226	+676 **7902**	+2 **7904**	+89 **7993**	+127 **8120**	+198 **8318**	√	
*M D HIGGINS	Lab	5213	+102 **5315**	+28 **5343**	+167 **5510**	+136 **5646**	+126 **5772**	+323 **6095**	+569 **6664**
*P McCORMACK	FG	4760	+90 **4850**	+9 **4859**	+401 **5260**	+58 **5318**	+184 **5502**	+363 **5865**	+136 **6001**
M Cox	FF	3269	+428 **3697**	+7 **3704**	+48 **3752**	+49 **3801**	+69 **3870**	+212 **4082**	+215 **4297**
N GREALISH	PD	2735	+52 **2787**	+4 **2791**	+67 **2858**	+18 **2876**	+245 **3121**	+112 **3233**	+82 **3315**
S Walsh	Ind	2439	+120 **2559**	+29 **2588**	+38 **2626**	+116 **2742**	+32 **2774**	+170 **2944**	+210 **3154**
M McDonagh	FG	2279	+21 **2300**	+6 **2306**	+313 **2619**	+13 **2632**	+38 **2670**	+78 **2748**	+60 **2808**
N Ó Brolcháin	GP	2193	+23 **2216**	+25 **2241**	+67 **2308**	+108 **2416**	+34 **2450**	+201 **2651**	+457 **3108**
D Lyons	PD	1995	+22 **2017**	+9 **2026**	+32 **2058**	+10 **2068**	+477 **2545**	+168 **2713**	+74 **2787**
D R Scallon	Ind	1677	+50 **1727**	+13 **1740**	+72 **1812**	+60 **1872**	+48 **1920**	eliminated	
D Callanan	SF	1468	+17 **1485**	+13 **1498**	+11 **1509**	+657 **2166**	+34 **2200**	+106 **2306**	elim'td
D McDonnell	PD	1462	+17 **1479**	+5 **1484**	+15 **1499**	+7 **1506**	eliminated		
F Healy-Eames	FG	1320	+20 **1340**	+7 **1347**	eliminated				
S Ac Coistealbha	SF	1311	+62 **1373**	+10 **1383**	+14 **1397**	eliminated			
E Manning	Ind	96	+1 **97**	eliminated					
J Nulty	Ind	76	+1 **77**	eliminated					
Non transferable			0	7	13	38	21	187	503

No change

9	10	11	12	13	14	15
Fahey's surplus	Votes of Lyons	Votes of McDonagh	Votes of Walsh	McCormack's surplus	Votes of Ó Brolcháin	Higgins' surplus
+18	+489	+327	+653	+93	+2336	
6682	7171	7498	8151	8244	10580 √	
+11	+273	+1338	+797			
6012	6285	7623	8420 √			
+17	+309	+159	+462	+29	+312	+321
4314	4623	4782	5244	5273	5585	5906
+8	+1221	+554	+227	+27	+332	+531
3323	4544	5098	5325	5352	5684	6215 √
+1	+79	+94				
3155	3234	3328	eliminated			
+4	+76					
2812	2888	eliminated				
+3	+156	+124	+358	+26		
3111	3267	3391	3749	3775	eliminated	
+11						
2798	eliminated					
0	195	292	831	0	795	1483

FIANNA Fáil had hopes of a third seat here, especially when veteran PD Bobby Molloy decided not to run again following adverse publicity about his direct representations to a judge on behalf of a constituent. It took three candidates to replace him. Between them they hoped to bring in all the parts of the constituency that the minister himself used to reach. Fianna Fáil put their faith in senator Margaret Cox to win them the third seat, and in two ministers of state, Frank Fahey and Éamon Ó Cuív, grandson of Eamon de Valera, to provide the cutting edge of their campaign. Before Bobby Molloy's retirement there had been much speculation concerning Dana Rosemary Scallon, MEP for Connaught-Ulster and prominent pro-life campaigner who was looking for a constituency base to run for the Dáil. If she ran she was expected to hurt Fianna Fáil. Fine Gael had no hope of winning more than one seat and chose to blood two new young candidates, but unfortunately both were from much the same area and close to the incumbent Pádraic McCormack on the edge of the city. The offer by Pól Ó Foighil to sweep up in the west of the constituency was firmly rejected.

To most people's surprise, the PDs held their seat here, Scallon ran and polled very poorly and Fianna Fáil failed to win the third seat.

The PDs succeeded in increasing the party vote marginally but spread across three candidates this still looked like an unlikely victory. Grealish was elected with the second smallest first count vote of any other sucessful candidate in 2002. Nor were transfers strong: 48% from McDonnell and then 44% from Lyons to Grealish. At this point Grealish was still 79 votes behind Cox, but Fine Gael transfers from McDonagh put him ahead and while things remained close he was never caught. The key point for the PDs was the lack of a strong opponent. Cox was struggling because the Fianna Fáil vote was marginally down; apart from Cox there was nobody even close.

Michael D Higgins once again held on to a seat for Labour with a marginal increase in the vote. Sinn Féin won 6% and the Greens 4%, and neither mounted the sort of challenge to Labour they posed in some other urban areas.

Scallon won only 1,600 votes, and seems unlikely to have dented Fianna Fáil at all. Her transfers went all over the place, but more often to Labour and Fine Gael than to Cox.

ÉAMON Ó CUÍV

FIANNA FÁIL

Éamon Ó Cuív – or 'Dev Óg' – was first elected to the Dáil in 1992. He is a cousin of Síle de Valera TD for Clare and grandson of Eamon de Valera. The Minister for Community, Rural and Gaeltacht Affairs was a junior minister in the last government. He surprised many when he claimed to have voted against the Nice Treaty in 2001 despite campaigning for it, but campaigned strongly for Nice in 2002.

OCCUPATION
Government Minister,
former co-op manager

ADDRESS
Corr na Mona, Conamara,
Contae na Gaillimhe

PHONE
Constituency
(091) 562 846
Fax (091) 562 844

Leinster House
(01) 647 3057
Fax (01) 647 3101

EMAIL
aire@pobail.ie

WEBSITE
www.ie/ealga/

BORN
Dublin, June 1950

EDUCATION
Oatlands College, Mount Merrion,
Dublin;
University College Dublin (BSc)

MARITAL STATUS
Married to Áine Ní Choincheannáin.
Three sons, one daughter

No such thing as a free launch: Bertie Ahern helps carry a curragh while canvassing in Galway West
PHOTOCALL IRELAND

3 SEATS

1 Fianna Fáil
1 Fine Gael
1 Sinn Féin

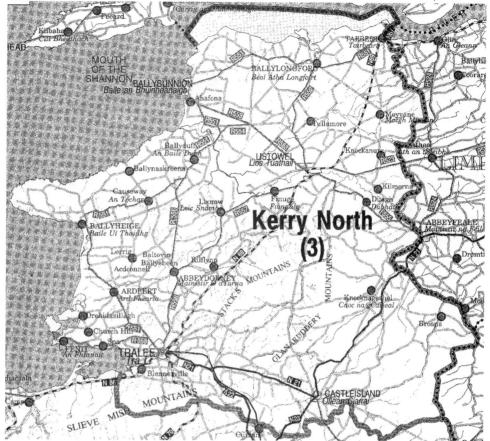

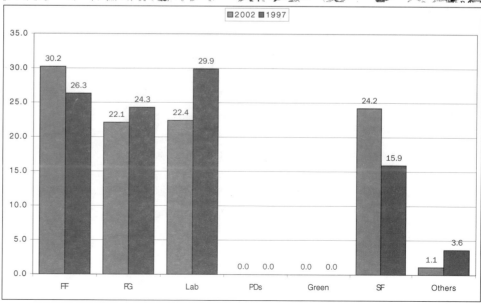

	2002	1997
FF	30.2	26.3
FG	22.1	24.3
Lab	22.4	29.9
PDs	0.0	0.0
Green	0.0	0.0
SF	24.2	15.9
Others	1.1	3.6

			1	**2**	**3**
				Votes of Kiely, Kennedy and O'Connor	McEllistrim's surplus
3 SEATS	M FERRIS	SF	9496	+520 10016 √	
	*D Spring	Lab	8773	+393 9166	+187 9353
	*J DEENIHAN	FG	8652	+886 9538	+304 9842 √
	T McELLISTRIM	FF	7884	+2401 10285 √	
	D Kiely	FF	3927	eliminated	
	J Kennedy	Ind	233	eliminated	
	A O'Connor	Ind	208	eliminated	
	Non transferable			168	0

ELECTORATE
55,476

TOTAL POLL
39,524

SPOILED
351

VALID POLL
39,173

QUOTA
9,794

* DENOTES OUTGOING TD

NEWLY ELECTED TDS IN CAPITALS

SF gain from Lab

THIS was the result that interested the world's media: Martin Ferris, one time IRA gun-runner taking a seat from Dick Spring, former Labour leader and, as Minister for Foreign Affairs in the rainbow coalition, who played his part in bringing the republican movement into democratic politics.

Spring won almost 9,000 votes, far more than any other defeated candidate in this election and with one of the largest shares of the vote won by a losing candidate on any occasion. Only Willie Penrose won more votes for Labour in 2002. Spring survived by the smallest of margins in 1987 but perhaps hindered by some indecision as to whether he would stand again, failed to beat the axe on this occasion.

Despite a campaign dogged by allegations of vigilantism, Ferris topped the poll. The votes of two independent candidates and the Listowel based Dan Kiely, the unsuccessful Fianna Fáil candidate, elected Fianna Fáil's Tom McEllistrim and the Listowel-based Jimmy Deenihan for Fine Gael. Away in Tralee, Spring missed out at the last.

The battle for the Fianna Fáil seat was one of the more interesting stories of the election. Incumbent deputy Denis Foley retired, damaged by his involvement in the Ansbacher scandal. Fearful of losing the seat to Ferris the government party poured considerable resources into the area but did not succeed in building anything like a unified team on the ground.

McEllistrim, the unsuccessful candidate in 1997, followed two generations of his family into representative politics in Kerry but did not endear himself to the party HQ whose favourite appeared to be Senator Dan Kiely. It often seems to be the case that this is the kiss of death for the chosen one. McEllistrim's thorough door-to-door effort paid off. Although the transfer from Kiely was not a strong one –below 60% – it was enough.

JIMMY DEENIHAN

FINE GAEL

A Dáil deputy since 1987. Appointed spokesperson on Arts, Sports and Tourism, June 2002. From 1994-1997 Minister of State at the Department of Agriculture, Food and Forestry. Member of Kerry County Council GAA member, won All Ireland football medals with Kerry in 1975, 1978, 1980 and in 1981(as captain).

OCCUPATION
Full-time public representative, former teacher

ADDRESS
Finuge, Lixnaw, Co Kerry

PHONE
Constituency
(068) 40154
Fax (068) 40383

Leinster House
(01) 618 3352
Fax (01) 618 4145

EMAIL
jimmy.deenihan@oireachtas.ie

WEBSITE

BORN
Listowel, Co Kerry, 1952

EDUCATION
Dromclough National School, Listowel;
St. Michael's College, Listowel;
National College of Physical Education, Limerick (BEd)

MARITAL STATUS
Married

MARTIN FERRIS

SINN FÉIN

Spent a total of 13 years in prison for IRA activities. A member of Sinn Féin's Ard Chomhairle since 1994, he was centrally involved in the negotiations leading up to the Good Friday Agreement. He is a member of Kerry County Council and Tralee UDC and Munster candidate in the 1999 European Parliament elections. he won an All Ireland under-21 football medal in 1973.

OCCUPATION
Former fisherman

ADDRESS
2 Moyderwell, Tralee, Co Kerry

PHONE
Constituency
(066) 712 9545
Leinster House
(01) 618 4248
(01) 618 4798

EMAIL
sinnfeinkerry@eircom.net
mferris@oireachtas.ie

BORN
Ardfert, Co Kerry, March 1952

EDUCATION
Tralee CBS

MARITAL STATUS
Married to Marie.
Six children

TOM McELLISTRIM

FIANNA FÁIL

Tom McEllistrim was a Dáil candidate for Fianna Fáil in 1997. He lost out to Denis Foley in the battle for the last seat but defeated Foley's daughter for the nomination this time. Apparently out of favour with the party hierarchy, he seemed set to succeed despite it. He comes from a long line of Tom McEllistrims who stood on the Fianna Fáil ticket – his father and grandfather were both TDs – and he was the youngest councillor on Kerry County Council.

OCCUPATION
Full-time public representative, former secondary school teacher

ADDRESS
Ahane, Ballymacalligott,
Tralee, Co Kerry

PHONE
Constituency
(066) 713 7127
Fax (066) 713 7127

Leinster House
(01) 618 3817
Fax (01) 618 4788

EMAIL
cllrtmcellistrim@eircom.net

BORN
Tralee, October 1968

EDUCATION
Presentation Convent, Tralee;
CBS Tralee;
St Patrick's College, Castleisland;
St Brendan's College, Killarney;
National University of Ireland
Maynooth (BA, HdipEd)

MARITAL STATUS
Single

Fianna Fáil senator Dan Kiely and supporters   PHOTOCALL IRELAND

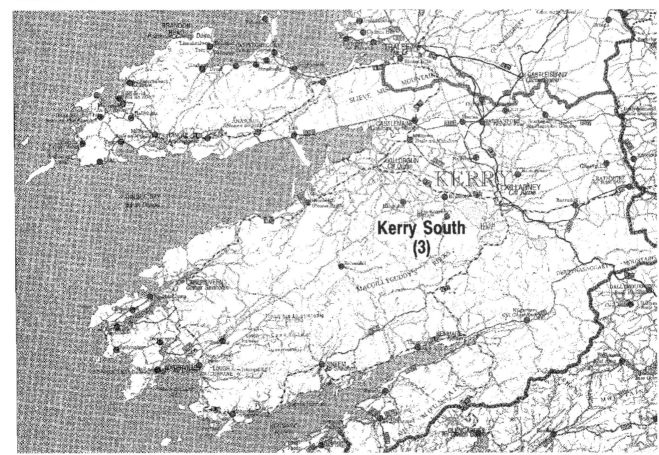

3 SEATS

1 Fianna Fáil
1 Labour
1 Independent

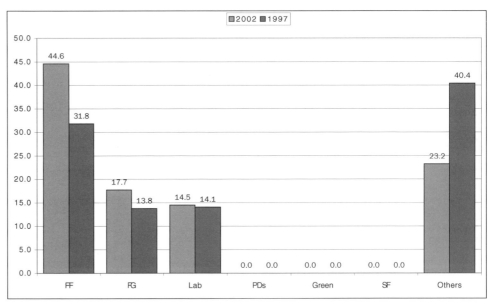

	2002	1997
FF	44.6	31.8
FG	17.7	13.8
Lab	14.5	14.1
PDs	0.0	0.0
Green	0.0	0.0
SF	0.0	0.0
Others	23.2	40.4

			1	2 Votes of Barry	3 Votes of Grady	4 O'Donoghue's surplus	5 Votes of Casey	6 Votes of Fitzgerald	7 Moynihan Cronin's surplus	
*J O'DONOGHUE	FF		**9445**	√						
T Fleming	FF		**6912**	+83 **6995**	+260 **7255**	+152 **7407**	+186 **7593**	+683 **8276**	+105 **8381**	
*J HEALY-RAE	Ind		**6229**	+226 **6455**	+364 **6819**	+74 **6893**	+254 **7147**	+1262 **8409**	+175 **8584**	√
*B MOYNIHAN CRONIN	Lab		**5307**	+173 **5480**	+466 **5946**	+33 **5979**	+453 **6432**	+3010 **9442**	√	
S Fitzgerald	FG		**4539**	+193 **4732**	+59 **4791**	+20 **4811**	+1272 **6083**	eliminated		
S Casey	FG		**1934**	+99 **2033**	+183 **2216**	+4 **2220**	eliminated			
D Grady	Ind		**1346**	+103 **1449**	eliminated					
D Barry	Ind		**934**	eliminated						
Non transferable				57	117	0	55	1128	0	

3 SEATS

ELECTORATE
51,761

TOTAL POLL
37,022

SPOILED
376

VALID POLL
36,646

QUOTA
9,162

* DENOTES
OUTGOING TD

NEWLY
ELECTED TDS
IN CAPITALS

No change

NO change in party representation, nor in personnel: one Fianna Fáil, one Labour and, not least, one independent. The one-time Fianna Fáil activist Jackie Healy-Rae, one of the gang of four independents who supported the last government, was made to fight hard by Fianna Fáil to keep his seat. The FF vote was up considerably here by almost 13%, an increase bettered only in Limerick East. Healy-Rae's vote was down slightly from 20% in 1997 to 17% and another independent from the FF family, Breandán Mac Gearailt, who won 4,000 votes in 1997, did not stand again. John O'Donoghue, the outgoing Minister for Justice replaced Healy-Rae on top of the poll with more than a quota, passing on 54% of his surplus of 283 votes to running mate Tom Fleming in second place. Fleming's failure to secure a seat given that placing was due to the strong transfer of votes from Fine Gael to both Healy-Rae and the fourth placed Labour candidate. Fine Gael have failed to win a seat here since 1987 but at least on this occasion they could determinewho would be the last TD to be elected.

Of Séamus Fitzgerald's 6,083 votes on the 5th count, almost half went to Labour's Moynihan Cronin and a further 21% to Healy-Rae with Fleming winning only 11%. This made the difference, electing Moynihan Cronin and placing Healy-Rae ahead of the second Fianna Fáil candidate for the first time. Moynihan Cronin's surplus, not surprisingly, elected the independent candidate. Geography often determines transfers; this time it was politics – anyone but Fianna Fáil.

JACKIE HEALY-RAE

INDEPENDENT

The colourful Jackie Healy-Rae gained many benefits for his constituency in his first term as an independent TD. It remains to be seen whether a stronger government will confer as many favours.

OCCUPATION
Full-time public representative, former farmer, publican and businessman

ADDRESS
Kilgarvan, Co Kerry

PHONE
Constituency
(064) 32 467
Fax (064) 37 375

Leinster House
(01) 618 3363
LoCall 1890 337 889

EMAIL
jhr@oireachtas.ie

WEBSITE
www.kerryweb.ie/destination-kerry/kilgarvan/rae.html

BORN
Kilgarvan, March 1931

EDUCATION
Kilgarvan NS;
Ballyvourney Secondary School

MARITAL STATUS
Separated.
Two sons, four daughters

BREEDA MOYNIHAN CRONIN

LABOUR

Breeda Moynihan Cronin took the seat held by her father, Michael Moynihan, in the 1992 General Election having been a member of Kerry County Council since 1991. She was Chairperson of the Joint Oireachtas Committee on Tourism, Sport and Recreation in the last Dáil.

OCCUPATION
Full-time public representative, former bank official

ADDRESS
10 Muckross Grove,
Killarney, Co Kerry

PHONE
Constituency
(064) 34 993

Leinster House
(01) 618 4441
Fax (01) 618 4640

EMAIL
bmoynihancronin@eircom.net

WEBSITE
www.breedamoynihancronin.ie

BORN
Killarney, March 1953

EDUCATION
St Brigid's Secondary School,
Killarney;
Sion Hill College, Dublin;
Skerry's College, Cork

MARITAL STATUS
Married to Daniel C Cronin

JOHN O'DONOGHUE

FIANNA FÁIL

The Minister for Arts, Sport and Tourism was first elected in 1987. Any hope that his present ministry would allow a little relaxation after the rigours of the Department of Justice in a time of unprecedented immigration must have been dashed by the drama of the withdrawal of the 'Bertie Bowl' funding. With Jackie Healy-Rae close by, John O'Donoghue operates more clinics than almost any other public representative.

OCCUPATION
Government minister,
former solicitor

ADDRESS
Garranearagh, Cahirciveen,
Co Kerry

PHONE
Constituency
(066) 947 3221
Fax (066) 947 3222

Leinster House
(01) 631 3804
Fax (01) 678 5906

EMAIL
ministersoffice@dasp.gov.ie

WEBSITE
www.gov.ie/arts-sport-tourism

BORN
Caherciveen, Co Kerry, May 1956

EDUCATION
CBS Caherciveen;
University College Cork;
Incorporated Law Society, Dublin
(BCL, LLB)

MARITAL STATUS
Married to Kate Ann Murphy.
Two sons, one daughter

3 SEATS

1 Fianna Fáil
1 Labour
1 Fine Gael

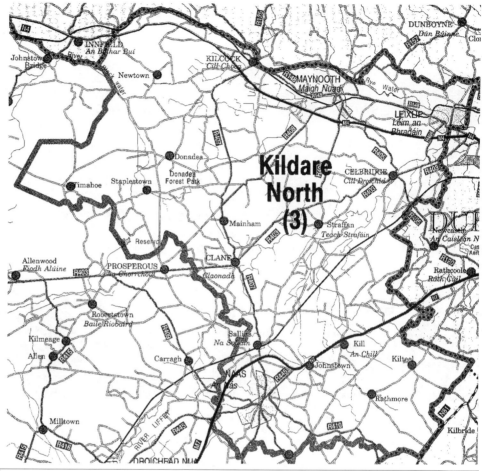

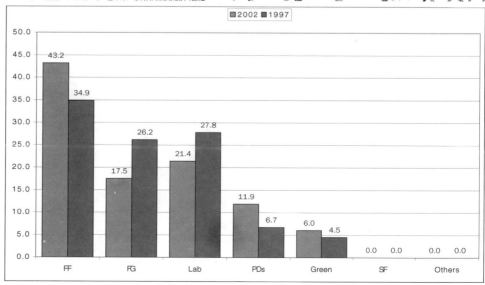

			1	**2** McCreevy's surplus	**3** Votes of Kelly-McCormack	**4** Votes of Walsh	**5** Stagg's surplus
3 SEATS	*C McCREEVY	FF	**9082**	√			
				+117	+837	+1467	
ELECTORATE 60,094	*E STAGG	Lab	**7051**	**7168**	**8005**	**9472**	√
				+73	+318	+1164	+684
TOTAL POLL 33,271	*B DURKAN	FG	**5786**	**5859**	**6177**	**7341**	**8025** √
				+513	+242	+1459	+508
SPOILED 291	P Kelly	FF	**5168**	**5681**	**5923**	**7382**	**7890**
				+108	+446			
VALID POLL 32,980	K Walsh	PD	**3919**	**4027**	**4473**	**eliminated**	
				+25			
QUOTA 8,246	A Kelly McCormack	GP	**1974**	**1999**	**eliminated**		
	Non transferable			0	156	383	34

* DENOTES OUTGOING TD

NEWLY ELECTED TDS IN CAPITALS

No change

CHARLIE McCreevy and Emmet Stagg were re-elected for Fianna Fáil and Labour respectively and the very experienced Mayo born Bernard Durkan hung on to his seat by just 135 votes from Fianna Fáil's Paul Kelly. McCreevy's personal vote was significantly up, reflecting his very high profile as Minister for Finance, and the party vote, as in neighbouring Kildare South, was up 8%. Fine Gael ran only one candidate this time but with a 9% drop in their vote they must have had a very nervous count. Durkan was 616 votes ahead of Kelly initially. McCreevy's surplus naturally favoured Kelly although he won only 53% of it, but Kelly McCormack's Green supporters did not flow to the part-namesake. The PDs almost made the difference. Kate Walsh ran as an independent in the 1999 local elections and did very well to push the PD vote up 4%, to the benefit of Paul Kelly. Only 33% of her transfers went to Fianna Fáil but these made a net difference of 295 votes, edging Kelly ahead.

Labour also ran only one candidate; both Stagg and a DL candidate stood in 1997. His vote was down almost 2% against the combined Labour/DL vote last time but his personal support went up by over 1000 votes, keeping him well out of the struggle further down the list. His surplus favoured Durkan over Kelly; it was only by a margin of 176 out of 1,192 votes but it was enough.

Charlie McCreevy: elected on first count

BERNARD DURKAN

FINE GAEL

First elected to the Dáil in 1981 Bernard Durkan was appointed Chief Whip in 2002. Despite some adverse publicity over earlier financial problems which Deputy Durkan revealed to the Public Accounts Committee legal team before the DIRT enquiry he emerged "with no cause to be embarrassed".

OCCUPATION
Full-time public representative, former agricultural contractor

ADDRESS
Timard, Maynooth, Co Kildare

TELEPHONE
Constituency
(01) 628 6063
Fax (01) 628 5215

Leinster House
(01) 618 3732
Fax (01) 618 4515

EMAIL
bernard.durkan@oireachtas.ie

BORN
Killasser, Co Mayo, 1945

EDUCATION
St John's, Carramore, Co Mayo

MARITAL STATUS
Married to Hilary Spence.
Two sons

CHARLIE McCREEVY

FIANNA FÁIL

Charlie McCreevy was first elected to the Dáil in 1977. His popularity waxes and wanes with the state of the nation's finances and his proposals regularly generate controversy. He is a strong advocate of firm control over government spending and the lowering of taxation.

OCCUPATION
Government Minister, chartered accountant

ADDRESS
Hillview House, Kilcullen Road, Naas, Co Kildare

PHONE
Constituency
(045) 876 816
Fax (045) 876 092

Leinster House
(01) 676 7571

EMAIL
webmaster@finance.irlgov.ie

WEBSITE
www.finance.gov.ie

BORN
Sallins, Co Kildare,
September 1949

EDUCATION
CBS, Naas, Co Kildare;
Franciscan College, Gormanston,
Co Meath;
University College Dublin
(BComm, FCA)

MARITAL STATUS
Separated.
Four sons, three daughters

EMMET STAGG

LABOUR

Labour Party chief whip since 1997, Emmet Stagg was elected to the Dáil in 1987. He left the party in early 1992 over the party's attitude to coalition but rejoined shortly afterwards and was Minister of State in both the Reynolds and the Rainbow coalitions. He is a brother of IRA hunger striker Frank Stagg.

OCCUPATION
Full-time public representative, former medical technologist

ADDRESS
736 Lodge Park, Straffan,
Co Kildare

PHONE
Constituency
(01) 627 2149
Fax (01) 627 0601

Leinster House
(01) 618 3013
Fax (01) 618 4538

EMAIL
emmet.stagg@oireachtas.ie

WEBSITE
www.labour.ie

BORN
Hollymount, Co Mayo,
October 1944

EDUCATION
Ballinrobe CBS;
College of Technology,
Kevin Street

MARITAL STATUS
Married to Mary Morris.
One daughter, one son

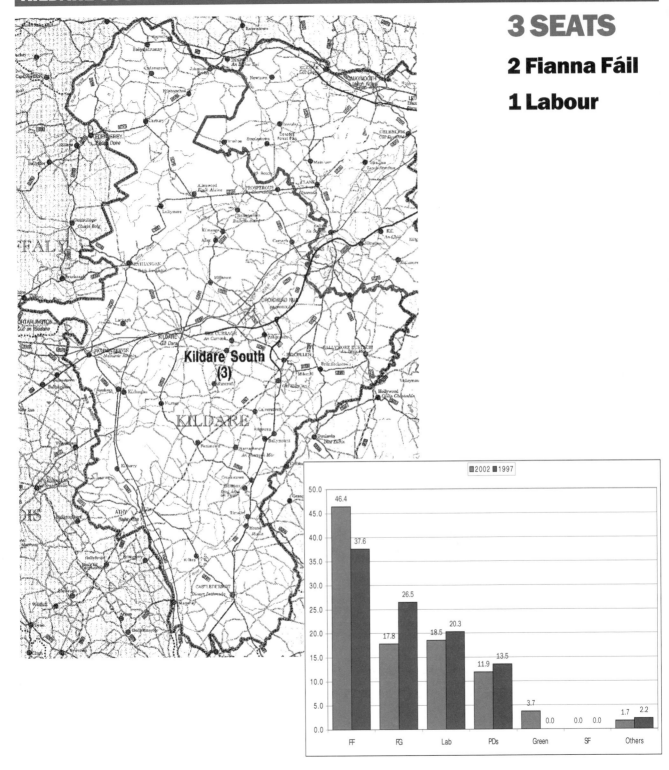

3 SEATS

2 Fianna Fáil

1 Labour

		1	2 Votes of Fitzgibbon	3 Votes of Hendy	4 Votes of Dardis, JJ Power	5 Seán Power's surplus	6 Ó Fearghail's surplus
*S POWER	FF	7782	+35 7817	+43 7860	+1309 9169 √		
S Ó FEARGHAIL	FF	7370	+88 7458	+43 7501	+925 8426 √		
*J WALL	Lab	6043	+105 6148	+116 6264	+1179 7443	+406 7849	+128 7977 √
*A Dukes	FG	4967	+73 5040	+506 5546	+1624 7170	+480 7650	+140 7790
J Dardis	PD	3887	+59 3946	+112 4058	eliminated		
JJ Power	GP	1208	+127 1335	+16 1351	eliminated		
R Hendy	FG	828	+22 850	eliminated			
G Fitzgibbon	Ind	546	eliminated				
Non transferable			37	14	372	125	0

3 SEATS

ELECTORATE
58,354

TOTAL POLL
33,132

SPOILED
501

VALID POLL
32,631

QUOTA
8,158

* DENOTES
OUTGOING TD

NEWLY
ELECTED TDS
IN CAPITALS

FF gain from FG

ONE of the real shocks of the election was Alan Dukes, former Fine Gael leader and prominent front bench spokesman, losing his seat to Fianna Fáil's Senator Seán Ó Fearghail. Fianna Fáil ran only two candidates this time but their vote was up almost 8%, one of their best performances, while Fine Gael's dropped by almost 9%. Dukes fell from first to fourth place in the poll, behind Jack Wall, the sitting Labour deputy. Transfers from Rainsford Hendy, his running mate, and JJ Power (Green) favoured Dukes but even with the added benefit of more votes from Seán Power's surplus Dukes remained 199 votes short of Wall.

The PD vote fell here despite the presence of a well-rooted candidate, Senator John Dardis, one of the Taoiseach's four PD nominees. (Interestingly, none of these was elected in 2002.) Dardis was eliminated along with JJ Power so the destination of his votes is not clear but with 41% of their combined vote going to Fianna Fáil it seems likely that at least 50% of Dardis' voters went on to support the other government party, which would be one of the strongest PD to Fianna Fáil transfers in 2002.

Real shock: the defeat of former Fine Gael finance minister and party leader Alan Dukes

PHOTOCALL IRELAND

SEÁN Ó FEARGHAÍL

FIANNA FÁIL

Seán Ó Fearghaíl was elected to the Seanad Agricultural Panel in June 2000, having been a member of Kildare County Council since 1985. He was narrowly defeated as a Fianna Fáil candidate in the South Kildare constituency in the 1997 General Election.

OCCUPATION
Full-time public representative,

ADDRESS
Fennor House, Kildare, Co Kildare

PHONE
Constituency
(045) 522 966
Fax (045) 522 966

Leinster House
(01) 618 3948
Fax (01) 618 4649

EMAIL
sean.ofearghail@oireachtas.ie

BORN
Kildare, April 1960

EDUCATION
St Joseph's Academy, Kildare

MARITAL STATUS
Married to Mary Clare.
Two daughters

SEÁN POWER

FIANNA FÁIL

Seán Power was first elected to the Dáil in 1989 and came to prominence in October 1991 when he tabled a vote of No Confidence in Taoiseach Charles Haughey. A firm believer in fiscal rectitude, he has suggested that all candidates for public office should be required to produce a tax clearance certificate. He is a son of Paddy Power, Kildare TD from 1969-89. He is Chair of the Oireachtas Committee on the Environment.

OCCUPATION
Public representative, publican

ADDRESS
Castlekealy, Caragh, Naas, Co Kildare

PHONE
Constituency
(045) 432 289
Fax (045) 435 380

Leinster House
(01) 618 3428
Fax (01) 618 4529

EMAIL
sean.power@oireachtas.ie

WEBSITE
www.fiannafail.ie/td_cv_38.htm

BORN
Caragh, Naas, Co Kildare, October 1960

EDUCATION
CBS, Naas

MARITAL STATUS
Married to Deirdre Malone.
Three sons, one daughter

JACK WALL

LABOUR

Jack Wall, a passionate member of the GAA whose constituency includes the Curragh Camp, was nominated to the Seanad in 1993 and elected to Dáil Éireann in 1997. He became Labour Party spokesperson on Defence following the revelation that his predecessor in the post, Michael Bell TD, had filed an army deafness claim.

OCCUPATION
Full-time public representative; former electrician

ADDRESS
Castlemitchell, Athy, Co Kildare

PHONE
Constituency Office
(059) 8632 874
Fax (059) 8633 157
Mobile
(087) 257 0275

Leinster House
(01) 618 3571
Fax (01) 618 4540

EMAIL
jackwall@oireachtas.ie

WEBSITE
www.labour.ie

BORN
Castledermot, Co Kildare, July 1945

EDUCATION
Castledermot Vocational School

MARITAL STATUS
Married to Anne Byrne.
Two sons, two daughters

5 SEATS

3 Fianna Fáil
1 PD
1 Fine Gael

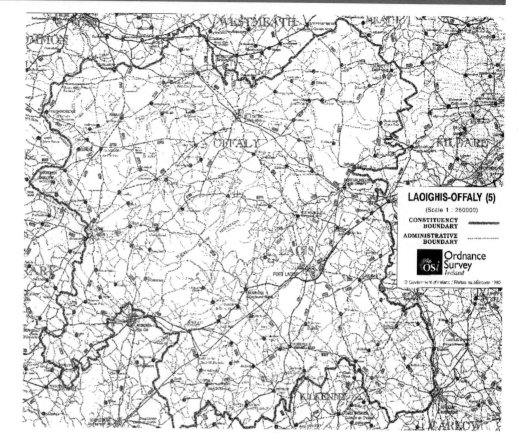

LAOIGHIS-OFFALY (5)

(Scale 1 : 250000)

CONSTITUENCY BOUNDARY

ADMINISTRATIVE BOUNDARY

Ordnance Survey Ireland

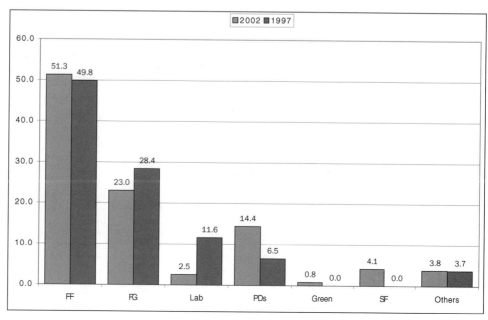

	FF	FG	Lab	PDs	Green	SF	Others
2002	51.3	23.0	2.5	14.4	0.8	4.1	3.8
1997	49.8	28.4	11.6	6.5	0.0	0.0	3.7

			1	2 Cowen's surplus	3 Votes of Fettes, Kelly, McCormack, Redmond	4 Votes of Dwyer	5 Votes of Stanley, Buckley	6 Votes of Killaly
*B COWEN	FF		12529 √					
T PARLON	PD		9088	+270 9358	+173 9531	+158 9689	+883 10572 √	
*J MOLONEY	FF		8093	+167 8260	+83 8343	+41 8384	+464 8848	+2124 10972 √
O ENRIGHT	FG		8053	+202 8255	+148 8403	+494 8897	+1308 10205	+800 11005 √
*S FLEMING	FF		7091	+439 7530	+112 7642	+86 7728	+633 8361	+2092 10453 √
*C Flanagan	FG		6500	+30 6530	+116 6646	+219 6865	+519 7384	+222 7606
G Killally	FF		4719	+668 5387	+50 5437	+93 5530	+532 6062	eliminated
B Stanley	SF		2600	+39 2639	+181 2820	+197 3017	eliminated	
M Buckley	Ind		1695	+88 1783	+183 1966	+390 2356	eliminated	
J Dwyer	Lab		1600	+75 1675	+134 1809	eliminated		
C Fettes	GP		520	+9 529	eliminated			
J McCormack	Ind		351	+2 353	eliminated			
J Kelly	Ind		236	+1 237	eliminated			
M Redmond	CSP		142	+2 144	eliminated			
Non transferable				0	83	131	1034	824

5 SEATS

ELECTORATE
95,373

TOTAL POLL
63,888

SPOILED
671

VALID POLL
63,217

QUOTA
10,537

* DENOTES
OUTGOING TD

NEWLY
ELECTED TDS
IN CAPITALS

PD gain from FG

FORMER IFA leader Tom Parlon sounded out both Fine Gael and the PDs about a candidacy, opted for the latter and then showed Fine Gael what they were missing by collecting the biggest PD vote in the country, coming second in the poll and winning a seat at the expense of Charlie Flanagan, thus restoring the geographic balance to the more traditional three deputies from Offaly.

Parlon gained over 14% of the vote, a big increase on the vote typically won by the party since 1987.

Brian Cowen, outgoing Minister for Foreign Affairs, topped the poll as Fianna Fáil pushed its support share back over 50%. 64% of his surplus went to his running mates and another 14% to Parlon. Sitting Fianna Fáil TDs Seán Fleming and John Moloney, both from Laois, also ran well. Ger Killally put in a good performance as the second Offaly candidate and delivered 70% of his votes to other party candidates when he was eliminated.

With the Fine Gael vote down by over 5% to only 23% someone was going to be in difficulties but it was not

PD leader Mary Harney and former IFA president Tom Parlon at the Progressive Democrats election manifesto launch at the Hilton Hotel, Dublin
PHOTOCALL IRELAND

BRIAN COWEN

FIANNA FÁIL

Brian Cowen was first elected to the Dáil in 1984 following the death of his father. Reappointed as Minister for Foreign Affairs, he has also served as Minister for Health and Children, Minister for Transport, Energy and Communications and Minister for Labour and been opposition spokesperson on Agriculture. He is a combative and effective speaker in the Dáil.

OCCUPATION
Government Minister, former solicitor

ADDRESS
Ballard, Tullamore, Co Offaly

PHONE
Constituency
(0506) 21 976
Fax (0506) 21 910

Leinster House
(01) 408 2137
Fax (01) 408 2400

EMAIL
minister@iveagh.irlgov.ie

WEBSITE
www.irlgov.ie/iveagh

BORN
Tullamore, Co Offaly,
January 1960

EDUCATION
Ard Scoil Naoimh Chiaráin, Clara;
Cistercian College, Roscrea;
University College Dublin;
Incorporated Law Society
of Ireland

MARITAL STATUS
Married to Mary Molloy.
Two daughters

the new candidate, Olwyn Enright, daughter of retiring TD Tom Enright, based in Offaly like Tom Parlon, but the Portlaoise-based Flanagan. Flanagan, the son of Oliver J, who represented the constituency for many years, was first elected in 1987. His support was down by over 1,600 votes while Enright dropped only 300 votes on her father's 1997 total.

Fine Gael would have hoped to pick up votes in the absence of Labour's Pat Gallagher, who had won a seat in 1992 and had always polled well.

Gallagher's successor, John Dwyer made little impression; his 2.5% was the second lowest ever for Labour in this constituency and he finished behind both Brian Stanley of Sinn Féin and Molly Buckley, another independent running on a health services platform.

OLWYN ENRIGHT

FINE GAEL

Olwyn Enright takes over the seat of her father Tom Enright who retired from politics in 2002 after a public service career spanning 35 years. A well-known local figure in her own right, she has been appointed spokeswoman on Education and Children.

OCCUPATION
Full-time public representative

ADDRESS
John's Place, Birr, Co Offaly

PHONE
Home
(0509) 23 893

Constituency
(0506) 29870
(0509) 22 326
Fax (0509) 20 802

Leinster House
(01) 618 4217
Fax (01) 618 4351

EMAIL
oenright@eircom.net
olwyn.enright@oireachtas.ie

WEBSITE
www.olwynenright.com

BORN
Ballinasloe, Co Galway, July 1974

EDUCATION
St Brendan's Community School;
University College Dublin (BCL);
Law Society of Ireland;
University College Galway
(Dip Community Development
Practice)

MARITAL STATUS
Single

SEÁN FLEMING

FIANNA FÁIL

Deputy Fleming, who was first elected in 1997, took over the administration of the Fianna Fáil party leader's allowance as Fianna Fáil's financial director following the resignation of Charles Haughey in 1992. He has argued strongly against all business donations to political parties. He is Chair of the Joint Committee on Finance and the Public Service.

OCCUPATION
Full-time public representative, former financial director of Fianna Fáil

ADDRESS
Silveracre, Castletown, Portlaoise, Co Laois

PHONE
Constituency
(0502) 32 692
Fax (0502) 32 922

Leinster House
(01) 618 3472
Fax (01) 618 4178

EMAIL
sean.fleming@oireachtas.ie

BORN
Castletown, Co Laois, February 1958

EDUCATION
Salesian College, Ballinakill;
University College Dublin
(BComm); Fellow of the Institute of Chartered Accountants in Ireland

MARITAL STATUS
Married to Mary O'Gorman.
One son

JOHN MOLONEY

FIANNA FÁIL

An unsuccessful candidate in the 1992 general election, John Moloney was first elected in 1997, having been co-opted to Laois County Council in 1981 on the death of his father. He has campaigned strongly against the downgrading of Portlaoise hospital in favour of Tullamore, even going so far as to threaten to resign his Dáil seat.

OCCUPATION
Full-time public representative, former undertaker and publican

ADDRESS
27 Patrick Street, Mountmellick, Co Laois

PHONE
Constituency
(0502) 24 392
Fax (0502) 24 011

Leinster House
(01) 618 4098
Fax (01) 618 4611

EMAIL
moloneyjo@eircom.net

BORN
Portlaoise, June 1953

EDUCATION
Patrician Brothers College, Ballyfin, Co Laois

MARITAL STATUS
Married to Patricia McEvoy.
Two sons, one daughter

TOM PARLON

PROGRESSIVE DEMOCRATS

Many were surprised when former IFA leader Tom Parlon chose to run with the PDs rather than Fine Gael for his first attempt at the Dáil but his faith in Mary Harney was justified by the result. Parlon should give farmers a very articulate voice in the 29th Dáil. He is Minister for State at the Department of Finance with special responsibility for the Office of Public Works.

OCCUPATION
Public representative, farmer

ADDRESS
Hamilton House, Emmet Street, Birr, Co Offaly

PHONE
Constituency
(0509) 23737
Fax (0509) 23739

Leinster House
(01) 661 9750
Fax (01) 661 2531

EMAIL
tomparlon@finance.gov.ie

WEBSITE
www.tomparlon.ie

BORN
Coolderry, Co Offaly, August 1953

EDUCATION
Roscrea CBS;
Gurteen Agricultural College, Co Tipperary

MARITAL STATUS
Married to Martha.
Five children

5 SEATS

2 Fianna Fáil
1 Fine Gael
1 PD
1 Labour

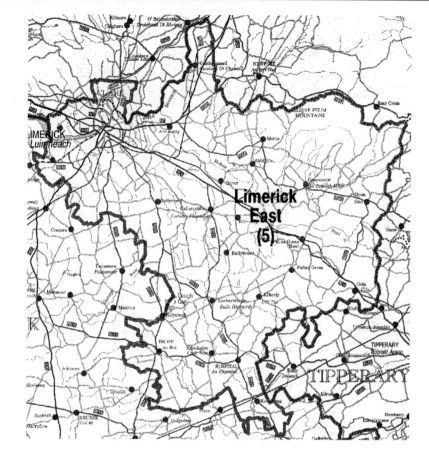

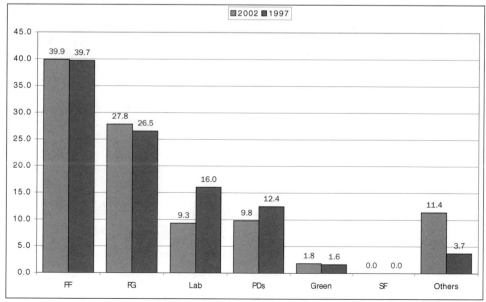

		1	2	3	4	5	6	7	8
			O'Dea's surplus	Noonan's surplus	Votes of Bennis O'Donoghue A Ryan	Votes of Kelly	Votes of Hourigan	Votes of T Ryan	Votes of Gilligan
*W O'DEA	FF	13174 √							
*M NOONAN	FG	9451 √							
T O'MALLEY	PD		+442	+88	+75	+16	+125	+151	+90
		4885	5327	5415	5490	5506	5631	5782	5872
*J O'SULLIVAN	Lab		+419	+145	+62	+101	+359	+212	+396
		4629	5048	5193	5255	5356	5715	5927	6323
M Jackman	FG		+244	+697	+88	+32	+128	+185	+137
		4468	4712	5409	5497	5529	5657	5842	5979
P POWER	FF		+1957	+41	+90	+38	+73	+173	+172
		3881	5838	5879	5969	6007	6080	6253	6425
*E Wade	FF		+1111	+13	+42	+21	+29	132	+57
		2918	4029	4042	4084	4105	4134	4266	4323
P Kennedy	Ind		+221	+53	+68	+133	+83	+190	+539
		2092	2313	2366	2434	2567	2650	2840	3379
J Gilligan	Ind		+139	+18	+46	+197	104	+240	
		1176	1315	1333	1379	1576	1680	1920	elim'td
T Ryan	Ind		+121	+20	+72	+44	+73		
		1148	1269	1289	1361	1405	1478	eliminated	
T Hourigan	GP		+53	+15	+68	+24			
		917	970	985	1053	1077	eliminated		
M Kelly	Ind		+59	+15	+13				
		677	736	751	764	eliminated			
N Bennis	Ind		+57	+9					
		479	536	545	eliminated				
C O'Donoghue	CSP		+9	+1					
		86	95	96	eliminated				
A Ryan	Ind		+8	+2					
		19	27	29	eliminated				
Non transferable			0	0	46	158	103	195	529

5 SEATS

ELECTORATE
80,593

TOTAL POLL
50,513

SPOILED
513

VALID POLL
50,000

QUOTA
8,334

* DENOTES OUTGOING TD

NEWLY ELECTED TDS IN CAPITALS

No change

9	10	11
Votes of Kennedy	Votes of Wade	Power's surplus
+452	+629	+770
6324	6953	7723 √
+635	+298	+211
6958	7256	7467 √
+590	+417	+176
6569	6986	7162
+426	+2640	
6851	9491 √	
+206		
4529	eliminated	
eliminated		
1070	*545*	*2646*

INTEREST here centred around the performance of Michael Noonan as party leader of Fine Gael: could he bring in his running mate, Senator Mary Jackman, who narrowly failed in the by-election following the death of Labour's Jim Kemmy in 1997? In addition, could the PDs win a seat here post-Dessie O'Malley (who struggled himself last time)? Less importantly, but still an interesting question: just how many votes would Willie O'Dea get this time?

The answers to the first question was 'no'. Michael Noonan polled quite well, holding the Fine Gael decline to just 1% but although he was elected on the first count, the surplus was not enough to bring in Jackman. A 62% transfer was fair, but it needed something closer to 90% and we don't very often see that sort of transfer pattern nowadays. Initially behind Jan O'Sullivan, the sitting Labour TD, Jackman pulled ahead with Noonan's votes but was generally second to O'Sullivan in later transfers and was over 300 votes down at the end. Pat Kennedy, a dissident Fine Gaeler running as an independent, polled over 2,000 votes, few of which found their way back to the party. He was one of several independents who together won over 11% of the vote, three times that won in 1997.

Tim O'Malley, a local PD councillor, polled better than his cousin had done in 1997, but with only one PD candidate this time the party vote was down by almost 3%. As in 1997 it proved sufficient thanks to the votes of the Fianna Fáil's second incumbent, Eddie Wade, who was eliminated after the 8th count. Wade's surplus in 1997 elected Dessie O'Malley; in 2002 his votes took O'Malley ahead of Jackman, and the surplus of Peter Power, the other Fianna Fáil candidate, pushed him ahead of O'Sullivan as well. More Fianna Fáil transfers went to O'Malley than to O'Sullivan and Jackman combined. This made the difference.

O'Dea surprised nobody by topping the poll with more than one-and-a-half quotas, increasing his own share of the vote and winning more than twice the votes of his running mates combined. 63% of his surplus transferred, 2% less than last time but enough to bring in a running mate. This time it was Peter Power. Wade's personal vote was well down, and Power's up. O'Dea's massive transfer also favoured Power.

Aidan Ryan, running as an independent candidate, achieved the dubious distinction of winning fewer votes than any other candidate in this election: just 19. At least he did not lose his deposit since these are no longer required.

MICHAEL NOONAN

FINE GAEL

The former leader of Fine Gael has been a TD since 1981. His career in recent times has been overshadowed by his reactions during the hepatitis C revelations, which came back to haunt him again in the run up to the general election. The promise to repay money lost by share-holders in Eircom also did nothing for his credibility. He was succeeded as party leader by Enda Kenny.

OCCUPATION
Full-time public representative, former teacher

ADDRESS
18 Gouldavoher Estate,
Fr Russell Road, Limerick

PHONE
Constituency
(061) 229 350

Leinster House
(01) 618 3125
Fax (01) 618 4504

EMAIL
michael.noonan@oireachtas.ie

BORN
Limerick, May 1943

EDUCATION
St Patrick's Secondary School, Glin, Co Limerick;
St Patrick's Teacher Training College, Dublin;
University College Dublin
(BA, HDipEd)

MARITAL STATUS
Married, three sons, two daughters

WILLIE O'DEA

FIANNA FÁIL

Despite Willie O'Dea's championing of the taxi drivers in November 2000 he has been appointed Minister of State at the Department of Justice, Equality and Law Reform (with special responsibility for Equality Issues including Disability Issues). A dissident during the Haughey administration, he was first elected in February 1982.

OCCUPATION
Minister of State, former accountant

ADDRESS
2 Glenview Gardens, Farranshore, Co Limerick

PHONE
Constituency
(061) 454 488
Fax (061) 328 849

Leinster House
(01) 663 2670
Fax (01) 667 0369

EMAIL
willie.odea@oceanfree.net

WEBSITE
www.willieodea.ie

BORN
Limerick, November 1952

EDUCATION
Patrician Brothers College, Ballyfin, Co Laois; University College Dublin; King's Inns; Institute of Certified Accountants (BCL, LLM, BL, Certified Accountant)

MARITAL STATUS
Married to Geraldine Kennedy

TIM O'MALLEY

PROGRESSIVE DEMOCRATS

Minister of State at the Department of Health, Tim O'Malley was not hotly tipped to succeed his cousin Dessie into the Dáil. The county councillor campaigned hard on Mid-West health issues.

OCCUPATION
Full-time public representative, former pharmacist

ADDRESS
Regional Pharmacy, Dooradoyle, Limerick

PHONE
Constituency
(061) 308 540
Fax (061) 228 718

Leinster House
(01) 635 4764
Fax (01) 635 4765

EMAIL
timomalley@limerickcoco.ie

WEBSITE
www.timomalley.ie

BORN
Limerick, July 1944

EDUCATION
Crescent College, Limerick; University College, Dublin (BSc Pharm), MPSI, FPSI

MARITAL STATUS
Married to Peg Kelly. Two daughters, two sons

JAN O'SULLIVAN

LABOUR

Jan O'Sullivan, one of the few members of the Church of Ireland in the Dáil, was elected in March 1998 in the by-election caused by the death of Jim Kemmy. She campaigned strongly but unsuccessfully for victims of physical abuse to be included in the amendment to the Statute of Limitations Act for those abused in State-sponsored institutions.

OCCUPATION
Full-time public representative, former pre-school teacher

ADDRESS
7 Lanahrone Avenue, Corbally, Limerick

PHONE
Constituency
(061) 312 316
(061) 313 707

Leinster House
(01) 618 3670
Fax (01) 618 4617

EMAIL
jan.osullivan@oireachtas.ie

WEBSITE
www.labour.ie

BORN
Clare, 1950

EDUCATION
Villiers School, Limerick; Trinity College Dublin

MARITAL STATUS
Married to Paul O'Sullivan. One son, one daughter

PETER POWER

FIANNA FÁIL

First elected TD in 2002, having been defeated in 1997, Peter Power comes from a well established Limerick Fianna Fáil background and is currently an Alderman on Limerick Corporation.

OCCUPATION
Public representative, solicitor

ADDRESS
Kilfeara, Ennis Road, Limerick

PHONE
Constituency
Fax (061) 317 148

Leinster House
(01) 618 4232

EMAIL
peter@peter-power.com

WEBSITE
www.peter-power.com

BORN
Limerick, January 1966

EDUCATION
Ard Scoil Rís, Limerick; University College Cork

MARITAL STATUS
Married to Lorraine. One daughter

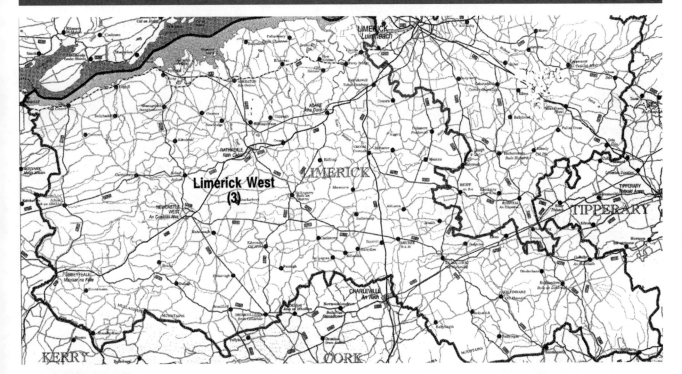

3 SEATS

2 Fianna Fáil
1 Fine Gael

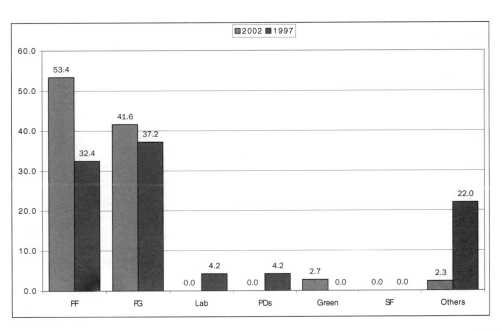

3 SEATS

ELECTORATE
53,879

TOTAL POLL
36,145

SPOILED
476

VALID POLL
35,669

QUOTA
8,918

* DENOTES
OUTGOING TD

NEWLY
ELECTED TDS
IN CAPITALS

			1	**2**	**3**	**4**	
				Cregan's surplus	Collins' surplus	Votes of Briody, MacDomhail and O'Riordan	
J CREGAN	FF		10823 √				
				+1290			
*M COLLINS	FF		8236	9526 √			
				+232	+184	+702	
*D NEVILLE	FG		7446	7678	7862	8564	√
				+274	+183	+696	
*M Finucane	FG		7410	7684	7867	8563	
				+54	+136		
M Briody	GP		948	1002	1138	eliminated	
				+48	+79		
M Mac Domhnaill	Ind		662	710	789	eliminated	
				+7	+26		
P O'Riordan	CSP		144	151	177	eliminated	
Non transferable				0	0	706	

FF gain from FG

This result provided more support for electronic voting. An extra seat here was a major Fianna Fáil target as 1997 was the first time they had failed to take two seats. The problem then was the presence of two disaffected Fianna Fáil candidates running as independents. This cut the party's vote to just 32% and allowed Fine Gael to win two seats with just 37% of the vote. In 2002 there was no such distraction for the faithful and the party's vote rose once again to stand above 50%. John Cregan, a local councillor and new senator, topped the poll and was elected on the first count. 68% of his surplus went to the brother of the former minister and now MEP Gerry Collins, Michael, who was elected next. With one Fine Gael TD in the firing line, the question was who would fall? It was as close as it could be. The Croagh based Dan Neville finished just a single vote ahead of his fellow Fine Gael incumbent Michael Finucane from Newcastle West. Finucane waived his right to a recount, which might well have been indecisive.

Had the two actually tied, Neville would have won anyway by virtue of a higher first preference vote.

MICHAEL COLLINS

FIANNA FÁIL

First elected in 1997, Michael Collins is a brother of Gerard Collins, MEP for Munster since 1994, Dáil Deputy for Limerick West 1967-1997 and former Government Minister. Son of James J Collins, Dáil Deputy for Limerick West 1948-1967. A long-serving county councillor, he has now resigned from local politics.

OCCUPATION
Full-time public representative, businessman

ADDRESS
White Oaks, Red House Hill, Patrickswell, Co Limerick

PHONE
Constituency
(061) 355 081
Fax (061) 355 902

Leinster House
(01) 618 3577
Fax (01) 618 4183

EMAIL
michael.collins@oireachtas.ie

WEBSITE
www.michaelcollins.ie

BORN
Abbeyfeale, Co Limerick,
November 1940

EDUCATION
St Munchin's College, Limerick

MARITAL STATUS
Married to Una O'Farrell.
One son, two daughters

Noel Dempsey and Pat Carey on the banks of the Grand Canal in Dublin at the launch of the FF environment policy   PHOTOCALL IRELAND!

JOHN CREGAN

FIANNA FÁIL

A Senator from 1997-2002, John Cregan has been an active member of the Communication Workers Union. He was first elected to Limerick Co Council in 1991 following the retirement of his late father Tom, and also became a member of the Mid-Western Health Board.

OCCUPATION
Full-time public representative, former employee of Telecom Éireann

ADDRESS
Church Street, Dromcollogher, Co Limerick

PHONE
Constituency
(069) 77671
Fax (069) 77672

Leinster House
(01) 618 3028
Fax (01) 618 4377

EMAIL
john.cregan@oireachtas.ie

BORN
Dromcollogher, Co Limerick, May 1961

EDUCATION
St Joseph's National School; St Mary's Secondary School, Dromcollogher

MARITAL STATUS
Married to Patsy.
Three children

DAN NEVILLE

FINE GAEL

Deputy Neville was first elected to Dáil Éireann in 1997, having previously stood in 1987 and 1992, and was appointed deputy spokesperson on Health and Children, June 2002. He has a particular interest in young people and suicide.

OCCUPATION
Full-time public representative

ADDRESS
Kiltannan, Croagh, Co Limerick

PHONE
Constituency
(061) 396 351
Fax (061) 396 351

Leinster House
(01) 618 3356
Fax (01) 618 4525

EMAIL
daniel.neville@oireachtas.ie

BORN
Limerick, December 1946

EDUCATION
Adare CBS;
University of Limerick;
University College Cork

MARITAL STATUS
Married.
Four children

4 SEATS

1 Fine Gael
2 Fianna Fáil
1 PD

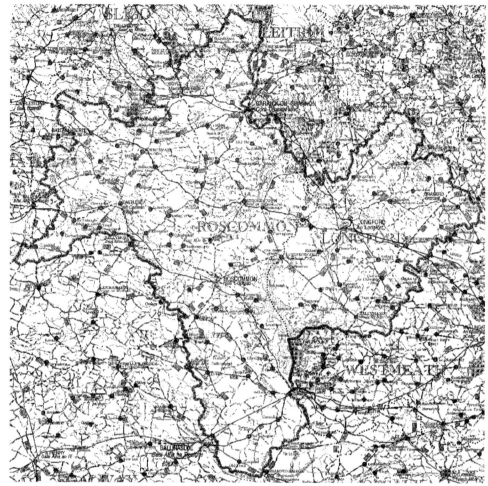

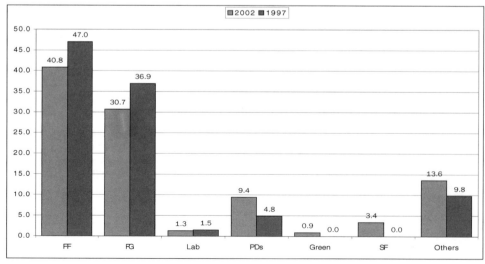

	2002	1997
FF	40.8	47.0
FG	30.7	36.9
Lab	1.3	1.5
PDs	9.4	4.8
Green	0.9	0.0
SF	3.4	0.0
Others	13.6	9.8

MICHAEL FINNERAN

FIANNA FÁIL

A long serving member of Roscommon County Council and Chairman of the General Council of County Councils, Michael Finneran was an active Senator on the administrative panel from 1989-2002.

OCCUPATION
Full-time public representative, former health board officer

ADDRESS
Riverside Avenue, Roscommon

PHONE
Constituency
(090) 662 2245
Fax (090) 662 2033

Leinster House
(01) 618 3579
Fax (01) 618 4588

EMAIL
michael.finneran@oireachtas.ie

BORN
Roscommon, September 1947

EDUCATION
Summerhill College, Sligo

MARITAL STATUS
Married to Elizabeth Walsh.
Two sons, two daughters

PETER KELLY

FIANNA FÁIL

Peter Kelly, whose family have been prominent in business and local politics in Longford since 1905, is a former chairman of the Midland Regional Authority, Longford Urban and County Councils, and Longford Tourism.

OCCUPATION
Full-time public representative, former funeral director, publican and general merchant

ADDRESS
Church Street, Battery Road, Longford

PHONE
Constituency
(043) 45070 or 45340
Fax (043) 41996

Leinster House
(01) 618 3913
Fax (01) 618 4792

EMAIL
cllrpeterkelly@eircom.net

WEBSITE
www.peterkelly.ie

BORN
Longford, August 1944

EDUCATION
St Michael's Boys NS, Longford;
Marist College, Dundalk

MARITAL STATUS
Married to Maura.
One daughter, two sons

DENIS NAUGHTEN

FINE GAEL

Denis Naughten, the son of the late Liam Naughten, was only 24 when he was first elected to the Dáil in 1997. Having been Fine Gael's front bench spokesman on Enterprise, Trade and Employment from June 2000 to February 2001, Deputy Naughten was appointed spokesman on Transport in June 2002.

OCCUPATION
Full-time public representative

ADDRESS
Ardkeenan, Drum, Athlone, Co Roscommon

PHONE
Home
(090) 643 7324
Constituency
(090) 662 7557
Fax (090) 662 7556

Leinster House
(01) 618 3545
Fax (01) 618 4581
LoCall 1890 337-889

EMAIL
denis.naughten@oireachtas.ie

WEBSITE
www.naughten.com

BORN
Drum, Co Roscommon, 1973

EDUCATION
St Aloysius College, Athlone;
University College Dublin (BSc);
University College Cork (MSc)

MARITAL STATUS
Single

MAE SEXTON

PROGRESSIVE DEMOCRATS

Independent Councillor to the Longford County Council and Longford UDC, she joined the PDs in 1997 and was re-elected in 1999. Stood as an independent in the constituency in 1992 and for the PDs in 1997, losing her deposit on each occasion. Has a long involvement with many local groups and charities. Her father, a local baker, was a Fianna Fáil councillor for 30 years.

OCCUPATION
Company secretary

ADDRESS
46 Demesne, Longford

PHONE
(043) 41142

Leinster House
(01) 618 3792
Fax (01) 618 4786

EMAIL
maesexton@eircom.net

BORN
April 1955

EDUCATION
Convent of Mercy Longford;
NUI Maynooth

MARITAL STATUS
Married to Tommy Sexton.
Two children

			1	2 Votes of Killalea, Lenehan	3 Votes of Ansbro	4 Votes of Flanagan, Baxter	5 Votes of Whelan	6 Votes of Crosby	7 Votes of Connor	8 Votes of Quinn
P KELLY	FF		7319	+4 7323	+11 7334	+73 7407	+227 7634	+238 7872	+33 7905	+75 7980
*D NAUGHTEN	FG		6660	+26 6686	+36 6722	+199 6921	+155 7076	+355 7431	+2075 9506	+2108 11614 √
M FINNERAN	FF		6502	+19 6521	+16 6537	+75 6612	+118 6730	+428 7158	+136 7294	+887 8181
G Kelly	FF		6430	+41 6471	+19 6490	+180 6670	+227 6897	+117 7014	+726 7740	+719 8459
*L Belton	FG		4762	+5 4767	+21 4788	+133 4921	+116 5037	+156 5193	+512 5705	+127 5832
M SEXTON	PD		4679	+20 4699	+52 4751	+154 4905	+293 5198	+299 5497	+61 5558	+513 6071
J Connor	FG		3829	+51 3880	+19 3899	+143 4042	+108 4150	+139 4289	eliminated	
U Quinn	Ind		3598	+52 3650	+88 3738	+262 4000	+331 4331	+528 4859	+506 5365	elim'td
T Crosby	Ind		2123	+10 2133	+11 2144	+107 2251	+171 2422	eliminated		
P Whelan	SF		1673	+13 1686	+16 1702	+170 1872	eliminated			
L M Flanagan	Ind		779	+11 790	+50 840	eliminated				
H Baxter	Lab		638	+2 640	+84 724	eliminated				
C Ansbro	GP		426	+9 435	eliminated					
V Killalea	Ind		191	eliminated						
B Lenehan	CSP		80	eliminated						
Non transferable				8	12	68	126	162	240	936

4 SEATS

ELECTORATE
70,650

TOTAL POLL
50,310

SPOILED
621

VALID POLL
49,689

QUOTA
9,938

* DENOTES
OUTGOING TD

NEWLY
ELECTED TDS
IN CAPITALS

PD gain from FG

A SHOCK result, at least for most of those outside the PD fold. Two sitting Fianna Fáil TDs, Albert Reynolds and Seán Doherty, the man whose 1992 revelations on the 1982 phone tapping helped to make Reynolds Taoiseach, retired. Fianna Fáil had votes to spare here in 1997, and if these went to PD Mae Sexton she would be in the hunt for the fourth seat, but few expected it would happen. In fact, the Fianna Fáil vote was down by 6% (their biggest drop anywhere in this election), but so too was the Fine Gael vote, while the PDs gathered an extra 6%, winning almost 10%. Mae Sexton, a

Longford councillor, was just a few votes behind Louis Belton, the outgoing Longford based Fine Gael deputy. She had edged ahead by the 7th count, favoured by most packets of transfers. The elimination of Una Quinn (an independent running on a Roscommon Hospital Action ticket) at that point, pushed Roscommon's Denis Naughten well over the quota and also put Sexton ahead of Belton again. His surplus should have taken his running mate Belton ahead of Sexton but that surplus was made up of votes from Quinn, and those Roscommon voters did not help Belton who won just

9	10
Naughten's surplus	Votes of Belton
+25	+1313
8005	**9318** √
+544	+191
8725	**8916** √
+228	+175
8687	**8862**
+383	
6215	**eliminated**
+230	+2616
6301	**8917** √
266	*1920*

Bertie Ahern shares a joke with former Taoisech Albert Reynolds while canvassing in Longford

PHOTOCALL IRELAND

17% of them. Sexton remained ahead and Belton was eliminated. His votes favoured the Longford candidates, and Sexton in particular, enabling her to overtake the two Roscommon based Fianna Fáil candidates.

Fianna Fáil ran two candidates from Roscommon and one from Longford, only one of whom, Michael Finneran, ran in 1997.

Peter Kelly, the Longford based deputy, was close to Reynolds and as a member of the county council was always a good bet for a seat. His namesake Greg, from west Roscommon lost out to the more centrally placed Finneran by only 54 votes.

The independent vote was well up here, but few of them went to Luke 'Ming the Merciless' Flanagan, campaigning to legalise cannabis, who is probably ahead of his time.

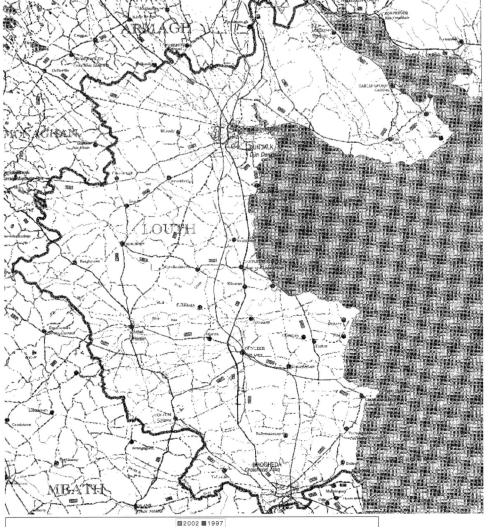

LOUTH

4 SEATS

2 Fianna Fáil
1 Fine Gael
1 Sinn Féin

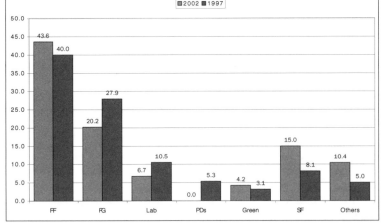

		1	2	3	4	5	6	7	8
			Votes of McMahon, Ó Gógáin, Short, Maguire	Votes of Bellew, Godfrey	Ahern's surplus	Votes of Martin	Votes of Grehan	Votes of Bell	Votes of Maher
*D AHERN	FF	9603	√						
A MORGAN	SF	7121	+154 7275	+213 7488	+7 7495	+310 7805	+669 8474	+518 8992	+485 9477√
*S KIRK	FF	6495	+66 6561	+207 6768	+43 6811	+182 6993	+651 7644	+316 7960	+2027 9987√
F O'DOWD	FG	5505	+35 5540	+146 5686	+2 5688	+410 6098	+248 6346	+1394 7740	+2435 10175√
F Maher	FF	4653	+15 4668	+139 4807	+4 4811	+135 4946	+72 5018	+625 5643	elim'td
T Brennan	FG	4130	+77 4207	+235 4442	+7 4449	+221 4670	+724 5394	+652 6046	+87 6133
*M Bell	Lab	3185	+52 3237	+151 3388	+3 3391	+341 3732	+385 4117	eliminated	
M Grehan	Ind	2384	+112 2496	+525 3021	+9 3030	+491 3521	eliminated		
B Martin	GP	1979	+130 2109	+197 2306	+3 2309	eliminated			
M Bellew	Ind	1307	+103 1410	eliminated					
F Godfrey	Ind	473	+29 502	eliminated					
A McMahon	Ind	294	eliminated						
L Ó Gogain	Ind	239	eliminated						
P Short	WP	176	eliminated						
M Maguire	CSP	79	eliminated						
Non transferable			15	99	0	219	772	612	609

4 SEATS

ELECTORATE
81,952

TOTAL POLL
48,274

SPOILED
651

VALID POLL
47,623

QUOTA
9,525

* DENOTES
OUTGOING TD

NEWLY
ELECTED TDS
IN CAPITALS

SF gain from Lab

THIS one was on Sinn Féin's list of possibles rather than probables but Arthur Morgan polled very well in the European elections for the Leinster constituency, and the waning of Michael Bell's long political career offered him the opportunity to win a seat at Labour's expense. Fianna Fáil's two seats were cemented by a small increase in their vote. Outgoing minister Dermot Ahern was just over the quota, and while the long-serving Séamus Kirk had to wait until the 8th count, he always had the cushion of Frank Maher's votes behind him.

Morgan came second and did not need the steady accumulation of transfers he received to keep ahead of the pack. Elected without reaching the quota, he was still over 3,000 votes ahead of the runner-up.

Ahern, Kirk and Morgan are all from north Louth. The other new deputy here is FG's Fergus O'Dowd, former Mayor of Drogheda. He succeeded the Dundalk-based Brendan McGahon who had held the seat since 1982. Bell, another ex-Mayor of Drogheda had held his seat since 1982, defeating O'Dowd for the last seat by only 381 votes in 1997. On this occasion Bell's transfers went heavily to the FG man and took him comfortably over the quota.

Independents also ran quite strongly, with Dr Mary Grehan, a well-known anti-Sellafield campaigner from Dundalk, polling almost 2,500 votes – just as she did wearing PD colours in 1997. But it is unlikely that the 669 votes she passed on to Morgan when she was eliminated were cast for her as a one-time PD.

DERMOT AHERN

FIANNA FÁIL

The Minister for Communications, Marine and Natural Resources was first elected in 1987. Chief Whip under Charles Haughey, he was Minister for Social, Community and Family Affairs in the last Dáil. He famously suffered from myopia when looking up the trees of Dublin North.

OCCUPATION
Government Minister, former solicitor

HOME ADDRESS
Hill Cottage, The Crescent, Blackrock, Dundalk, Co Louth

PHONE
Constituency
(042) 933 9609
Fax (042) 932 9016

Leinster House
(01) 678 2005
Fax (01) 678 2029

EMAIL
dahern@iol.ie

BORN
Drogheda, Co Louth, February 1955

EDUCATION
Marist College, Dundalk; University College Dublin; Incorporated Law Society of Ireland (BCL)

MARITAL STATUS
Married to Maeve Coleman. Two daughters

SÉAMUS KIRK

FIANNA FÁIL

The former Louth footballer has been elected continuously since November 1982 and served as a junior minister at the Department of Agriculture under Charles Haughey, but has not found favour with succeeding party leaders.

OCCUPATION
Full-time public representative, former farmer

ADDRESS
Rathiddy, Knockbridge, Dundalk, Co Louth

PHONE
Constituency
(042) 933 1032
Fax (042) 935 5680

Leinster House
(01) 618 3468

EMAIL
seamus.kirk@oireachtas.ie

BORN
Drumkeith, Co Louth, April 1945

EDUCATION
CBS, Dundalk, Co Louth

MARITAL STATUS
Married to Mary McGeogh. Three sons, one daughter

ARTHUR MORGAN

SINN FÉIN

A member of Sinn Féin's Ard Chomhairle and chairman of the Irish Seafood Wholesalers and Retailers Association. Arthur Morgan is the Sinn Féin spokesperson on the Environment. Describing himself as an active Republican from the age of 14 and as educated in Long Kesh, his current preoccupations are Sellafield and waste management. When he contested the European election in 1999 he topped 20,000 first preferences.

OCCUPATION
Director in the family fish processing company

ADDRESS
Williamson's Place, Dundalk, Co Louth

PHONE
Constituency
(042) 932 8859
Fax (042) 932 8859

Leinster House
(01) 618 3719
Fax (01) 618 4785

EMAIL
arthur.morgan@oireachtas.ie

BORN
Omeath, July 1958

EDUCATION
St Michael's College, Omeath

MARITAL STATUS
Married to Marian

FERGUS O'DOWD

FINE GAEL

New to the Dáil, Fergus O'Dowd has been a member of Drogheda Corporation since 1974 and a member of Louth County Council since 1979. He was elected to the Seanad on the Administrative Panel in 1997 and has been appointed Fine Gael spokesperson on Community, Rural and Gaeltacht Affairs. Fergus is the founding chairman of the Droichead Arts Centre and a qualified remedial teacher.

OCCUPATION
Full-time public representative, former teacher

ADDRESS
24 St Mary's Villas, Drogheda, Co Louth

PHONE
Constituency
(041) 984 2275
Fax (041) 987 0282

Leinster House
(01) 618 3078
Fax (01) 618 4628

EMAIL
fergus.odowd@oireachtas.ie

BORN
Thurles, Co Tipperary September 1948

EDUCATION
Drogheda CBS; Seán Crawford Technical Institute (teaching qualification in rural science)

MARITAL STATUS
Married, three sons

5 SEATS

2 Fine Gael
1 Independent
2 Fianna Fáil

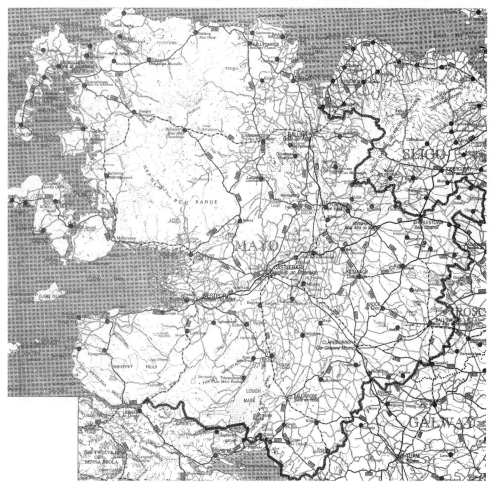

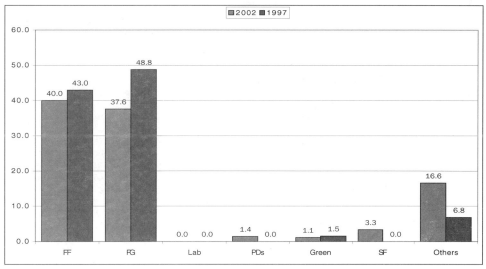

	FF	FG	Lab	PDs	Green	SF	Others
2002	40.0	37.6	0.0	1.4	1.1	3.3	16.6
1997	43.0	48.8	0.0	0.0	1.5	0.0	6.8

5 SEATS

ELECTORATE
94,854

TOTAL POLL
64,270

SPOILED
790

VALID POLL
63,480

QUOTA
10,581

* DENOTES
OUTGOING TD

NEWLY
ELECTED TDS
IN CAPITALS

Candidate	Party	1	2 Votes of Heffron, Crowley King	3 Votes of Holmes	4 Votes of Wood	5 Votes of Caffrey	6 Cowley's surplus	7 Ring's surplus	8 Votes of Chambers
*M RING	FG	9880	+165 / 10045	+339 / 10384	+192 / 10576	+331 / 10907 √			
J COWLEY	Ind	8709	+504 / 9213	+595 / 9808	+765 / 10573	+555 / 11128 √			
*B COOPER FLYNN	FF	6661	+80 / 6741	+145 / 6886	+237 / 7123	+44 / 7167	+11 / 7178	+9 / 7187	+2330 / 9517
*T Moffatt	FF	6536	+213 / 6749	+143 / 6892	+192 / 7084	+437 / 7521	+140 / 7661	+36 / 7697	+928 / 8625
J CARTY	FF	6457	+55 / 6512	+43 / 6555	+201 / 6756	+61 / 6817	+5 / 6822	+2 / 6824	+1460 / 8284
*J Higgins	FG	5858	+113 / 5971	+64 / 6035	+120 / 6155	+678 / 6833	+165 / 6998	+102 / 7100	+120 / 7220
*E KENNY	FG	5834	+120 / 5954	+91 / 6045	+97 / 6142	+336 / 6478	+98 / 6576	+131 / 6707	+600 / 7307
F Chambers	FF	5726	+66 / 5792	+253 / 6045	+221 / 6266	+41 / 6307	+8 / 6315	+4 / 6319	elim'td
E Caffrey	FG	2290	+129 / 2419	+67 / 2486	+72 / 2558	eliminated			
V Wood	SF	2085	+96 / 2181	+93 / 2274	eliminated				
M Holmes	Ind	1754	+119 / 1873	eliminated					
B Heffron	PD	919	eliminated						
A Crowley	GP	669	eliminated						
T King	Ind	102	eliminated						
Non transferable			30	40	177	75	120	42	881

Ind gain from FG

FINE Gael won three out of five here in 1997 and early local polls suggested that they could keep this lead in 2002 but an independent candidate, Jerry Cowley, a local doctor campaigning on a platform of improving the local health services in particular and developing the West in general, ran a hugely successful campaign which brought him a seat at the expense of Fine Gael.

The Fine Gael vote was down more than 10% to just 38%, while the Fianna Fáil vote held firm. Crowley polled 8,709 votes, coming second, and was elected on the 5th count with big transfers from all sides: he won 32% of all votes transferred up to this point.

Fine Gael transfers were quite good, with 64% of them staying within the party, but with the vote well under 40% there were only two seats there. Michael Ring, the energetic auctioneer from Westport, surprised nobody by topping the poll with the biggest vote in the country for a FG candidate but one of the two sitting TDs, either Enda Kenny from Castlebar or Jim Higgins from Ballyhaunis, had to lose out.

In the end it was Higgins but he was only 87 votes behind Kenny when he was eliminated. Higgins was ahead early but transfers from Fianna Fáil's Frank Chambers from Newport favoured Kenny in nearby Westport over Higgins in faraway Ballyhaunis, 600 going to Kenny and only 102 to Higgins, and that sealed Higgins' fate. It also determined the future path for Fine Gael as Kenny succeeded Michael Noonan in the leadership.

9	**10**
Votes of Higgins	Kenny's surplus

+232	+161
9749	**9910** √
+253	+309
8878	**9187**
+1247	+626
9531	**10157** √

eliminated
+4615
11922 √

873   245

P-Reg: the Beverley Cooper-Flynn mobile patrols the streets of Mayo

JOHN CARTY

FIANNA FÁIL

Involved in a number of local organisations, and with a keen interest in the history of South County Mayo, John Carty has been a member of Mayo County Council since 1999.

OCCUPATION
Agricultural officer, farmer

ADDRESS
Carrowmore, Knock, Co Mayo

PHONE
Home
(094) 937 2707

Constituency
(094) 938 8149
Fax (094) 938 8154

Leinster House
(01) 618 4213
Fax (01) 618 4700

EMAIL
jcarty@mayococo.ie

BORN
Knock, Co Mayo, August 1950

EDUCATION
St. Patrick's College, Ballyhaunis;
Warrenstown Agricultural College,
Co Meath;
National University of Ireland,
Maynooth

MARITAL STATUS
Married to Kathleen Regan.
Two daughters and six sons

There was no less competition for the Fianna Fáil seats, with reports of confrontations between rival sets of supporters during the campaign.

Castlebar's Beverly Cooper Flynn was ratified as a candidate, despite having lost the party whip following a failed libel case, along with the other incumbent Tom Moffatt from Ballina, first elected in 1992 and an outgoing junior minister. These were complemented by Senator Frank Chambers from Newport and John Carty from Knock.

Carty and Moffatt were very close on the first count, an excellent performance by the new man. In the end Carty displaced Moffatt, largely because of 1,200 votes from his near neighbour Jim Higgins while Moffatt received only 250.

Sinn Féin polled 3% here, standing for the first time since 1987 but PDs and Greens attracted only a handful of votes.

DR JERRY COWLEY

INDEPENDENT

Dr Cowley who is based in Mulranny, Co Mayo is a former Mayoman of the Year who has made his reputation via a number of projects in the county including the St Brendan's Village Project, which is dedicated to the care of older and disabled people, and the Irish Institute of Rural Health, which seeks to aims to encourage good health and standards of practice in rural Ireland and to promote research.

OCCUPATION
Medical practitioner

ADDRESS
Mulranny, Co Mayo

PHONE
Constituency
(098) 36298
Fax (098) 36299

Leinster House
(01) 618 3333
Fax (01) 618 4795

EMAIL
jerry.cowley@oireachtas.ie

WEBSITE
www.jerrycowley.com

BORN
Galway, November 1952

EDUCATION
St Muirdeach's College, Ballina;
NUI Galway (MB BCh DCh DObst,
MRCGP, LLB BL)

MARITAL STATUS
Married to Teresa.
Three sons, two daughters

BEVERLEY COOPER FLYNN

FIANNA FÁIL

Deputy Cooper Flynn was first elected to her father's former seat in 1997. In February 1999 she was expelled from the party when she voted against a Dáil motion calling on her father to clarify his position in the Gilmartin political donation affair. She also lost a libel action against RTE which left her with an estimated legal bill of €2.5m. Despite all this she subsequently topped the poll in the local elections and became the first woman to be elected to the Chair of the Western Health Board.

OCCUPATION
Full-time public representative,
former financial services manager

ADDRESS
Newtown, Castlebar, Co Mayo

PHONE
Constituency
(094) 902 7035
Fax (094) 902 7036

Leinster House
(01) 618 3562
Fax (01) 618 4608

EMAIL
b.cooper.flynn@oireachtas.ie

BORN
Tuam, Co Galway, June 1966

EDUCATION
St Joseph's, Castlebar;
University College Dublin

MARITAL STATUS
Married to John Cooper

ENDA KENNY

FINE GAEL

Deputy Kenny was elected as leader of Fine Gael in June 2002 following the resignation of Michael Noonan, despite considerable feeling in the party that the leadership elections should be postponed until the new electoral rules were implemented. He is spokesman on Northern Ireland. He followed his father into the Dáil in 1975, and has held a wide range of posts.

OCCUPATION
Full-time public representative,
former national school teacher

ADDRESS
Home
Lightfort, Hawthorn Avenue,
Castlebar, Co Mayo
Constituency office
Tucker Street, Castlebar, Co Mayo

PHONE
Constituency
(094) 902 5600
Fax (094) 902 6554

Leinster House
(01) 618 3105
Fax (01) 618 4502

EMAIL
enda.kenny@oireachtas.ie

WEBSITE
www.endakennytd.com

BORN
Castlebar, Co Mayo, 1951

EDUCATION
St Gerald's College, Castlebar;
St Patrick's Teacher Training
College, Drumcondra:
University College Galway

MARITAL STATUS
Married, three children

MICHAEL RING

FINE GAEL

A member of Dáil Éireann since the by-election following the departure for the European Commission of Pádraig Flynn in 1994 Michael Ring, famous as one of the most effective constituency workers in the country, topped the poll again and is spokesman on Social and Family Affairs.

OCCUPATION
Full-time public representative,
former auctioneer

ADDRESS
Home
The Paddock, Westport, Co Mayo
Constituency
Quay Street, Westport

PHONE
Home
(098) 25734
Fax (098) 26744

Constituency
(098) 27012
Fax (098) 27644

Leinster House
(01) 618 4367
Fax (01) 618 4602

EMAIL
michael.ring@oireachtas.ie

BORN
Westport, Co Mayo,
December 1953

EDUCATION
Westport Vocational School

MARITAL STATUS
Married, three children

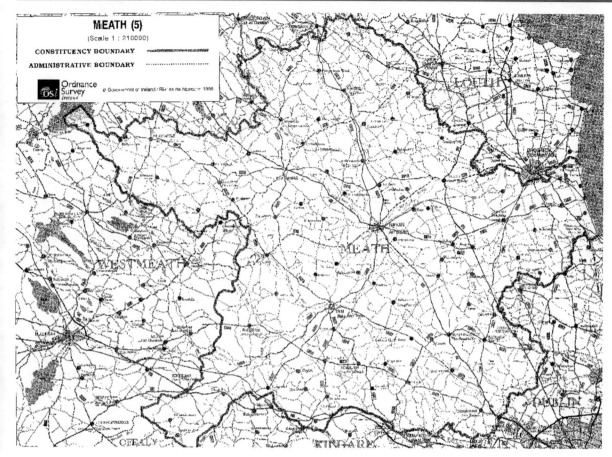

MEATH (5)
(Scale 1 : 210000)

CONSTITUENCY BOUNDARY ━━━━━━━━━

ADMINISTRATIVE BOUNDARY ⋯⋯⋯⋯⋯

Ordnance Survey Ireland

© Government of Ireland / Rialtas na hÉireann 1998

5 SEATS

3 Fianna Fáil
2 Fine Gael

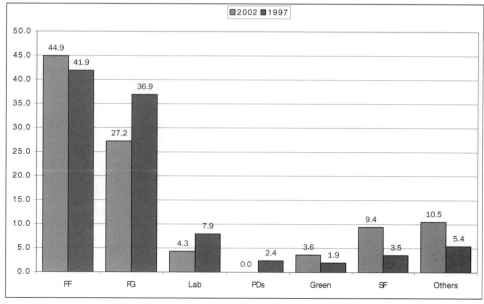

☐ 2002 ■ 1997

	FF	FG	Lab	PDs	Green	SF	Others
2002	44.9	27.2	4.3	0.0	3.6	9.4	10.5
1997	41.9	36.9	7.9	2.4	1.9	3.5	5.4

5 SEATS

ELECTORATE
108,717

TOTAL POLL
64,081

SPOILED
0

VALID POLL
64,081

QUOTA
10,681

* DENOTES
OUTGOING TD

NEWLY
ELECTED TDS
IN CAPITALS

			1	2 Dempsey's surplus	3 Votes of Colwell, Redmond	4 Votes of O'Brien	5 Votes of Kelly	6 Votes of O'Byrne	7 Votes of Ward	8 Votes of Farrelly
*N DEMPSEY	FF		11534 √							
*M WALLACE	FF		8759	+313 9072	+32 9104	+180 9284	+361 9645	+362 10007	+254 10261	+113 10374
*J BRADY	FF		8493	+258 8751	+36 8787	+46 8833	+46 8879	+108 8987	+123 9110	+467 9577
*J BRUTON	FG		7617	+76 7693	+32 7725	+155 7880	+241 8121	+333 8454	+694 9148	+1733 10881 √
J Reilly	SF		6042	+51 6093	+51 6144	+123 6267	+118 6385	+325 6710	+412 7122	+226 7348
D ENGLISH	FG		5958	+61 6019	+52 6071	+68 6139	+126 6265	+374 6639	+737 7376	+1349 8725
*J Farrelly	FG		3877	+15 3892	+11 3903	+34 3937	+41 3978	+74 4052	+221 4273	elim'td
B Fitzgerald	Ind		3722	+29 3751	+56 3807	+113 3920	+185 4105	+359 4464	+675 5139	+119 5258
P Ward	Lab		2727	+21 2748	+21 2769	+75 2844	+120 2964	+631 3595	eliminated	
F O'Byrne	GP		2337	+16 2353	+53 2406	+224 2630	+200 2830	eliminated		
T Kelly	Ind		1373	+7 1380	+23 1403	+163 1566	eliminated			
P O'Brien	Ind		1199	+3 1202	+42 1244	eliminated				
J Colwell	Ind		263	+2 265	eliminated					
M Redmond	CSP		180	+1 181	eliminated					
Non transferable				0	37	63	128	264	479	733

No change

FIANNA Fáil won three out of five here in 1997 despite John Bruton's personal popularity and looked like doing so again. The question mark was over Fine Gael: could the party stave off a challenge from Labour, and from the independent Labour candidate Brian Fitzgerald. This they did easily. It was Joe O'Reilly running in his second Dáil election for Sinn Féin who provided the real threat. But the second seat was won not by the incumbent John Farrelly but by a new young candidate, Damien English.

Fianna Fáil's vote was up here by 3%, as Fine Gael's dropped by almost 10% to only 27%, well short of two quotas. Labour's vote was also down, but Sinn Féin won over 9% and independents over 10%. It was this fragmentation that enabled Fine Gael to hold its second seat, as it was in 1987 when the party won two seats with 26% of the vote. Labour votes did not transfer to Brian Fitzgerald, the former Labour TD who broke with his party over the merger with DL. Nor did they go to Sinn Féin. More in fact went to Fine Gael. Fitzgerald's votes broke almost equally between Fianna Fáil and Fine Gael, with only a few falling to Sinn Féin.

9

Votes of
Fitzgerald

+1261
11635 √
+299
9876 √

+732
8080
+1429
10154 √

---

eliminated

1836

Money where her mouth is: Mary Harney – pictured here in Lucan – bet on the
PDs winning eight seats – and she was right   PHOTOCALL IRELAND

JOHNNY BRADY

FIANNA FÁIL

First elected in 1997 and a member of Meath County Council since 1974, Brady has once again benefit-ed from FF's fine vote-management strategy. Brady used damage sustained by the Book of Kells during a trip to Australia to campaign for its repatriation to Kells. Chair of Oireachtas Commit-tee on Agriculture and Food.

OCCUPATION
Public representative, farmer

ADDRESS
Springville, Kilskyre, Kells, Co Meath

PHONE
Constituency
(046) 924 0852
Fax (046) 924 9566

Leinster House
(01) 618 3592
Fax (01) 618 4552

EMAIL
johnny.brady@oireachtas.ie

BORN
Kells, January 1948

EDUCATION
Kells Vocational School

MARITAL STATUS
Married to Kathleen Clarke.
One son

Thus although Joe Reilly came fifth on the first count the transfers, particularly those from the second Fine Gael candidate and from Fitzgerald, went against him.

English, a young county councillor from the Navan area ran almost 2,000 votes ahead of Kells based Farrel-ly, but some 1,600 votes behind Bruton, (whose vote was only about half as big as it was in 1997) so Farrelly always looked like the man who would have to give way.

Fianna Fáil's main aim was to secure their three seats and this they accomplished in some comfort with their three incumbent TDs coming in 1, 2 and 3 in first

preferences. 67% of Noel Demsey's surplus went to his running mates. Mary Wallace generally picked up more transfers than her running mate John Brady, but they were elected together on the 9th count.

JOHN BRUTON

FINE GAEL

John Bruton has been a member of Dáil Éireann since 1969, was party leader from 1990-2001, and Taoiseach in the Rainbow Coalition from December 1994-June 1997. He is Fine Gael spokesperson without portfolio, and a member of the Praesidium of the Convention on the Future of Europe. He was appointed Chair of the EU Crime and Justice Taskforce in July 2002.

OCCUPATION
Full-time public representative

ADDRESS
Cornelstown, Dunboyne, Co Meath

PHONE
Constituency/Leinster House
(01) 618 3107
Fax (01) 618 4141

EMAIL
john.bruton@oireachtas.ie

WEBSITE
www.johnbruton.net

BORN
Dublin, May 1947

EDUCATION
St Dominic's College, Cabra; Clongowes Wood College, Naas; University College Dublin; King's Inns Dublin (BA, BL)

MARITAL STATUS
Married to Finola Gill. One son, three daughters

NOEL DEMPSEY

FIANNA FÁIL

Noel Dempsey, the Minister for Education and Science, will long be remembered as the man who cleared the plastic bags from the roadsides of Ireland and introduced the voting machine. First elected in 1987, he was Minister for the Environment and Local Government in the last Dáil. Never one to avoid controversy, he often announces policy before negotiating with interested parties.

OCCUPATION
Government minister, former career guidance counsellor

ADDRESS
Newtown, Trim, Co Meath

PHONE
Constituency
(046) 943 1146
Fax (046) 943 6643

Leinster House
(01) 889 2277
Fax (01) 872 9093

EMAIL
noelmin@eircom.net

WEBSITE
www.noeldempseytd.ie

BORN
Trim, Co Meath, January 1953

EDUCATION
St Michael's CBS, Trim; University College Dublin; St Patrick's College, Maynooth (BA, DipCG)

MARITAL STATUS
Married to Bernadette Rattigan. Two sons, two daughters

DAMIEN ENGLISH

FINE GAEL

The possessor of surely the Dáil's most upbeat website, his accountancy career indefinitely postponed, 24-year-old English was appointed deputy spokesperson on Arts, Sport and Tourism in June 2002. He was previously the youngest member of Meath County Council, having been elected in 1999 at 21 years of age.

OCCUPATION
Full-time public representative

ADDRESS
16 Bridge Street, Navan, Co Meath

PHONE
Constituency
(046) 907 1667
Fax (046) 907 2225

Leinster House
(01) 618 4012
Fax (01) 618 3430

EMAIL
damien.english@oireachtas.ie
denglish@members.meathcoco.ie

WEBSITE
homepage.eircom.net /~denglish

BORN
Drogheda, Co Louth, February 1978

EDUCATION
Kells Community School; CIMA

MARITAL STATUS
Single

MARY WALLACE

FIANNA FÁIL

Mary Wallace is rumoured to have had a somewhat heated discussion with the Taoiseach when not reappointed Minister of State in the new administration and expressed her lack of interest in a consolation committee chair. First elected in 1989, her main first-preference catchment area is the east of the county from her home in Ratoath to the coast.

OCCUPATION
Full-time public representative, former personnel executive

ADDRESS
Fairyhouse Road, Ratoath, Co Meath

PHONE
Constituency
(01) 825 6259
Fax (01) 825 6848

Leinster House
(01) 618 4467
Fax (01) 618 4602

EMAIL
mary.wallace@oireachtas.ie

BORN
Dublin, June 1959

EDUCATION
Loreto Convents, Balbriggan and Dublin; College of Commerce, Rathmines

MARITAL STATUS
Married to Declan Gannon. One son

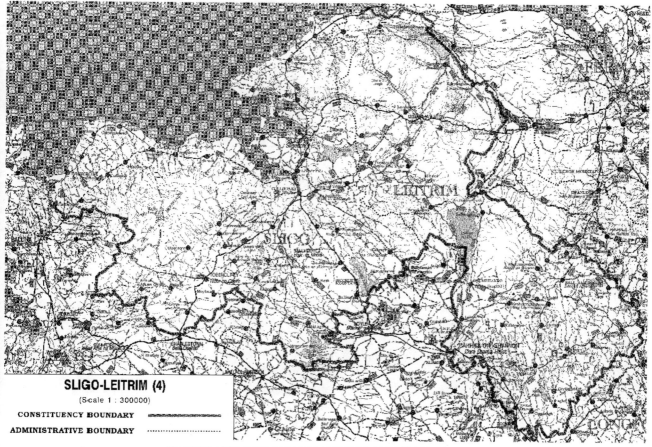

SLIGO-LEITRIM (4)
(Scale 1 : 300000)

CONSTITUENCY BOUNDARY
ADMINISTRATIVE BOUNDARY

4 SEATS

1 Independent
2 Fianna Fáil
1 Fine Gael

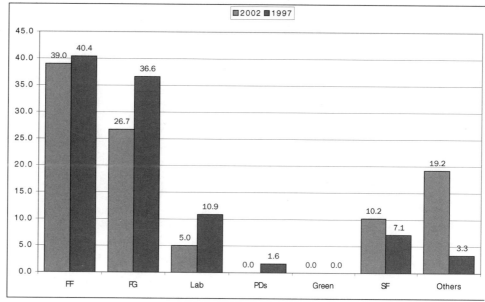

Legend: ☐ 2002 ■ 1997

	FF	FG	Lab	PDs	Green	SF	Others
2002	39.0	26.7	5.0	0.0	0.0	10.2	19.2
1997	40.4	36.6	10.9	1.6	0.0	7.1	3.3

		1	2 Votes of McSharry, Ford, Lacken, McCrea	3 Votes of Bree	4 Votes of McManus	5 Harkin's surplus	6 Votes of Scanlon	7 Devins' surplus
M HARKIN	Ind	8,610	+186 8,796	+828 9,624	+1,773 11,397√			
*J PERRY	FG	6,897	+86 6,983	+308 7,291	+408 7,699	+224 7,923	+2,516 10,439√	
*J ELLIS	FF	6,434	+31 6,465	+41 6,506	+776 7,282	+221 7,503	+996 8,499	+772 9,271 √
E Scanlon	FF	6,345	+36 6,381	+82 6,463	+393 6,856	+125 6,981	eliminated	
J DEVINS	FF	6,307	+120 6,427	+397 6,824	+767 7,591	+303 7,894	+2,727 10,621√	
*G Reynolds	FG	6,162	+74 6,236	+202 6,438	+501 6,939	+212 7,151	+152 7,303	+54 7,357
S MacManus	SF	5,001	+99 5,100	+516 5,616	eliminated			
D Bree	Lab	2,429	+101 2,530	eliminated				
A McSharry	Ind	303	eliminated					
M Ford	Ind	203	eliminated					
J Lacken	CSP	166	eliminated					
J McCrea	Ind	114	eliminated					
Non transferable			53	156	998	517	590	0

4 SEATS

ELECTORATE
70,460

TOTAL POLL
49,494

SPOILED
523

VALID POLL
48,971

QUOTA
9,795

* DENOTES OUTGOING TD

NEWLY ELECTED TDS IN CAPITALS

Ind gain from FG

A PROMINENT campaigner for the development of the West, who would probably have won a place in Europe in the 1999 elections but for Dana Rosemary Scallon, Marian Harkin had been tipped to win a seat here for some time, and had been courted by the major parties in consequence. And win a seat she did, topping the poll with almost a full quota and pushing out Gerry Reynolds, one of the two Fine Gael incumbents. Reynolds, whose father and grandfather were both TDs, has had an intermittent Dáil career, losing the seat in 1992 that he first won in 1989, only to recapture it in 1997. The final tally gave Leitrim only one TD instead of the two it had held in 1997 but with Sligo having twice the population this result was always likely.

Labour were also looking to win back the seat held by Declan Bree in 1992, and Sinn Féin were hopeful of making an impact in this border constituency but did not come very close to success on this occasion.

Fianna Fáil maintained most of their first preference share, dropping just 1%, while Fine Gael were down 10%. Labour's hopes were dashed as Bree's vote was also down 6% and although Seán McManus pushed the Sinn Féin vote up to 10% he could not hope to displace anyone else once Marian Harkin had done so well.

One of the incumbent FF deputies, Mattie Brennan from Sligo, retired, and the other, John Ellis from Leitrim, had suffered more adverse publicity stemming from the collapse of his business several years ago. Yet Fianna Fáil rose above such potential disadvantatage. Perry's vote was up by 1,000 and Ellis' was down only 500; Eamon Scanlon from Ballymote and Jimmy Devins, another Sligo Town candidate, polled well enough to make up for missing Brennan. Many of Scanlon's transfers leaked away to Perry (36%) with only 53% going on to his party colleagues but they were still more than sufficient. Devins became the first Fianna Fáil TD from the town since Ray MacSharry.

Bree's votes favoured Harkin and to a lesser extent McManus, and certainly did not help FG here; McManus was eliminated on the 4th count and his votes strongly favoured Harkin over any other.

DR JIMMY DEVINS

FIANNA FÁIL

Newcomer to the Dáil Jimmy Devins was first elected to Sligo County Council in 1991. He slugged it out with fellow Fianna Fáil candidate Éamon Scanlan for the last seat in a constituency which has seen considerable acrimony over vote management strategies.

OCCUPATION
Full-time public representative, former medical practitioner

ADDRESS
Mail Coach Road, Sligo

PHONE
Constituency
(071) 915 2970
Fax (071) 915 2971

Leinster House
(01) 618 3338
Fax (01) 618 4132

EMAIL
devins@iol.ie

WEBSITE
www.jimmydevins.ie

BORN
September 1948

EDUCATION
Blackrock College, Dublin;
University College Dublin
(MB DCh);
Trinity College Dublin (MSc)

MARITAL STATUS
Married.
Four children

JOHN ELLIS

FIANNA FÁIL

First elected in 1981, he lost his seat in November 1982 but was re-elected in 1987 and at each subsequent election. Best known for the failure of his meat company, Stanlow Trading, with considerable debts to suppliers, and for his revelation to the Moriarty Tribunal that he had received £26,000 from Charles Haughey to prevent creditors from bankrupting him. Vice-chairman of the Oireachtas Committee on Transport.

OCCUPATION
Public representative, farmer and businessman

ADDRESS
Fenagh, Ballinamore, Co Leitrim

PHONE
Home
(071) 964 4252
Fax (071) 964 4017

Leinster House
(01) 618 3289
Fax (01) 618 4180

EMAIL
john.ellis@oireachtas.ie

BORN
Fenagh, Co Leitrim, May 1952

EDUCATION
St Felim's College, Ballinamore, Co Leitrim

MARITAL STATUS
Married to Patricia Donnelly.
Two sons, one daughter

MARIAN HARKIN

INDEPENDENT

Started organising development organisations when she lived in Manorhamilton and played a major role in initiating the Council for the West on which she originally represented Leitrim of which she has been Chair for several years. Stood for the Connaght-Ulster constituency in the 1999 European Parliament election.

OCCUPATION
Secondary school teacher

ADDRESS
24 The Park, Strandhill Road, Sligo

PHONE
Constituency
(071) 914 5888
Fax (071) 914 5690

Leinster House
(01) 618 4293
Fax (01) 618 4514

EMAIL
marianh@marianharkin.com

WEBSITE
www.marianharkin.com

BORN
Ballintogher, Co Sligo,
November 1953

EDUCATION
Marist Convent, Tubercurry;
University College Dublin
(BSc, H.DipEd)

MARITAL STATUS
Widow.
Two sons

JOHN PERRY

FINE GAEL

First elected in 1997, John Perry has been nominated as Chairman of the Public Accounts Committee. Former Fine Gael spokesperson on Science, Technology, Small Business and Enterprise and the Border Counties, and assistant Director of Organisation. A strong campaigner for the development of regional infrastructure and decentralisation.

OCCUPATION
Public representative, businessman

ADDRESS
Teeling Street, Ballymote, Co Sligo;
Westward Town Centre, Bridge Street, Sligo

PHONE
Constituency
(071) 915 1011
Fax (071) 915 1119

Leinster House
(01) 618 3765
Fax (01) 618 4610

EMAIL
john_perry@oireachtas.ie

WEBSITE
www.johnperry.ie

BORN
Ballymote, Co Sligo, August 1956

EDUCATION
Corran College, Ballymote,
Co Sligo

MARITAL STATUS
Married to Marie.
One son

3 SEATS

1 Independent
2 Fianna Fáil

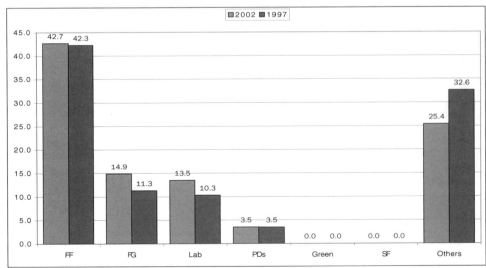

		1	**2** Votes of Dwan	**3** Votes of O'Meara	**4** Hoctor's surplus
*M LOWRY	Ind	**10400** √			
M HOCTOR	FF	**8949**	+371 **9320**	+1720 **11040** √	
*M SMITH	FF	**8526**	+316 **8842**	+800 **9642**	+446 **10088** √
N Coonan	FG	**6108**	+328 **6436**	+2649 **9085**	+352 **9437**
K O'Meara	Lab	**5537**	+340 **5877**	eliminated	
B Dwan	PD	**1446**	eliminated		
Non transferable			*91*	*708*	*0*

3 SEATS

ELECTORATE
59,427

TOTAL POLL
41,412

SPOILED
446

VALID POLL
40,966

QUOTA
10,242

* DENOTES
OUTGOING TD

NEWLY
ELECTED TDS
IN CAPITALS

No change

WOULD the news from the Moriarty Tribunal damage Michael Lowry? It seems not. His support was down by over 1,000 votes on a higher valid vote but with more than a quota all to himself this is the sort of setback easily overcome. While Lowry's star shines so brightly, Fine Gael continue to be eclipsed. Although their vote was up almost 4% in what was their second biggest gain anywhere and Labour's was also up, FG candidate Noel Coonan was over 500 votes behind the outgoing Minister for Defence Michael Smith on the final count. A 45% transfer from Labour Senator Kathleen O'Meara brought Coonan to within a few hundred votes of Smith, but Coonan would have needed more like 55% to catch him. In 1997, O'Meara transferred 60% of her votes to the Fine Gael candidate. That would have been more than enough this time. Michael Lowry also had a surplus of 158 votes that were never distributed.

Fianna Fáil's vote share was up marginally, despite the retirement of the long standing TD and former Minister for Foreign Affairs, Michael O'Kennedy. Máire Hoctor, like O'Kennedy from Nenagh, amply filled in for the departed deputy.

The PDs also ran a candidate here, Bill Dwan a local businessman from Thurles, but he made little impact.

MÁIRE HOCTOR

FIANNA FÁIL

Máire Hoctor takes over the seat from Michael O'Kennedy. First elected to Nenagh UDC in 1994, she topped the local poll in 1999 and is chair or vice-chair of many local organisations and committees. Her Nenagh interests balance those of Michael Smith in Roscrea to maximise the party vote in the constituency.

OCCUPATION
Full-time public representative, secondary teacher

ADDRESS
Teach Ruadhain, 40 Melrose, Nenagh, Co Tipperary

TELEPHONE
Constituency
(067) 32943
Fax (067) 50470

Leinster House
(01) 618 4204
Fax (01) 618 4320

EMAIL
maire.hoctor@oireachtas.ie

WEBSITE
www.mairehoctor.com

BORN
Nenagh, January 1963

EDUCATION
St Mary's Convent of Mercy, Nenagh;
St Patrick's College, Maynooth (BA Th HDipEd)

MARITAL STATUS
Single

Sister Raphael from Nenagh General Hospital speaks to Ruairí Quinn TD during the Labour leader's visit to the hospital

PHOTOCALL IRELAND

MICHAEL LOWRY

INDEPENDENT

Michael Lowry was first elected to Dáil Éireann in 1987 as a Fine Gael TD. He has topped the poll in both elections since his departure and it is believed that he would still welcome a return to the party fold. Minister for Transport, Energy & Communications 1994-1996, he resigned due to tax problems in his relationship with businessman Ben Dunne.

OCCUPATION
Public representative, company director

ADDRESS
Glenreigh, Holycross, Thurles, Co Tipperary

PHONE
Constituency
(0504) 22022

EMAIL
michael.lowry@oireachtas.ie

BORN
March 1954

EDUCATION
Thurles CBS

MARITAL STATUS
Married to Catherine McGrath. Two sons, one daughter

MICHAEL SMITH

FIANNA FÁIL

A member of Dáil Éireann from 1969-1973, 1977-1982 and since 1987, Michael Smith was re-appointed Minister for Defence in the 29th Dáil in the Cabinet reshuffle following the resignation of Ray Burke only to find himself embroiled in the army deafness compensation claims. He has held posts in both Dáil and Seanad since 1980.

OCCUPATION
Government minister, former farmer

ADDRESS
Lismackin, Roscrea, Co Tipperary

PHONE
Constituency
(0505) 21933
Fax (0505) 22004

Leinster House
(01) 618 3258
Fax (01) 678 9328

Department of Defence
(01) 804 2101
Fax (01) 804 2805

EMAIL
info@defence.irlgov.ie
michael-smith@defence.irlgov.ie

BORN
Roscrea, Co Tipperary,
November 1940

EDUCATION
CBS Templemore, Co Tipperary;
University College Cork (DPA)

MARITAL STATUS
Married to Mary Therese Ryan.
One son, six daughters

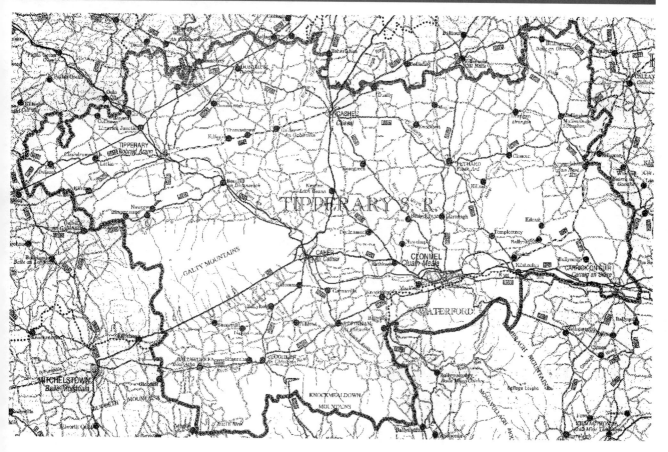

3 SEATS

1 Fine Gael
1 Fianna Fáil
1 Independent

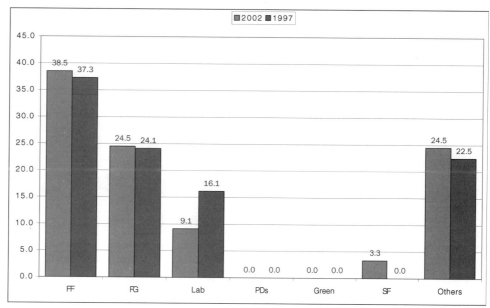

	FF	FG	Lab	PDs	Green	SF	Others
2002	38.5	24.5	9.1	0.0	0.0	3.3	24.5
1997	37.3	24.1	16.1	0.0	0.0	0.0	22.5

			1	**2**	**3**	
				Votes of Ó Súilleabháin and Larkin	Votes of Landy and Wood	
				+136	+1591	
3 SEATS	*T HAYES	FG	8997	9133	10724 √	
				+197	+944	
ELECTORATE 56,092	*N DAVERN	FF	8888	9085	10029 √	
				+415	+1712	
TOTAL POLL 37,056	*S HEALY	Ind	7350	7765	9477 √	
				+200	+455	
SPOILED 390	M Mansergh	FF	5233	5433	5888	
				+202		
VALID POLL 36,666	D Landy	Lab	3353	3555	eliminated	
				+116		
QUOTA 9,167	T Wood	Ind	1515	1631	eliminated	
	M Ó Súilleabháin	SF	1210	eliminated		
	M Larkin	CSP	120	eliminated		
	Non transferable			64	484	

3 SEATS

ELECTORATE
56,092

TOTAL POLL
37,056

SPOILED
390

VALID POLL
36,666

QUOTA
9,167

* DENOTES
OUTGOING TD

NEWLY
ELECTED TDS
IN CAPITALS

Ind gain from Lab

THIS change is relative to 1997; in fact, there was no change from the position at the dissolution of the last Dáil as Labour lost its seat to Séamus Healy in 2000 in the first of the two by elections that took place here in the lifetime of the Dáil. This was caused by the death of Michael Ferris. Later, Theresa Ahearn's death led to another by election, which brought in Tom Hayes.

Fianna Fáil's failure to win either by election in a constituency where it won almost 40% of the vote in the last general election and, prior to 1987, had usually won two seats, helped open the door to the selection this time of Martin Mansergh, a local landowner who has been a vital special advisor to Fianna Fáil leaders since 1982 and who has played a significant role in the development of the peace process in Northern Ireland. Released from the backroom, Mansergh polled better than his predecessor in 1997 while Noel Davern's vote stood still.

However, there is only one Fianna Fáil seat here and Davern kept a firm hold on it this time. Support for Fianna Fáil and Fine Gael were both up slightly, but Labour's vote was down 7% and the party could mount no serious challenge to Healy for the left-wing seat in the Dáil that has been there (apart from in 1987) since 1961.

NOEL DAVERN

FIANNA FÁIL

A member of the Dáil 1969-81 and since 1987, MEP 1979-84, Minister for Education 1991-92, and Minister of State at the Department of Agriculture, Food and Rural Development in the last government, Noel Davern, the son of Michael Davern TD and brother of Dan Davern TD, easily held off the challenge from headquarters colleague Martin Mansergh.

OCCUPATION
Full-time public representative, former farmer and publican

ADDRESS
Tannersrath, Fethard Road, Clonmel, Co Tipperary

PHONE
Home
(052) 22991
Constituency
(052) 25707
Fax (052) 29800

Leinster House
(01) 618 4215
Fax (01) 618 4345

EMAIL
noel.davern@oireachtas.ie

BORN
Cashel, Co Tipperary, December 1945

EDUCATION
CBS Cashel;
Franciscan College, Gormanston, Co Meath

MARITAL STATUS
Married to Anne Marie Carroll. Two sons, one daughter

The dealmaker: former political adviser to three taoisigh, Martin Mansergh failed in his bid to become a TD for Tipperary South

PHOTOCALL IRELAND

TOM HAYES

FINE GAEL

Tom Hayes was elected to the Seanad (Agricultural Panel) in 1997 and fought both the Tipperary South by-elections, losing to Séamus Healy in the first and winning the one that followed the death of popular party colleague Theresa Ahearn. A county councillor since 1991, he is Fine Gael deputy spokesman on Agriculture and Food.

OCCUPATION
Public representative, farmer

ADDRESS
Home
Cahervillahow, Golden,
Co Tipperary

PHONE
Constituency
(062) 62892
(052) 80731
Fax (052) 82895

Leinster House
(01) 618 3168
Fax (01) 618 4634

EMAIL
tom.hayes@oireachtas.ie

BORN
Golden, Co Tipperary, 1952

EDUCATION
Mount Melleray College, Waterford;
Tipperary Vocational School
University College, Cork

MARITAL STATUS
Married.
Three sons

SÉAMUS HEALY

INDEPENDENT

Séamus Healy posed a serious challenge to the late Michael Ferris in the 1997 general election, and topped the poll in the 2000 by-election which followed Ferris's death. The Workers and Unemployed Action Group candidate, a long-time trade union official and former hospital administrator, was third in the poll this time and draws his main support from his native Clonmel.

OCCUPATION
Full-time public representative, former hospital administrator

ADDRESS
Scrouthea, Old Bridge, Clonmel,
Co Tipperary

PHONE
Constituency
(052) 21883
Fax (052) 70860

Leinster House
(01) 618 3859
Fax (01) 618 4643

EMAIL
seamus.healy@oireachtas.ie

BORN
Scrouthea, August 1950

EDUCATION
Christian Brothers High School, Clonmel

MARITAL STATUS
Widowed.
Four daughters

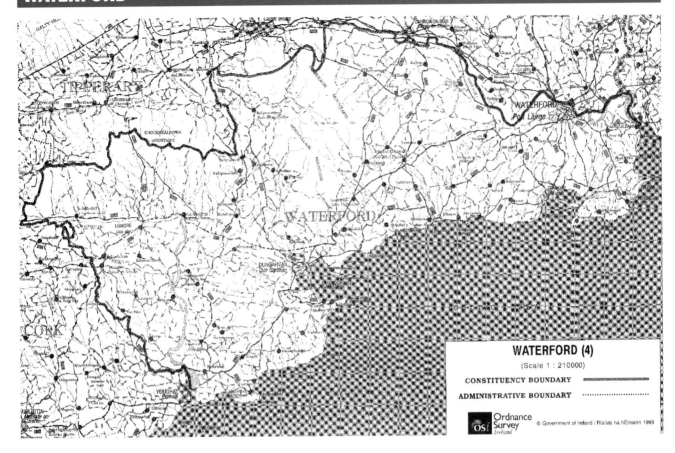

4 SEATS
2 Fianna Fáil
1 Fine Gael
1 Labour

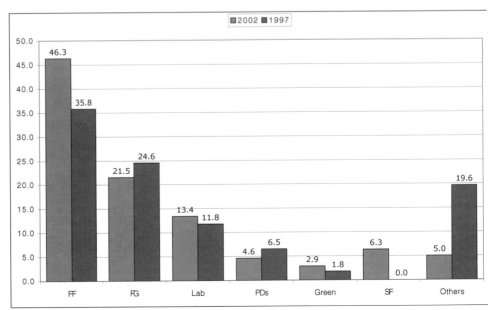

2002 ■ 1997

	FF	FG	Lab	PDs	Green	SF	Others
2002	46.3	21.5	13.4	4.6	2.9	6.3	5.0
1997	35.8	24.6	11.8	6.5	1.8	0.0	19.6

		1	2 Votes of Waters, Kelly, Halpin, Walsh	3 Votes of Halligan	4 Votes of McCann	5 Votes of Flynn	6 Votes of Cummins	7 Votes of Cullinane
*M CULLEN	FF	8,529	+77 8,606	+128 8,734	+120 8,854	+578 9,432 √		
O WILKINSON	FF	7,312	+55 7,367	+16 7,383	+60 7,443	+192 7,635	+88 7,723	+481 8,204 √
J DEASY	FG	7,204	+99 7,303	+60 7,363	+218 7,581	+537 8,118	+1,880 9,998 √	
*B O'SHEA	Lab	6,219	+145 6,364	+285 6,649	+533 7,182	+467 7,649	+667 8,316	+1,208 9,524 √
*B Kenneally	FF	5,735	+45 5,780	+140 5,920	+49 5,969	+196 6,165	+260 6,425	+692 7,117
D Cullinane	SF	2,955	+135 3,090	+320 3,410	+175 3,585	+129 3,714	+157 3,871	eliminated
M Cummins	FG	2,799	+63 2,862	+147 3,009	+112 3,121	+220 3,341	eliminated	
M Flynn	PD	2,137	+50 2,187	+64 2,251	+213 2,464	eliminated		
B McCann	GP	1,361	+172 1,533	+113 1,646	eliminated			
J Halligan	WP	1,270	+128 1,398	eliminated				
D Waters	Ind	335	eliminated					
J Kelly	SWP	300	eliminated					
C Halpin	Ind	289	eliminated					
E Walsh	Ind	118	eliminated					
Non transferable			55	16	60	192	88	481

4 SEATS

ELECTORATE
73,725

TOTAL POLL
47,120

SPOILED
557

VALID POLL
46,563

QUOTA
9,313

* DENOTES
OUTGOING TD

NEWLY
ELECTED TDS
IN CAPITALS

No change

A LOT of votes shifted party here and there were some changes in personnel, but the bottom line remained the same: two Fianna Fáil, one Fine Gael and one Labour deputy elected. Fianna Fáil's vote went up more than 10% but this was not anything like enough to squeeze out a third seat although Brendan Kenneally was the runner-up. Their vote increase was at the expense of Fine Gael, the PDs and independents, all of whom lost votes, with independents in particular dropping almost 15%. This last is accounted for by the absence this time of two big vote winners from 1997. There was a change of Workers' Party candidate. Martin O'Regan polled 9% for that party in 1997 but his successor, John Halligan, fell well short of that figure, obtaining less than 3%

(although this was still the party's highest vote anywhere). One of the more successful of the TV deflector candidates, Dermot Kirwan, was also absent in 2002. As well as gains for Fianna Fáil, Sinn Féin won 7%, not having stood in 1997, and Labour's vote was up marginally too.

Personnel change involved John Deasy taking the place of his retired father and Ollie Wilkinson, from Lismore, displacing Waterford's Brendan Kenneally for the second FF seat. Martin Cullen, also from the city and a junior coalition minister, topped the poll with votes to spare. Cullen was once a PD deputy and was put over the quota on this occasion by a generous transfer from the eliminated PD candidate.

MARTIN CULLEN

FIANNA FÁIL

Previously Minister of State at the Department of Finance, Martin Cullen has now been appointed Minister for the Environment. First elected in 1987 for the PDs, he lost his seat in 1989 but was re-elected in 1992. In 1994 "irreconcilable differences" with Mary Harney led to his move to Fianna Fáil.

OCCUPATION
Full-time public representative, former businessman

ADDRESS
Abbey House, Abbey Road, Ferrybank, Co Waterford

PHONE
Constituency
(051) 844 860
Fax (051) 876 943

Leinster House
(01) 888 2572
Fax (01) 888 2627
Fax (01) 618 3522

EMAIL
minister@environ.irlgov.ie

BORN
Waterford, November 1954

EDUCATION
Waterpark College; Waterford RTC (Member Marketing Institute of Ireland)

MARITAL STATUS
Married to Dorthe Larsen. Three sons, one daughter

JOHN DEASY

FINE GAEL

The newly elected John Deasy, son of former Fine Gael TD Austin Deasy, was appointed spokesman on Justice, Equality and Law Reform in June 2002. A member of Waterford County Council and Dungarvan District Council, he has worked as a legislative assistant in both the United States Senate and the House of Representatives.

OCCUPATION
Full-time public representative, former legislative assistant in USA, former public relations manager

ADDRESS
Kilrush, Dungarvan, Co Waterford

PHONE
Constituency
(058) 43003
Fax (058) 45315

Leinster House
(01) 618 3596
Fax (01) 618 4517

EMAIL
jdeasy@cablesurf.com
john.deasy@oireachtas.ie

BORN
Abbeyside, Dungarvan, 1967

EDUCATION
Coláiste na Rinne, Ring, Dungarvan; St Augustine's College, Dungarvan; Mercyhurst College, Erie, Pennsylvania USA (BA); University College Cork (BCL)

MARITAL STATUS
Single

BRIAN O'SHEA

LABOUR

A member of Dáil Éireann since 1989, Brian O'Shea was a junior minister in both the Fianna Fáil-Labour coalition and the rainbow coalition. As a former primary school teacher he has campaigned for a ban on television advertising aimed at children.

OCCUPATION
Full-time public representative, former teacher

ADDRESS
61 Sweetbriar Lawn, Tramore, Co Waterford

PHONE
Constituency
(051) 381 913
Fax (051) 386 427

Leinster House
(01) 618 3780
Fax (01) 618 4198

EMAIL
brian.oshea@oireachtas.ie

WEBSITE
www.labour.ie

BORN
Waterford, 1944

EDUCATION
Mount Sion CBS Waterford; St Patrick's Training College, Drumcondra

MARITAL STATUS
Married to Eileen Walsh. Two sons, four daughters

OLLIE WILKINSON

FIANNA FÁIL

Born in Parliament Street, Waterford, Wilkinson is an effective grass-roots politician who first contested a general election in 1997 and was elected chairperson of Waterford County Council in July 2001. His Lismore electoral base gave him the edge over city-based party colleague Brendan Kenneally this time around.

OCCUPATION
Full-time public representative, former farmer

ADDRESS
Killahala, Cappoquin, Co Waterford

PHONE
Constituency
(058) 23652
(058) 23653
Fax (058) 23654

Leinster House
(01) 618 3446
Fax (01) 618 4780

EMAIL
ollie.wilkinson@oireachtas.ie

BORN
Waterford, October 1944

EDUCATION
Tourin NS; CBS Lismore

MARITAL STATUS
Married to Bridget. Ten children

3 SEATS

1 Labour
1 Fine Gael
1 Fianna Fáil

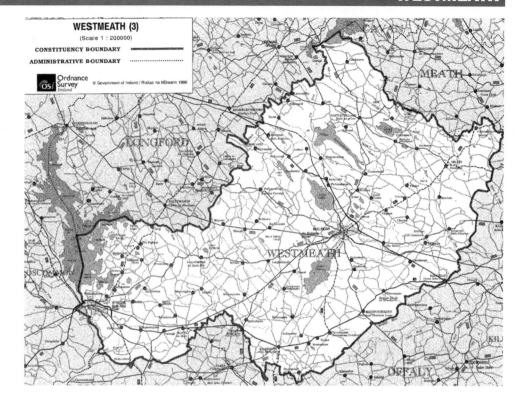

WESTMEATH (3)
(Scale 1 : 200000)

CONSTITUENCY BOUNDARY

ADMINISTRATIVE BOUNDARY

Ordnance Survey Ireland

© Government of Ireland / Rialtas na hÉireann 1998

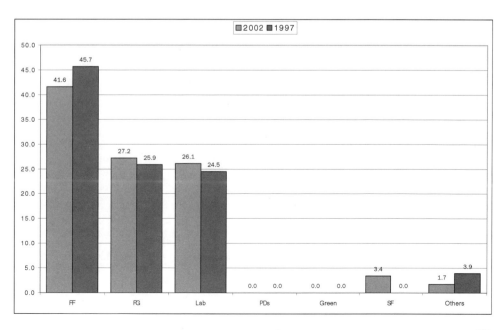

	2002	1997
FF	41.6	45.7
FG	27.2	25.9
Lab	26.1	24.5
PDs	0.0	0.0
Green	0.0	0.0
SF	3.4	0.0
Others	1.7	3.9

3 SEATS

ELECTORATE
56,012

TOTAL POLL
34,978

SPOILED
557

VALID POLL
34,421

QUOTA
8,606

* DENOTES
OUTGOING TD

NEWLY
ELECTED TDS
IN CAPITALS

		1	2 Penrose's surplus	3 Votes of McFadden, Hogg, Lynam and Walsh	
*W PENROSE	Lab	8967	√		
D CASSIDY	FF	7892	+90 7982	+576 8558	√
*M O'Rourke	FF	6444	+47 6491	+1544 8035	
*P McGRATH	FG	5570	+145 5715	+2770 8485	√
N McFadden	FG	3793	+31 3824	eliminated	
N Hogg	SF	1185	+31 1216	eliminated	
V Lynam	Ind	444	+16 460	eliminated	
P Walsh	CSP	126	+1 127	eliminated	
Non transferable			0	737	

No change

NO change in party shares, but there was a significant change of personnel. Senator Donie Cassidy, who was standing for the first time, edged out Mary O'Rourke, Fianna Fáil's deputy leader, minister and very experienced politician.

Fianna Fáil thought they had a chance of two seats here at the expense of Fine Gael with the right vote management. Cassidy actually came out some 1,500 votes ahead of O'Rourke on the first count but the real problem was that the votes were not there. Party support was down 4% with Fine Gael and Labour both marginally up. The elimination of the last four candidates en bloc favoured O'Rourke over Cassidy as may have been expected but she was still 500 votes adrift of Cassidy and McGrath, the Fine Gael incumbent, who took the third seat.

Once again Willie Penrose topped the poll, and this time won more votes than any other Labour Party candidate in this election. He increased his vote, as he had done when bucking the anti-Labour trend in 1997, and was elected on the first count.

DONIE CASSIDY

FIANNA FÁIL

The high-profile Donie Cassidy has been a Senator since 1982 and was appointed Leader of the Seanad in 1997. The anxieties rumoured to have been expressed during the campaign by Mary O'Rourke that she had given up too much territory in the interest of vote management to attempt a second seat seem to have been justified.

OCCUPATION
Public representative, businessman, impresario

ADDRESS
Castlepollard, Co Westmeath

PHONE
Constituency
(044) 61176
Fax (044) 61678

Leinster House
(01) 618 3578

EMAIL
donie.cassidy@oireachtas.ie

BORN
Castlepollard, September 1945

EDUCATION
St Michael's, Castlepollard

MARITAL STATUS
Married to Anne Geraghty.
Four sons

A wide array of options for voters in Dublin South east   PHOTOCALL

PAUL McGRATH

FINE GAEL

Member of Westmeath County Council since 1991 and elected to the Dáil in 1989, McGrath is deputy spokesperson on Finance, June 2002, having previously been Fine Gael junior spokesperson on Social, Community and Family Affairs, spokesperson on Public Works 1993-1994 and front bench spokesperson on Education.

OCCUPATION
Full-time public representative, former teacher

ADDRESS
Carna, Irishtown, Mullingar, Co Westmeath

PHONE
Constituency
(044) 40746
Fax (044) 40087

Leinster House
(01) 618 3747
Fax (01) 618 4601

EMAIL
paul.mcgrath@oireachtas.ie

WEBSITE
www.paulmcgrathtd.com

BORN
Ballymore, Co Westmeath, February 1948

EDUCATION
St Finian's College, Mullingar; Trinity and All Saints College, Leeds

MARITAL STATUS
Married.
Two sons, two daughters

WILLIE PENROSE

LABOUR

Once more Willie Penrose topped the poll as he did in 1997. The first Labour TD in Westmeath in 65 years when he was elected in 1992, he is enormously popular in the Mullingar area and, coming from a large rural working-class family, he is in a strong position to highlight the problems of rural poverty. He has now retired as a member of Westmeath County Council. Runner-up in the election to be deputy leader of the Labour Party.

OCCUPATION
Public representative, barrister

ADDRESS
Ballintue, Ballynacargy, Co Westmeath

PHONE
Constituency Office
(044) 43987
Fax (044) 43966

Leinster House
(01) 618 3734
Fax (01) 618 4541

EMAIL
willie.penrose@oireachtas.ie

BORN
Mullingar, August 1956

EDUCATION
St Mary's CBS Mullingar; Multyfarnham Agricultural College; University College Dublin; King's Inns

MARITAL STATUS
Married to Anne Fitzsimons.
Three daughters

5 SEATS

2 Fianna Fáil
1 Labour
1 Fine Gael
1 Independent

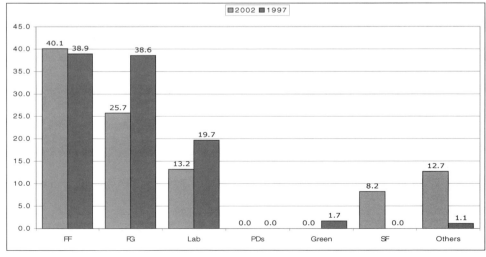

	2002	1997
FF	40.1	38.9
FG	25.7	38.6
Lab	13.2	19.7
PDs	0.0	0.0
Green	0.0	1.7
SF	8.2	0.0
Others	12.7	1.1

		1	2 Votes of Ó Bolguidhir, O'Connor	3 Votes of S Doyle	4 Votes of A Doyle	5 Votes of Dwyer	6 Votes of D'Arcy	7 Kehoe's surplus	8 Browne's surplus
*J BROWNE	FF	9150	+31 9181	+337 9518	+91 9609	+569 10178 √			
*B HOWLIN	Lab	7995	+78 8073	+128 8201	+723 8924	+1211 10135 √			
*H Byrne	FF	7556	+18 7574	+46 7620	+135 7755	+481 8236	+466 8702	+311 9013	+59 9072
T DEMPSEY	FF	7520	+40 7560	+75 7635	+158 7793	+403 8196	+627 8823	+279 9102	+48 9150 √
P KEHOE	FG	7048	+51 7099	+288 7387	+1404 8791	+404 9195	+3436 12631 √		
L TWOMEY	Ind	5815	+195 6010	+203 6213	+361 6574	+1488 8062	+678 8740	+1342 10082 √	
J Dwyer	SF	4964	+56 5020	+128 5148	+69 5217	eliminated			
*M D'Arcy	FG	4564	+33 4597	+28 4625	+1020 5645	+190 5835	eliminated		
A Doyle	FG	3940	+29 3969	+42 4011	eliminated				
S Doyle	Ind	1274	+41 1315	eliminated					
M Ó Bolguidhir	Ind	424	eliminated						
M O'Connor	CSP	173	eliminated						
Non transferable			25	40	50	471	628	628	0

5 SEATS

ELECTORATE
61,440

TOTAL POLL
61,440

SPOILED
1,017

VALID POLL
60,423

QUOTA
10,071

* DENOTES
OUTGOING TD

NEWLY
ELECTED TDS
IN CAPITALS

Ind gain from FG

THE news that Fine Gael's big vote winner here, Ivan Yates, would not stand in 2002 was always going to make things hard for the party. Avril Doyle MEP was drafted in from Brussels to shore up the dyke but in vain. In fact, things proved even worse than expected.

The party's vote was down a whopping 12% to just 26%; Avril Doyle was eliminated on the 3rd count and Michael D'Arcy, the second incumbent, on the 4th. Paul Kehoe, aided by a 60% transfer within the party, was elected on the 6th count.

The beneficiary of the collapse was Liam Twomey, a Rosslare based doctor who ran as an independent with health as his big issue and the general neglect of the area as a fall back. His was a late candidacy, and he won only 5,815 first preferences, placing him sixth on the first count. Fifteen hundred transfer votes from Sinn Féin's John Dwyer then put him in the running and another 1,300 votes from Kehoe's surplus put him over the quota, the first ever independent TD for Wexford.

There was more change within the Fianna Fáil camp with Tony Dempsey, manager of the county hurling team, just edging out the sitting TD and junior minister, Hugh Byrne by 78 votes. Byrne was injured before the start of the campaign, like several other defeated TDs including Nora Owen and Jim Mitchell of Fine Gael, and he felt he had not been able to knock on enough doors.

At the top of the poll was John Browne for Fianna Fáil, first elected in 1982, and the Labour deputy leader Brendan Howlin. The Labour vote was down more than 5% here on the 1997 Labour/DL vote but Howlin was safe. He was put over the quota with 1,200 votes from John Dwyer, who took 8% of the vote for Sinn Féin in an area where they had made no impact at all before 2002.

JOHN BROWNE

FIANNA FÁIL

Former Minister of State at both Environment and Agriculture, John Browne takes over for Fianna Fáil the Enniscorthy local votes and poll-topping position left vacant by the surprise departure of Fine Gael's Ivan Yates from political life and has been rewarded with the post of Minister of State at the Department of Communications, Marine and Natural Resources. He was first elected in November 1982.

OCCUPATION
Public representative, former salesman

ADDRESS
Kilcannon, Enniscorthy, Co Wexford

PHONE
Constituency
(054) 35046
Fax (054) 35049

Leinster House
(01) 678 2021
(01) 618 3094
Fax (01) 618 4527
Fax 901) 678 2059

EMAIL
john.browne_ff@oireachtas.ie

BORN
Marshalstown, Co Wexford, August 1948

EDUCATION
St Mary's CBS, Enniscorthy, Co Wexford

MARITAL STATUS
Married to Judy Doyle.
One son, three daughters

TONY DEMPSEY

FIANNA FÁIL

A member of the GAA Central Council for over 20 years, Tony Dempsey has been involved with every inter-county hurling and football team in County Wexford. Formerly one of the youngest ever school principals in a vocational school in Ireland, he retired from teaching three years ago to use his Wexford town base to take up politics.

OCCUPATION
Full-time public representative, former school principal

ADDRESS
Ardbracan House, Barntown, Co Wexford

PHONE
Constituency
(087) 203 7586
Fax (053) 20011

Leinster House
(01) 618 3629
Fax (01) 618 4783

EMAIL
tdempseyff@eircom.net

BORN
Davidstown, Co Wexford, May 1944

EDUCATION
St Mary's CBS, Enniscorthy; University College Dublin; NUI Maynooth

MARITAL STATUS
Married to Gemma.
Four sons, one daughter

BRENDAN HOWLIN

LABOUR

Member of Dáil Éireann since 1987, Labour Chief Whip 1987-93 and Deputy Leader of the Labour Party 1997-2002, he has held the ministries of Environment and Health and been spokesperson on the Environment and on Justice. Lost the 1997 leadership contest to Ruairí Quinn and lost to Pat Rabbitte in 2002. Member of Wexford County Council, 1985-93 and since 1999. Member of Wexford Borough Council, 1981-93.

OCCUPATION
Full-time public representative, former teacher

ADDRESS
Whiterock Hill, Wexford

PHONE
Constituency
(053) 24036

Leinster House
(01) 618 4366
Fax (01) 618 4542

EMAIL
brendan.howlin@oireachtas.ie

WEBSITE
www.brendanhowlin.ie

BORN
Wexford, May 1956

EDUCATION
CBS Wexford; St Patrick's College, Drumcondra

MARITAL STATUS
Single

PAUL KEHOE

FINE GAEL

Many had expected Avril Doyle to be the front-runner for Fine Gael in the constituency where she formerly held a seat but in the event Paul Kehoe, whose local base is close to that of Ivan Yates, finds himself elected to the 29th Dáil and has been appointed deputy spokesperson on Communications, Marine and Natural Resources.

OCCUPATION
Full-time public representative

ADDRESS
7 Weyfer Street, Enniscorthy, Co Wexford

PHONE
Home
(054) 47852
Fax (054) 47566

Constituency
(054) 43558
Fax (054) 39562

Leinster House
(01) 618 4438
Fax (01) 618 4130

EMAIL
paul.kehoe@oireachtas.ie

BORN
Ball, Enniscorthy, 1972

EDUCATION
St Mary's CBS, Enniscorthy; Kildalton Agricultural College

MARITAL STATUS
Single

Quids in: Mary Harney puts €20 on the PDs doubling their tally of seats to eight

PHOTOCALL IRELAND

DR LIAM TWOMEY

INDEPENDENT

Dr Liam Twomey is a general practitioner in Rosslare who has not previously held office outside his profession. He decided to stand for election to make sure that Health issues would be taken seriously, and once having decided to run he campaigned hard and professionally, knocking on a very high percentage of the doors of his new constituency and intends to be an equally professional presence in the Dáil.

OCCUPATION
Public representative, medical practitioner

ADDRESS
Rosslare Medical Centre, Rosslare Strand, Co Wexford

PHONE
(053) 32484
Fax (053) 32483

Leinster House
(01) 618 4299
Fax (01) 618 4536

EMAIL
ltwomey@oireachtas.ie

BORN
Cork, April 1967

EDUCATION
St Finbar's Seminary, Farranferris, Cork;
Trinity College Dublin (BA. BAO. BCh. MB.DGM. MICGP.)

MARITAL STATUS
Married.
Two children

5 SEATS

2 Fianna Fáil
1 Labour
1 Fine Gael
1 Independent

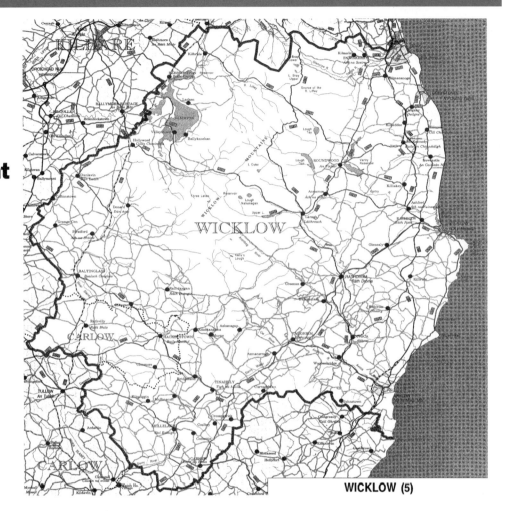

WICKLOW (5)

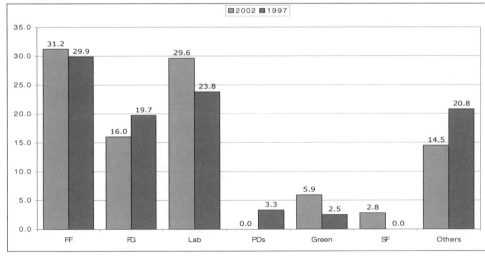

	2002	1997
FF	31.2	29.9
FG	16.0	19.7
Lab	29.6	23.8
PDs	0.0	3.3
Green	5.9	2.5
SF	2.8	0.0
Others	14.5	20.8

MILDRED FOX

INDEPENDENT

Mildred Fox was first elected to the Dáil in June 1995 following a by-election caused by the death of her father, the independent deputy Johnny Fox. One of the four independent TDs who gave stable support to the last government, she was outspoken on the need for another referendum on abortion.

OCCUPATION
Full-time public representative, former hotel front office manager

ADDRESS
Lower Calary, Kilmacanogue, Co Wicklow

PHONE
Constituency
(01) 287 6386

Leinster House
(01) 618 3548
Fax (01) 618 4188

EMAIL
mildred.fox@oireachtas.ie

WEBSITE
www.mildredfox.com

BORN
Dublin, June 1971

EDUCATION
St Kilian's Community School, Ballywaltrim, Bray; University College Dublin (BA)

MARITAL STATUS
Married to Daryl Tighe. One daughter

JOE JACOB

FIANNA FÁIL

Elected to Wicklow Co Council in 1985, the Dáil in 1987 and chairman of the Fianna Fáil parliamentary party and Leas-Cheann Comhairle under Albert Reynolds, Joe Jacob was Minister of State at the Department of Public Enterprise with special responsibility for Energy in the last government, in which capacity he gave his infamous interview with Marian Finucane to explain Ireland's (un)readiness in the event of a nuclear disaster.

OCCUPATION
Publican

ADDRESS
Main Street, Rathdrum, Co Wicklow

PHONE
Constituency
(0404) 46528
Fax (0404) 43026

Leinster House
(01) 618 3067
Fax (01) 618 4776

BORN
Kilrush, Co Clare, April 1939

EDUCATION
De La Salle College, Wicklow; Terenure College, Dublin

MARITAL STATUS
Married to Patti Grant. Three sons, three daughters

BILLY TIMMINS

FINE GAEL

A TD since 1997, when he resigned his commission to contest the seat formerly held by his father Godfrey, and a member of Wicklow County Council since 1999, Deputy Timmins is spokesman on Agriculture and Food, and has also held the posts of spokesman on Defence and on Housing.

OCCUPATION
Full-time public representative, former army officer

ADDRESS
Home
Sruhaun, Baltinglass, Co Wicklow

Constituency Office
Weaver Square, Baltinglass, Co Wicklow

PHONE
Constituency
(059) 648 1016
Fax (059) 648 1068

Leinster House
(01) 618 3384
Fax (01) 618 4604

EMAIL
billy.timmins@oireachtas.ie

WEBSITE
www.billytimmins.com

BORN
Baltinglass, October 1959

EDUCATION
Patrician College, Ballyfin, Co Laois; University College Galway

MARITAL STATUS
Married to Madeleine Hyland. Three daughters, two sons

DICK ROCHE

FIANNA FÁIL

A member of Wicklow County Council since 1985, Dick Roche was first elected to the Dáil in 1987 but lost in 1992 to former Fianna Fáil County Councillor Johnny Fox, running as an Independent. He regained his seat in 1997 after five years in the Seanad. He is now Minister of State at the Department of the Taoiseach and at the Department of Foreign Affairs and represents the government at the Convention on the Future of Europe.

OCCUPATION
Public representative, university lecturer

ADDRESS
2 Herbert Terrace, Herbert Road, Bray, Co Wicklow

PHONE
Constituency
(01) 286 3211
Fax (01) 286 7666

Leinster House
(01) 619 4309

EMAIL
dick.roche@oireachtas.ie

WEBSITE
www.dickroche.com

BORN
Wexford, March 1947

EDUCATION
Wexford CBS; University College Dublin (DPA, BComm, MPA)

MARITAL STATUS
Married to Eleanor Griffin. Three sons, one daughter

		1	2 Roche's surplus	3 Votes of Hyland	4 Votes of Kenny	5 Votes of Kearns, Kennedy, Keddy	6 Votes of O'Rourke	7 Votes of Keane	8 Votes of de Burca, O'Shaughnessy
*D ROCHE	FF	9222 √							
			+63	+14	+13	+119	+28	+233	+663
*J JACOB	FF	7836	7899	7913	7926	8045	8073	8306	8969
			+17	+24	+57	+208	+219	+190	+2210
*L McMANUS	Lab	7595	7612	7636	7693	7901	8120	8310	10520 √
			+5	+11	+10	+68	+930	+80	+634
*B TIMMINS	FG	7372	7377	7388	7398	7466	8396	8476	9110 √
			+3	+4	+19	+107	+29	+219	+899
N Kelly	Lab	6529	6532	6536	6555	6662	6691	6910	7807
			+18	+22	+46	+232	+84	+249	+1272
*M FOX	Ind	6324	6342	6364	6410	6642	6726	6975	8247
			+4	+28	+37	+223	+61	+465	
D de Burca	GP	3208	3212	3240	3277	3500	3561	4026	elim'td
			+2	+1	+0	+96	+20	+40	
J O'Shaughnessy	Lab	2029	2031	2032	2032	2128	2148	2188	elim'td
			+3	+6	+10	+103	+10		
M Keane	SF	1527	1530	1536	1546	1649	1659	eliminated	
			+1	+20	+19	+25			
R O'Rourke	FG	1332	1333	1353	1372	1397	eliminated		
			+0	+6	+6				
R Kearns	Ind	406	406	412	418	eliminated			
			+1	+12	+13				
C Kennedy	SWP	399	400	412	425	eliminated			
			+1	+8	+12				
C Keddy	Ind	383	384	392	404	eliminated			
			+1	+10					
B Kenny	Ind	236	237	247	eliminated				
			+0						
B Hyland	Ind	171	171	eliminated					
Non transferable			0	5	5	66	16	183	536

5 SEATS

ELECTORATE
89,797

TOTAL POLL
55,296

SPOILED
736

VALID POLL
54,560

QUOTA
9,094

* DENOTES
OUTGOING TD

NEWLY
ELECTED TDS
IN CAPITALS

No change

LABOUR wanted to win back the seat lost to an independent candidate, Mildred Fox, in 1997 and co-opted Nicky Kelly, another independent who had won almost 5,000 votes last time to help them. The party's vote was up by 6% to almost 30%, close to two quotas. Former DL TD Liz McManus, the Labour incumbent, won 7,500 votes and was safe enough and Kelly was in fifth place on the 1st count. However, Mildred Fox's vote held up well. One of the 'gang of four' who voted for Ahern as Taoiseach and who had given firm support to the government, her constituents seem to have appreciated what she had been able to accomplish. Kelly and Fox were neck and neck though seven counts. The key was probably the transfers from the double elimination of De Burca (Green) and Shaughnessy, the third Labour candidate. Normally these would have been expected to favour Kelly but Fox gained a net 378 votes at this point. De Burca and Fox are both from the Bray area in the

9	10
McManus' surplus	Jacob's surplus

156	
9125 √	

+848	+12
8657	**8669**
+422	+19
8669	**8688** √

Mildred Fox with her daughter Caoilfhionn Tighe during the long count at Arklow Leisure Centre
PHOTOCALL IRELAND

0	*0*

LIZ McMANUS

LABOUR

The new Deputy Leader of the Labour Party, completing a clean sweep by former Democratic Left TDs, was first elected in 1992. McManus was Minister of State for Housing & Urban Renewal 1994-7, and is a long serving member of Wicklow County Council and Bray Town Council. A writer, she is a past winner of the Hennessy, Listowel and Irish PEN awards in fiction, and a long-time columnist with *The Sunday Tribune.*

OCCUPATION
Full-time public representative, writer, former architect

ADDRESS
1 Martello Terrace, Bray, Co Wicklow

PHONE
Constituency
(01) 276 0583
Fax (01) 276 0584

Leinster House
(01) 618 3131
(01) 618 4591

EMAIL
liz.mcmanus@oireachtas.ie

WEBSITE
www.labour.ie

BORN
United States, March 1947

EDUCATION
Holy Child Convent, Killiney;
University College Dublin

MARITAL STATUS
Married to Dr John McManus.
Four children

North east of Wicklow while Kelly is from Arklow in the South east. Shaughnessy is located between the two. A net 401 votes from Liz McManus's surplus at the subsequent count (and these would have come from the same source) could not undo the damage. Fox held on by just 47 votes.

In Fianna Fáil the key question was which of its two candidates could top the poll: Dick Roche, or his rival Joe Jacob, a junior minister in the coalition government. Jacob's credibility took more than a slight dent following an embarrassing RTE interview in which he explained his department's lack of plans in the event of a nuclear disaster. This may have helped Roche, who not only topped the poll but also won more than a quota.

CONSTITUENCY	VALID	SEATS	FF VOTES	SEATS	FG VOTES	SEATS	LABOUR VOTES	SEATS	PDS VOTES	SEATS	GREEN VOTES	SEATS	SF VOTES	SEATS	OTHERS** VOTES	SEATS
Carlow-Kilkenny	62.7	5	50.2	3	21.9	1	13.2	1*	0	0	8.2	0	3.4	0	3.2	0
Cavan-Monaghan	70.6	5	34.9	2	25.2	1	0.9	0	1.8	0	1.8	0	17.5	1	17.9	1
Clare	61.9	4	45.4	2	25.5	1	3.5	0	0	0	5.8	0	0	0	19.9	1
Cork East	63.0	4	41.3	2	29.1	1	21.0	1	0	0	2.5	0	5.7	0	0.4	0
Cork North Central	57.1	5	41.5	3	20.4	1	11.8	1	6.9	0	2.6	0	6.3	0	10.6	0
Cork North West	72.3	3	50.1	2	42.1	1	6.9	0	0	0	0	0	0	0	1.0	0
Cork South Central	61.6	5	48.6	3	19.4	1	5.9	0	0	0	9.0	1	3.7	0	13.4	0
Cork South West	69.5	3	39.5	2	32.3	1	9.1	0	0	0	0	0	5.9	0	13.2	0
Donegal North East	62.4	3	49.4	2	21.0	0	2.8	0	0	0	0	0	9.9	0	16.9	1
Donegal South West	65.0	3	42.1	2	25.4	1	3.0	0	0	0	0	0	10.7	0	18.7	0
Dublin Central	54.7	4	39.6	2	11.1	0	12.2	1	0	0	4.3	0	14.6	0	18.3	1
Dublin Mid West	51.6	3	32.1	1	11.5	0	9.0	0	20.1	1	12.3	1	6.5	0	8.5	0
Dublin North	60.7	4	38.2	2	11.8	0	14.5	1	0	0	16.6	1	3.1	0	15.8	0
Dublin North Central	61.1	4	50.0	2	17.0	1	10.5	0	0	0	5.7	0	5.7	0	11.0	1
Dublin North East	56.3	3	40.1	2	15.4	0	16.2	1	4.2	0	5.6	0	10.2	0	8.2	0
Dublin North West	54.9	3	47.5	2	8.0	0	16.8	1	0	0	2.3	0	18.3	0	7.1	0
Dublin South	59.7	5	36.6	2	19.8	1	9.5	0	15.0	1	9.4	1	3.9	0	5.7	0
Dublin South Central	51.1	5	34.3	2	16.9	1	19.7	1	3.1	0	5.2	0	12.7	1	8.0	0
Dublin South East	54.1	4	27.0	1	16.1	0	12.4	1	18.8	1	16.2	1	7.4	0	2.1	0
Dublin South West	54.2	4	38.7	2	12.7	0	19.8	1	0	0	3.1	0	20.3	1	5.4	0
Dublin West	55.8	3	34.6	1	12.3	0	12.7	1	7.9	0	2.5	0	8.0	0	21.9	1
Dún Laoghaire	58.6	5	30.3	2	15.0	0	22.7	1	13.4	1	9.3	1	4.0	0	5.3	0
Galway East	67.1	4	46.8	2	31.5	1	0	0	0	0	2.1	0	3.7	0	15.9	1
Galway West	60.2	5	41.3	2	16.9	1	10.5	1	12.5	1	4.4	0	5.6	0	8.7	0
Kerry North	70.6	3	30.2	1	22.1	1	22.4	0	0	0	0	0	24.2	1	1.1	0
Kerry South	70.8	3	44.6	1	17.7	0	14.5	1	0	0	0	0	0	0	23.2	1
Kildare North	54.9	3	43.2	1	17.5	1	21.4	1	11.9	0	6.0	0	0	0	0	0
Kildare South	55.9	3	46.4	2	17.8	0	18.5	1	11.9	0	3.7	0	0	0	1.7	0
Laoighis-Offaly	66.3	5	51.3	3	23.0	1	2.5	0	14.4	1	0.8	0	4.1	0	3.8	0
Limerick East	62.0	5	39.9	2	27.8	1	9.3	1	9.8	1	1.8	0	0	0	11.4	0
Limerick West	66.2	3	53.4	2	41.7	1	0	0	0	0	2.7	0	0	0	2.3	0
Longford-Roscommon	70.3	4	40.8	2	30.7	1	1.3	0	9.4	1	0.9	0	3.4	0	13.6	0
Louth	58.1	4	43.6	2	20.2	1	6.7	0	0	0	4.2	0	15.0	1	10.4	0
Mayo	66.9	5	40.0	2	37.6	2	0	0	1.4	0	1.1	0	3.3	0	16.6	1
Meath	58.9	5	44.9	3	27.2	2	4.3	0	0	0	3.6	0	9.4	0	10.5	0
Sligo-Leitrim	69.5	4	39.0	2	26.7	1	5.0	0	0	0	0	0	10.2	0	19.2	1
Tipperary North	68.9	3	42.7	2	14.9	0	13.5	0	3.5	0	0	0	0	0	25.4	1
Tipperary South	65.4	3	38.5	1	24.5	1	9.1	0	0	0	0	0	3.3	0	24.5	1
Waterford	63.2	4	46.3	2	21.5	1	13.4	1	4.6	0	2.9	0	6.3	0	5.0	0
Westmeath	61.4	3	41.6	1	27.2	1	26.1	1	0	0	0	0	3.4	0	1.7	0
Wexford	63.9	5	40.1	2	25.7	1	13.2	1	0	0	0	0	8.2	0	12.7	1
Wicklow	60.8	5	31.2	2	16.0	1	29.6	1	0	0	5.9	0	2.8	0	14.5	1
Total	61.9	166	41.4	81	22.5	31	10.8	21	4.0	8	3.8	6	6.5	5	10.9	14

* Séamus Pattison was returned unopposed as Ceann Comhairle
** Others includes 0.80% of the vote for the Socialist Party (1 seat), 0.18% for the Socialist Workers' Party, 0.26% for Comhar Críostaí – Christian Solidarity Party, 0.22% for The Workers' Party and 9.49% (13 seats) for non-party candidates.

Terry Leyden celebrates with wife Mary after being re-elected to the Seanad after nine years out of the Oireachtas   PHOTOCALL IRELAND

There is a total of 60 Members of Seanad Éireann

PANELS: 43
UNIVERSITIES: 6
NOMINATED BY TAOISEACH: 11

CULTURAL AND EDUCATIONAL PANEL (5)

Paschal Mooney FF
Ann Ormonde FF
Labhras Ó Murchú FF
Brian Hayes FG
Noel Coonan FG

ADMINISTRATIVE PANEL (7)

Camillus Glynn FF
Tony Kett FF
Joanna Tuffy LAB
Frank Feighan FG
Timmy Dooley FF
Diarmuid Wilson FF
Joe McHugh FG

AGRICULTURAL PANEL (11)

Francis O'Brien FF
Kathleen O'Meara LAB
Paddy Burke FG
Peter Callanan FF
Jim Walsh FF
Rory Kiely FF
Paul Bradford FG
Dr Martin Mansergh FF
Ulick Burke FG
John Paul Phelan FG
Eamon Scanlon FF

INDUSTRIAL AND COMMERCIAL PANEL (9)

Derek McDowell LAB
Kieran Phelan FF
James Bannon FG
Eddie Bohan FF
Margaret Cox FF
Marc MacSharry FF
Mary White FF
Paul Coghlan FG
Sheila Terry FG

LABOUR PANEL (11)

Liam Fitzgerald FF
Jim Higgins FG
Don Lydon FF
Michael McCarthy LAB
Brendan Daly FF
Terry Leyden FF
Geraldine Feeney FF
Hanafin, John Gerard FF
Maurice Cummins FG
Michael Finucane FG
Fergal Brown FG

NATIONAL UNIVERSITY OF IRELAND (3)

Fergal Quinn IND
Brendan Ryan LAB
Joe O'Toole IND

UNIVERSITY OF DUBLIN (3)

Shane Ross IND
David Norris IND
Mary Henry IND

NOMINATED BY THE TAOISEACH (11)

Mary O'Rourke FF
Dr Maurice Hayes, Other
Brendan Kenneally FF
Michael Kitt FF
Michael Brennan FF
Cyprian Brady FF
Pat Moylan FF
Tom Morrissey PD
John Dardis PD
Kate Walsh PD
John Minihan PD

Seanad for second thoughts

Michael Marsh on how the little understood, often irrelevant Upper House of the Oireachtas is elected – and what it does

THE Seanad is a curious institution filled by a combination of appointment, election and indirect election, with an arcane nomination process. Many parliaments have a second chamber (although many states have abandoned them), and typically these are filled by a process that is quite different from that by which the first one is elected.

There are three pathways to the Seanad. One is to be elected by county councillors and TDs. This quite small but very sophisticated electorate decides on who will fill 43 of the 60 seats. A second route is to be voted in by graduates of Dublin University (TCD) and the National University of Ireland, who each elect a further 3 senators. Most non-party senators arrive through this channel. A third way is to be appointed by the Taoiseach to one of the 11 seats in his gift.

Those who seek to be elected by other public representatives must be nominated to one of five panels, which each elect between five and 11 senators: the Cultural and Educational Panel (5), the Agricultural Panel (11), the Labour Panel (11), the Industrial and Commercial Panel (9) and the Administrative Panel (7). There are many nominating bodies but the most important are the parties themselves. More importantly, it is the elected public representatives of the major parties themselves who fill most of the seats so the Seanad is comprised mostly of members of Fianna Fail and Fine Gael and usually provides strong support for the government.

For many members it is a resting place where would-be TDs are prepared, and prepare themselves for, the next election. A majority of members with party affiliation either have stood, or intend to stand for the Dáil. As a channel of recruitment to the Dáil it is important but otherwise it is a body little understood by the public whose deliberations are generally ignored by the media. It can seem to be, and often is, an irrelevance. The government has at least 34 seats out of the 60. Yet it is a place where second thoughts are aired, and at times legislation is amended significantly or even withdrawn. Certainly it is over-due for reform, but it will have to wait a while yet.

	FF	FG	LAB	PD	IND	TOTAL
Elected by public representatives						
Administration	4	3	1	0	0	7
Agriculture	6	4	1	0	0	11
Culture and Education	3	2	0	0	0	5
Industry and Commerce	5	3	1	0	0	9
Labour	6	4	1	0	0	11
Elected by graduates of NUI and Dublin University						
NUI	0	0	1	0	2	3
Dublin University	0	0	0	0	3	3
Nominated by the Taoiseach						
	6	0	0	4	1	11
Total	**30**	**15**	**5**	**4**	**6**	**60**

Joe O'Toole: returned to the Seanad by NUI voters PHOTOCALL IRELAND

7 SEATS

4 Fianna Fáil
2 Fine Gael
1 Labour

FIRST PREFERENCES

GLYNN, CAMILLUS (FF) **128**   Elected 1st count

TUFFY, JOANNA (Lab) **114**   Elected 9th count

KETT, ANTHONY (FF) **85**   Elected 7th count

FEIGHAN, FRANK (FG) **82**   Elected 9th count

Nolan, Enda (FF) **70**

WILSON, DIARMUID (FF) **63**   Elected 12th count

DOOLEY, TIMMY (FF) **61**   Elected 12th count

Fitzgerald, Frances (FG) **57**

Coogan, Fintan (FG) **55**

McHUGH, JOE (FG) **51**   Elected 13th count

Kitt, Michael P (FF) **49**

McFadden, Nicky (FG) **42**

McGennis, Marian (FF) **39**

O'Donnell, Kieran (FG) **30**

Bonner, Enda (FF) **27**

TIMMY DOOLEY

FIANNA FÁIL

The Fianna Fáil spokesman on Transport in the Seanad has been a member of the party's National Executive for the last five years and is a member of the National Forum on Europe. Outside politics he finds time for membership of the GAA, the IFA and the Irish/US business committee and supports the MS Society of Ireland.

OCCUPATION
Business Development Manager, Octagon Technologies

ADDRESS
Sellernane, Mountshannon, Co Clare

PHONE
Leinster House
(01) 618 3514
Fax (01) 618 4558

EMAIL
timmy.Dooley@oireachtas.ie

BORN
Clare, February 1960

EDUCATION
Scariff Community College;
University College Dublin
(Computer Science)

MARITAL STATUS
Married.
One child

FRANK FEIGHAN

FINE GAEL

Frank Feighan is a new Senator elected to Seanad Éireann in July 2002. Senator Feighan was first elected to Roscommon County Council in 1999 for the Boyle electoral area, where Fine Gael took four out of the five seats. He is spokesman for Health and Children's Affairs.

OCCUPATION
Full time public representative

ADDRESS
Bridge St, Boyle, Co Roscommon

PHONE
Constituency
(071) 966 2115/62 383
Fax (071) 966 2115

Leinster House
(01) 619 4289
Fax (01) 618 4799

EMAIL
frank.feighan@oireachtas.ie
feighanf@eircom.net

BORN
Boyle, Co Roscommon, July 1962

EDUCATION
St Mary's College, Boyle

MARITAL STATUS
Single

CAMILLUS GLYNN

FIANNA FAIL

A new Senator, Camillus Glynn contested the 1997 General Election in Westmeath. He has been a member of Westmeath County Council since 1979, was President of theAssociation of Municipal Authoritative of Ireland in 1989/1990 and has been a member of the Midland Health Board since 1980.

OCCUPATION
Public representative,
psychiatric nurse,
abuse therapist

ADDRESS
8 Newbrook Road, Clonmore,
Mullingar, Co Westmeath.

PHONE
(044) 47 151
(044) 47 318

Leinster House
(01) 618 3648
Fax (01) 618 4565

BORN
Grehanstown, Killucan,
Co Westmeath, October 1941

EDUCATION
St Mary CBS, Mullingar:
St Loman's School of Nursing,
Mullingar

MARITAL STATUS
Married to Margaret Fallon.
Two sons, two daughters

TONY KETT

FIANNA FAIL

Tony Kett has been a member of Dublin City Council since 1988 when he was co-opted to fill the vacancy following the retirement of Bertie Ahern, having been a constituency worker since 1977, and is a member of the Drumcondra "Kitchen Cabinet". Uses his experience in the CRC as Spokesperson on Disability in the Seanad.

OCCUPATION
Administrator,
Central Remedial Clinic, Dublin

ADDRESS
54 Whitethorn Road, Dublin 5

PHONE
(01) 837 4129

Leinster House
(01) 618 3503

EMAIL
tkett@crc.ie

BORN
Ballinasloe, Co Galway, June 1951

EDUCATION
St Joseph's College, Garbally Park,
Ballinasloe;
College of Commerce, Rathmines,
Dublin.

MARITAL STATUS
Married to Noreen Kilkenny.
One son, two daughters.

JOE McHUGH

FINE GAEL

Joe McHugh is a new Senator. He was elected to Donegal County Council in 1999 for the Milford electoral area. A secondary school teacher from 1994 – 1996 he became a Community Youth Worker in 1996.

OCCUPATION
Full time public representative,
former secondary teacher and
youth worker

ADDRESS
Claggan, Carrigart, Letterkenny

PHONE
Constituency
(074) 915 5968
Fax (074) 915 5968

Leinster House
(01) 618 4242
Fax (01) 618 3669

EMAIL
joe.mchugh@oireachtas.ie
joe.mchugh@donegalcoco.ie

BORN
Letterkenny, July 1971

EDUCATION
Loreto Milford;
St Patrick's College, Maynooth

MARITAL STATUS
Single

JOANNA TUFFY

LABOUR

Joanna Tuffy contested the General Election in Dublin Mid-West in May. She is currently a Councillor on South Dublin County Council to which she was first elected in 1999 and is a member of Dublin Regional Authority.

OCCUPATION
Solicitor

ADDRESS
111 Esker Lawns, Lucan.
Co Dublin

PHONE
Constituency
Phone and fax (01) 628 0765

Leinster House
(01) 618 3822
Fax (01) 6184392

EMAIL
Joanna.tuffy@oireachtas.ie
jtuffy@sdublincoco.ie

BORN
London, 1965

EDUCATION
Trinity College, Dublin (BA);
DIT, Rathmines (Dip Legal
Studies)

MARITAL STATUS
Single

DIARMUID WILSON

FIANNA FAIL

In 1991 Diarmuid Wilson failed narrowly in the County Council elections but he topped the poll in the Cavan electoral area in 1999. Involved in local voluntary work as Director of County Cavan Partnership Board and Tullachmongan Resource Centre he is Seanad Spokesperson on Transport.

OCCUPATION
Director of YouthReach, Co Cavan

ADDRESS
45 Carrickfern, Keadue Lane,
Co Cavan

PHONE
Constituency
(049) 436 2256

Leinster House
(01) 618 3561
Fax (01) 618 4791

EMAIL
diarmuid.Wilson@oireachtas.ie

BORN
Cavan, November 1965

EDUCATION
Cavan Vocational School;
St Patrick's College, Maynooth;
Brunel University, London (Extern)

MARITAL STATUS
Married to Marian Kelly.
One boy, one girl

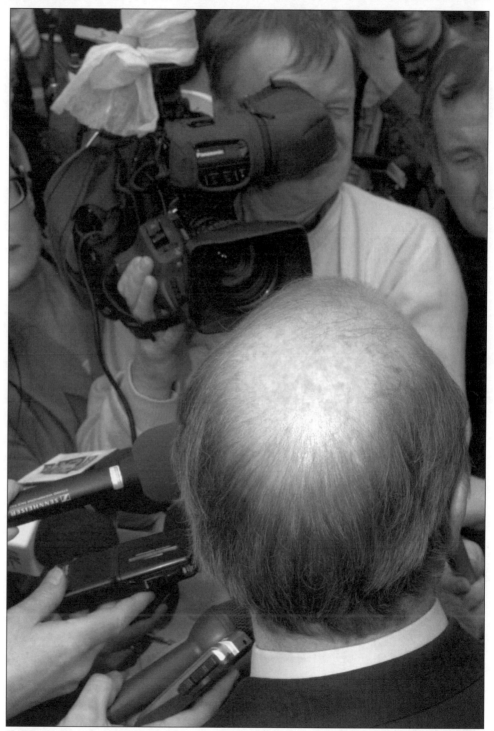

Fine Gael leader Michael Noonan started his party's 2002 general election campaign with a walk about in Dublin's Grafton Street

PHOTOCALL IRELAND

9 SEATS

5 Fianna Fáil

3 Fine Gael

1 Labour

FIRST PREFERENCES

O'BRIEN, FRANCIS (FF)	**91**	Elected 1st count
O'MEARA, KATHLEEN (Labour)		
	87	Elected 1st count
BURKE, PADDY (FG)	**69**	Elected 14th count
WALSH, JIM (FF)	**65**	Elected 17th count
KIELY, RORY (FF)	**63**	Elected 18th count
CALLANAN, PETER (FF)	**61**	Elected 17th count
MANSERGH, MARTIN (FF)		
	52	Elected 23rd count
BRADFORD, PAUL (FG)	**50**	Elected 22nd count
Moylan, Pat (FF)	**45**	
BURKE, ULICK (FG)	**39**	Elected 25th count
Bailey, John (FG)	**37**	
Connor, John (FG)	**37**	
Phelan, John Paul (FG)	**36**	
Fleming, Thomas (FF)	**28**	
Scanlon, Eamon (FF)	**27**	
Fitzgerald, Michael (FG)	**26**	
Hoade, Mary (FF)	**26**	
Boylan, Andrew (FG)	**25**	
McGowan Patrick (FF)	**23**	
Murphy, Kevin (FG)	**19**	
Chambers, Frank (FF)	**17**	
Killilea, D-M (FF)	**13**	
Higgins, Albert (FF)	**10**	
Kelly, Gerry (FG)	**8**	
Moynihan, Bernard (np)	**1**	
Farrell, Mary (np)	**0**	
Hunt, Bridget (np)	**0**	
Sharkey, Paddy (np)	**0**	

PAUL BRADFORD

FINE GAEL

Bradford lost in Cork East to party colleague David Stanton and returns to the Seanad. He became the youngest ever member of Cork County Council at the age of 21 in 1985 and was the youngest ever elected Senator between 1987 and 1989. He became a TD in 1989 aged 26 and was a member of the Fine Gael front bench until the formation of the 'Rainbow Coalition' but did not gain ministerial rank. He was Fine Gael's Chief Whip and a member of the Leader's Cabinet from February 2001 to May 2002.

OCCUPATION
Full-time public representative, farmer

ADDRESS
Mourne Abbey, Mallow, Co Cork

PHONE
Constituency
(022) 29375
Fax (022) 42457

Leinster House
(01) 618 3760
Fax (01) 618 4519

EMAIL
paul.bradford@oireachtas.ie

BORN
Mallow, 1963

EDUCATION
Patrician Academy, Mallow

MARITAL STATUS
Single

PADDY BURKE

FINE GAEL

The Leas-Chathaoirleach has been a Senator on the Agricultural Panel since 1993. and a member of Mayo County Council since 1979. A former regional development officer and former member of Mayo County Committee of Agriculture, he is a member of Mayo-Galway Regional Development Organisation.

OCCUPATION
Full-time public representative

ADDRESS
Knockaphunta, Westport Road, Castlebar, County Mayo

PHONE
Constituency
(094) 902 2568

Leinster House
(01) 618 3570
Fax (01) 618 4570

EMAIL
paddy_burke@oireachtas.ie

BORN
Castlebar, January 1955

EDUCATION
Ballinafad College, Castlebar; Rockwell College of Agriculture; Franciscan Brothers Agricultural College, Mount Bellew, Co Galway

MARITAL STATUS
Married to Dolores Barrett. One son

ULICK BURKE

FINE GAEL

Ulick Burke was a member of Seanad Éireann from 1981 to 1982 and from 1983 to 1987 and was elected to the Dáil for Galway East in 1997. He was Fine Gael Junior Spokesperson on heritage from 2000 - 2001 and was Deputy Spokesperson on Education from 2001-2002. He is a member of Galway County Council and has served on the Central Executive Committee of the association of Secondary Teachers of Ireland.

OCCUPATION
Full-time public representative, former secondary school teacher

ADDRESS
Eagle Hill, Abbey, Loughrea, Co Galway

PHONE
Constituency
(091) 847 437
Fax (091) 847 438

Leinster House
(01) 618 3387
LoCall 1890 337 889
Fax (01) 618 4580

EMAIL
ulick.burke@oireachtas.ie

BORN
Loughrea, Co Galway, 1943

EDUCATION
St Molaise College, Portumna, Co Galway;
University College Galway.
(BA, HDipEd)

MARITAL STATUS
Married.
Five sons, two daughters

PETER CALLANAN

FIANNA FAÍL

A Senator since 1997 Peter Callanan has been a member of the Joint Committees on Agriculture, Food and the Marine and on Public Enterprise and Transport. He has been a member of Cork County Council since 1979.

OCCUPATION
Public representative, farmer.

ADDRESS
Ballymountain, Innishannon, Co Cork.

PHONE
Constituency
(021) 477 5192,
Fax (021) 477 5204,

Leinster House
(01) 618 3257
Fax (01) 618 4632

EMAIL
peter.callanan@oireachtas.ie

BORN
Clonakilty, Co Cork. June 1935

EDUCATION
Mount Melleray College, Co Waterford.

MARITAL STATUS
Married to Sheila Harrington
Four sons, two daughters

RORY KIELY

FIANNA FÁIL

The Cathaoirleach was a Senator from 1977-1982 and has been elected on each occasion since 1983. As Cathaoirleach he is Chairman of the Committee on Procedure and Privileges of Seanad Éireann and of the Select Committee on members interests and a member of the Presidential Commission and the Council of State. The former selector of the Limerick Senior Hurling Team has been Limerick delegate to Munster GAA Council since 1982.

OCCUPATION
Public representative, farmer.

ADDRESS
Cloncrippa, Feenagh, Kilmallock, Co Limerick.

PHONE
Constituency
(063) 85 033
Fax (063) 85 150

Leinster House
(01) 618 3227
Fax (01) 618 4101

EMAIL
rory.kiely@oireachtas.ie

BORN
Feenagh, Co Limerick, May 1934

EDUCATION
Charleville CBS, Co Cork; UCC (Dip Social and Rural Science)

MARITAL STATUS
Married to Eileen O'Connor.
Two sons, two daughters

MARTIN MANSERGH

FIANNA FAIL

Martin Mansergh resigned from the civil service in 1981 to become Special Advisor to successive Fianna Faíl Taoisigh from Charles Haughey onwards and Fianna Fáil's Head of Research in opposition. Widely credited with playing a very significant role in the process which led to the Good Friday Agreement he was winner of the Tipperary Peace Prize with Fr. Reid and Rev. Roy Magee. Candidate for Tipperary South in the general election.

OCCUPATION
Co-owner of family farm, former senior civil servant

ADDRESS
Friarsfield House, Tipperary Town, Co Tipperary

PHONE
Constituency
(062) 51 226
Fax (062) 31 028

Leinster House
(01) 618 3233
Fax (01) 618 4793

EMAIL
mmansergh@oireachtas.ie

BORN
England, 1946

EDUCATION
King's School, Canterbury;
Christ Church, Oxford
(PPE) MA, D Phil

MARITAL STATUS
Married to Liz.
Four daughters, one son

KATHLEEN O'MEARA

LABOUR

Kathleen O'Meara once again fought well for the Tipperary North seat she first campaigned for in 1997. She is currently a Councillor on Tipperary North Riding County Council and a Councillor on Nenagh Urban District Council.

OCCUPATION
Full time Public Representative, former RTÉ Journalist

ADDRESS
15 Knights Crescent, Nenagh, Co Tipperary

PHONE
Constituency
(067) 34190
Fax (067) 34011

Leinster House
(01) 618 3573
Fax (01) 618 4163

EMAIL
kathleen.omeara@
oireachtas.ie

BORN
Shinrone, Birr, January 1960

EDUCATION
Sacred Heart Convent, Roscrea;
University College, Dublin

MARITAL STATUS
Married.
Two children

FRANCIS O'BRIEN

FIANNA FÁIL

Francis O'Brien has been a member of Seanad Éireann since 1989, and is Spokesprson on Rural Development and a member of the Joint Oireachtas Committee on Agriculture and Food.Hehas been a member of Monaghan County Council since 1979 and a member of the East Border Region Committee since 1987. He continues to be involved with local GAA activities and is an active IFA member.

OCCUPATION
Public representative,
dairy farmer

ADDRESS
Corwillan, Latton, Castleblaney,
Co Monaghan

PHONE
(042) 974 1152
Fax (042) 974 8064

Leinster House
(01) 618 3388
Fax (01) 618 4173

BORN
Corwillan, Latton, Castleblaney,
April 1943

EDUCATION
Drumfeehan NS, Co Monaghan

MARITAL STATUS
Married to Gertrude Smith.
Three sons, one daughter

JOHN PAUL PHELAN

FINE GAEL

Senator Phelan is the youngest elected member of the new Seanad. Although he has no family background in politics, he was only 20 when he was elected to Kilkenny County Council in 1999 for the Piltown Electoral Area, the youngest person elected to this council.

OCCUPATION
Full-time public representative

ADDRESS
Smithstown, Tullogher, via
Mullinavat, Co Kilkenny

PHONE
Constituency
(051) 427 326

Leinster House
(01) 618 4202
Fax (01) 618 4303

EMAIL
johnpaul2000@eircom.net

WEBSITE
www.johnpaulphelan.com

BORN
Waterford, September 1978

EDUCATION
Good Counsel College, New Ross
WIT Waterford (BBS)

MARITAL STATUS
Single

EAMON SCANLON

FIANNA FÁIL

Eamon Scanlon, who was less that a hundred first preferences behind sitting party colleague John Ellis, has long political experience with seven years on the National Executive and as Director of Elections for Matt Brennan TD, whose seat he was expected to take, since 1981. He topped the poll for the Ballymote area in the 1999 council elections but fell victim to the Harkin effect. Seanad spokesman on Food and Horticulture.

OCCUPATION
Senator, auctioneer

ADDRESS
Keenaghan, Ballymote, Co Sligo

PHONE
Constituency
(071) 918 9224
Fax (071) 918 9339

Leinster House
(01) 618 4087
Fax (01) 618 4794

EMAIL
eamonscanlonmcc@eircom.net

BORN
Ballymote, Co Sligo, 1954

EDUCATION
Coran College Ballymote

MARITAL STATUS
Married to Ann.
Four boys and two girls

JIM WALSH

FIANNA FÁIL

The former President of the Irish Road Hauliers' Association was first elected to the Agricultural Panel in 1997 and has been a member of Wexford County Council since 1979. Currently Fianna Fáil Spokesperson on Environment and Local Government.

OCCUPATION
Company director, farmer.

ADDRESS
Mountgarrett Castle, New Ross, Co Wexford.

PHONE
Constituency
(051) 421 771

Leinster House
(01) 618 3763
Fax (01) 618 4558

EMAIL
jim.walsh@oireachtas.ie

BORN
New Ross, May 1947

EDUCATION
New Ross CBS.

MARITAL STATUS
Married to Marie Furlong.
One son, two daughters

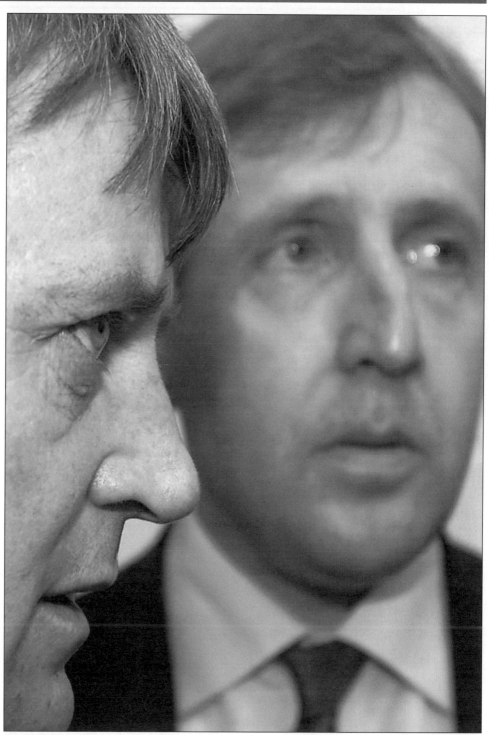

Gerard Murphy (LEFT) who pipped Fine Gael running mate Michael Creed by just 47 votes in Cork North West

MARK CONDREN

5 SEATS

3 Fianna Fáil
2 Fine Gael

FIRST PREFERENCES

MOONEY PASCHAL (FF)	**114**	Elected 12th count
HAYES BRIAN (FG)	**109**	Elected 16th count
Ó MURCHÚ LABHRÁS (FF)	**106**	Elected 14th count
COONAN NOEL (FG)	**101**	Elected 16th count
ORMONDE ANN (FF)	**101**	Elected 17th count
Brassil John Joseph (FF)	**72**	
Taylor-Quinn Madeleine (FG)	**68**	
Harty Mary (FG)	**64**	
McKenna Tony (FF)	**59**	
Ó Baoill Seán (np)	**47**	
Kelly Paul (FF)	**44**	
Ó Murchú Helen (np)	**22**	
Maher Frank (FF)	**14**	
Herity Michael (np)	**12**	
Crowley Aidan (FF)	**10**	
Hammond Richard (FG)	**8**	
Spearman David (np)	**4**	
Dillon Ellen B (np)	**1**	
Hoy Kevin (np)	**0**	

NOEL COONAN

FINE GAEL

Noel Coonan has been a member of Tipperary North County Council since 1991 and was a Dáil candidate in that constituency in 2002, gaining over 6,108 first preferences. Mid West health board

OCCUPATION
Full-time public representative

ADDRESS
Gortnagoona, Roscrea, Co Tipperary

PHONE
Constituency
(0504) 32 544
Fax (0504) 31 830

Leinster House
(01) 618 3842
Fax (01) 618 4789

EMAIL
noelcoonan@eircom.net/
noel.coonan@oireachtas.ie

BORN
Tipperary, January, 1951

EDUCATION
CBS Templemore

MARITAL STATUS
Married

BRIAN HAYES

FINE GAEL

Former Fine Gael National Youth & Education Officer Brian Hayes was a member of Seanad Éireann from 1995 to 1997, nominated by the then Taoiseach, John Bruton, and was elected to Dáil Éireann in 1997 for Dublin South West. Before the General Election he was Fine Gael Front Bench Spokesperson on Social and Community Affairs. He has been a member of South Dublin County Council since 1995.

OCCUPATION
Full-time public representative, former secondary school teacher

ADDRESS
48 Dunmore Park, Kingswood Heights, Tallaght, Dublin 24

PHONE
Constituency
(01) 462 6545

Leinster House
(01) 618 3567
Fax (01) 618 4563

EMAIL
brian.hayes@oireachtas.ie

BORN
Dublin, August 1969

EDUCATION
Garbally Park, Ballinasloe, Co Galway;
St Patrick's College, Maynooth (BA);
Trinity College Dublin (HdipEd)

MARITAL STATUS
Married. One son

PASCHAL MOONEY

FIANNA FÁIL

This well-known voice from the airwaves and professional Leitrim man has been a Senator since 1987 and a member of Leitrim County Council since 1991 as well as being active across the sport and cultural sector in the county and nationally. He is a member of the Fianna Fáil National Executive.

OCCUPATION
Public representative, journalist, broadcaster and businessman

ADDRESS
Carrick Road, Drumshambo, Co Leitrim

PHONE
Constituency
(071) 964 1236
Fax (071) 964 1237

Leinster House
(01) 618 3483
Fax (01) 618 4171

EMAIL
paschal.mooney@oireachtas.ie

BORN
Dublin, October 1947

EDUCATION
Carrick-on-Shannon Vocational College;
Camden Institute, London

MARITAL STATUS
Married to Sheila Baldrey.
Three sons, two daughters

LABHRÁS Ó MURCHÚ

FIANNA FÁIL

The Ard-stiurthoir of Comhaltas Ceoltóirí Éireann is now in his second term in the Seanad. His report on the needs of the Irish music industry, prepared for Minister Síle de Valera during the last administration, caused considerable controversy.

OCCUPATION
Public representative, Director General of Comhaltas Ceoltóirí Éireann

ADDRESS
An Bhoithrín Glas, Caiseal, Coe Thiobraid Árann

PHONE
Constituency
(062) 61 122

Leinster House
(01) 618 4018
Fax (01) 618 4588

BORN
August 1939

EDUCATION
CBS Cashel, Co Tipperary

MARITAL STATUS
Married to Úna Ni Ronáin

ANN ORMONDE

FIANNA FÁIL

First elected to the Seanad in 1993, Ann Ormonde contested the 1987, 1989, 1992 and 1997 General Elections for Fianna Fáil in Dublin South. She has been a member of Dublin County Council since 1985.

OCCUPATION
Public representative, counsellor

ADDRESS
2 Auburn Road, Dublin 4

PHONE
Constituency
(01) 260 5435

Leinster House
(01) 618 3030
Fax (01) 618 4573

EMAIL
ann.ormonde@oireachtas.ie

BORN
Kilmacthomas, Co Waterford

EDUCATION
Presentation Convent, Clonmel; UCD (MA[Psych], BComm, HdipEd, DC [Diploma in Career Guidance]).

MARITAL STATUS
Single

9 SEATS

6 Fianna Fáil
2 Fine Gael
1 Labour

FIRST PREFERENCES

McDOWELL, DEREK (Labour)	84	Elected 32nd count
BOHAN, EDDIE (FF)	60	Elected 32nd count
COGHLAN, PAUl (FF)	47	Elected 32nd count
BANNON, JAMES (FG)	46	Elected 30th count
MacSHARRY, MARC (FF)	42	Elected 32nd count
WHITE, MARY M (FF)	39	Elected 33rd count
Butler, Larry (FF)	38	
Clune, Deirdre (FG)	35	
PHELAN, KIERAN (FF)	35	Elected 29th count
Caffrey, Ernie (FG)	33	
McPadden, James (FG)	33	
Hughes, Brendan (FF)	32	
White, Mary A (Green)	32	
COX, MARGARET (FF)	29	Elected 32nd count
Kenneally, Brendan (FF)	26	
McGrath, Michael (FF)	25	
Colleary, Aidan (FF)	24	
Cahill, Michael (FF)	23	
Egan, John (FF)	23	
TERRY, SHIELA (FG)	23	Elected 33rd count
Jackman, Mary (FG)	22	
Hanley, Val (FF)	20	
O'Keeffe (FF)	18	
O'Meara, Pat (FF)	18	
McDonagh, Michael (FG)	17	
Keogh, Helen (FG)	14	
Moffatt, Dr Tom (FF)	14	
Fitzgerald, Ted (FF)	13	
Killally, Gerard (FF)	13	
Reilly, Jim (FG)	13	
Dowling, Patrick (FG)	12	
Lucey, Cormac (FG)	10	
Regan, Michael (FF)	9	
Mullins, John (FG)	7	
Bridgett, Andrew (FF)	3	
Hunter-McGowan, Thomas (np)	3	
Hennessy, Séamus (np)	0	
O'Muire, Toal (np)	0	

JAMES BANNON

FINE GAEL

Senator Bannon, who is now General Secretary of theLocal Authority Members Association, has been a member of Longford County Council since 1985, topping the poll in County Longford each time.

OCCUPATION
Full-time public representative, former farmer and auctioneer

ADDRESS
Newtown, Legan, Co Longford

PHONE
Constituency
(044) 57575

Leinster House
(01) 618 4226
Fax (01) 618 4398

EMAIL
james.bannon@oireachtas.ie

BORN
Legan, Co Longford

EDUCATION
Legan National School,
Convent of Mercy, Ballymahon

MARITAL STATUS
Single

EDDIE BOHAN

FIANNA FÁIL

A former President of the Vintner's Federation of Ireland and an Executive Member of the Dublin Licensed Vintners Association Eddie Bohan, a friend of fellow Longford man Albert Reynolds, has been a Senator since 1987.

OCCUPATION
Public representative, publican and auctioneer

ADDRESS
18 Orwell Park, Dublin 6.

PHONE
Constituency
(01) 475 4068/4753973

Leinster House
(01) 618 3391
Fax (01) 618 4171

EMAIL
eddie.bohan@oireachtas.ie

BORN
Longford, November 1932

EDUCATION
Longford Secondary School

MARITAL STATUS
Married to Betty Lambert.
One son, three daughters

PAUL COGHLAN

FINE GAEL

Paul Coghlan was first elected to the Industrial and Commercial Panel in 1997. A former member of Kerry County Council, Killarney UDC, and Dingle Harbour Commissioners, he is Vice Chairman of Kerry Fisheries and Coastal Management Committee and is a trustee and former Chairman of Muckross House. He is a member of the Institute of Bankers in Ireland.

OCCUPATION
Full-time public representative, auctioneer & valuer, insurance broker

ADDRESS
Ballydowney, Killarney, Co Kerry

PHONE
Constituency
(064) 31 733

Leinster House
(01) 618 3762
Fax (01) 618 4156

EMAIL
paul.coghlan@oireachtas.irl.ie

BORN
Killarney, June 1944

EDUCATION
St Brendan's College, Killarney

MARITAL STATUS
Married to Peggy O'Shea.
Two sons, three daughters

MARGARET COX

FIANNA FÁIL

Senator Cox, daughter of the late Tim Cox, well known in Galway politics and business, has been a member of the Seanad since 1997. Once again unsuccessful in the closely fought Galway West constituency, she is a member of Galway Corporation, the Western Health Board, the West Regional Authority, Galway County & City Enterprise Board and the General Council of County Councils.

OCCUPATION
Senator, Managing Director of ICE Group

ADDRESS
5 Fr Griffin Road, Galway

PHONE
Constituency
(091) 520 440
Fax (091) 585 070

Leinster House
(01) 618 3000
Fax (01) 618 4558

EMAIL
margaret.cox@oireachtas.ie

WEBSITE
www.margaretcox.ie

BORN
Galway, September 1963

EDUCATION
NUI Galway;
University of Limerick;
ACCA

MARITAL STATUS
Married to Felim McDonnell.
Two sons and two daughters

DEREK McDOWELL

LABOUR

Derek McDowell has been a member of Dublin Corporation since 1991 and was first elected to Dáil Éireann in 1992 in Dublin North Central. He has been Labour Spokesperson on both Health and Finance and was the key figure in the drafting of the economic policies in the Labour manifesto at the last election. During the "Spring Tide" he topped the poll with over 10,000 votes only to see his first preferences fall to under 3,000 in 1997 and 4,203 this time around.

OCCUPATION
Public representative, solicitor

ADDRESS
3 Dunluce Road. Clontarf, Dublin 3

PHONE
Constituency
(01) 833 6138

Leinster House
(01) 618 3251
Fax (01) 618 4664

EMAIL
derek.mcdowell@oireachtas.ie

WEBSITE
www.derekmcdowell.ie

BORN
Dublin, September 1958

EDUCATION
Árd Scoil Rís, Marino;
University College Dublin;
Incorporated Law Society of Ireland.

MARITAL STATUS
Married to Vicki Barrett

MARC MacSHARRY

FIANNA FÁIL

Senator Mac-Sharry was a Member of Fianna Fail National Youth Committee in 1994 and Assistant Director of Elections for the European Parliament in Sligo/Leitrim Constituency for Fianna Fail in the same year. A member of the.Seanad Spokesperson for Marine and Natural Resources All Ireland Amateur One Act Drama Champion in 1997

OCCUPATION
Seanator, CEO Sligo Chamber of Commerce 2000

ADDRESS
'Fatima', Pearse Road, Sligo

PHONE
Constituency
086 2674 764

Leinster House
(01) 618 4221
Fax: (01) 618 4357

EMAIL
mmacsharry@oireachtas.ie

BORN
Dublin, July, 1973

EDUCATION
Castleknock College, Dublin;
Cert. in Advanced Spanish in El Colegio De Espana, Alicante, Spain

MARITAL STATUS
Recently engaged to Marie Murphy

KIERAN PHELAN

FIANNA FÁIL

This new senator is a life-long member of Fianna Fáil and a member of Laois Co Council since 1991, topping the poll in his area in 1999. He is chairman of the East Coast and Midland Tourism Board and vice chair of Midland Regional Authority and the Laois VEC.

OCCUPATION
Farmer, Senator

ADDRESS
Raheen Upper, Donaghmore, Portlaoise, Co Laois

PHONE
Leinster House
(01) 618 4476
Fax (01) 618 4558

EMAIL
kieran.phelan@ oireachtas.ie

BORN
Rathdowney, Co Laois, November 1949

EDUCATION
Roscrea CBS;
Multifarnham, Co Westmeath
(Dip. Ag.)

MARITAL STATUS
Married to Mary.
Four girls, one boy

SHEILA TERRY

FINE GAEL

Originally from Cork, former PD Sheila Terry has represented Castleknock and Blanchardstown on the County Council since 1991 and was elected Chairperson of Fingal County Council after the 1999 election. A Board Member of the Draiocht Arts Centre and Blanchardstown Area Partnership, organiser for the Chernobyl Children's appeal.and a committee member of ROOFS – Blanchardstown housing for the homeless - she obtained 3.694 first preferences in Dublin West in 2002.

OCCUPATION
County councillor, mother, wife, former substitute teacher and childcare worker

ADDRESS
65 College Grove, Castleknock, Dublin 15

PHONE
Leinster House
(01) 6184219
Fax (01) 6184354

EMAIL
sheila.terry@fingalcoco.ie
sheila.terry@oireachtas.ie

WEBSITE
www.sheilaterry.com

BORN
Cork, 1950

EDUCATION
St Aloysius School, Carrigtwohill, Co Cork;
secretarial course
Skerries College, Cork

MARITAL STATUS
Married to Michael.
Four sons

MARY M WHITE

FIANNA FÁIL

In the 1970s Mary White's interest in politics sent her back to UCD to study th subject at night. Her political activities are driven by her passion for peace in the North. She represented Dublin women on the Fianna Faíl National Executive from 1993-98 and is the party spokesperson in the Seanad on Enterprise, Trade and Employment (Trade and commerce).

OCCUPATION
Senator, marketing director/sales manager Lir Chocolates

ADDRESS
6 Wickham Park Road, Dundrum, Dublin 6

PHONE
Leinster House
(01) 618 3233
Fax 6184793

EMAIL
lirchocolates@eircom.net

BORN
Dundalk 1944

EDUCATION
Holy Family Convent, Droichead Nua, Co Kildare;
College of Technology, Bolton Street, Dublin;
University College Dublin
(Politics and Economics)

MARITAL STATUS
Padraig White.
One daughter

11 SEATS

6 Fianna Fáil
4 Fine Gael
1 Labour

FIRST PREFERENCES

FITZGERALD, LIAM (FF)	**85**	Elected 1st count
HIGGINS, JIM (FG)	**68**	Elected 7th count
LYDON, DON (FF)	**66**	Elected 9th count
McCARTHY, MICHAEL (Labour)	**64**	Elected 12th count
CUMMINS, MAURICE (FG)	**54**	Elected 19th count
FINUCANE, MICHAEL (FG)	**51**	Elected 20th count
Cregan, Denis (Dino) (FG)	**50**	
LEYDEN, TERRY (FF)	**50**	Elected 14th count
BROWNE, FEARGAL (FG)	**48**	Elected 21st count
DALY, BRENDAN (FF)	**45**	Elected 14th count
FEENEY, GERALDINE (FF)	**45**	Elected 14th count
HANAFIN, JOHN (FF)	**44**	Elected 15th count
Sinnott, Kathryn (Ind)	**44**	
Geraghty, Des (Labour)	**39**	
Wade, Eddie (FF)	**36**	
Kiely, Dan (FF)	**32**	
Ridge, Thérèse (FG)	**30**	
Andrews, Chris (FF)	**25**	
Collins, Seán (FF)	**25**	
Kelly, Rody P (FF)	**23**	
Keegan, Garry (FF)	**18**	
Lyons, Seán (Ind)	**13**	

FERGAL BROWNE

FINE GAEL

Fergal Browne who stood for the Dáil in Carlow-Kilkenny is a new Senator, elected to the Labour Panel in July 2002. He is the son of Deputy John Browne, TD for Carlow-Kilkenny 1989–2002 and was elected to Carlow Town Council, where he is currently Vice-Chairman, in June 1999, gaining a seat for Fine Gael.

OCCUPATION
Public representative, former primary school teacher

ADDRESS
61, Old Burrin, Carlow

PHONE
Constituency
(059) 913 5356
Fax (059) 913 3159

Leinster House
(01) 618 3295
Fax (01) 618 4522

EMAIL
brownefergal@eircom.net
fergal.browne@oireachtas.ie

BORN
Carlow, September 1973

EDUCATION
St Mary's Academy, Station Road, Carlow;
NUI Maynooth
(Higher Diploma in ICT);
St Patrick's College, Drumcondra, Dublin (B.Ed.)

MARITAL STATUS
Single

MAURICE CUMMINS

FINE GAEL

Maurice Cummins, a new Senator, elected to Seanad Éireann (Labour Panel) in July 2002 Maurice Cummins has been a member of Waterford City Council since 1979. was Mayor of Waterford 1995-1996, and in Brussels represents the South east on the Council for the Regions. He is a former President of the FAI Schoolboys and Youth and Chairman of the Waterford International Festival of Light Opera.

OCCUPATION
Full-time public representative, former claims manager with transport and shipping company

ADDRESS
34 Ursuline Court, Waterford

PHONE
Constituency
(051) 855 486
Fax (051) 856 702

Leinster House
(01) 618 4206

EMAIL
maurice.cummins@indigo.ie/
maurice.cummins@oireachtas.ie

BORN
Waterford, 1953

EDUCATION
De la Salle College, Waterford;
Cert Planning Law

MARITAL STATUS
Married, two children

BRENDAN DALY

FIANNA FÁIL

Brendan Daly represented Clare in the Dáil from 1973-92 and from 1997 but fell victim to health campaigner and former Fianna Fáil councillor James Breen this time around. He was elected to the Seanad in 1993 and returns there in 2002. First elected 1973. He has been Minister for Social Welfare (1991), Defence (1991), Marine (1987-89, during the rod licence dispute) and Fisheries and Forestry (1982).

OCCUPATION
Full-time public representative

ADDRESS
Cooraclare, Kilrush, Co Clare

PHONE
Constituency
(065) 905 9040

Leinster House
(01) 618 3033
Fax (01) 618 4534

EMAIL
brendan.daly@oireachtas.ie

BORN
Cooraclare, Co Clare
February 1940

EDUCATION
Kilrush CBS, Co. Clare

MARITAL STATUS
Married to Patricia Carmody.
Two sons and one daughter

GERALDINE FEENEY

FIANNA FÁIL

Senator Feeney has been a member of the Fianna Fáil National Executive, elected to the Committee of Fifteen, since 1993. She has just completed five years on An Bord Altranais. As a member of the Medical Council attracted adverse publicity in 2001 over over her wish to see the "X" case verdict on termination incorporated into Irish medical practise. She is now, as Chair of its Ethics Committee, the first lay person to chair any committee of the Medical Council.

OCCUPATION
Senator,
former public relations consultant

ADDRESS
Ard Caoin, Sligo, Co Sligo

PHONE
(071) 914 5690
Fax (071) 914 5606

Leinster House
(01) 618 3905
Fax (01) 618 4791

EMAIL
geraldine.feeney@oireachtas.ie

BORN
Tullamore, Co Offaly

EDUCATION
Tullamore;
University College Galway

MARITAL STATUS
Widowed, two boys and two girls

MICHAEL FINUCANE

FINE GAEL

A member of Limerick County Council since 1985, Finucane was Fine Gael Spokesman on Defence from June 2000 the position after Michael Noonan's election as party leader. He represented Limerick West from 1989 until 2002 when Fianna Fáil solved local problems to win the seat. As spokesperson on Marine and Natural Resources 1997-2000 he fought to prevent EU cutbacks in the Irish fishing fleet. He has also been spokesperson on Commerce and Technology and Taxation.

OCCUPATION
Senator,
formerly recruitment and training consultant and shipping agency manager

ADDRESS
Ardnacrohy, Newcastle West,
Co Limerick

PHONE
Constituency
(069) 40154
Fax (069) 61946

Leinster House
(01) 618 3745
Fax (01) 618 4507

EMAIL
michael.finucane@oireachtas.ie

BORN
Limerick, February 1943

EDUCATION
St Senan's Secondary School,
Foynes;
Dip Ind Eng.

MARITAL STATUS
Married.
One son, two daughter

LIAM FITZGERALD

FIANNA FÁIL

The former TD for Dublin North East from 1981–February 1982 and November 1982-1997 joined the Senate Labour Panel in 1997. Chairman of the City of Dublin VEC from 1985-88 and on the DIT governing body from 1985-91 he has been a member of Dublin City Council since 1985, and was elected an Alderman 1991.

OCCUPATION
Public Representative,
former primary school teacher

ADDRESS
117 Tonlegee Road, Raheny,
Dublin 5

PHONE
Constituency
(01) 847 0632

Leinster House
(01) 618 3152
Fax (01) 618 4587

EMAIL
liam.fitzgerald@oireachtas.ie

BORN
Doon, Co Limerick,
September 1949

EDUCATION
CBS, Doon;
St Patrick's Teacher Training College, Drumcondra, Dublin;
UCD (BA, HDipEd).

MARITAL STATUS
Married to Brid Lynch.
Three sons, two daughters

JOHN GERARD HANAFIN

FIANNA FÁIL

John Hanafin, is the son of former Senator Des Hanafin and brother of Minister Mary Hanafin. Co-opted to North Tipperary County Council on the death of his aunt Jane (Binkie) Hanafin in 1998 he chairs its Economic, Social and Cultural Special Policiy Committee. In the Seanad he is government spokesperson at Enterprise, Trade and Employment on Labour and Training.

OCCUPATION
Senator, auctioneer and valuer

ADDRESS
The Retreat, Richmond, Templemore, Co Tipperary

PHONE
Constituency
Phone and fax (0504) 31560

Leinster House
(01) 618 3000

EMAIL
hanafinj@eircom.net

BORN
Thurles, September 1960

EDUCATION
CBS Thurles;
Cistercian College, Roscrea;
College of Marketing and Design, Dublin;
University College Cork;
University College Dublin

MARITAL STATUS
Married to Linda Cummins.
One daughter, two sons

JIM HIGGINS

FINE GAEL

Jim Higgins was was first elected to the Dáil for Mayo in 1987 having contested the General Elections of June 1981, February and November 1982, He was on the Fine Gael Front Bench from 1997-2002 having previously been a Minister of State from 1995-97 He served two Seanad terms between June 1981 and 1987 and was a member of Mayo County Council from 1979-95. An outstanding public debater he was outspoken in the Dáil over the appointment of former Supreme Court Judge Hugh O'Flaherty to the European Investment Bank.

OCCUPATION
Full-time public representative, former community school teacher

ADDRESS
Devlis, Ballyhaunis, Co Mayo

PHONE
Constituency
(094) 963 0052
Fax (094) 963 1356

Leinster House
(01) 618 3109
Fax (01) 618 4582

EMAIL
jim.higgins @oireachtas.ie

BORN
Ballyhaunis, May 1945

EDUCATION
St Jarlath's College, Tuam;
University College Galway
(BA, HDipEd)

MARITAL STATUS
Married to Marian Hannan.
Four daughters

TERRY LEYDEN

FIANNA FÁIL

Senator Leyden is a rarity in that he returns to the Oireachtas after an absence of nine years. The former Minister for Trade and Marketing ((1989-92) is a member of Roscommon County Council and the Western Regional Authority. His work as an Election Monitor in Bosnia in September 1998 led to the founding of Kosova Regional Aid, which is still functioning and a keen interest in return to normal life for the peoples of the Balkans.

OCCUPATION
Full-time public representative, former trade and marketing consultant

ADDRESS
Castlecoote, Roscommon

PHONE
Constituency
(090) 662 6422
Mobile: 087-797 8922

Leinster House
(01) 618 3000

EMAIL
leydenterry@eircom.net

WEBSITE
www.geocities.com/leydenterry

BORN
October 1945

EDUCATION
Vocational School, Roscommon;
National University of Ireland Galway (Extra-mural Diploma in Politics, Sociology and Economics)

MARITAL STATUS
Married to Mary O'Connor.
Three girls, one boy

DON LYDON

FIANNA FÁIL

Don Lydon has been a County Councillor in Dublin since 1985, currently serving on Dun Laoghaire Rathdown CC, is a member of the Dublin Regional Authority and has been a member of Seanad Éireann since 1987 where he is Spokesperson for Foreign Affairs with special responsibility for Human Rights. He has served on the Dublin County Local Health Committee. He is an Associate Fellow of the Psychological Society of Ireland and the British Psychological Society.

OCCUPATION
Public Representative, psychologist

ADDRESS
Santo Antonio, Stillorgan Park Avenue, Stillorgan, Co Dublin.

PHONE
Constituency
(01) 288 8741

Leinster House
(01) 618 3677
Fax (01) 618 4173

EMAIL
don.lydon@oireachtas.ie

BORN
August 1938

EDUCATION
St Eunan's College, Letterkenny;
University College Galway;
University College Dublin

MARITAL STATUS
Married to Maeve Ryan

MICHAEL McCARTHY

LABOUR

At 25, Michael McCarthy, who is a Councillor on Cork County Council, is Labour's youngest member of the Oireachtas. His 3,442 votes in the General Election represents an increase of over 1,000 in the Labour vote. A cousin of former Senator Michael Calnan he was co-opted to the Labour National Youth Committee in 1997 and continues the strong tradition of Labour Party politicians throughout the country who have hailed from Dunmanway

OCCUPATION
Senator, former process operator Schering Plough

ADDRESS
Castle Street, Dunmanway, Co Cork

PHONE
and Fax (023) 45 011

Leinster House
(01) 618 3844
Fax (01) 618 4330

EMAIL
michaelmccarthyccc@eircom.net

BORN
Bantry, November 1976

EDUCATION
Colaiste Chairbe, Dunmanway

MARITAL STATUS
Single

Oisín O Driscoll takes a nap during the Cork East count in Mallow

MARK CONDREN

Taoiseach picks 6 FF and 4 PDs for Seanad

ELEVEN members of the Seanad are appointed by the Taoiseach of the day. They most important aspect of this power is that it helps to ensure that the government has a majority in the Seanad. Those appointed thus typically come from the government party or parties, and Bertie Ahern's list is unexceptional in this regard, containing six Fianna Fáil members and four PDs. For some time now the Taoiseach has also appointed someone from Northern Ireland. This time, again, it was Dr Maurice Hayes, who has become well known around the country as Chairman of the Forum on Europe. Unlike 1997, when the businessman Dr Edward Haughey was also appointed, in 2002 there is only one such appointment.

The PD senators, their party's only representation in the Seanad, include the party chairman John Minihan.

The Seanad supposedly provides an aspiring TD with a good base to win a Dáil seat, but none of the 1997 PD senators made such use of their position. Jim Gibbons and Mairín Quill did not stand. John Dardis stood unsuccessfully, as did Helen Keogh – but for Fine Gael! Three of the party's 2002 nominees stood for the Dáil in 2002, and all four might be expected to be candidates in the future – perhaps with a little more success.

The Fianna Fáil nominees are all new senators, although Mary O'Rourke was once in the Seanad before, and several of them will also hope to be candidates for the Dáil next time around.

CYPRIAN BRADY

FIANNA FÁIL

Cyprian Brady is a former civil servant, a member of Fianna Fáil for the past 23 years and a close associate of the Taoiseach for whom he has acted as constituency organiser and manager. He had been viewed as Ahern's choice for running mate in his Dublin Central constituency but Dr Dermot Fitzpatrick was selected at the convention and subsequently won a Dáil seat. Senator Fitzpatrick was one of the Taoiseach's Eleven in 1997.

OCCUPATION
Public representative, former civil servant

ADDRESS
St Luke's, 161 Lower Drumcondra Road, Dublin 9

PHONE
Constituency
(01) 847 6020

Leinster House
(01) 618 4249
Fax (01) 618 4784

EMAIL
cbrady@oireachtas.ie

BORN
Dublin, July 1962

EDUCATION
St Joseph's CBS, Fairview, Dublin

MARITAL STATUS
Married to Valerie.
One boy, one girl

MICHAEL BRENNAN

FIANNA FÁIL

The Chairman of Limerick County Council has had a stormy relationship with his party over the years. Co-opted onto Limerick County Council in 1983 to replace Fine Gael's Michael Noonan, he stood as an independent in the 1997 general election when he failed to get the party nomination. When Michael Collins TD did not retire this time around Brennan stood down, expecting to be added to the ticket. The Seanad seat perhaps indicates a reward for good behaviour and a pledge for the future. Senator Brennan is a firm believer in the abolition of the Dual Mandate.

OCCUPATION
Full-time public representative, former manager, Adare Heritage Centre

ADDRESS
14 Park Avenue, Adare, Co Limerick

PHONE
Constituency
(061) 396408

Leinster House
(01) 618 3845
Fax (01) 618 4655

EMAIL
michael.brennan@oireachtas.ie

BORN
Adare, Co Limerick, 1945

MARITAL STATUS
Married to Rose Houlihan.
Five children

JOHN DARDIS

PROGRESSIVE DEMOCRATS

John Dardis has been a member of Kildare County Council since 1989 and a member of Seanad Éireann since 1991 and is a member of the Mid East Regional Authority. He was PD candidate for Kildare South in 1997 and 2002. As well as his farming interests he has a keen interest in angling, the arts, and rugby.

OCCUPATION
Farmer, agricultural journalist, public representative

ADDRESS
Belmont House, Athgarvan, Newbridge, Co Kildare

PHONE
Constituency
(045) 431 665
Fax (045) 434 794

Mobile (087) 255 5205

Leinster House
(01) 618 3559

EMAIL
johndardis@eircom.net

BORN
Newbridge, Co Kildare, 1945

EDUCATION
Dominican College, Newbridge; University College Dublin (BAgrSc)

MARITAL STATUS
Married to Beatrice Lane.
One son, two daughters

MAURICE HAYES

OTHER

First appointed in 1997, he sits as an independent and has been Chairman of the National Forum on Europe since 2001. After seven years teaching and many more in local government, Hayes became Chairman of the Community Relations Council in Northern Ireland in 1969. In 1972, with the introduction of direct rule from Westminster, he left local government for the civil service where he served in several departments and was Ombudsman 1987-91. In 1998 he was appointed to the Patten Commission. He is chairman of the Advisory Committee of the Ireland Funds and a director of Independent Newspapers.

OCCUPATION
Former teacher, local government official, civil servant, ombudsman, author

ADDRESS
5 Bullseye Park, Downpatrick, Co Down, BT30 63X

PHONE
Constituency
(0044) 776 429 0900

Leinster House
(01) 618 3418
Fax (01) 618 4565

EMAIL
maurice.Hayes@oireachtas.ie

BORN
Killough, Co Down, July 1927

EDUCATION
Queen's University, Belfast
(BA Eng.Lit.)

MARITAL STATUS
Married to Joan Ross.
Three sons, two daughters

BRENDAN KENNEALLY

FIANNA FÁIL

Kenneally was TD for Waterford from1989-2002 and Minister of State 1992-93. Personal Record:. He was a Member of Waterford Corporation 1985 – 1992 and Mayor of Waterford 1988/1989. The son of Billy Kenneally TD for Waterford 1965 - 1982 and grandson of William Kenneally, TD 1952 – 1961, he suggested on occasion that newcomers to the Fianna Fáil party, and allied independents, get more recognition than faithful backbenchers.

OCCUPATION
Full-time public representative, former accountant

ADDRESS
'Hillside House', Dunmore Road, Waterford

PHONE
Constituency
(051) 855 964
Fax (051) 850 597

Leinster House
(01) 618 3474
Fax (01) 618 4528

EMAIL
brendan.kenneally@oireachtas.ie
bwk@eircom.net

WEBSITE
www.brendankenneally.com

BORN
Waterford, April 1955

EDUCATION
De La Salle College, Waterford;
Waterford RTC

MARITAL STATUS
Married to Martina Crotty.
One son, three daughters

MICHAEL KITT

FIANNA FÁIL

Michael Kitt first represented Galway East in the 1975 by-election following the death of his father Michael F Kitt, lost the seat in 1977, and was re-elected in 1981 and at each subsequent election. A member of Galway Co. Council from 1975-91 he was Minister of State 1991-92 and lost his seat to party colleague Joe Callanan in 2002. Brother of Tom Kitt, Dáil Deputy for Dublin South and Minister of State.

OCCUPATION
Full-time public representative, former teacher

ADDRESS
Castleblakeney, Ballinasloe, Co Galway.

PHONE
Constituency
(090) 967 8147
Fax: (090) 967 8148

Leinster House
(01) 618 3473
Fax (01) 618 4555

EMAIL
michaelp.kitt@oireachtas.ie

WEBSITE
www.mpkitt.com

BORN
Tuam, Co Galway, May 1950

EDUCATION
St Jarlath's College, Tuam;
St Patrick's Teacher Training College, Drumcondra, Dublin;
UCD (BA, HdipED); UCG

MARITAL STATUS
Married to Catherine Mannion.
Three sons, one daughter

JOHN MINIHAN

PROGRESSIVE DEMOCRATS

John Minihan was commissioned in 1976 and served in the army both at home and with the United Nations until he retired in 1996 to take over the family chemist's shop in Cork. In 1999 he joined the PDs, was elected to Cork City Council and, in late 1999, became Chairman of the PDs. Although he failed to gain a seat in Cork North Central he was nominated to the Seanad by the Taoiseach and is Chairman of the Parliamentary Party.

OCCUPATION
Former army officer, businessman

ADDRESS
Loreto Park, Douglas Road, Cork.

PHONE
Constituency
(021) 480 3624
Fax (021) 480 6309

Leinster House
(01) 618 4347
Fax (01) 618 4651

EMAIL
minihan@indigo.ie
jminihan@corkcorp.ie

BORN
Cork, 1958

EDUCATION
Farranferris College, Cork;
Army Cadet School

MARITAL STATUS
Married to Trish.
Two sons

TOM MORRISSEY

PROGRESSIVE DEMOCRATS

Elected to Dublin County Council in June 1991 as a Fine Gael councillor and re-elected to Fingal County Council in June 1999 for the PDs Senator Morrissey represented Castleknock from 1991-97 and was one of those who voted against the Quarryvale development.

OCCUPATION
Self employed printing company managing director

ADDRESS
34 Castleknock View, Castleknock, Dublin 15

PHONE
Constituency
(01) 820 2218
Fax (01) 822 0125

Leinster House
(01) 618 4236
Fax (01) 618 4796

EMAIL
icdp@indigo.ie

WEBSITE
www.icdp.ie

BORN
July 1956

EDUCATION
College of Commerce, Limerick (BSc Marketing)

MARITAL STATUS
Married to Betty. Two sons

PAT MOYLAN

FIANNA FÁIL

Pat is a new Senator and has been a member of Offaly CC since 1975. He is also a member of the Midland Health Board: Midland Regional Authority and the EU Committee of the Regions. He is the Fianna Fáil Spokesperson on Tourism, Sport & Recreation in An Seanad and is a member of the Joint House Services Committee.

OCCUPATION

ADDRESS
Harbour Road, Banagher, Co Offaly

PHONE
Constituency
(0509) 51 113
Fax (0509) 51858

Leinster House
(01) 618 3698
Fax (01) 618 4614

BORN
Banagher, Co Offaly

EDUCATION
Banagher Vocational School

MARITAL STATUS
Married to Mary Dunne. Three sons, one daughter

MARY O'ROURKE

FIANNA FÁIL

O'Rourke was a Senator from 1981 to 1982 and was elected to the Dáil in November 1982 and at each subsequent Election, being Deputy leader of Fianna Fáil from 1994 until she came to grief in a Westmeath vote management accident. She has held various ministerial portfolios, most recently that of Public Enterprise in the outgoing government. She is a sister of the late Brian Lenihan, TD and Minister, daughter of PJ Lenihan, TD 1965-70 and aunt of Deputies Brian and Conor Lenihan. She is Leader of Seanad Eireann and Spokeswoman on Northern Ireland.

OCCUPATION
Full-time public representative; former teacher

ADDRESS
Aisling, Arcadia, Athlone, Co Westmeath.

PHONE
Constituency
(090) 647 2313
Fax (090) 647 8218

Leinster House
(01) 618 3703
Fax (01) 618 4790

EMAIL
mary.o.rourke@oireachtas.ie

BORN
Athlone, Co Westmeath, May 1937

EDUCATION
Loreto Convent, Bray, Co Wicklow; University College Dublin; St Patrick's College, Maynooth (BA, HDipEd)

MARITAL STATUS
Married to the late Enda O'Rourke. Two sons

KATE WALSH

PROGRESSIVE DEMOCRATS

Kate Walsh fought the General Election in Kildare North and considerably increased the Progressive Democrat vote. A community activist with a long record of service to local charities she was elected to Kildare County Council in 1999, topping the poll in Celbridge with a quota and a half and is honorary Lord Mayor of Celbridge, a position she has held for most of the last 20 years. She is a Taoiseach's nominee to the Seanad on the recommendation of the Tanaiste.

OCCUPATION
Family business

ADDRESS
Main Street, Celbridge, Co Kildare.

PHONE
Constituency
(01) 628 8118
Mobile (087) 259 7766

Leinster House
(01) 618 4078
Fax (01) 618 3655

EMAIL
kate@katewalsh.ie

WEBSITE
www.katewalsh.ie

BORN
Ballyfoyle, Mageney, Co Laois, March 1947

EDUCATION
St Leo's Convent of Mercy, Carlow

MARITAL STATUS
Married to the late Eugene

NATIONAL UNIVERSITY 3 SEATS

2 Independents
1 Labour

FIRST PREFERENCES

QUINN, FEARGAL	**5640**	Elected 11th count
O'TOOLE, JOE	**5463**	Elected 12th count
RYAN, BRENDAN (LAB)	**4264**	Elected 12th count
O'Sullivan, Bernadine	**4054**	
Bresnihan, Valerie	**2856**	
Price, Brendan	**2035**	
O'Shea-Farren, Linda	**1533**	
Purcell, Pierce	**1295**	
Mac Carthaigh, Daithí	**1273**	
O'Callaghan, Jim	**1239**	
Griffin, Michael	**961**	
Harmey, Matthew	**590**	
Murphy, Noel	**354**	
Cosgrave, Michael	**273**	
O'Higgins, Colm	**226**	
ó Gógáin, Liam	**191**	

DUBLIN UNIVERSITY 3 SEATS

3 Independents

FIRST PREFERENCES

NORRIS, DAVID	**3493**	Elected 4th count
ROSS, SHANE	**3465**	Elected 5th count
HENRY, MARY	**2123**	Elected 9th count
Bacik, Ivana	**1591**	
Barrett, Seán	**994**	
Guéret, Maurice	**780**	
McDonagh, Rosaleen	**733**	
O'Meara, PJ	**265**	
Martin, David	**212**	
Kulkarni, Prabhu	**185**	
McHugh, Gerard	**156**	
O'Donnell, Anthony	**142**	
Boland, Declan	**98**	

Senator David Norris pushes his bicycle through the disinfecting mats at Leinster House during the foot and mouth crisis

JOE O'TOOLE

INDEPENDENT

Joe O'Toole, a senator since 1987, is a teacher by profession, and the former General Secretary of the Irish National Teachers' Organisation and President of the Irish Congress of Trade Unions (ICTU). He is also an executive member of the European Trade Union Committee on Education (ETUCE).

OCCUPATION
Public representative, former teacher, President ICTU

ADDRESS
Kilsallaghan, Co Dublin

PHONE
Leinster House
(01) 618 3786
Fax 618 4155,

EMAIL
jotoole@oireachtas.ie

WEBSITE
www.senator-joeotoole.ie

BORN
Dingle, Co Kerry, July 1947

EDUCATION
CBS Dingle;
St Patrick's Teachers' Training College, Dublin;
Maynooth College (H.dipEd);
UCD (BA)

MARITAL STATUS
Married to Joan Lynam.
Five children

FEARGAL QUINN

INDEPENDENT

First elected as an NUI senator in 1993, Fergal Quinn developed and runs the Superquinn chain of supermarkets. He is also a former chairman of An Post. His website is one of the most useful for those wishing to follow Oireachtas affairs.

OCCUPATION
Public representative, grocer

ADDRESS
Sutton Cross, Dublin 13

PHONE
(01) 816 7163
Fax (01) 816 7162

Leinster House
(01) 618 4346
Fax (01) 618 4155

EMAIL
himself@feargalquinn.ie

WEBSITE
www.feargalquinn.ie

BORN
Dublin, 1936

EDUCATION
Newbridge College;
University College Dublin (Bcomm)

MARITAL STATUS
Married to Denise Prendergast.
Three sons, two daughters

BRENDAN RYAN

LABOUR

Unique among the university senators in listing a political affiliation, in being a current Dail candidate and in not being based in Dublin, Brendan Ryan, Cork South Central Labour candidate was elected to Seanad Eireann 1981-93 and re-elected 1997 and 2002.

OCCUPATION
Senator, Lecturer in Chemical Engineering, Cork Institute of Technology

ADDRESS
16 The Orchards,
Middle Glanmire Road, Cork

PHONE
Leinster House
(01) 618 3417
Fax (01) 618 4192

EMAIL
brendan.ryan@oireachtas.ie
brryan@indigo.ie

BORN
Dublin, August 1946

EDUCATION
CBS, Athy;
Divine Word Seminary;
University College Dublin

MARITAL STATUS
Married.
Three children

MARY HENRY

INDEPENDENT

Senator for Dublin University and a practising hospital consultant Mary Henry is President elect of The Irish Association and also finds time to be President of Cherish, to be a trustee of the TCD Association and Trust, and to be a member of the Ethics Committee of the Irish Hospitals Consultants Association, the Royal Irish Academy of Medicine, the National Economic and Social Forum and numerous other professional, charitable and educational bodies.

OCCUPATION
Senator, Consultant, Rotunda and Adelaide Hospitals

ADDRESS
12 Burlington Road, Dublin 4

PHONE
Constituency
(01) 668 3663

Leinster House
(01) 618 3346
Fax: (01) 618 4155

EMAIL
mary.henry@oireachtas.ie

WEBSITE
www.senatormaryhenry.ie

BORN
Blackrock, Cork, May 1940

EDUCATION
Rochelle School, Cork; Alexandra College, Dublin; Trinity College Dublin (MD, MB, BA, BCh, MA)

MARITAL STATUS
Married to John McEntagart.
One daughter, two sons

DAVID NORRIS

INDEPENDENT

Senator for Dublin University since 1987, and one of the more colourful contributors to Seanad debates, Norris is a noted Joyce scholar, a prominent gay rights campaigner and a member of An Taisce, Amnesty International and the Irish Georgian Society.

OCCUPATION
Senator, former university lecturer, TCD

ADDRESS
Seanad Éireann, Kildare Street, Dublin 2

PHONE
Leinster House
(01) 618 3104
Fax (01) 618 4155

EMAIL
david.norris@oireachtas.ie

WEBSITE
www.davidnorris.ie

BORN
Belgian Congo, July 1944

EDUCATION
St Andrew's College;
The High School, Dublin;
Reade Pianoforte School;
Trinity College Dublin.

MARITAL STATUS
Single

SHANE ROSS

INDEPENDENT

Son of former senator John A Ross, and a senator since for Dublin University since 1981, Shane Ross ran as a Fine Gael Candidate in the 1992 General Election but has since left the party. Identified flaws in the government's bill to restrict opinion polling during election campaigns, which led to the bill being dropped.

OCCUPATION
Public representative, Business Editor, *Sunday Independent*

ADDRESS
Askefield House, Dublin Road, Bray, Co Wicklow

PHONE
(01) 295 4276

Leinster House
(01) 618 4475

EMAIL
shane.ross@oireachtas.ie

WEBSITE
www.shane-ross.ie

BORN
Dublin, July 1939

EDUCATION
Rugby School;
Trinity College Dublin

MARITAL STATUS
Married to Ruth Buchanan.
One son, one daughter

The new government assembles before the start of the first cabinet meeting of the 29th Dáil at Farmleigh in the Phoenix Park

PHOTOCALL

David Trimble addresses a Unionist Party election rally

OVERALL RESULTS

Party	Votes	Share	Seats
UUP	216,839	26.8%	6
DUP	181,999	22.5%	5
Sinn Féin	175,392	21.7%	4
SDLP	169,865	21.0%	3
Alliance	28,999	3.6%	
UKUP	13,509	1.7%	
PUP	4,781	0.6%	
NIWC	2,968	0.4%	
Conservatives	2,422	0.3%	
WP	2,352	0.3%	
NIUP	1,794	0.2%	
Others	8,913	1.5%	

ANTRIM EAST
UUP hold

R Beggs	UUP	13101	36.4%
S Wilson	DUP	12973	36.0%
J Matthews	All	4483	12.5%
D O'Connor	SDLP	2641	7.3%
R Mason	Ind	1092	3.0%
J Graffi	SF	903	2.5%
A Greer	Con	807	2.2%
TOTAL		36000	59.1%
Electorate		60897	
Majority UUP		**128**	**0.36%**

ANTRIM NORTH
DUP hold

I Paisley	DUP	24539	49.9%
L Scott	UUP	10315	20.9%
S Farren	SDLP	8283	16.8%
J Kelly	SF	4822	9.8%
J Dunlop	All	1258	2.6%
TOTAL		49217	66.1%
Electorate		74451	
Majority DUP		**14224**	**28.9%**

ANTRIM SOUTH
UUP hold

D Burnside	UUP	16366	37.1%
W McCrea	DUP	15355	34.8%
S McKee	SDLP	5336	12.1%
M Meehan	SF	4160	9.4%
D Ford	All	1969	4.5%
N Boyd	NIUP	972	2.2%
TOTAL		44158	62.50%
Electorate		70651	
Majority UUP		**1011**	**2.29%**

BELFAST EAST
DUP hold

P Robinson	DUP	15667	42.5%
T Lemon	UUP	8550	23.2%
D Alderdice	All	5832	15.8%
D Ervine	PUP	3669	9.9%
J O'Donnell	SF	1237	3.4%
C Farren	SDLP	880	2.4%
T Dick	Con	800	2.2%
J Bell	WP	123	0.3%
R G Weiss	VFYP	71	0.2%
TOTAL		36829	63.0%
Electorate		58455	
Majority DUP		**7117**	**19.3%**

BELFAST SOUTH
UUP hold

M Smyth	UUP	17008	44.8%
A McDonnell	SDLP	11609	30.6%
M McWilliams	NIWC	2968	7.8%
A Maskey	SF	2894	7.6%
G Rice	All	2042	5.4%
D Purvis	PUP	1112	2.9%
P Lynn	WP	204	0.5%
RG Weiss	VFYP	115	0.3%
TOTAL		37952	63.8%
Electorate		59436	
Majority UUP		**5399**	**14.23%**

BELFAST NORTH
DUP gain from UUP

N Dodds	DUP	16718	40.8%
G Kelly	SF	10331	25.2%
A Maginness	SDLP	8592	21.0%
C Walker	UUP	4904	12.0%
M Delaney	WP	253	0.6%
RG Weiss	VFYP	134	0.3%
TOTAL		40932	67.17%
Electorate		60941	
Majority DUP		**6387**	**15.60%**

BELFAST WEST
SF hold

G Adams	SF	27096	66.1%
A Attwood	SDLP	7754	18.9%
E Smyth	DUP	2641	6.4%
C McGimpsey	UUP	2541	6.2%
J Lowry	WP	736	1.8%
D Kerr	U3W	116	0.3%
RG Weiss	VFYP	98	0.2%
TOTAL		40982	68.7%
Electorate		59617	
Majority SF		**19342**	**47.20%**

DOWN NORTH
UUP Gain from UKUP

S Hermon	UUP	20833	56.0%
R McCartney	UKUP	13509	36.3%
M Farrell	SDLP	1275	3.4%
J Robertson	Con	815	2.2%
C Carter	Ind	444	1.2%
E McConvey	SF	313	0.8%
TOTAL		37189	58.8%
Electorate		63212	
Majority UUP		**7324**	**19.69%**

DOWN SOUTH
SDLP hold

E McGrady	SDLP	24136	46.4%
M Murphy	SF	10278	19.7%
D Nesbitt	UUP	9173	17.6%
J Wells	DUP	7802	15.0%
B Campbell	All	685	1.3%
TOTAL		52074	70.83%
Electorate		73519	
Majority SDLP		**13858**	**26.61%**

FERMANAGH-SOUTH TYRONE
SF Gain from UUP

M Gildernew	SF	17739	34.1%
J Cooper	UUP	17686	34.0%
T Gallagher	SDLP	9706	18.7%
J Dixon	Ind	6843	13.2%
TOTAL		51974	77.99%
Electorate		66640	
Majority SF		**53**	**0.10%**

FOYLE
SDLP hold

J Hume	SDLP	24538	50.2%
M McLaughlin	SF	12988	26.6%
W Hay	DUP	7414	15.2%
A Davidson	UUP	3360	6.9%
C Cavanagh	All	579	1.2%
TOTAL		48879	68.90%
Electorate		70943	
Majority SDLP		**11550**	**23.63%**

LAGAN VALLEY
UUP hold

J Donaldson	UUP	25966	56.5%
S Close	All	7624	16.6%
E Poots	DUP	6164	13.4%
P Lewsley	SDLP	3462	7.5%
P Butler	SF	2725	5.9%
TOTAL		45941	63.22%
Electorate		72671	
Majority UUP		**18342**	**39.93%**

LONDONDERRY EAST
DUP gain from UUP

G Campbell	DUP	12813	32.1%
W Ross	UUP	10912	27.4%
J Dallat	SDLP	8298	20.8%
F Brolly	SF	6221	15.6%
Y Boyle	All	1625	4.1%
TOTAL		39869	66.2%
Electorate		60215	
Majority DUP		**1901**	**4.77%**

MID ULSTER
SF hold

M McGuinness	SF	25,502	51.1%
I McCrea	DUP	15,549	31.1%
E Haughey	SDLP	8,376	16.8%
E Bogues	All	509	1.0%
TOTAL		49,936	81.34%
Electorate		61,390	
Majority SF		**9,953**	**19.93%**

NEWRY & ARMAGH
SDLP hold

S Mallon	SDLP	20784	37.4%
C Murphy	SF	17209	30.9%
P Berry	DUP	10795	19.4%
S McRoberts	UUP	6833	12.3%
TOTAL		55621	76.75%
Electorate		72466	
Majority SDLP		**3575**	**6.43%**

STRANGFORD
DUP gain from UUP

I Robinson	DUP	18532	42.8%
D McNarry	UUP	17422	40.3%
K McCarthy	All	2902	6.71%
D McCarthy	SDLP	2646	6.12%
L Johnston	SF	930	2.15%
C Wilson	NIUP	822	1.90%
TOTAL		43254	59.92%
Electorate		72192	
Majority DUP		**1110**	**2.57%**

TYRONE WEST
Gain from UUP

P Doherty	SF	19814	40.8%
W Thompson	UUP	14774	30.4%
B Rodgers	SDLP	13942	28.7%
TOTAL		48530	79.9%
Electorate		60739	
Majority SF		**5040**	**10.39%**

UPPER BANN
UUP hold

D Trimble	UUP	17095	33.5%
D Simpson	DUP	15037	29.5%
D O'Hagan	SF	10771	21.1%
D Kelly	SDLP	7607	14.9%
T French	WP	527	1.0%
TOTAL		51037	70.3%
Electorate		72574	
Majority UUP		**2058**	**4.03%**

BELFAST WEST

GERRY ADAMS

SINN FÉIN

President Sinn Féin since 1983, Gerry Adams first came to public attention as a member of a republican delegation which had talks with the British government in 1972. Interned in the 1970s. Elected as MP for West Belfast first in 1983. Played a central role with John Hume in building the nationalist coalition which was a pillar of the peace process. A member of PEN, the international guild of writers Gerry Adams has also published several books.

OCCUPATION
Former bartender
Campaigner for rights of Irish Nationalists, Elected President of Sinn Fein in 1983

ADDRESS/PHONE
Constituency
53 Falls Road, Belfast, Co Antrim, BT12 4PD
(048) 9022 3000
Fax (048) 9022 5553

Westminster
(0044) (20)72 193 000

EMAIL
sfadmin@eircom.net

BORN
Belfast, October 1948

EDUCATION
St Mary's CBS, Belfast

MARITAL STATUS
Married to Colette McArdle.
One son

EAST ANTRIM

ROY BEGGS

ULSTER UNIONIST PARTY

Mayor of Larne from 1978 – 1983 and MP for East Antrim since 1983, Roy Beggs is the UUP's Chief Whip and Spokesperson for Education and Skills, and a member of the Public Accounts Commission. His son is Roy Beggs MLA. He is a member of the Ulster Farmers' Union and a committee member of Raloo Presbyterian Church.

OCCUPATION
Former secondary school teacher

ADDRESS/PHONE
Constituency
41 Station Road, Larne BT40 3AA
(048) (28) 273 258
Fax (048) (28) 273 007

Westminster
(0044) (20) 721 963 05
Fax (0044) (20) 721 938 89

BORN
Belfast, February 1936

EDUCATION
Ballyclare High School;
Stranmillis Training College (Cert.Ed.)

MARITAL STATUS
Married to Wilma Lorimer.
Two sons, two daughters

SOUTH ANTRIM

DAVID BURNSIDE

ULSTER UNIONIST PARTY

One of David Trimble's most prominent critics, he was unsuccessful in the by election in 2000 but was elected in 2001 and is on the Environment, Food and Rural Affairs Committee. He was press officer for the Vanguard Unionist Party 1974-77; director of public relations at the Institute of Directors 1979-84; and director of public affairs at British Airways 1984-93.

OCCUPATION
Chair New Century Holdings and David Burnside Associates

ADDRESS/PHONE
Home
24 Fountain Street, Antrim BT41 4BB
(048) (94) 461 211

Westminster
(0044) (20) 72 193 000

BORN
Ballymoney. August 1951

EDUCATION
Coleraine Academical Institution;
Queens University, Belfast

MARITAL STATUS
Married to Fiona Rennie.
One daughter from first marriage

EAST LONDONDERRY

GREGORY CAMPBELL

DEMOCRATIC UNIONIST PARTY

On Derry City Council since 1981, and a member of the NI Assembly, he is security spokesperson for the DUP and held the Regional Development portfolio in the power sharing executive. In Westminster was on the Transport, Local Government and the Regions committee 2001-2002

OCCUPATION
Civil servant 1972-82, 1986-94;
self-employed businessman 1994-

ADDRESS/PHONE
Constituency
25 Bushmills Road, Coleraine, BT52 2BP
(048) (70) 327 327
Fax (048) (70) 327 328

Westminster
(0044) (20) 72 198 495

EMAIL
gregory.campbell@dup2win.com

BORN
Londonderry, February 1953

EDUCATION
Londonderry Technical College;
Magee College (Pol Studies 1982)

MARITAL STATUS
Married to Frances Patterson.
One son, three daughters

BELFAST NORTH

NIGEL DODDS

DEMOCRATIC UNIONIST PARTY

1988-91: Lord Mayor of Belfast, A member of Belfast City Council and former Lord Mayor, Nigel Dodds is also a member of the Northern Ireland Assembly. He is the DUP Chief Whip.

OCCUPATION
Former barrister

ADDRESS/PHONE
Home
210 Shore Road, Belfast
(048) (90) 774 774
Fax (048) (90) 777 685

Westminster
(0044)(20) 7219 8419

BORN
Derry, August, 1958

EDUCATION
Portora Royal School, Enniskillen;
St John's College, Cambridge
(BA Law);
Guenn's University;
Belfast Institute of Prefessional
Legal Studies (Cert PLS)

MARITAL STATUS
Married to Diana Harris.
Two sons, one daughter

WEST TYRONE

PAT DOHERTY

SINN FÉIN

Vice-President of Sinn Féin since 1988 and a new MP, Pat Doherty has contested elections unsuccessfully both in Northern Ireland and in the Republic of Ireland: West Tyrone 1997 in the 1997 Westminster general election, Donegal North East in three Dail elections and Connaght/Ulster in the 1989 and 1994 European Parliament elections. He is also a member of the Northern Ireland Assembly.

OCCUPATION
Site engineer

ADDRESS/PHONE
Constituency
1a Melvin Road, Strabane,
County Tyrone, BT82 9AE
(048) 7188 6466
Fax (048) 7188 6466

Westminster
(0044) (20) 72 193 000

EMAIL
sfadmin@eircom.net

BORN
Glasgow, July 1945

MARITAL STATUS
Married.
Two sons, three daughters

LAGAN VALLEY

JEFFREY DONALDSON

ULSTER UNIONIST PARTY

David Trimble's *de facto* heir apparent, Jeffrey Donaldson has been the most prominent critic of the Good Friday Agreement from within the UUP. Party spokesperson for Treasury; Transport, Local Government and the Regions; and Work and Pensions. A former Chairman of the Ulster Young Unionist Council, he also spearheaded Enoch Powell's election campaigns in 1983 and 1987.

OCCUPATION
Partner in a Financial Services and Estate Agency business

ADDRESS/PHONE
Constituency
2 Sackville St, Lisburn, BT27 4AB
(048) (92) 668 001
Fax (048) (92) 671 845

Westminster
(0044) (20) (72) 193 407
Fax (0044) (20) (72) 190 696

EMAIL
laganvalley@uup.org

BORN
Kilkeel, Co Down, December 1962

EDUCATION
Kilkeel High School; Castlereagh College (Dip Electrical Engineering)

MARITAL STATUS
Married to Eleanor Cousins.
Two daughters

FERMANAGH/SOUTH TYRONE

MICHELLE GILDERNEW

SINN FÉIN

Michelle Gildernew was elected to the Northern Ireland Assembly in 1998 and Westminster in 2001. As a full-time member of staff of Sinn Féin she was a member of the first Sinn Féin delegation to meet Tony Blair and has been involved in negotiations ever since.

OCCUPATION
Political researcher

ADDRESS/PHONE
Constituency
40 Irish Street, Dungannon,
Co Tyrone
Phone and Fax (048) 8772 2776

Westminster
(0044) (20) (72) 193 000

BORN
March, 1970

EDUCATION
St Catherine's College, Armagh;
University of Ulster, Coleraine

MARITAL STATUS
Married.
One son

NORTH DOWN

SYLVIA HERMON

ULSTER UNIONIST PARTY

First elected in 2001, and one of only three women to represent Northern Ireland in Westminster at present, Sylvia Hermon is the UUP spokesperson for Home Affairs; Trade and Industry; Youth and Women's Issues. She is the wife of former RUC Chief Constable Sir John Hermon.

OCCUPATION
Former Law Lecturer

ADDRESS/PHONE
Constituency
(048) 91 275 858

Westminster
(0044) (20) 72 198 491
Fax (0044) (20) 72 194 953

EMAIL
uup@uup.org

BORN
Dungannon, August 1955

EDUCATION
Dungannon High School for Girls; Aberystwyth University, Wales (Law); Part II Solicitors' Qualifying Examinations

MARITAL STATUS
Married to Sir John Hermon.
Two sons

FOYLE

JOHN HUME

SDLP

Former leader of the SDLP until 2001 and a recipient of the Nobel Peace Prize for his part in bringing about the Good Friday Agreement, Hume has been an SDLP MP since 1979 (he succeeded Gerry Fitt) as well as an MEP for Northern Ireland since 1979 and was earlier a member of the Northern Ireland Assembly 1973-5 and later in 1982-6, and the New NI Assembly 1998-2001.

OCCUPATION
Lecturer in international affairs; French and History teacher

ADDRESS/PHONE
Constituency
5 Bayview Terrace, Derry BT48 7EE
(048) 71 265 340
Fax (048) 71 363 423

Westminster
(0044) (20) 72 193 485

EMAIL
she@humblemp-freeserve.co.uk

BORN
Derry, January 1937

EDUCATION
St Columb's College, Derry; NUI (BA French and History); St Patrick's College, Maynooth (MA)

MARITAL STATUS
Married to Patricia Hone.
Two sons, three daughters

NEWRY AND ARMAGH

SÉAMUS MALLON

SDLP

Séamus Mallon has been the MP Newry and Armagh since he beat Jim Nicholson in a by-election in 1986. He has enjoyed a long career as a nationalist politician, the high point of which was the position of deputy First Minister of the power sharing executive, 1998-2001.He was a member of the Northern Ireland Assembly 1973-74, and has been in the New Northern Ireland Assembly since 1998. He was also a member of Seanad Éireann in 1982.

OCCUPATION
Former primary school headmaster

ADDRESS/PHONE
Constituency
2 Bridge Street, Newry, Co Down BT35 8AE
(048) 30 267 933
Fax (048) 30 267 828

Westminster
(0044) (20) 72 194 018

BORN
Markethill, Armagh, August 1936

EDUCATION
Christian Brothers Abbey Grammar School, Newry; St Joseph's College of Education, Belfast

MARITAL STATUS
Married to Gertrude Cush.
One daughter

SOUTH DOWN

EDDIE McGRADY

SDLP

First Chairman of the SDLP in 1970, he is one of the less prominent SDLP representatives, Eddie McGrady has been an MP since 1992 and is also a member of the Northern Ireland Assembly. SDLP Parliamentary Group Leader, and a member Northern Ireland Affairs Committee since 1997. A fomer member and chairman of Down District Council and Downpatrick Urban District Council.

OCCUPATION
Chartered Accountant, Fellow of the Institute of Chartered Accountants

ADDRESS/PHONE
Constituency
Cois Na Cille, Saul Brae, Downpatrick, County Down, BT30 6NL
(048) 44 612 882
Fax (048) 44 619574

Westminster
(0044) (20) 72 194 481

EMAIL
e.mcgrady@sdlp.ie

WEBSITE
http://www.epolitix.com/webminster/eddie-mcgrady

BORN
Downpatrick, Co Down, June 1935

EDUCATION
St Patrick's Grammar School, Downpatrick; Belfast Technical College

MARITAL STATUS
Married to Patricia Swail.
Two sons, two daughters

MID ULSTER

MARTIN McGUINNESS

SINN FÉIN

MP for Mid Ulster since 1997 and politically involved since the late 1960s, Martin McGuinness was a leading republican representative in the 1972 talks with the then British Secretary of State, Willie Whitelaw. Sinn Féin's chief negotiator since the mid-1980s and member of the Northern Ireland Assembly of 1983-4 and the New Northern Ireland Assembly set up in 1998, he has been Minister for Education in the power sharing executive. An obsessive fly fisherman.

OCCUPATION
Negotiator

ADDRESS
Sinn Féin, 55 Falls Road, Belfast, BT12 4PD

PHONE
(048) 90 521 470
Fax (048) 86 766 734

Westminster
(0044) (20) 72 193 000

EMAIL
midulstersf@ireland.com

BORN
Derry, May 1950

EDUCATION
Christian Brothers Technical College

MARITAL STATUS
Married.
Four children

NORTH ANTRIM

REV IAN PAISLEY

DEMOCRATIC UNIONIST PARTY

Leader and co-founder of DUP; Ian Paisley has been the voice of unionist defiance for several decades, has represented North Antrim in Westminster since 1970 and has been an MEP for Northern Ireland since 1979. He has been a member of all Northern Ireland Assemblies over the last 30 years.

OCCUPATION
Minister of religion

ADDRESS/PHONE
Constituency
46 Hill Street, Ballymena, BT43 6BH
(048) 90 454 255
Fax (048) 90 457 783

Home
(048) 25 641 421

Westminster
(0044) (20) 72 193 457
Fax(0044) (20) 72 195 854

EMAIL
ian.paisley@virgin.net

BORN
Armagh, April, 1926

EDUCATION
Ballymena Technical High School; South Wales Bible College; Reformed Presbyterian Theological College, Belfast

MARITAL STATUS
Married to Eileen Emily Cassells. Two sons, three daughters

STRANGFORD

IRIS ROBINSON

DEMOCRATIC UNIONIST PARTY

Elected to Castlereagh Borough Council in 1989, Mayor in 1992, and a Northern Ireland Assembly member, Iris Robinson, the wife of Peter Robinson, deputy leader of the DUP, is a new MP.

OCCUPATION
Councillor, former secretary

ADDRESS
2b James Street, Newtownards

PHONE
(028) 9182 7701
Fax (028) 9182 7703

Westminster
(0044) (20) 72 198 323

EMAIL
iris.robinson@dup2win.com

BORN
Belfast, September 1949

EDUCATION
Knockbreda Intermediate School; Castlereagh Technical College

MARITAL STATUS
Married to Peter Robinson MP. Two sons, one daughter

BELFAST EAST

PETER ROBINSON

DEMOCRATIC UNIONIST PARTY

The Deputy Leader of the Democratic Unionist Party, Peter Robinson has been MP for East Belfast for 19 years. He was a member of the Northern Ireland Assembly 1982-6; Deputy Leader, Democratic Unionist Party: resigned 1987, re-elected 1988; and the New Northern Ireland Assembly 1998-; Minister for Regional the power sharing executive. He is also a member of Castlereagh Borough Council and his wife Iris is also an MP.

OCCUPATION
Estate agent

ADDRESS /PHONE
Constituency
Strandtown Hall, 96 Belmont Avenue, Belfast, BT4 3DE
(048) 90 658 217
Fax (048) 90 471 161

Westminster
(0044) (20) 72 193 506

EMAIL
info@dup.org.uk

BORN
Belfast, December 1948

EDUCATION
Annadale Grammar School; Castlereagh College of Further Education

MARITAL STATUS
Married to Iris (née Collins) MP. Two sons, one daughter

BELFAST SOUTH

REV MARTIN SMYTH

ULSTER UNIONIST PARTY

A former Grand Master of the Grand Orange Lodge of Ireland, and past chairman of the Ulster Unionist Council, Martin Smyth has represented Belfast South since 1982. he is the UUP spokesperson for Foreign and Commonwealth Affairs, International Development, and Health, and is a member of the Northern Ireland Affairs Select Committee since 2001.

OCCUPATION
Presbyterian Minister

ADDRESS/PHONE
Constituency
117 Cregagh Road, Belfast,
BT6 0LA
(048) (90) 457 009
Fax (048) (90)45 0837

Westminster
(0044) (20) 7219 4098

BORN
Belfast, June 1931

EDUCATION
Methodist College, Belfast;
Magee University College, Derry;
Trinity College, Dublin (BA, BD);
Presbyterian College, Dublin;
San Francisco Theological Seminary

MARITAL STATUS
Married to Kathleen Johnston.
Two daughters and one daughter deceased

UPPER BANN

DAVID TRIMBLE

UUP

Leader of the UUP in succession to Sir James Molyneaux, David Trimble has been the MP for Upper Bann since he won the 1990 by-election caused by the death of his party's deputy leader, Harold McCusker. Has moved politically from the hardline fringe of unionism with Bill Craig's Vanguard Party to negotiate the Good Friday Agreement, a journey which won him a share of the Nobel Peace Prize. First Minister, Northern Ireland Assembly since 1998.

OCCUPATION
Former Law Lecturer

ADDRESS/PHONE
Constituency
2 Queen Street, Lurgan BT66 8BQ
(048) 38 328 088
Fax (048) 38 322 343

Westminster
(0044) (20) 72 196 987

EMAIL
upperbann@uup.org

BORN
Belfast, October 1944

EDUCATION
Bangor Grammar School;
Queens University, Belfast

MARITAL STATUS
Married to Daphne Orr.
Two sons, two daughters

Assembly Elections 1998 - results by party

	VOTES	VOTE%	SEATS
SDLP	177,963	22.0%	24
UUP	172,225	21.3%	28
DUP	145,917	18.0%	20
Sinn Féin	142,858	17.7%	18
Alliance	52,636	6.5%	6
UKUP	36,541	4.5%	5
Ind Unionists	24,339	3.0%	3
PUP	20,634	2.6%	2
Women's Coalition	13,019	1.6%	2
UDP	8,651	1.1%	
Others	9548	1.2%	

Assembly - current state of the parties

PARTY	SEATS	NOTES
Ulster Unionist Party	26	(A)
Social Democratic and Labour Party	24	
Democratic Unionist Party	21	(B)
Sinn Fein	18	
The Alliance Party	6	
Northern Ireland Unionist Party	3	(C)
United Unionist Assembly Party	3	(D)
Northern Ireland Women's Coalition	2	
Progressive Unionist Party	2	
UK Unionist Party	1	
Independent Unionist	2	

(A) Peter Weir and Pauline Armitage ceased to be members of the Ulster Unionist Party with effect from 9 November 2001

(B) Peter Weir became a member of the Democratic Unionist Party with effect from 30 April 2002

(C) Elected as UK Unionist Party, resigned and formed Northern Ireland Unionist Party (NIUP) with effect from 15 January 1999. Roger Hutchinson was expelled from the NIUP with effect from 2 December 1999.

(D) Elected as Independent Candidates, formed United Unionist Assembly Party with effect from 21 September 1998

NAME	PARTY	CONSTITUENCY
GERRY ADAMS	Sinn Féin	West Belfast
IAN ADAMSON	UUP	East Belfast
FRASER AGNEW (1)	UUAP	North Belfast
LORD ALDERDICE	SPEAKER	East Belfast
PAULINE ARMITAGE (8)	Ind Unionist	East Londonderry
BILLY ARMSTRONG	UUP	Mid Ulster
ALEX ATTWOOD	SDLP	West Belfast
ROY BEGGS Jnr	UUP	East Antrim
BILLY BELL	UUP	Lagan Valley
EILEEN BELL	Alliance	North Down
PAUL BERRY	DUP	Newry & Armagh
ESMOND BIRNIE	UUP	South Belfast
NORMAN BOYD (2)	NIUP	South Antrim
PJ BRADLEY	SDLP	South Down
JOE BYRNE	SDLP	West Tyrone
GREGORY CAMPBELL	DUP	East Londonderry
MERVYN CARRICK	DUP	Upper Bann
JOAN CARSON	UUP	Ferm & Sth Tyrone
SEAMUS CLOSE	Alliance	Lagan Valley
WILSON CLYDE	DUP	South Antrim
FRED COBAIN	UUP	North Belfast
ROBERT COULTER	UUP	North Antrim
ANNIE COURTNEY (5)	SDLP	Foyle
MICHAEL COYLE (9)	SDLP	East Londonderry
JOHN DALLAT	SDLP	East Londonderry
DUNCAN SHIPLEY-DALTON	UUP	South Antrim
IVAN DAVIS	UUP	Lagan Valley
BAIRBRE DE BRUN	Sinn Féin	West Belfast
NIGEL DODDS	DUP	North Belfast
PAT DOHERTY	Sinn Féin	West Tyrone
BOYD DOUGLAS (1)	UUAP	East Londonderry
MARK DURKAN	SDLP	Foyle
REG EMPEY	UUP	East Belfast
DAVID ERVINE	PUP	East Belfast
SEAN FARREN	SDLP	North Antrim
JOHN FEE	SDLP	Newry & Armagh
DAVID FORD	Alliance	South Antrim
SAM FOSTER	UUP	Ferm & Sth Tyrone
TOMMY GALLAGHER	SDLP	Ferm & Sth Tyrone
OLIVER GIBSON	DUP	West Tyrone
MICHELLE GILDERNEW	Sinn Féin	Ferm & Sth Tyrone
JOHN GORMAN (4)	UUP	North Down
TOM HAMILTON (6)	UUP	Strangford
CARMEL HANNA	SDLP	South Belfast
DENIS HAUGHEY	SDLP	Mid Ulster
WILLIAM HAY	DUP	Foyle
JOE HENDRON	SDLP	West Belfast
DAVID HILDITCH	DUP	East Antrim
DEREK HUSSEY	UUP	West Tyrone
BILLY HUTCHINSON	PUP	North Belfast
ROGER HUTCHINSON (3)	Ind Unionist	East Antrim
GARDINER KANE	DUP	North Antrim
GERRY KELLY	Sinn Féin	North Belfast
JOHN KELLY	Sinn Féin	Mid Ulster
DANNY KENNEDY	UUP	Newry & Armagh
JAMES LESLIE	UUP	North Antrim
PATRICIA LEWSLEY	SDLP	Lagan Valley
ALBAN MAGINNESS	SDLP	North Belfast
SEAMUS MALLON	SDLP	Newry & Armagh
ALEX MASKEY	Sinn Féin	West Belfast
KIERAN McCARTHY	Alliance	Strangford

NAME	PARTY	CONSTITUENCY
ROBERT McCARTNEY	UKUP	North Down
DAVID McCLARTY	UUP	East Londonderry
WILLIAM McCREA	DUP	Mid Ulster
DONOVAN McCLELLAND (4)	SDLP	South Antrim
ALASDAIR McDONNELL	SDLP	South Belfast
BARRY McELDUFF	Sinn Féin	West Tyrone
ALAN McFARLAND	UUP	North Down
MICHAEL McGIMPSEY	UUP	South Belfast
EDDIE McGRADY	SDLP	South Down
MARTIN McGUINNESS	Sinn Féin	Mid Ulster
GERRY McHUGH	Sinn Féin	Ferm & Sth Tyrone
MITCHEL McLAUGHLIN	Sinn Féin	Foyle
EUGENE McMENAMIN	SDLP	West Tyrone
PAT McNAMEE	Sinn Féin	Newry & Armagh
MONICA McWILLIAMS	NIWC	South Belfast
FRANCIE MOLLOY	Sinn Féin	Mid Ulster
CONOR MURPHY	Sinn Féin	Newry & Armagh
MICK MURPHY	Sinn Féin	South Down
JANE MORRICE (4)	NIWC	North Down
MAURICE MORROW	DUP	Ferm & Sth Tyrone
SEAN NEESON	Alliance	East Antrim
MARY NELIS	Sinn Féin	Foyle
DERMOT NESBITT	UUP	South Down
DANNY O'CONNOR	SDLP	East Antrim
DARA O'HAGAN	Sinn Féin	Upper Bann
EAMONN ONEILL	SDLP	South Down
IAN PAISLEY	DUP	North Antrim
IAN PAISLEY jr	DUP	North Antrim
EDWIN POOTS	DUP	Lagan Valley
SUE RAMSEY	Sinn Féin	West Belfast
IRIS ROBINSON	DUP	Strangford
KEN ROBINSON	UUP	East Antrim
MARK ROBINSON	DUP	South Belfast
PETER ROBINSON	DUP	East Belfast
PATRICK ROCHE (2)	NIUP	Lagan Valley
BRID RODGERS	SDLP	Upper Bann
GEORGE SAVAGE	UUP	Upper Bann
JIM SHANNON	DUP	Strangford
JOHN TAYLOR	UUP	Strangford
JOHN TIERNEY	SDLP	Foyle
DAVID TRIMBLE	UUP	Upper Bann
DENIS WATSON (1)	UUAP	Upper Bann
PETER WEIR (7)	DUP	North Down
JIM WELLS	DUP	South Down
CEDRIC WILSON (2)	NIUP	Strangford
JIM WILSON	UUP	South Antrim
SAMMY WILSON	DUP	East Belfast

(1) Elected as independent candidates, formed United Unionist Assembly Party (UUAP) with effect from 21 September 1998.

(2) Elected as UK Unionist candidates, formed Northern Ireland Unionist Party (NIUP) with effect from 15 January 1999

(3) Hutchinson was expelled from the NIUP with effect from 2 December 1999

(4) Elected as deputy speakers of the Assembly 31 January 2000

(5) Hume resigned from the assembly with effect from 1 December 2000. He was replaced by Annie Courtney who took her seat on 11 December 2000.

(6) Tom Benson died on 24 December 2000. He was replaced by Tom Hamilton with effect from 17 January 2001.

(7) Weir ceased to be a member of the UUP with effect from 9 November 2001. He became a member of the DUP with effect from 30 April 2002.

(8) Pauline Armitage was suspended from the UUP with effect 9 November 2001.

(9) Arthur Doherty resigned from the assembly with effect from 1 September 2002. He was replaced by Michael Coyle.

Connacht-Ulster

3 seats   11 candidates   6 counts
electorate: 541,552   quota: 80,038

First Preference Votes

candidate	party	votes	% share
P C GALLAGHER	FF*	66,055	20.6%
J McCARTIN	FG*	63,632	19.9%
D R SCALLON	Ind	51,086	16.0%
N Treacy	FF	47,933	16.0%
M Harkin	Ind	47,372	14.8%
S MacManus	SF	20,457	6.4%
G Gibbons	Lab	10,522	3.3%
L Sharkey	Ind	5,334	1.7%
M L Flanagan	Ind	5,000	1.6%
P Campbell	NLP	1,920	0.6%
P Raymond	Ind	840	0.3%
Total valid		320,151	59.1%
Spoilt votes		12,085	3.6%
Total poll		332,236	61.4%

Dublin

4 seats   13 candidates   8 counts
electorate: 793,200   quota: 56,135

First Preference Votes

candidate	party	votes	% share
M BANOTTI*	FG	56,593	20.2%
N ANDREWS*	FF	44,176	15.7%
P McKENNA*	GP	35,659	12.7%
P DE ROSSA	LAB	28,748	10.2%
J Mitchell	FG	27,873	10.0.%
B Briscoe	FF	25,065	8.9%
S Crowe	SF	18,633	6.6%
B Malone*	LAB	15,890	5.7%
J Higgins	SOC	10,619	3.8%
G Casey	CSP	9,425	3.4%
C Goulding	Ind	5,546	2.0%
A Goodwin	Ind	1,438	0.5%
J Burns	NLP	1,006	0.4%
Total valid		280,671	35.4%
Spoilt votes		6,013	2.1%
Total poll		286,684	36.1%

Leinster

4 seats   8 candidates   3 counts
electorate: 706,200   quota: 68,468

First Preference Votes

candidate	party	votes	% share
A DOYLE	FG	67,881	19.8%
N AHERN*	GP	47,184	13.8%
J FITZSIMONS*	FF	58,750	17.2%
L HYLAND*	FF	58,477	17.1%
A Gillis*	FG	48,729	14.2%
S Butler	LAB	38,112	11.1%
A Morgan	SF	20,015	5.9%
D Garrett	NLP	3,191	0.9%
Total valid		342,339	48.5%
Spoilt votes		14,725	4.1%
Total poll		357,064	50.6%

Munster

4 seats   10 candidates   6 counts
electorate: 823,008   quota: 89,716

First Preference Votes

candidate	party	votes	% share
B CROWLEY*	FF	154,195	34.4%
G COLLINS*	FF	83,106	18.5%
P COX*	IND	63,954	14.3%
J CUSHNAHAN*	FG	46,100	10.3%
P Desmond	LAB	28,270	6.3%
J Corr	FG	31,363	7.0%
M Ferris	SF	29,060	6.5%
B Nutty	GP	10,257	2.3%
S Luck	NLP	1,267	0.3%
D Riordan	Ind	1,007	0.2%
Total valid		448,579	54.5%
Spoilt votes		13,724	3.0%
Total poll		462,303	56.2%

*Denotes outgoing MEP

Northern Ireland

3 seats
electorate: 1,190,190

8 candidates
quota: 169,703

3 counts

First Preference Votes

candidate	party	votes	% share
* I PAISLEY	DUP	192,762	28.4%
* J HUME	SDLP	190,731	28.1%
J NICHOLSON	UUP	119,507	17.6%
M McLaughlin	SF	117,643	17.3%
D Ervine	PUP	22,494	3.3%
R McCartney	UKU	20,283	3.0%
S Neeson	ALL	14,391	2.1%
J Anderson	NLP	998	0.2%
Total valid		*678,809*	*57.0%*
Spoilt votes		*8,764*	*1.3%*
Total poll		*687,573*	*57.8%*

How the Irish MEPs line up in the European Parliament

Union for Europe of the Nations Group
ANDREWS, Niall (FF)
COLLINS, Gerard (FF)
CROWLEY, Brian (FF)
FITZSIMONS, Jim (FF)
HYLAND, Liam (FF)
Ó NEACHTAIN, Seán (FF)

Group of the European People's Party (Christian Democrats) and European Democrats
BANOTTI, Mary (FG)
CUSHNAHAN, John (FG)
DOYLE, Avril (FG)
McCARTIN, Joe (FG)
NICHOLSON, Jim (UUP)
SCALLON, Dana Rosemary (Ind)

Group of the Party of European Socialists
DE ROSSA, Proinsias (Labour)
HUME, John (SDLP)

Group of the Greens/ European Free Alliance
AHERN, Nuala (Green)
McKENNA, Patricia (Green)

Group of the European Liberal, Democrat and Reform Party
COX, Pat (Ind)

Non-attached
PAISLEY, Ian (DUP)

How the country voted – by party

	Dublin	Leinster	Munster	Connacht-Ulster	IRELAND
FF	24.7%	34.2%	52.9%	35.6%	**38.6%**
FG	30.1%	34.1%	17.3%	19.9%	**24.6%**
Lab	15.9%	11.1%	6.3%	3.3%	**8.7%**
GP	12.7%	13.8%	2.3%		**6.7%**
SF	6.6%	5.8%	6.5%	6.4%	**6.3%**
Soc	3.8%				**0.8%**
CSP	3.4%				**0.7%**
NLP	0.4%	0.9%	0.3%	0.6%	**0.5%**
Inds	2.5%		14.5%	34.2%	**13.0%**
Turnout	36.1%	50.5%	56.2%	61.3%	**50.2%**

JOE McCARTIN

FINE GAEL

Joe McCartin has represented the constituency of Connacht / Ulster since 1979. He has served as vice-president of the European People's Party and is a member of the Budgets committee. He was elected to the Dáil for Sligo-Leitrim in 1981 and in November 1982 and was a member of Seanad Éireann 1973-81.

OCCUPATION
Full Time Public Representative, former agriculturalist and businessman

ADDRESS/PHONE
Mullyaster, Newtowngore, Carrick-on-Shannon, Leitrim

CONSTITUENCY
(049) 433 3395 Fax (049) 433 3026

Brussels Office
Phone 00322 284 5214 Fax 00322 284 9214

EMAIL
jmccartin@europarl.eu.int

BORN
Dernasmallin, Ballinamore April 1939

EDUCATION
Clogher NS;
St Patrick's College, Cavan

MARITAL STATUS
Married to Anne.
Two sons

SEAN Ó NEACHTAIN

FIANNA FÁIL

The second substitute for Pat 'the Cope' Gallagher, he moved to the European Parliament when the latter was re-elected to the Dáil and appointed as Minister of State. A member of the committees for Industry, External Trade, Research and Energy, and for Fisheries. Re-elected in 1999 to Galway County Council for Connemara, he is a former chairman of Galway County Council, Údarás na Gaeltachta and of the EU Committee of the Regions.

OCCUPATION
County councillor, former secondary teacher

ADDRESS
42 Prospect Hill, Galway

PHONE
Constituency
(091) 560020
Fax: (091) 560023
Brussels
(00) (322) 2845611
Fax: (00) (322) 2849611
Strasbourg
(00) (333) 88175611
Fax: (00) (333) 88179611

EMAIL
seanoneachtain@eircom.net
soneachtain@europarl.eu.int

BORN
Galway, May 1947

EDUCATION
St Joseph's College, Galway

MARITAL STATUS
Married to Christine

DANA ROSEMARY SCALLON

INDEPENDENT

Scallon is a member of the Regional Policy, Transport and Tourism committee and the Culture, Youth, Education, Media and Sport committee in the parliament. She is an associate member of the EPP group. Dana won the Eurovision Song Contest in 1970 but more recently became prominent as a pro-Life campaigner and was stood in the 1997 presidential election winning 14% of the vote. She was an unsuccessful Dáil candidate for Galway West in 2002.

OCCUPATION
Entertainer

ADDRESS/PHONE
Constituency
6 Colonial Buildings,
Eglinton Street, Galway
Tel (091) 562 111
Fax (091) 562 974.

Brussels
(0032) 22 84 5570
Fax (0032) 22 84 9570

Strasbourg
(0033) (388) 17 5570
Fax (0033) (388) 17 9570

EMAIL
dscallon@europarl.eu.int
danamep@eircom.net

WEBSITE
www.danascallon.ie

BORN
London, 1951

EDUCATION
Thornhill College, Derry

MARITAL STATUS
Married to Damien Scallon.
Two girls, two boys

NIALL ANDREWS

FIANNA FÁIL

Andrews has been MEP for Dublin since 1984 and is a member of the Citizens' Freedoms and Rights, Justice and Home Affairs committee. He is a former TD (1977-87) and Minister of State and is a brother of David Andrews, former Minister for Foreign Affairs, and uncle of Barry Andrews, a new TD for Dun Laoghaire. He was an active anti-apartheid campaigner.

OCCUPATION
Former RTE programme executive

ADDRESS
43 Molesworth St, Dublin 2

PHONE
Constituency
(01) 679 4368
Fax (01) 679 0024

EMAIL
niall.andrews.mep@indigo.ie
nandrews@europarl.eu.int

BORN
Dundrum, Co Dublin, 1938

EDUCATION
CBS Synge Street, Dublin;
Presentation College, Bray,
Co Wicklow.

MARITAL STATUS
Married to Bernadette McCarthy.
One son, two daughters

MARY BANOTTI

FINE GAEL

An MEP since 1984, Banotti is a member of the committee on Citizens' Freedoms and Rights, Justice and Home and of the College of Quaestors. She has worked on a variety of issues including environmental and women's and children's rights. Runner-up for FG in the 1997 presidential election. She ran for the Senate in 1982 and 1983 and as a by-election candidate in Dublin Central in 1983. A grandniece of Michael Collins, her sister Nora Owen, is a former Fine Gael TD and Minister for Justice.

OCCUPATION
Formerly nurse, social worker,
TV presenter

ADDRESS/PHONE
Constituency
3 Molesworth St, Dublin 2
(01) 662 5100 Fax (01) 662 5132

Brussels Office
European Parliament, Rue Weirtz,
1047 Brussels, Belgium

(0032) 2 284 5225
Fax (0032) 2 284 9225

EMAIL
banotti@indigo.ie
mbanotti@europarl.eu.int
info@banotti.ie

WEBSITE
www.banotti.ie

BORN
Dublin, 1939

EDUCATION
Dominican Convent, Wicklow;
Royal London Hospital

MARITAL STATUS
Widowed, one daughter

PROINSIAS DE ROSSA

LABOUR PARTY

Proinsias De Rossa was a MEP 1989-92 as a member of The Workers' Party and was re-elected for Labour in 1999. Formerly leader of The Workers' Party and then Democratic Left, he is now president of the Labour Party. He was a Dáil deputy for Dublin NW (1982-2002) and served as Minister for Social Welfare (1994-7). A member of the Convention on the Future of Europe, he is also on the Employment and Social Affairs committee and the Petitions committee of the parliament.

OCCUPATION
Full-time public representative

ADDRESS/PHONE
Constituency
43 Molesworth Street, Dublin 2
Tel: (0)1 678 9740
Fax: (0)1 678 9737

Brussels Office
Tel (0032)2 2847681
Fax 00322 2849681

Strasbourg Office
(0033) 3881 75681
Fax (0033) 3881 79681

EMAIL
E-mail: pderossa@europarl.eu.int

WEBSITE
www.derossa.com

BORN
Dublin, May 1940

EDUCATION
Scoil Colmcille, Marlborough St,
Dublin;
Kevin St College of Technology

MARITAL STATUS
Married.
Two sons, one daughter

PATRICIA McKENNA

GREEN

An MEP since 1994 and a former vice president of the Green group, she is a member of the committees on Environment, Public Health and Consumer Policy and on Fisheries. Her case against the Irish government for using public money to fund only one side of a referendum campaign led to the McKenna Judgement in 1995 which has influenced the way all referendums since that time have been conducted.

OCCUPATION
Former art teacher

ADDRESS/PHONE
Constituency
43 Molesworth St, Dublin 2
Tel (01) 661 6833
Fax (01) 676 3969

EMAIL
mckennap@iol.ie
pmckenna@europarl.eu.int

WEBSITE
www.pmckenna.com

BORN
Castleshane, Co Monaghan, 1957

EDUCATION
St Louis Convent, Monaghan, College of Art and Design, Limerick

MARITAL STATUS
Married.
One son

NUALA AHERN

GREEN

Nuala Ahern was first elected to the European Parliament in 1994, She is the vice-president of the European Parliament's committee on Industry, External Trade, Research & Energy. She is also a member of the Legal Affairs Committee and president of the intergroup on Complimentary and Natural Medicine. A member of Wicklow County Council 1991-94.

OCCUPATION
Counselling psychologist

ADDRESS/PHONE
Constituency
(01) 287 6574
Fax (01) 287 2638

EMAIL
nahern@eircom.net

WEBSITE
www.nualaahern.net

BORN
Northern Ireland

EDUCATION
"Various"

MARITAL STATUS
Married to Barry

AVRIL DOYLE

FINE GAEL

First elected in 1999 she is a member of the committee on Environment, Public Health and Consumer Policy. Doyle was TD for Wexford 1982-89 and 1992-97 and a member of the Seanad 1989-92. She was a Minister of State 1986-87, 1994-97, and mayor of Wexford in 1976. Defeated by Banotti for the FG nomination in the 1997 presidential election, she was also an unsuccessful candidate in the 2002 general election.

OCCUPATION
Full time public representative

ADDRESS/PHONE
Home
Kitestown House, Crossabeg,
Co Wexford
(053) 42 873
Fax (053) 47 810

Leinster Euro Office,
3 Upper Allen Street, Wexford
(053) 21 862
Fax (053) 21 863

Brussels Office
(0032)22 84 5784
Fax (0032) 22 84 9784

EMAIL
avrildyl@indigo.ie
office@avrildoyle.ie
adoyle@europarl.eu.int

WEBSITE
www.avrildoyle.com

BORN
Dublin, 1949

EDUCATION
Holy Child Convent, Killiney,
Co Dublin; UCD (BSc, Biochemistry)

MARITAL STATUS
Married, three daughters

JIM FITZSIMONS

FIANNA FÁIL

An MEP since 1984, Fitzsimons is a member of the committees on Petitions and on Environment, Public Health and Consumer Policy. Formerly a Meath TD (1977-87), he was a Minster of State in 1982. He was a member of Meath County Council (1973-84) and captained Meath at gaelic football.

OCCUPATION
Full time public representative

ADDRESS/PHONE
Constituency
43 Molesworth St, Dublin 2
Tel (01) 662 3065
Fax (01) 662 3040

EMAIL
jfmep1@indigo.ie
jfitzsimons @ europarl.eu.int

BORN
Navan, December 1936

EDUCATION
St Finian's College, Mullingar

MARITAL STATUS
Married to Aoife O'Farrell.
Four children

LIAM HYLAND

FIANNA FÁIL

First elected in 1994, Liam Hyland is a member of the committee on Agriculture and Rural Development. Formerly a TD for Laois-Offaly (1981-97), a member of Seanad Éireann (1977-81) and was a Minister of State (1992-94)

OCCUPATION
Farmer

ADDRESS/PHONE
Constituency
Fearagh, Ballacolla, Portlaoise,
Co Laois
(0502) 34051
Fax (0502) 34030

EMAIL
liamhyland@eircom.net
lhyland@europarl.eu.int

BORN
Portlaoise, April 1933

EDUCATION
Ballacolla NS;
UCD (Diploma in Political and Social Science)

MARITAL STATUS
Married to Agnes Rafter
Five sons, one daughter

GERARD COLLINS

FIANNA FÁIL

First elected in 1994, Gerry Collins is vice-president of the Union for Europe of the Nations Group and a member of the committee on Regional Policy, Transport and Tourism and was vice-president of the European Parliament in 1998-99. he followed his father James to be TD for Limerick W (1967-97) (and was succeeded by his brother Michael) he served as minister in several departments including Minister for Posts and Telegraphs (1970-73), Minister for Justice, Security and Home Affairs (1977-81, 1987-89) and Minister for Foreign Affairs (1982, 1989-92). He was assistant general secretary of Fianna Fáil from 1964-67.

OCCUPATION
Former teacher

ADDRESS/ PHONE
Constituency
The Hill, Abbeyfeale, Co Limerick

Tel (01) 662 3042
Fax (01) 662 3040

EMAIL
gcollins@europarl.eu.int

BORN
Abbeyfeale, Co Limerick

EDUCATION
Patrician Brothers College,
Ballyfin, Co Laois;
UCD (BA)

MARITAL STATUS
Married to Hilary Tatton

PAT COX

INDEPENDENT

First elected in 1989 for the PDs, he broke with his party to run as an independent in 1994. A former president of the Liberal Democratic and Reformist Group, he was elected President of the European Parliament in 2002. Cox exercised a key role in insisting on executive accountability of the commission before the parliament, a demand that led in March 1999 to the unprecedented resignation of the commission. General secretary of the PDs at its foundation, TD for Cork South Central 1992-94, deputy leader 1993-94.

OCCUPATION
Former economics lecturer,
journalist, television presenter

ADDRESS/PHONE
Constituency
Crawford Hall, Western Road, Cork
(021) 497 5833
Fax (021) 497 5834

Brussels
Rue Wiertz, PHS 11B11, B - 1047
Brussels, Belgium
(0032) 2 284 53 63
Fax (0032) 2 284 93 63

EMAIL
pcoxmep@eircom.net
pcox@europarl.eu.int

WEBSITE
www.patcox.ie
www.europarl.eu.int/president

BORN
Limerick, 1952

EDUCATION
CBS Limerick;
Trinity College Dublin BA(Mod), MA

MARITAL STATUS
Married, six children

BRIAN CROWLEY

FIANNA FÁIL

An MEP since 1994, and re-elected in 1999 with the highest first preference vote (154,195) ever won by an MEP in Ireland, Brian Crowley is a member of the committee on Legal Affairs and the Internal Market. He was a member of Seanad Éireann (1992-94) and was appointed to the Council of State in 1997. Brian is the son of Flor Crowley, a Cork TD (1965-77, 1981-82). He has required a wheelchair following an accident in 1980.

OCCUPATION
Full time public representative,
former disc jockey

ADDRESS/PHONE
Constituency
39 Sundays Well Road, Cork
(021) 439 4598
Fax (021) 439 5831

Brussels
(0032) 22 84 5751
Fax (0032) 22 84 9751

Strasbourg (0033) 38 817 5751
Fax (0033) 38 817 9751

EMAIL
briancrowleymep@eircom.net
bcrowley@europarl.eu.int

WEBSITE
www.briancrowleymep.ie

BORN
Dublin, March 1965

EDUCATION
Hamilton High School, Bandon,
UCC (Dip. Law)

MARITAL STATUS
Single

JOHN CUSHNAHAN

FINE GAEL

Elected first in 1989, John Cushnahan is a member of the committee on Foreign Affairs, Human Rights, Common Security and Defence Policy. He is also a representative to the Convention on the Future of Europe. A leader of the Alliance Party in Northern Ireland from 1984-87, he was also a member of Belfast City Council and the Northern Ireland Assembly (1982-86) before moving to Munster.

OCCUPATION
Former teacher, Leader of the Alliance Party (NI), Member of the NI Assembly

ADDRESS/PHONE
Constituency
2nd Floor, 31 Cecil Street, Limerick
(061) 418289
Fax (061) 419736

Brussels
(0032) 2 284 5228
Fax (0032) 2 284 9228

EMAIL
jcushnahan@tinet.ie
jcushnahan@europarl.eu.int

BORN
Belfast, 1948

EDUCATION
CBS, Falls Road Belfast;
Queens University Belfast (BEd.)

MARITAL STATUS
Married to Alice
Five children

JOHN HUME

SDLP

An MEP for Northern Ireland since 1979, he belongs to the Party of European Socialists group and is a member of the committee for Regional Policy, Transport and Tourism. Former leader of the SDLP until 2001 and a recipient of the Nobel Peace Prize for his part in bringing about the Good Friday Agreement, John Hume has also been an SDLP MP since 1979, succeeding Gerry Fitt.

OCCUPATION
Lecturer in international affairs;
French and History teacher

ADDRESS/PHONE
Constituency
5 Bayview Terrace, Derry BT48 7EE
Tel (048 71) 265 340
Fax (048 71) 363 423

Brussels
(0032) 2 284 9190

Strasbourg
(0033) 3 88 17 9190

EMAIL
jhume@europarl.eu.int

BORN
Derry, January 1937

EDUCATION
St Columb's College, Derry;
NUI (BA French and History);
St Patrick's College, Maynooth (MA)

MARITAL STATUS
Married to Patricia Hone
Two sons, three daughters

JIM NICHOLSON

ULSTER UNIONIST PARTY

Jim Nicholson is now a member of the European People's Party group and is on the committee on Regional Policy, Transport and Tourism and currently president of the EU/USA delegation. He is Vice-President of the UUP and a former councillor on Armagh City and District Council (1976-97), the Northern Ireland Assembly (1982-86) and the UK Parliament (1983-86). Former Vice-Chairman of the Group of Independents for a Europe of Nations.

OCCUPATION
Farmer

ADDRESS/PHONE
Constituency
429 Holywood Road,
Belfast BT4 2LN
(048) 90 765 504
Fax:(048) 90 694 419

Brussels
European Parliament, Rue Wiertz,
ASP 9E205
B-1047 BRUSSELS
(0032) 322 284 5933
Fax (0032) 322 284 9933

Strasbourg
(0033) 3 88 17 5933
Fax (0033) 3 88 17 9933

EMAIL
jnicholson@europarl.eu.int

BORN
Armagh, January 1945

IAN PAISLEY

DEMOCRATIC UNIONIST PARTY

An MEP for Northern Ireland since 1979 he is a member of the committee on Development and Cooperation and is not affiliated to any group. Leader and co-founder (in 1971) of Democratic Unionist Party; Ian Paisley has been the voice of unionist defiance for several decades. He has represented North Antrim in Westminster since 1970 and has been a member of all Northern Ireland Assemblies over the last 30 years.

OCCUPATION
Minister of Religion

ADDRESS/PHONE
Constituency
256 Ravenhill Road, Belfast BT6 8GF
(048 90) 454 255
Fax (048 90) 457 783

EMAIL
ipaisley@europarl.eu.int
ianrkpaisley@btinternet.com

WEBSITE
www.ianpaisley.org

BORN
Armagh, April 1926

EDUCATION
Ballymena Technical High School;
South Wales Bible College;
Reformed Presbyterian
Theological College, Belfast

MARITAL STATUS
Married to Eileen Emily Cassells.
Two sons, three daughters

Bertie Ahern and Mary Harney pose for photographers on the completion of their agreement to form a government in June 1997

The years of the tiger, then the snail

It was a time of joy, and a time of sorrow. And a time of unprecedented plenty before it all went horribly wrong. It was a time of unprecedented mayhem in the North with the Omagh bombing, and a time of great hope for permanent peace. Political Correspondent **Shane Coleman** reviews the last five years in the life of the nation

1997

June
Bertie Ahern is elected Taoiseach by 85 votes to 78. Ahern is forced to drop a proposal to give David Andrews not only the position of Minister for Defence but also a special role on Europe in the Department of Foreign Affairs.

An embarrassing row erupts when the Taoiseach's partner and constituency adviser Celia Larkin moves into an office in government buildings. This follows strict guidelines from Ahern to colleagues warning them about giving preferential jobs to friends.

July
The Orange Order is granted permission at the last minute to march down Garvaghy Road.

The Sunday Tribune names Foreign Affairs Minister Ray Burke as the politician who had received the much speculated upon payment of £30,000 from builders. The Taoiseach says he has gone "to extraordinary lengths" to clear up the situation before appointing Burke to cabinet.

The IRA announces that, from July 20, it has ordered the unequivocal restoration of the ceasefire of 1994.

August
Ray Burke strongly denies receiving up to £80,000 from a development company and claims that the £30,000 he received from JMSE was a legitimate political donation.

September
Mary McAleese secures the Fianna Fáil nomination for the presidential election in a surprise victory over Albert Reynolds. Mary Banotti narrowly beats Avril Doyle to win the Fine Gael nomination. Dana Rosemary Scallon also secures a presidential nomination after being nominated by five county councils. Labour's candidate is the founder of Chernobyl Children's Project, Adi Roche. Victim Support founder Derek Nally completes the list of candidates.

The Government appoints Judge Michael Moriarty to chair the forthcoming tribunal on payments to politicians.

Labour Party chairman Jim Kemmy dies at the age of 61.

As opposition politicians call on Ray Burke to step down until the outcome of the Tribunal, Bertie Ahern announces that a separate judicial tribunal will investigate 730 acres of land in north county Dublin with which Burke is accused of being involved.

October
A newspaper report states that Ray Burke granted 11 passports to a wealthy Arab banker in 1990 in return for investment in the country. Government sources accept that Burke's future as Minister for Foreign Affairs is short lived. Three days later, he announces his resignation both as a Minister and a TD. The Taoiseach says in the Dáil that Burke is an honourable man and that he has been hounded out of office on the basis of innuendo

Mary McAleese waves to supporters at the count in Dublin Castle for the presidential election on Hallowe'en 1997 PHOTOCALL IRELAND

and unproven allegations. David Andrews replaces him at Foreign Affairs, with Michael Smith joining the cabinet as Minister for Defence.

On a visit to Stormont, Tony Blair shakes hands with republican leaders, including Gerry Adams, behind closed doors.

A memo leaked from the Department of Foreign Affairs implies that the presidential frontrunner is sympathetic towards Sinn Féin. McAleese insists that she has always voted for the SDLP and that the document had been "totally denuded" of its content. After further leaks on the same issue, the Taoiseach accuses Fine Gael of engaging in a "dirty tricks" campaign to halt McAleese's campaign.

The election is held on 30 October. Mary McAleese is elected the eighth president of Ireland by a record margin. A referendum limiting cabinet confidentiality is passed on the same day.

Both John Bruton and Dick Spring come under pressure due to the respective performances of the Fine Gael and Labour candidates.

November

The Sunday Tribune exclusively reports on Dick Spring's pending resignation as Labour leader, which occurs just days later.

Mary McAleese is inaugurated as President of Ireland.

The 'C' case or X case mark II emerges. The High Court upholds the Children's Court decision that the child, who is in the care of the Eastern Health Board, is free to travel to the UK for an abortion if she wishes.

December

Finance minister Charlie McCreevy introduces tax cuts to the basic and upper rates of taxation. He also announces £20m will be given to the GAA to assist with the re-development of Croke Park. The budget is criticised in some quarters as favouring better off.

1,400 jobs are lost in Clonmel as Seagate Technology closes.

1998

January

Charles Haughey unsuccessfully challenges the Moriarty Tribunal's inquiry into his family affairs.

The British Government announces a new judicial inquiry into Bloody Sunday.

Agreement at last: Bertie Ahern, George Mitchell and Tony Blair after the signing of the Good Friday agreement   PHOTOCALL IRELAND

March

Labour scores two by-election victories, with Jan O'Sullivan retaining the Labour seat previously held by Jim Kemmy in Limerick East and Seán Ryan regaining the seat lost to Fianna Fáil in the general election and subsequently vacated by Ray Burke in Dublin North.

Fine Gael deputy and former Minister Hugh Coveney drowns off the Cork coast. His son Simon subsequently wins the by-election in Cork South central.

NIB admits taking money improperly from customer accounts after a report by RTE's Charlie Bird and George Lee. The two journalists had also broken a story two months earlier about offshore deposits held by NIB account holders amounting to £23m.

A baggage handler dispute at Ryanair escalates, leading to the closure of Dublin Airport.

April

On Good Friday, around 18 hours after deadline, and amid intense interest from the media, the parties in the Stormont peace talks reach an historic agreement on a new Northern Assembly. It was a traumatic week for the Taoiseach Bertie Ahern who had to deal with his mother's death during one of the most demanding weeks of his political life.

The Bacon Report, completed by economist Peter Bacon on the housing crisis, is published.

May

The first day of the month is 'Blue Flu' day, when 80% of the gardaí, who are prohibited from striking, fail to show up for work, citing "sickness" as the reason.

Bertie Ahern comes under pressure in the Dáil as he attempts to explain his handling of the Ray Burke affair

Ireland, North and South, votes overwhelmingly in favour of the Belfast Agreement. The Amsterdam Treaty is also passed.

July

The cabinet approves a national convention centre on Dublin's docklands.

Official figures show an economic growth rate of 7.5%.

The Orange Order is refused permission to march down the Garvaghy Road. The bitter stand-off effectively ends just over a week later, however, when news emerges that three young brothers, Jason, Mark and Richard Quinn have been killed in a sectarian attack on their house in Ballymoney, Co Antrim

August

In the County Tyrone town of Omagh a Real IRA bomb murders 28 people, including a woman eight months pregnant with twins.

September

The first Irish alternative to RTÉ on television, TV3, is launched.

Hugh O'Flaherty speaking to the media during the Philip Sheedy controversy in April 1999
PHOTOCALL IRELAND

SDLP leader John Hume and UUP leader David Trimble are awarded the Nobel Peace Prize in Oslo.

The Labour Party and Democratic Left agree to merge, adding four DL deputies to the 18 Labour TDs to give a combined Dáil strength of 22 TDs.
Charlie Haughey has a tax assessment of £2m controversially dismissed by the appeals commissioners. The tax charge had been based on the findings of the McCracken Tribunal.

1999

January
The Euro makes its first appearance on the international financial markets

James Gogarty, former chief executive at JMSE, begins his evidence to the Flood Tribunal

The Football Association of Ireland (FAI) announces ambitious plans for a £65m stadium at Citywest.

February
The Sunday Tribune reveals that businessman and Fianna Fáil donor Ken Rohan was the sole beneficiary of an amendment to the Finance Act introduced by the then Finance Minister Bertie Ahern in 1994

Former assistant Dublin city and county manager George Redmond is arrested at Dublin Airport with £200,000 in cash

March
Lurgan solicitor Rosemary Nelson is murdered in a car bomb in Portadown

Second report into housing by Peter Bacon is published

April
Unemployment falls to its lowest level since 1983 as the economy continues to boom

The Philip Sheedy affair causes enormous controversy in politics and the judiciary. On 16 April, High Court Judge Cyril Kelly resigns over his role in the affair. Supreme Court Hugh O'Flaherty also resigns.

May
Taoiseach Bertie Ahern is forced to defend countersigning a £25,000 Fianna Fáil cheque that turns up in a bank account controlled by Charles Haughey's financial advisor Des Traynor.

June
The Taoiseach's advisor Paddy Duffy resigns after it emerges he was a director and shareholder of a PR firm Dillon Consultants, which advised communications company NTL on its purchase of the state owned Cablelink.

Local and European elections are held. Dana Rosemary Scallon wins a seat in Connaught-Ulster at the expense of Fianna Fáil

October
Unemployment falls below 9%. The Government commissions a study on the National Stadium – the issue proves to be a major source of tension between the two government parties over the next four years.

November
The Cabinet agrees a new regionalisation plan for maximising EU funds, with counties Clare and Kerry last minute beneficiaries.

British Prime Minister Tony Blair delivers an historic address to a packed Leinster House.

December
Public Enterprise Minister Mary O'Rourke ends Ireland's EU derogation from introducing competition in telecommunications and de-regulates the sector.

Charlie McCreevy's second budget has a strong emphasis on the lower paid and is well received. Bookies also benefit.

In Donegal, 700 workers lose their jobs at Fruit of the Loom.

Euro mover David Byrne headed off to Brussels as EU commissioner

but otherwise the party representation is unchanged in the European elections, with Fianna Fáil holding six seats; Fine Gael four; the Green Party, two, Independents, two; and one Labour seat. No change either in the North, where Ian Paisley (DUP), John Hume (SDLP) and Jim Nicholson (UUP) take the three seats.
In the local elections Fianna Fáil has a strong performance gaining 25 seats. Fine Gael is also up seven seats, while Sinn Féin wins 21 seats, up from just seven in the 1991 election. Labour and the PDs lose 22 and 12 seats respectively.

The State buys the Guinness family Farmleigh estate in the Phoenix Park for £23m.

July
Half a million people buy shares in Telecom Eireann, which is floated on the stock market. The subsequent fall in the share price leaves many shareholders facing a loss on their investment.

David Byrne is appointed Ireland's new EU commissioner, replacing Padraig Flynn. Michael McDowell fills his role as Attorney-General.

The Comptroller and Auditor General says that tax evasion is widespread.

An IRA gun smuggling plot is discovered in Florida.

Former Fianna Fáil minister Maire Geoghegan-Quinn is nominated to the European Court of Auditors.

August
The new planning bill contains a radical new provision that 20% of building land must be set aside for affordable housing

September
The Public Accounts Committee, chaired by Fine Gael's Jim Mitchell, begins its high profile and successful inquiry into the Dirt tax evasion bank scandal.

In the North, the Patten Report says the RUC should be renamed, re-organised and that its emblems should be changed.

The High Court is told that more than half of the directors of CRH in 1987 held Ansbacher accounts.

Jim Culliton, the man behind the highly regarded 'Culliton Plan' for industrial development in Ireland and former CRH chairman, becomes the first Ansbacher casualty. He resigns from the board of three companies two days after it is claimed that his name is on the list of 120 business figures connected with Ansbacher (Cayman).

October
The Cabinet approves Irish entry into Partnership for Peace, despite a commitment from Fianna Fáil that when in government it will hold a referendum before taking any such action.

The Haughey family is told to pay the £500,000 legal cost of challenging Moriarty.

It emerges at the Moriarty Tribunal that in 1989/90 Sligo-Leitrim Fianna Fáil deputy John Ellis was paid £26,000 in cash by Haughey to rescue him from the threat of bankruptcy. Counsel for the Tribunal John Coughlan says the money appears to have come from the party leaders allowance account. It also emerges that Haughey sent almost £16,000 from the state funded party leader's allowance to the Paris firm of Charvet, which makes expensive, hand-tailored shirts.

The Tribunal also questions claims by the former Taoiseach about money raised for the medical expenses of the late Brian Lenihan which was deposited in the leader's account.

Peter Mandelson, one of those credited with the repackaging of old Labour into new Labour in Britain, replaces Mo Mowlam as the new Northern Secretary.

Labour's Mary Upton wins the by-election in Dublin South central. Her late brother Pat Upton had held the seat.

November
John Ellis resigns from the chair of the Oireachtas committee on agriculture after a five week controversy, which includes the revelation that Ellis' debt of £243,000 to NIB was written off in 1991 while his family's failed abattoir business Stanlow Trading did not honour substantial debts to farmers. Ellis has since made a settlement with the farmers.

The £6bn National Development Plan is announced outlining major capital expenditure on infrastructure such as roads, rail and telecommunications.

The Northern Ireland Assembly elects a power sharing executive after David Trimble agrees to enter government in advance of IRA disarmament.

The Irish Pound falls to its lowest level against sterling for 15 years, with one Irish pound buying just 79.63p sterling.

December
A massive give-away Budget from Charlie McCreevy runs into major controversy over the introduction of individualisation. The government is later forced to give an increased tax-free allowance where one person stays home to care for a dependent.

The direct rule of Northern Ireland by Britain ends and a new executive meets for the first time. The government scraps articles two and three of the constitution as it committed to doing in the Belfast Agreement. Less than a fortnight later, the North-South Ministerial Council meet for the first time in Armagh.

George Redmond pleads guilty to failing to make tax returns.

The Public Accounts Committee's report into the Dirt scandal is published.

2000

January
David Andrews stands downs as Minister for Foreign Affairs. Brian Cowen moves over from the Department of Health to replace him. As part of the re-shuffle, Michael Martin moves to Health; Michael Woods to Education and Frank Fahey is promoted to the Cabinet as Minister for the Marine.

February
Fianna Fáil deputy for Kerry North Denis Foley agrees to resign the party whip in the wake of the disclosure that he held over £130,000 in two Ansbacher accounts.

Peter Mandelson suspends the Northern Ireland Executive and the other institutions of the Good Friday Agreement after General de Chastelain reports that he received "no information from the IRA as to decommissioning".

Charlie McCreevy signals plans for a major decentralisation programme and says he hopes to have plans well advanced by the summer. This does not happen and the plans are later put on hold in advance of the 2002 general election.

March
In his keynote address to the Ard Fheis, the Taoiseach says that "all the armies must be stood down" in Northern Ireland.

The chairman of CIE Brian Joyce resigns citing "fundamentally differing views" from Public Enterprise Minister Mary O'Rourke over the autonomy of the group. O'Rourke famously tells Morning Ireland that she was "in the bath" when she heard of Joyce's resignation.

The Sunday Tribune reveals that there is disagreement within cabinet over plans to part-privatise Aer Rianta.

It also reveals details of a deal between the Revenue Commissioners and former assistant Dublin city and county manager George Redmond to pay almost £800,000 in tax, interest and penalties.

The Sunday Tribune reveals who PR man Frank Dunlop called 'Mr Big' and 'Mr Insatiable'

April
PR consultant Frank Dunlop rocks the Flood Tribunal with dramatic revelations of payments to councillors in Dublin county.

May
The British and Irish governments in a bid to restore devolved government to Northern Ireland broker an historic deal. The IRA says it will "initiate a process that will be completely and verifiably put IRA arms beyond use".

Though policing remains an issue of contention, the Ulster Unionist Council votes to re-enter the Northern Executive and days later the institutions are restored.

Fine Gael concludes its inquiry, prompted by Frank Dunlop's revelations, into payments to Dublin County Councillors. The inquiry quickly runs into controversy with some Fine Gael councillors disputing its findings.

At the Tribunal, Dunlop details 38 payments he made to members or former members of Dublin County Council and other politicians since 1991.

The Sunday Tribune reveals that Liam Lawlor is the "Mr Big" who was given money by Dunlop, while Colm McGrath is the man Dunlop described as "Mr Insatiable".

Lowry and O'Brien and how the *Tribune* broke the Telenor story

The Government runs into political trouble when it emerges that former Supreme Court judge Hugh O'Flaherty is being nominated to a plum £147,000 a year job at the European Investment Bank (EIB).

June
Liam Lawlor resigns from Fianna Fáil in the wake of the Fianna Fáil committee report on standards in public life.

Séamus Healy of the Workers Unemployed Action Group wins the by-election In Tipperary South caused by the death of Labour TD Michael Ferris. Fianna Fáil's vote collapses and its candidate is eliminated.

The third Bacon Report on Housing is published. *The Sunday Tribune* reveals that an urban-rural split at cabinet led to some dilution of the initial proposals presented to government.

The Sunday Tribune also reports that Mary Harney offered to resign as Tanaiste and leader of the PDs following the indefinite postponement of Charles Haughey's trial on a charge of obstructing the McCracken Tribunal because of her remark that he should go to jail. She is persuaded to stay on.

Fianna Fáil is criticised at the Moriarty Tribunal for not disclosing important information to the inquiry. Tribunal barrister John Coughlan criticised the party for not telling the Tribunal about internal inquiries that Ahern had carried out in 1996 into a £100,000 donation to Charles Haughey seven years earlier.

July
A challenge in the Supreme Court to Hugh O'Flaherty's appointment to the EIB fails but the pressure on the government grows.

Tom Hayes wins the Tipperary South by election occasioned by the death of Theresa Ahearn

The Flood Tribunal begins probing Century Radio.

August
The ten week train drivers strike collapses when ILDA announces its members will be returning to work.

The row escalates over Hugh O'Flaherty's nomination to the EIB position. O'Flaherty withdraws his name for nomination to the EIB after a summer of controversy.

September
The Sunday Tribune reports that the PDs are considering a name change as part of a revamp that would see Michael McDowell return as party president. Talks between McDowell and the party later break down only to be revived in advance of the 2002 General Election.

October
A ruling by the High Court effectively clears the way for the deregulation of the taxi market.

Justice Peter Kelly threatens to jail three government ministers unless they provide a safe place of detention for a disturbed 17 years old girl.

David Trimble toughens his position and the Ulster Unionist Council backs proposals that will immediately bar Sinn Féin ministers from attending North South ministerial meetings until the Provisional IRA "substantively" re-engages with the De Chastelain decommissioning body.

December
A *Sunday Tribune* investigation reveals that Food Minister of State Ned O'Keeffe failed to tell the Dáil that a farm belonging to his family is licensed to used meat and bone meal during a debate on its proposed ban. O'Keeffe subsequently resigns from his junior ministry.

Charlie McCreevy introduces the most populist budget in the history of the state, with £1.2bn in tax cuts and £850m in social welfare increases.

Bill Clinton visits Ireland for the last time as President of the US.

2001

January
Dublin West TD Liam Lawlor goes to jail for a week and is fined £10,000 for failing to provide the Flood Tribunal with all his financial records

Dr John Reid replaces Peter Mandelson as Northern Secretary.

John Bruton loses the leadership of Fine Gael after ten years. A new "dream team" leadership of Michael Noonan, as leader, and Jim Mitchell, as his deputy, takes over.

February
The Sunday Tribune reports that Fine Gael received a cheque

Farmers and officials from the Department of Agriculture load sheep on to a lorry in Ravensdale, Co Louth, which will take them to an abattoir to be slaughtered during the foot and mouth crisis

PHOTOCALL IRELAND

for $50,000 from Telenor/Esat six weeks after the Esat Digifone consortium was announced as winner of the second mobile phone licence. The Moriarty Tribunal later begins to investigate the awarding of the mobile phone licence and finds evidence of payments to disgraced communications minister Michael Lowry that originated from accounts held by Esat Telecom founder Denis O'Brien.

Strict measures are put in place to prevent a foot and mouth outbreak in Britain spreading to Ireland. A five mile exclusion zone is placed around a mid Ulster farm.

March
Foot and mouth is discovered at a farm on the Cooley Peninsula. An exclusion zone is created and all farmyard animals in that area are slaughtered.

Beverley Cooper-Flynn's libel case versus RTE fails. She is later expelled from the parliamentary party.

St Patrick's Day events are cancelled due to the threat of foot and mouth.

April
The Flood Tribunal creates its first barrister millionaires. The Department of Environment confirms the fees earned by Pat Hanratty and John Gallagher are on the brink of exceeding £1m each.

May
Fine Gael admits it gave £120,000 in illegal 'under the counter' cash payments to staff over a nine year period.

The appearance of Celia Larkin's name on the invitation for a state reception for Cardinal Desmond Connell causes controversy.

June
Despite the support of all the main political parties, the Nice Treaty is rejected in a referendum. Just over a third of the electorate vote.

July
The Supreme Court overturns a High Court ruling that Jamie Sinnott, an autistic man had an entitlement to education for as long as it was beneficial, irrespective of age.

August
The IRA makes a statement on decommissioning.

Aer Lingus chairman Bernie Cahill dies in a drowning accident.

Three Republicans are arrested in Colombia for alleged terrorist activity.

September
In the wake of the 11 September terrorist attacks, the Taoiseach says he will allow US forces engaged in a military response to refuel at Irish Airports.

John Hume says he will stand down as SDLP leader.

The Rail Signalling Inquiry, examining how a 17.78m contract ended up costing 63.49m, begins. However, there is a challenge in the courts to an Oireachtas inquiry into the circumstances surrounding the death of John Carty, who was shot by Gardaí. The Supreme Court finds that the Oireachtas does not have the right to make findings of fact against non-Oireachtas members. This effectively ends the Rail Signalling Inquiry.
Sunday World journalist Martin O'Hagan is shot dead by the LVF.

October
Ten IRA volunteers executed during the War of Independence, including Kevin Barry, are given state funerals. Thousands line the streets to pay their respects.

Aer Lingus indicates that it will have to introduce 2,500 job cuts from its workforce in order to survive as the aviation sector is badly hit by the September 11 attacks.

The Government takes legal action against the UK to block the commissioning of the controversial MOX plant at Sellafield.

November
GAA abolishes Rule 21, barring members of the British security forces from membership.

A row over the new director of the Irish Museum of Modern Art is revived when two board members resign.

December
Tánaiste Mary Harney marries Brian Geoghegan, a director with business group IBEC.

Charlie McCreevy introduces his fifth budget, which contains further tax cuts and large social welfare increases.

Liam Lawlor is sent back to jail by the Supreme Court. His sentence is deferred so he can enjoy Christmas in New York.

2002

January
The Sunday Tribune reports that the Fianna Fáil businessman Dermot O'Leary, who controversially arranged special treatment at Dublin Airport for Liam Lawlor, was re-appointed to the board of Aer Rianta at the insistence of the Taoiseach Bertie Ahern in 1997. The appointment was made despite the fact that O'Leary was involved in a major legal action for damages against the state after his removal from office as chairman of CIE by John Bruton's rainbow government two years earlier.

Mary Harney lands herself in trouble when it emerged she used the Casa fisheries patrol aircraft for a trip to open a friend's off-licence.

The PDs get a huge boost with the news that Tom Parlon and Michael McDowell will stand for the party in the general election.

Fine Gael proposes a plan to compensate Eircom shareholders which attracts great criticism.

The High Point Rendal report on the National Stadium is published. Its finding that the plans would cost the exchequer almost 900m – twice the initial estimate – attracts most attention. A decision on the National Stadium is effectively 'parked' until after the general election.

February
The Sunday Tribune reveals that the country's leading conservative politician, Dana Rosemary Scallon, will oppose the abortion referendum, dealing a major blow to the government's hopes of getting it passed.

Brian Geoghegan and Mary Harney celebrate their wedding with champagne at the Mansion House in Dublin   PHOTOCALL IRELAND

Progressive Democrats junior environment minister Bobby Molloy leaving RTE after being interviewed on the Six-One news about acting improperly when approaches were made to Judge Philip O'Sullivan about a rape case   PHOTOCALL IRELAND

March

The abortion referendum is narrowly defeated.

There is enormous embarrassment for the government when *The Irish Times* reports that Waterworld UK, the company contracted to operate the National Aquatic centre, is a dormant shelf company with assets of stg£4.

The Sunday Tribune reveals that CSID, the company responsible for managing the project, did not tell the government that it had been warned by outside consultants about Waterworld UK's dormant status the day before the cabinet approved its bid to build and operate the centre.

Paddy Teahon resigns from his role as CSID's executive chairman.

April

Brendan Comiskey resigns as Bishop of Ferns in the wake of his criticism of his handling of child abuse claims in his diocese.

Health and Children Minister Michael Martin announces the establishment of an inquiry into the handling of the abuse cases in Ferns.

Fine Gael runs into fresh controversy after *The Sunday Tribune* reports its plans to reform the public service if elected to government.

PD junior Minister Bobby Molloy resigns after Justice Philip O'Sullivan revealed that an assistant acting for Molloy had made "improper" approaches to him. Molloy also announces that he will not be contesting the next election.

The 28th Dáil effectively ends on 24th April when the Taoiseach announces that he intends to go to Aras an Uachtaráin to seek a dissolution the following day.

Bertie Ahern in Oughterard during the election campaign: his affable style conceals a huge capacity for work

PHOTOCALL IRELAND

The ultimate political pro

With apparently little of the brilliance and accomplishment of his predecessors as Taoiseach, is Bertie Ahern an icon for the emptiness of our times? Or is there more than meets the eye to the Dubs fan from Drumcondra? **Joe Lee** assesses the evidence and finds that Ahern may yet be judged as one of the most effective taoisigh of them all

AT FIRST sight Bertie Ahern is remarkable only for being unremarkable. It may, of course, be true that nobody would bother crossing the street to talk to many a politician if they didn't hold office. Their stature derives entirely from office, and not at all from themselves. But that holds for office holders in many an activity besides politics. It just happens that in the case of politics a higher public profile is involved.

In Bertie Ahern's case it is much easier at first sight to list what he isn't than what he is, what he doesn't have compared with what he has. He has none of the charismatic public persona of an O'Connell, a Parnell, a Collins, a de Valera, none of the oratorical flourish of a John Redmond, of the gravelly determination of a WT Cosgrave or of his son Liam, of the driving urgency to get things done of a Seán Lemass, of the incisive grasp of issues of Charlie Haughey, or the intellectual distinction of Garret FitzGerald, or the enthusiasm for ideas of John Bruton. He brings no distinction in any other field to politics – not an outstanding barrister like John A Costello, a legendary sportsman like Jack Lynch, or a successful businessman like Albert Reynolds. He is, in short, in the succession lists of Irish leaders, distinguished for being undistinguished.

Nor have there been spectacular policy successes with which his name is indelibly associated, despite his dogged contribution to the search for a settlement of the Northern Ireland problem, in the sense they couldn't have happened without him. The one thing about him that the bulk of the public can immediately identify concerns his private rather than his public life, in that he is the first Taoiseach to have reconstructed his domestic arrangements outside the traditional norms. That would not have been possible in earlier generations, nor could he himself have been certain it would not cost him a high political price even in this one.

Is he then an icon for our times, for the descent from on high of political leadership, or simply a reflection of the growing marginalisation of politics in a consumer age, where there are no great issues left to fight over, and where drugs, sex, and television increasingly provide the emotional fulfillment that politics and religion once did for so many, as multitudes grope to find some way of filling the void in their lives between birth and death? Or has the electorate become less discerning, despite recurring rumours that it is now more educated than ever before?

And yet the more one looks at the public record , the more one realises how first impressions can be misleading. Is he not the youngest-ever leader of his party? Is he not the first Taoiseach since 1969 to see his government re-elected? If a majority felt he lost the television debates with Bruton and Noonan before the 1997 and 2002 general elections, did he not have the last laugh on polling day? What politician wouldn't settle for losing every debate in sight provided they could win the vote every time? Is he not a leader whose poll ratings for years ran further ahead of his party than those of any of his contemporaries? That is certainly not the record of a political nobody.

All this warns against the danger of underrating him, as many have learned to their cost.

The significance of his role as Minister for Labour during the economic recovery after 1987, during which he proved a gifted finder of the middle ground between contending factions, remains to be fully evaluated. It could certainly be surmised that he was the right man in the right place at the right time. If his style was hardly that of the diplomatic circuit, his negotiating and brokerage skills were enormous. It was almost certainly a

Ahern: many have paid the price of underrarting him PHOTOCALL IRELAND

period when he did the state some service, although his subsequent stint as Minister for Finance is more difficult to assess.

His period in office can have left him with few illusions about human nature, if he had any before. And it would have been difficult for any faith in the inherent goodness of humanity to have survived his earlier experience as Chief Whip of Fianna Fáil during so turbulent a period of its history

The art, and arts, of party leadership are constantly underrated in the public mind. The finest human resource managers in Ireland are to be found in the offices of party leaders, and above all Fianna Fáil. To get so many strong-willed, eternally calculating creatures, to pull together – particularly in our electoral system – and to subordinate their individual wills to the idea of the unity of the party, is an extraordinary achievement, taken casually for granted by the media and the public because in fact it works so well. Party unity is not news. Party disunity is. Yet maintaining party unity is a constant challenge.

In that sense, and irrespective of the final verdict on his performance as Taoiseach, Ahern has been a notable leader. Inheriting a badly divided party, seething with internal hatreds for a generation, he turned it around to at least give the impression of pulling together.

Unlike almost all previous Fianna Fáil leaders, he came into office without a party newspaper to back him. Media management is an even more demanding art than party management. Party loyalty can be invoked, however hollowly at times, to bring recalcitrant members along. Playing the media when the loyal *Irish Press* was no longer available to convey the party message, has to be a game of ceaseless clinical calculation, particularly in an age of tribunal inquiries that allows the public to salivate on innuendo.

As Taoiseach, his style is the polar opposite of that of Reynolds. He is, at least in public, consensual and collegial, where Reynolds was confrontational. His instinct is to play down differences where that of Reynolds was to highlight them. In stark contrast to Reynolds, who seized the first opportunity to strike at his enemies in the party, and immediately created a sullen troop of disgruntled backbenchers, simply biding their time for revenge, Ahern sought to conciliate his enemies. There was no Night of the Long Knives. The unity of the party came first. Displaying enormous emotional self-discipline, he controlled the natural instinct to return blow for blow. Supremo of waffle, many a time must he have concealed in honeyed mumbles the desire to sink the knife in. He must have swallowed very, very hard in offering cabinet positions to some of his critics. But he had extraordinary emotional self-discipline, as well as a capacity for strategic thinking in party political terms, that allowed him swallow the vomit. He is the ultimate party political professional.

Self-discipline in the face of his enemies and detractors in the party provided useful training for dealing with the dervish dance of Northern Ireland affairs, where his level-headed approach has helped bring some calm to stormy waters.

If his inheritance as party leader was a potentially poisoned chalice, in many ways he has been lucky. One might call him Taoiseach by accident. It looked as if Reynolds was set fair to be Taoiseach for as long as he wished once Dick Spring brought Labour into government with him in 1992. Until Reynolds alienated Spring, Ahern's best hope was to be able to continue as finance minister. Even when Reynolds fell in grotesque circumstances, and Ahern wound up as leader of the party, it was in opposition. There could be no guarantee that he would win the

Suffer little children: Ahern poses for the cameras with some local children in Virginia, Co Cavan

Ahern TD watches the FA Cup final while canvassing in Kildare: he isn't happy doing the vision thing   PHOTOCALL IRELAND

next election. Indeed how the Bruton-Spring government managed to lose in the midst of the Celtic Tiger boom in 1997 still remains something of a mystery.

Ahern had fortunate legacies from his immediate predecessors as well. There were hardly any taboos left for Fianna Fáil, except perhaps coalition with Fine Gael, if even that, after Haughey had jettisoned virtually every core value. If Haughey could bed down with Dessie O'Malley in 1989, the range of possible nuptial partners was legion. In addition, the Fianna Fáil vote in 1992 had already fallen to a level that made coalition inevitable. And coalition suits Ahern's style. Indeed he could claim that he was the party leader best qualified to make it work.

It was not for nothing that Charlie Haughey is reputed to have called him 'the most cunning, the most devious, the most ruthless of all my ministers'. Given the unimpeachable authority of the source on the subject matter, and the intense competition for the accolade, could there be a more glowing encomium?

Cunning, devious, ruthless? One would need to know the inside story of many a murky episode before delivering a verdict. It is true that while friends fade from the scene, Bertie long remains top of the heaving heap, and without apparently losing the friendship of those he has deemed it politic to abandon. Emollient and conciliatory by instinct and calculation, he can strike with ruthless political efficiency. Didn't Albert Reynolds, not exactly unfamiliar with the ways of politics by that stage, go into a meeting as the Presidential candidate-elect to succeed

Mary Robinson in 1997, and come out as the ex-presidential candidate-elect, visibly dazed at the efficiency of the ambush, victim of a lightning cobra strike?

Haughey ought to have added two more accolades – hard working and realistic. An affable style conceals an enormous capacity for work, from constituency level to international level. He knows, too, that a week is a very long time in politics, and that the trap door is always waiting for party leaders, even Taoisigh. If the image-makers have been hard at work on everything from his clothes to his vowels, there is still no side to him, none of the pretensions of the *arriviste nouveau-riche* of the 'nineties. His sense of self-importance has not swollen on going to Europe and rubbing shoulders with Gerhard and Jacques, codding himself that he is at the top table. He knows well Ireland isn't, whatever had to be said to get the Nice Referendum through, and he keeps his feet firmly on the ground. He publicly supports both the Dubs and Manchester United – a combination inconceivable in the ideological atmosphere a generation or so earlier. And he does it without any fuss, as if it is the most natural thing in the world – as indeed it is for many Dubliners.

Bertie Ahern isn't happy doing the vision thing. Not naturally given to pontificating, he just does. And because much of what he does is more sensible than what many of the pontificators would have him do, he may come to be deemed one of the most effective of all Taoisigh in achieving his objectives, whatever opinion may be held of the objectives themselves.

Enda Kenny celebrates his election as Fine Gael leader as Gay Mitchell, Phil Hogan and Richard Bruton look on

PHOTOCALL IRELAND

FG opt for Kenny – but need luck more

A disastrous performance in the election ended with the departure of Michael Noonan, writes Political Editor **Stephen Collins**

THE Fine Gael election disaster happened like a crash in slow motion. The party made one mistake after another but, even so, the scale of the rout on election day was worse than anybody could have imagined. Fine Gael lost 23 seats and slumped to its lowest share of the vote since 1948.

As the calamity unfolded on the day of the count the party leader, Michael Noonan, resigned after less than 18 months in the post.

There were a number of reasons for the party's poor performance: a leadership contest held far too close to the election, a string of wrong policy options in the run-up to the campaign, the refusal of Labour to consider an election pact, and misleading opinion polls which marginalised the party during the campaign. To cap it all, Fine Gael won considerably fewer seats than its share of the national vote warranted.

The seeds of the disaster were sown in the wake of the 1997 election in which Fine Gael had done well and gained nine seats. Despite the improvement the party failed to get into office because Labour did so badly on that occasion. The party leader, John Bruton, had done well as Taoiseach and obtained good satisfaction ratings in the polls but back in opposition he soon struggled to make an impact. As time wore on this led to dissatisfaction and frustration in the party as TDs blamed the leader for the failure to put a dent in the popularity of the Fianna Fáil–Progressive Democrat coalition. Fine Gael TDs did not recognise that the primary reason for the party's failure to make an impact was that Ireland found itself in the unaccustomed position of being in the throes of an economic boom as the Celtic Tiger economy roared ahead. In hindsight it is difficult to see how any opposition party could have hoped to do well against such a background. Fine Gael strategists attempted to find ways to capitalise on the downside of the Celtic Tiger by focusing on issues like traffic chaos, rising house prices and the trend towards individualisation, which was undermining traditional social values. One of the few hiccups in the government's economic policy was the announcement of the individualisation of the tax code, which helped two income families at the expense of those with a single-income. Fine Gael opposed this strenuously in the Dáil and believed the public reaction indicated it was on to something in stressing the values of society in contrast to the government's policy of individualisation.

The outcome of the party's deliberations was a publicity campaign focusing on the downside of the Celtic Tiger. The party chose the slogan of 'the Celtic Snail' to make its point. It proved to be an unmitigated disaster and provided an eerie foretaste of what it was to be like for Fine Gael in the general election. The Celtic Snail campaign was lampooned and the description was quickly applied to Fine Gael itself. Bruton's already precarious hold on leadership was undermined and his leadership was challenged in November 2000. He survived a vote of confidence but two months later he was challenged again and, after an intense struggle, a motion of no confidence in his leadership, sponsored by Michael Noonan and Jim Mitchell, was carried narrowly. In the subsequent leadership contest Noonan defeated Mitchell and Enda Kenny for the post. Noonan's core support came from a group of Munster TDs such as Paul Bradford, Michael Creed and Michael Finucane, who felt they had been relegated to the political wilderness under Bruton. Cork city TDs Simon Coveney and Deirdre Clune also backed Noonan. When it came to the succession contest Noonan got the backing of some senior figures like Phil Hogan who had supported Bruton to the end, but most of the Bruton camp transferred its support to Kenny.

The election of Noonan as leader was designed by his supporters as a key element of the party strategy in advance of the election. They believed that Bruton was the problem and that a new leader would inevitably improve things. It was a complete miscalculation. From the very beginning opinion polls showed that Noonan was even more unpopular than Bruton and as the election drew near things only got worse. Noonan was handicapped by the negative publicity he had received for his handling of the hepatitis C issue as Minister for Health in the rainbow government from 1995 to 1997. "The ghost of Bridget McCole hung over him all through his leadership", said one senior Fine Gael figure, referring to a woman who had died as a result of hepatitis C while, as minister, Noonan was arguing with her over compensation. This problem for Noonan was compounded by an RTE

Michael Noonan: didn't clean up at the polls   PHOTOCALL IRELAND

television drama broadcast in the early months of 2002 which unfavourably represented his actions during that period. Noonan's decision not to appoint his defeated rival, Enda Kenny, to a front bench position only confirmed the negative image.

As the election drew near the party made one mistake after another. A decision was made to focus on quality of life issues like traffic and housing, the very ones that had underpinned the Celtic Snail campaign. Although the slogan changed the message remained the same and, whatever its underlying validity, the message did not make any greater impact the second time around. Noonan tried to articulate a "caring" alternative social vision to the individualistic emphasis on tax cuts which underpinned the government's record. Whatever chance his alternative vision had of being taken seriously was undermined in any case in the months before the election when Noonan and others in Fine Gael made the mistake of making extravagant promises to the electorate. Noonan himself announced that if Fine Gael was elected the party would introduce tax relief for those who had lost money buying Eircom shares. His deputy leader and Finance spokesman, Jim Mitchell, announced there would be a compensation package for taxi drivers who had suffered as a result of the deregulation of their industry. The government and many media commentators poured scorn on these promises as being totally inappropriate, particularly at a time when the public finances were slipping badly.

Fine Gael's manifesto – entitled 'Towards a Better Quality of Life' – promised a range of improvements in public services. On health the party promised an extension of the free GP service to

60% of the population and an end to the division between public and private patients with the state paying insurance for public patients. A big increase in old age pensions, more tax breaks for young house purchasers, state funding and tax breaks for child-care and the introduction of a youth wage for disadvantaged kids who stay in the educational system were only some of the "goodies" promised by Fine Gael. Most people just did not believe these promises were feasible. Behind the scenes in Fine Gael there was consternation that the party had chosen to fight the election on a give-away platform rather than concentrating on the state of the public finances on which the government was vulnerable. Former Taoiseach and Fine Gael leader, Garret FitzGerald, wrote a series of articles in *The Irish Times* vainly urging the opposition parties and media commentators to focus on the central issue of the public finances but few did until very late in the campaign.

By promising a package of goodies based on Department of Finance projections, Fine Gael fatally compromised its traditional image of being sound on the public finances. On the potentially damaging issue for Fianna Fáil of sleaze, Fine Gael did not seem to know what to do. Many in the party judged that the voters were just not interested and that raising the issue

After almost 27 years in the Dáil he took over a position few would have thought likely to come his way... Enda Kenny faces a huge task in attempting to rebuild morale in a shattered party and the prophets of doom have already written Fine Gael's obituary

could be counter-productive. On the basis of its focus group research Fianna Fáil had come to the same conclusion independently. While there was some discussion in the party about the issue, Fine Gael did not raise the matter until three days before polling when Noonan issued a detailed and damning indictment of Fianna Fáil's record on sleaze. The media did not pay the slightest bit of attention at that stage as the party had become irrelevant to the election outcome.

On a political level the party also had a problem from the beginning of the campaign. Months before the election Jim Mitchell publicly called for an election pact between Fine Gael and Labour, predicting that unless that happened Fianna Fáil was home and dry. However, Labour had refused to do a deal to offer the electorate an alternative government. Instead the party said Fine Gael was its preferred option for government but it did not rule out Fianna Fáil. That left Fine Gael stranded and the party was not widely regarded as having any chance of making it into government. With nobody believing the party's manifesto and few, even of its own supporters, believing it could get into government, Fine Gael was heading for disaster.

The trend was accelerated by the IMS and MRBI opinion polls carried out for the national media during the campaign which all significantly overestimated Fianna Fáil support. The effect

was to marginalise Fine Gael and give added force to the message of the PDs. Facing such odds Noonan was not able to lift the party. Even though an RTE/Lansdowne exit poll credited him with beating the Taoiseach in the only television debate between the two during the campaign, it made no difference. It is interesting that although Bruton easily outpointed Ahern in the televised debate during the 1997 election and Noonan did the same in 2002 in both cases the winner lost the election.

In the aftermath of the election many TDs conceded that they would probably have done better under Bruton but they would still have lost the election. Again, with hindsight, it is clear that Noonan snatched the poisoned chalice of responsibility for all of Fine Gael's woes out of Bruton's grasp. Fine Gael was always going to be up against it in the 2002 election, given the economic boom and Labour's refusal to present an alternative government to the voters, but the party made a large contribution to its own problems. It changed leaders at precisely the wrong time, it produced a manifesto which was not credible and it failed to focus on the one issue on which the government was most vulnerable: the public finances.

Noonan's decision to resign on the day of the count threw the leadership issue wide open again. There was considerable discussion within the party about allowing the choice to be made by the membership in the autumn on foot of a decision (which was not eventually ratified) at the February *ardfheis*. In the event the TDs and senators decided to make the choice themselves almost immediately rather than allow a vacuum to develop and persist for several months. There was an effort to find consensus at a two-day meeting of the parliamentary party at a Dublin hotel. Of course many of the leading figures who had dominated Fine Gael politics for the previous two decades had lost their seats in the election. The roll call of the defeated included many of the most talented politicians in the party such as Alan Dukes, Jim Mitchell, Alan Shatter, Nora Owen, Charlie Flanagan, Jim Higgins and Brian Hayes. Ironically the core Noonan supporters like Bradford, Creed and Gerry Reynolds were among the fallen. There was much talk about making a huge leap and handing the baton on to one of the very young TDs like Denis Naughten or Simon Coveney, both of whom are in their late 20s. However, both men declined to put themselves forward. A straw poll at the party meeting revealed that Enda Kenny was the most likely to succeed – but there was no consensus and a contest took place.

The contenders for the leadership in the depleted party were Kenny, Richard Bruton, Phil Hogan and Gay Mitchell. Each of the candidates conducted their own campaigns with little outside assistance. The campaign was low-key and little bitterness was evident. The survivors of the election deluge were still in a state of shock, while the new TDs found it all a novelty, so there was none of the hard-nosed campaigning that is usually associated with leadership contests. When it came to the vote the result was the same as in the straw poll and Kenny was elected leader. After almost 27 years in the Dáil he took over a position few would have thought likely to come his way even a short number of years earlier. Kenny faces a huge task in attempting to rebuild morale in a shattered party and the prophets of doom have already written Fine Gael's obituary. In the past, however, the party has outlasted quite a few of its obituarists and may do so again. To survive and prosper, though, Fine Gael will need to find the courage and determination to stake out its own territory ad defend it. The party will also need a big dose of something that it has eluded it for a long time now – luck.

He got the call: Pat Rabbitte on the night of the Labour leadership count

MARK CONDREN

Labour looks to its former enemies

Pat Rabbitte's election as Labour Party leader – with Liz McManus as his deputy – completed a remarkable clean sweep by former Democratic Left TDs, writes **Stephen Collins**

It sure is: Joe Costello and Ruairí Quinn canvassing in Moore Street, Dublin, prior to the announcement of the general election   PHOTOCALL

WHEN Pat Rabbitte announced in December 2001 on Vincent Browne's radio programme that he would not serve as a minister if Labour did a coalition deal with Fianna Fáil, most of his colleagues thought he was mad. At the end of October 2002 Rabbitte was elected leader of the Labour Party precisely because he took a stand on a point of principle that had the potential to cost him dearly if things had turned out differently.

The disappointing election performance in May, which consigned Labour to another term in opposition, vindicated Rabbitte's stand. The strategy of opening the door to coalition with Fianna Fáil clearly damaged the party's credibility during the election campaign. Many people in the party came around to this view after the election but Rabbitte was the only prominent figure to say it well in advance.

His stand gave Rabbitte the perfect platform to run for the party leadership in the wake of a disappointing result.

The fact that the Labour leader was selected by the ordinary members and not the parliamentary party was greatly to his advantage.

The members were looking for a new broom after the let-down of the election and Rabbitte, as the only candidate who had taken a stand against the coalition strategy, was well-positioned from the very beginning.

A sizeable number of Labour members around the country clearly share Rabbitte's view that the party should be in the business of providing an alternative government to Fianna Fáil rather than seeking merely to prop up Fianna Fáil in a different kind of coalition. The scale of Rabbitte's victory is as clear a message as Labour TDs could be given about what the party members want.

Rabbitte has made no bones about the fact that he believes cooperation with other opposition forces, and that includes Fine Gael, is the only way the electorate can be offered a real choice at the next election. That is not to suggest that Labour should be "the mud guard" of Fine Gael or any other party, as some of its more defensive TDs are inclined to suggest. What it means is that Labour has to be seen as willing to participate in an alternative to Fianna Fáil as well as offering full-blooded opposition to it over the next couple of years.

Of course Rabbitte's election victory was not solely due to his stand before the last election. Members responded to his considerable talent, his wit and his combativeness. They clearly saw him as the best equipped of the candidates to take on Bertie Ahern in the Dáil and also to capture the role as leader of the opposition from the Fine Gael leader, Enda Kenny.

Rabbitte is one of a small number of TDs with an intellectual ability and a facility with words that give him a real cutting edge in debate. He has an ability to dominate the Dáil chamber which only a few other TDs have. Brian Cowen, Michael McDowell and John Bruton spring to mind as being in the same league, but there are few others who have it. Such ability does not necessarily mean Rabbitte will be successful, but it will certainly give him a head start.

The new leader is sometimes derided by his Labour colleagues because he is perceived as the "darling of the media". He is undoubtedly popular with the media because, as well as being the best political performer around, he is also highly accessible. He has the confidence to talk uninhibitedly to journalists as well as being prepared to appear on a variety of radio programmes.

As the votes were being counted other Labour TDs ruefully accepted that Rabbitte's mastery of the airwaves had played a critical part in his success as Labour members all over the country felt they knew him as well, if not better, than their local TD. At the count there was no disguising the deep disappointment felt by some of the old Labour TDs, not so much that Rabbitte had won the leadership but that his former Democratic Left colleague, Liz McManus, had surprisingly taken the deputy leadership. The clean sweep by the former DL, allied to the fact that Proinsias De Rossa is the party president, was a bitter pill for some TDs to swallow.

They can't escape the fact, however, that the decision was made by the party membership and not by some clique in Leinster House. As DL brought very few foot soldiers to the merger four years ago, the choice was made by a party dominated by old Labour members. That gives old Labour TDs little to complain about and it also gives Rabbitte huge authority.

How he uses that authority will be the real test of his leadership. Given the size of the parliamentary party there is a job for nearly everyone on the front bench, but the way he allocates responsibilities will be interesting.

On the wider front, Rabbitte will have a dilemma about how to position the party. Should he move to the left and try to recapture some of the working-class vote that has slipped to Sinn Féin, the Greens and the Socialist Party, or should he go after the Fine Gael middle-class voters, many of whom admire him already? Of course he would like to get support from both these segments of the electorate but he will have to take a strategic decision about which should be a priority.

If an alternative government is to be put in place after the next election then both Fine Gael and Labour need to gain seats. In the past both have very rarely risen in tandem; the pattern has been for one to gain at the expense of the other. Fine Gael has now fallen so far back that it will require a massive swing against Fianna Fáil for the two main opposition parties to gain enough seats to form a government.

The lesson of May's election, though, is that decisive swings are possible. Rabbitte's task will be to ensure that Labour is positioned to benefit most from any drop in the FF vote. If that allows him to form an alternative government, well and good, and who knows what might happen before the next election to change the political landscape again?

Liz McManus: the surprise winner of the deputy leadership PHOTOCALL

HOW THE PARTY VOTED

		Gilmore and Shortall's votes
PAT RABBITTE	1587	+541 **2128**
Brendan Howlin	1005	+306 **1311**
Eamon Gilmore	598	eliminated
Róisín Shortall	282	eliminated
Non transferable		*43*

Hard times ahead for the man that bought the election

Charlie McCreevy's failure to control public spending in the two years prior to the election  ensured that the government parties were returned – but also that they have serious problems ahead, writes **Matt Cooper**

CHARLIE McCreevy is the man who bought the Fianna Fáil/Progressive Democrats government the 2002 general election and who has left it well placed to win the next should it come in 2007 – almost irrespective of how hard the present economic downturn strikes.

McCreevy deliberately failed to control increases in public spending in the two years prior to the election, lest cutbacks impact on the electoral consciousness. He wrote two election budgets, the first in December 2000 in case the election came in 2001, and the second in December 2001, giving away money like confetti, through tax cuts and higher social welfare spending. He introduced the Special Savings and Investment Accounts scheme in 2001 as an incentive for those who could afford to save (in other words, those more likely to vote) and the government can hope to benefit from the feelgood factor of all the cash in the pockets of voters come 2007.

He accompanied all of this with a lot of posturing about how tough and reforming a minister he was, despite mounting evidence that current expenditure was running amok, storing up problems for the future and at the expense of infrastructural spending.

But, incredibly, and fortunately for the government, the opposition failed to inform the electorate of the growing problems (or convince it that it would do anything differently). Worse, it had to listen to the government talking as if the economy was still booming – despite the international downturn – and that if any major problems were to arise perchance then only it could manage to put things right.

It wasn't for the want of trying on the media's part, but the electorate simply didn't seem to want to know about the deteriorating public finances during the election campaign. It wasn't until September 2002 – and *The Sunday Tribune*'s publication of a secret government memo outlining the full extent of the cuts to this year's spending being sought by McCreevy – that the cent dropped. Too late, the government's mishandling of the economy – and the consequences that would follow – had been exposed.

So what went wrong? McCreevy's stewardship of the Department of Finance suggests that he seemed to fall for the myth that Ireland had entered a permanent virtuous cycle of positive economic growth, a "new Celtic paradigm" so to speak, as we caught up with the output levels of the rest of Europe. While it is unlikely that he ever believed that tax revenues would continue to be so strong that budget surpluses would become permanent, he miscalculated by spending too much on day-to-day public services, thereby committing the State to permanently higher costs. He also tried too hard to return the surpluses to the electorate by the way of tax cuts.

McCreevy's budgets have been "pro-cyclical", in that they have pumped more money into the economy at just the time it was booming. In other words, he did not save enough money for a rainy day. What money he decided to save was invested badly, by gambling on world stock markets through the National Pension Reserve Fund instead of on infrastructure that would have been of long term economic benefit.

All of this might have been excused had revenues continue to outpace spending. But they didn't and McCreevy can't say he didn't see it coming. The economy clearly began to slow sharply from early 2001. This meant that McCreevy's predictions for tax revenue growth in 2002 – of near enough to 9% – were heroic and it was no surprise when it failed to materialise.

It also confirmed that his decision to allow for public spend-

McCreevy: deliberately failed to control increases in public spending in the two years prior to the election

ing increases of 14.4% in total in 2002 was excessively optimistic. His only excuse can be that a public system that had become used to increases of 20% plus in spending in the previous two years probably could not slim down to a single digit increase immediately. But that only serves to illustrate how badly McCreevy lost control during that preceding period. Instead of tricking about with how to use the surpluses he could have fought harder to control current spending increases, to provide an umbrella for the rainy day.

It was always inevitable that the domestic economy would slow and enough people tried to warn him of this. Double digit growth in 2000, on top of accelerating growth in the previous five, was never sustainable. It was certain that growth would decline, either because of domestic capacity constraints or because of global slowdown, the worry being how quickly. There was no doubt Ireland, as an open economy that trades 110% of its gross domestic product, was extremely reliant on

outside events yet McCreevy continued as if we were immune.

McCreevy has been left now to explain a sizeable deficit for 2002 – projected at 750m at the time of writing, compared to a projected surplus (after accounting tricks) of 170m. He is having to prepare for a substantial deficit, possibly of up to 4bn plus, next year. Even that will be achieved only after considerable sacrifices in "adjusting" (downwards) the present level of public services.

It is now certain that he will have to borrow substantially in 2003. The government will be unable to offer tax cuts as part of the new national pay deal at a time when wage competitiveness is becoming a major issue for employers. It will also have stand firm on pay demands from the public sector unions, and may struggle to pay any of the benchmarking awards. If it gives in then tax increases may accompany higher borrowing, but the former could suck demand out of the economy at the worst possible time. He will struggle to find the extra money for the

Health, Housing, Traffic,
Health, Housing, Traffic,
Health, Housing, Traffic,
Health, Housing, Traffic,
Health, Housing, Traffic,
Health, Housing, Traffic,
Health, Housing, Traffic,

Sick Waiting?

Vote Labour

Labour

www.labour.ie

Red fly the banners: the Labour Party show their colours down the front of Liberty Hall in Dublin PHOTOCALL IRELAND

implementation of the long awaited new health strategy.

He may not be saved by a global economic recovery either. In the summer Department of Finance officials were preparing estimates for the Irish economy based on average GDP growth of 5% over the next three years. But they admitted that this "is achievable provided there are no major economic shocks and that the international economic pickup and Ireland's competitiveness are sustained". In other words this level of growth will be very difficult to achieve and many independent economists simply don't see it happening.

If it doesn't happen – and it is combined with a significant strengthening of the euro against the dollar and sterling – major competitiveness losses against the UK and US could ensue. This would add further to the pressure on public spending as well as reducing the potential growth rate in revenue from economic growth.

Department of Finance officials were preparing estimates for the Irish economy based on average GDP growth of 5% over the next three years... this level of growth will be very difficult to achieve and many independent economists simply don't see it happening

McCreevy is now talking tough but a sudden clampdown in spending after years of largesse may be both economically and politically unwise (although he seems determined to restore his hard man image). In the overall scheme of things borrowing of 750m this year compared to all the surpluses of recent years is minuscule and virtually irrelevant given the overall size of the exchequer finances. Even borrowing of up to 4bn in 2003 is affordable (and probably desirable), suggesting a debt to GNP ratio of less than 2% and a general government balance ratio of less than 0.5%.

There are problems with borrowing, however, as this country's history shows. It can become a bad habit and can result in a lot of money being wasted on unnecessary spending whereas the discipline of trying to maintain surpluses can reduce waste. What borrowed money is spent on is also an important issue. If it is on capital investments that will provide a real and measurable return then it can be justified. If it is to pay wages – that will have to be paid next year again and the year after – it is much harder to justify, especially if the number of public sector jobs is excessive and wage rates are too high.

McCreevy's solution may lie in the proposals of the ESRI's Danny McCoy. He points out that it could make sense to return to separating current and capital spending more definitively. The aim should be to achieve an excess of revenue over current spending. This surplus, and whatever borrowed money is required, can then be used to fund capital spending. The objective should be to fund all of the capital spending out of current revenues but, bearing in mind the economic life cycle, to borrow when this is not possible and to then balance this out over time. Such an approach, however, would require an "adjustment" in McCreevy's economic philosophy. It may be forced upon him.

A lot done, but lots more to do for Moriarty and Flood

One serious headache: Ray Burke arrives at the Flood tribunal, February 2001

The revelations at the tribunals did not have a major impact on the election, but they did spell the end for two senior Fianna Fáil figures, writes **Michael Clifford**

POLITICS finally felt the full brunt of the tribunals in April 2000, nearly half way through the 28th Dáil. For over a decade tribunals had threatened, but never delivered, a serious blow to politics through revelations presented under oath. The Beef tribunal was expected to uncover links between business and politics and the unhealthy way that things were done, but the report ultimately failed to point fingers.

Then the McCracken tribunal, set up to investigate payments to Charles Haughey and Michael Lowry cast a shadow over the general election looming in 1997. While the final report reprimanded Haughey, the only alleged criminality was in relation to obstructing the work of McCracken. There was 'no' linking of payments to favours, and therefore no question of bribery. The main feature of McCracken was that it spawned a son, the Moriarty tribunal, charged with a detailed examination of Haughey and Lowry's finances.

Moriarty was set up within months of the general election and around the same time as the Flood tribunal, the latter being

Liam Lawlor addresses the Dáil on a brief outing from Mountjoy

the one that threatens to break all records of longevity and cost is chaired by Justice Feargas Flood and was set up to investigate the payment of £30,000 to Ray Burke, who had held a number of ministerial portfolios, including Justice and Foreign Affairs.

Burke received the money in June 1989 from James Gogarty, an executive for Joseph Murphy Structural Engineering (JMSE), which was attempting to get lands rezoned in north County Dublin. Gogarty alleged that the money was in connection with the rezoning. Burke denied this and made a statement in the Dáil defending his record as a politician. But following mounting pressure Burke resigned not just his office but his Dáil seat in September 1997.

The Flood tribunal was set up just as the new government was getting into its stride. Pretty soon it emerged that Burke was accustomed to receiving large sums, often many times his salary, from business interests. Flood's investigations quickly extended to a payment of £35,000 Burke received in 1989 from

Oliver Barry, a director of what was then the fledgling Century Radio. The payment was made at a time when Burke was Minister for Communications and Century was attempting to have a "level playing pitch" with RTE installed in the communications sector. Yet more investigations of Burke's finances revealed that he had received a number of large payments from companies controlled by two builders, Tom Brennan and Joseph McGowan, who were at one time the largest house builders in the state.

These three modules formed the core of Flood's investigations during the course of the 28th Dáil, and bit by bit morsels of information arrived in the public domain, putting Burke in a bad light. At the far end of Dublin Castle, Moriarty was probing deeper into Haughey's financial background. That also threw up some unsavoury facts about politics and the way wealthy interests might fire money at their favourite politicians.

However, despite what many had expected, there was nothing that rocked the establishment. Haughey and Burke were yesterday's men and as far as the current crop of politicians were concerned, both were merely getting their just deserts.

Others were caught up in the emerging scandals. Former minister and EU commissioner Padraig Flynn was accused of having received £50,000 from developer Tom Gilmartin, a sum which never found its way to Fianna Fáil headquarters. Flynn said he would tell all at the tribunal and not before.

Slowly but surely, the Flood investigations began to close in on Liam Lawlor TD, a man who had flirted around the edges of controversy for most of his political life.

Up the yard at Moriarty, Fianna Fáil backbench Denis Foley TD was unmasked as an account holder in Ansbacher, the controversial accounts which were run by Haughey's late financial advisor Des Traynor. The accounts were largely utilised to stash away money undeclared to the revenue commissioners. Foley parted ways with the Fianna Fáil parliamentary party, but still the fall-out was regarded as minor. Evidence at Moriarty also revealed that Taoiseach Bertie Ahern had signed blank cheques which were subsequently used by Haughey for his own use. There were no political repercussions for what was largely seen as a lapse of judgement; it was all such a long time ago and Ireland was a different country now. So they said, anyway.

The blank cheque revelations, like a number of others, were regarded as minor in themselves. And therein lay one of the principal reasons for a lack of political impact in the tribunals. The morsels of information that fell out over a five year period were, as far as they effected the current body politic, inconsequential. However, if they had all entered the public arena at the same time the impact might well have been different.

Meanwhile, the public was growing weary of the tribunals. The vast sums of money being paid in legal fees, and the belief that nobody would be brought to book for the apparent crimes and misdemeanors that were being uncovered, led to fatigue among the public. Even elements of the media that had been supportive of the work of the Flood tribunal began to question its value. Then, Frank Dunlop walked onto the stage.

Dunlop had been a press secretary to the government at 29 and went on to enjoy a lucrative career as a public relations consultant, especially in the employ of developers. He had been a major influence in Dublin County Council in the early 1990s, acting on behalf of a number of clients looking to have land rezoned.

The tribunal had discovered an bank account through which thousands of pounds had been channelled at times that coincided with vital decisions on land rezoning and it wanted answers. Dunlop declined to give a statement to the inquiry and was invited in to give evidence in public.

As Paul Cullen wrote in *With A Little Help From My Friends*: "The tribunal chairman invited the witness to 'reflect' on his evidence overnight, and Dunlop took his advice to heart. He arrived in Dublin Castle on 19 April – Spy Wednesday – a different man. Haltingly at first, he revealed the details of payments to 15 different county councillors ranging in size from £500 to £48,500. The cash was handed over in various locations: homes, offices, Conway's pub on Parnell Street and even the Dáil bar."

Further revelations of payments were added the following week. The cat was finally out of the bag. For decades, it had been assumed that councillors were in the pay of developers because of a number of suspicious rezonings. Three garda investigations into payments had come to naught, including a probe in the late 1980s in which a superintendent characterised the council's dealings on rezoning as "a nest of vipers". Now, at

last, proof was at hand. The most vital link in the chain of bribery, the middle man, was spilling the beans.

The reaction was immediate. Fianna Fáil and Fine Gael set up inquiries into payments to politicians who were Dublin county councillors. As a result of those inquiries, Liam Lawlor resigned from the Fianna Fáil parliamentary party and Fine Gael's inquiry led to fresh controversy, with some of those named in a resulting report saying they were not afforded due process.

The issues exposed by Dunlop are scheduled for hearing in late 2002 or early 2003 and therefore did not impact on the general election in May 2002, but they did shake the political system. For the majority of politicians who never engaged in the sordid behaviour it was a confirmation of their worst suspicions. For those who had, it was the beginning of many sleepless nights.

One politician named by Dunlop had plenty of problems of

The public was growing weary of the tribunals. The vast sums of money being paid in legal fees, and the belief that nobody would be brought to book that were being uncovered, led to fatigue. Even elements of the media that had been supportive of the work of the Flood tribunal began to question its value. Then, Frank Dunlop walked onto the stage

his own, apart from the public relations consultant's confession. Liam Lawlor was not co-operating with Flood and the tribunal was growing weary of his intransigence. In December 2000, the chairman declared that he'd had enough and referred the matter to the High Court. The following month, on a cold January day, Lawlor became the first person to lose his liberty as a result of the tribunals' work. He was jailed for seven days with the remainder of a three month sentence suspended. Over the subsequent 18 months he would endure another two spells behind bars.

The interim Flood report was published in September 2002 and found that Burke had received corrupt payments from Gogarty – on behalf of JMSE, from Barry on behalf of Century and in a number of instances from Brennan and McGowan. The only serious political fall-out resulting from the findings related to Bertie Ahern's judgement in appointing Burke as Minister for Foreign Affairs in 1997, when a dark cloud was already forming above the latter's head. But a new Dáil term was just under way, so there would be no electoral fall-out.

Flood and Moriarty will continue well into the 29th Dáil, and the chances are that Flood at least will outlive the Dáil, such is the extent of the investigations which it is due to undertake. The biggest political impact from the tribunals is the reappraisal of how political parties raise money. New legislation has made the process more transparent and less open to the kind of extensive abuse that occurred in the cases of Haughey and Burke.

Thumbs up: Brian Cowen and Bertie Ahern campaigning for a Yes vote second time round

PHOTOCALL IRELAND

Nice works if you can get it

Unlike the 2001 referendum on the Nice Treaty, the second campaign was marked by real debate, a better informed electorate and, crucially, a more passionate advocacy of the case by the 'Yes' side. **Michael Marsh** analyses the 2002 Nice vote

ASKED to think again the electorate decided by 63% to 37% to endorse the Nice treaty, having rejected it in 2001 by 54% to 46%. Why the difference? The government put its failure to carry the Nice treaty at the first time of asking down to a number of things. One was the Referendum Commission, which was given insufficient time to inform the public and the counter-productive task of arguing both sides of the case. If you were not confused you were not here. On this second occasion the Commission was given more time to do less: its task was simply to get out the vote. Its key message was: 'Its no good giving out afterwards', and it provided voters with a simple and straightforward booklet explaining the meaning of the treaty.

Thus a second change was that the job of debate was not subcontracted out but given to those best equipped for it – the parties, and a number of ad-hoc citizen groups – and it must be said that they did a much better job of it. There was more passion, particularly on the 'yes' side, more real debate, more information, and this time the voters were able to identify who was putting forward a particular case. This is particularly important as voters inevitably find the details of treaties complicated. They need 'information shortcuts', and knowing something about who is arguing what case is a useful shortcut for many people. In the end it is doubtful if many knew very much about the treaty, but the majority felt they at least knew enough to make a decision this time. In 2001, very few did, and so opted to stay home, or to vote 'no'.

The third change was that an effort was made to identify the source of voter discontent. Neutrality concerns were obvious and were addressed, however imperfectly, by adding a constitutional prohibition against a common defence policy. The democratic deficit is a problem that defies any quick fix but at least 'yes' campaigners could point to a greater role for the Oireachtas in future when EU decisions are being made. The 'yes' campaign also made a much stronger effort to identify the key issue as one of enlargement, which most voters favoured, and no little use was made of visiting dignitaries from Eastern Europe to boost that case.

Finally, the effort was made to push up turnout by holding the vote on a Saturday and by employing the canvassing techniques typically employed in elections. There was a theory that the 'yes' voters, those who had carried previous EU referendums, stayed home in 2001. If they could be persuaded to vote, to convert their undoubted support for enlargement and the EU project into a 'yes', then the referendum would be carried. The government treated the referendum as they would an election campaign and even if activists on the ground were fewer than they had been in May, an organisation was put in place to carry the campaign into every constituency and district electoral division and the other pro-Nice parties provided important support.

A major fear for the 'yes' side was that people might use the vote to protest against the economic cutbacks introduced after the general election. It was clear that the popularity of the government in general, and of the Taoiseach in particular, was low and there is evidence from Ireland and elsewhere of voters using referendums to express an adverse judgement on the government rather than the substantive issue. The resignation of PJ Mara following criticism of him in the preliminary report of the Flood tribunal added to those fears. Fine Gael and Labour asked their voters to hold their fire, and it seemed to have worked.

The result was everything 'yes' campaigners could have wished for. The margin was 26%, similar to that in the Amsterdam and Maastricht treaty referendums.

It is hard to escape the conclusion that the higher turnout was the key to the result. The 'no' vote was very similar to last time in every constituency, but the 'yes' vote roughly doubled in almost every constituency. In most of those where it did not, boundary changes make comparisons difficult anyway. But in reality things are rarely quite as simple as that, and there is no coherent explanation available for why the 'yes' vote should be 'soft' and the 'no' vote 'hard'.

Still, the link between the increase in the 'yes' vote and the increase in turnout is very clear, if a long way from being perfect. There was certainly a conversion of individual voters from a 'no' to a 'yes', notably in those places where 'yes' was strong anyway, such as Dublin South and Dun Laoghaire-Rathdown. Despite a huge increase in turnout there the 'no' vote fell considerably. In other places, the increase in turnout added both 'yes' and 'no' voters: Galway East, Mayo and Longford-Roscommon

Romano Prodi congratulates Bertie Ahern after the Nice treaty was passed by 63% to 37%
PHOTOCALL IRELAND

are examples. The increased turnout was generally a little greater outside the capital. Turnout rose in Dublin by over 12%, compared with almost 15% nationally. Even so the turnout pattern was that of a referendum, not a general election: in Dublin it was close to general election levels, elsewhere it was well down.

In the end, the treaty was endorsed in all constituencies; in 2001, it had been rejected in all but two. This nationwide support should not blind us to some significant variations. As in previous votes on EU treaties, the poorer parts of Dublin, and the some of the less affluent and geographically peripheral constituencies, such as Kerry and Donegal, are at best lukewarm in their support. Polls show that an intention to vote 'yes' was significantly weaker amongst the unskilled working class than the middle class. It is also weaker amongst the younger voters, who will become more influential in such votes in future.

There are clear lessons for the future here, most obviously, for the next EU referendum. Referendums can serve a valuable purpose by encouraging citizen participation and debate, but they are a very poor way to make decisions unless this occurs.

The second is that there is now an even better case to be made to facilitate voting by holding elections at weekends. Saturday is better than Thursday, but why not Saturday and Sunday?

A third point, which is less likely to keep the establishment awake at night is the huge diversity of financial resources available to both sides. Business wanted a 'yes', and coughed up, the big parties were not hoarding scarce resources for an imminent election, and so by most counts the 'yes' side outspent the 'no' side by a huge margin. Possibly it did not matter this time, but we have started to control spending in elections. There is also a strong argument for greater controls in referendums.

	2002						**2001**				
	Turnout %	Turnout % increase from 2001	YES	% YES	NO	% NO	YES	% YES	NO	% NO	YES % increase from 2001
Carlow-Kilkenny	48.9%	14.8%	31,402	66.9%	15,546	33.1%	14,799	47.7%	16,197	52.3%	19.2%
Cavan-Monaghan	50.5%	15.9%	27,262	62.5%	16,370	37.5%	14,031	48.1%	15,145	51.9%	14.4%
Clare	47.1%	16.3%	24,839	68.4%	11,484	31.6%	11,265	48.7%	11,853	51.3%	19.7%
Cork East	50.0%	14.4%	21,960	61.9%	13,504	38.1%	10,490	43.5%	13,613	56.5%	18.4%
Cork North-Central	47.0%	13.6%	19,751	55.0%	16,146	45.0%	10,127	40.9%	14,648	59.1%	14.1%
Cork North west	55.3%	17.8%	18,552	64.2%	10,360	35.8%	8,224	45.2%	9,978	54.8%	19.0%
Cork South central	52.0%	14.8%	28,506	62.3%	17,282	37.7%	15,428	46.2%	17,952	53.8%	16.0%
Cork South west	52.6%	15.5%	16,694	62.0%	10,243	38.0%	8,725	47.3%	9,704	52.7%	14.6%
Donegal North east	39.3%	11.7%	11,647	52.5%	10,555	47.5%	5,953	39.9%	8,980	60.1%	12.6%
Donegal South west	41.8%	13.2%	12,227	55.0%	10,022	45.0%	5,879	39.6%	8,961	60.4%	15.3%
Dublin Central	40.0%	6.3%	16,460	57.2%	12,305	42.8%	8,115	40.0%	12,197	60.1%	17.3%
Dublin Mid West*	44.9%		14,716	60.4%	9,657	39.6%					
Dublin North	52.8%	15.0%	24,839	66.5%	12,532	33.5%	12,635	48.0%	13,695	52.0%	18.5%
Dublin North-Central	56.6%	13.3%	22,763	62.5%	13,676	37.5%	11,752	42.9%	15,636	57.1%	19.6%
Dublin North east	51.6%	11.8%	15,953	60.5%	10,414	39.5%	10,291	43.6%	13,338	56.5%	17.0%
Dublin North west	47.2%	8.9%	11,961	54.0%	10,176	46.0%	9,078	41.8%	12,621	58.2%	12.2%
Dublin South	56.4%	13.8%	37,096	72.4%	14,133	27.6%	20,369	51.9%	18,894	48.1%	20.5%
Dublin South central	47.0%	7.9%	21,454	54.3%	18,048	45.7%	11,199	44.2%	14,141	55.8%	10.1%
Dublin South east	51.5%	11.8%	19,720	67.7%	9,407	32.3%	11,327	49.3%	11,650	50.7%	18.4%
Dublin South west	46.6%	14.7%	17,820	56.9%	13,516	43.1%	9,856	38.4%	15,797	61.6%	18.5%
Dublin West	49.7%	15.3%	15,935	62.1%	9,724	37.9%	11,708	44.7%	14,856	55.9%	17.4%
Dun Laoghaire	56.6%	13.8%	36,695	73.3%	13,375	26.7%	19,654	53.6%	17,030	46.4%	19.7%
Galway East	47.5%	17.9%	22,177	63.5%	11,986	36.5%	9,009	47.3%	10,034	52.7%	16.2%
Galway West	45.2%	15.7%	21,649	60.5%	14,146	39.5%	10,100	42.0%	13,951	58.0%	18.5%
Kerry North	46.3%	13.5%	13,887	55.6%	11,097	44.4%	6,786	39.4%	10,426	60.6%	16.2%
Kerry South	50.1%	18.1%	14,958	60.5%	9,766	39.5%	6,924	44.9%	8,486	55.1%	15.6%
Kildare North	50.5%	16.0%	19,868	68.6%	9,080	31.4%	9,923	49.3%	10,196	50.7%	19.3%
Kildare South	46.4%	14.1%	17,123	66.0%	8,808	34.0%	7,771	47.7%	8,513	52.3%	18.3%
Laois-Offaly	49.2%	17.0%	30,120	65.7%	15,742	34.3%	13,950	48.6%	14,736	51.4%	17.1%
Limerick East	49.3%	14.8%	23,876	61.5%	14,921	38.5%	12,720	46.6%	14,593	53.4%	15.0%
Limerick West	50.2%	15.4%	16,581	63.1%	9,701	36.9%	8,246	49.3%	8,476	50.7%	13.8%
Longford-Roscommon	50.9%	18.9%	21,549	62.1%	13,153	37.9%	9,988	47.3%	11,128	52.7%	14.8%
Louth	47.7%	13.7%	22,739	59.5%	15,513	40.6%	12,203	46.6%	13,972	53.4%	12.8%
Mayo	46.1%	16.0%	24,647	58.5%	17,510	41.5%	11,799	44.3%	14,865	55.8%	14.2%
Meath	46.7%	14.1%	32,712	65.3%	17,374	34.7%	15,712	48.0%	17,005	52.0%	17.3%
Sligo-Leitrim	49.3%	14.1%	20,981	63.2%	12,214	36.8%	10,303	44.9%	12,671	55.2%	18.4%
Tipperary North	51.3%	17.3%	19,705	67.5%	9,484	32.5%	9,260	49.4%	9,472	50.6%	18.1%
Tipperary South	51.5%	14.5%	18,167	65.4%	9,602	34.6%	9,410	48.6%	9,965	51.4%	16.9%
Waterford	50.5%	16.5%	23,291	63.7%	13,297	36.3%	11,919	48.2%	12,795	51.8%	15.5%
Westmeath	48.4%	16.8%	16,235	63.7%	9,249	36.3%	7,233	45.1%	8,814	54.9%	18.6%
Wexford	48.8%	15.4%	28,065	62.4%	16,937	37.6%	14,461	48.7%	15,220	51.3%	13.6%
Wicklow	53.9%	15.6%	29,710	63.8%	16,832	36.2%	14,839	46.2%	17,274	53.8%	17.6%
TOTAL	**49.5%**	**14.7%**	**906,292**	**62.9%**	**534,887**	**37.1%**	**453,461**	**46.1%**	**529,478**	**53.9%**	**16.8%**

* New constituency made up of parts of Dublin West and South West

Nice II: what the vote meant

Brigid Laffan, who advocated a 'Yes' vote, analyses why that campaign was successful and the lessons it holds for the future of Europe

Brigid Laffan: motivated by a number of factors   PHOTOCALL IRELAND

W HAT follows should be read as the views of an analyst turned advocate for the duration of the second campaign on the Nice Treaty. In opting to play an active campaigning role in Nice II and help to establish a civil society alliance, I was motivated by a number of factors.

First, Ireland's 30 years of EU membership was on balance very positive from an economic, political and public policy perspective. Ireland was perceived as a constructive small state that was broadly *communautaire* in its policies and practices while protecting its core preferences and ensuring that it had headroom for domestic policy. Moreover, Ireland has benefited from very high per capita transfers from the EU budget from 1973 onwards. A failure to ratify Nice, a treaty designed to accommodate enlargement, would undermine Ireland's position in the EU and would lose her goodwill and allies in negotiations. Second, the states of central Europe were looking to Ireland to endorse the treaty that would enable them to conclude their enlargement negotiations. Third, I found that many of the assertions of the 'no' campaign could not be supported by evidence. The language being deployed to characterise the EU was in many instances borrowed from the Tory right. Fourth, Nice I was characterised by a very weak campaign on the 'yes' side. The Government ran a lacklustre campaign that failed to engage or persuade the electorate. The low turnout (34%) and the energy of the 'no' campaign led to the defeat of the Treaty. For all of the above reasons, a coalition of the willing came together to actively campaign for Nice II.

The 'yes' campaign launched for Nice II bore no resemblance to Nice I. The context had changed following the deliberations of the Forum on Europe, new instruments of parliamentary scrutiny, and the Seville Declaration on neutrality. Moreover, it was clear by September 2002 that this would be a big bang enlargement involving up to ten states. The second time around, the Government parties knew what was at stake and devoted the necessary human and material resources to ensuring that they mobilised their voters. This was a major challenge given the unpopularity of the Government because of the deteriorating public finances and the revelations of the Flood Tribunal. The main opposition parties, particularly Fine Gael with John Bruton as director of elections, campaigned actively. Pat Cox, President of the European Parliament, did a country-wide tour with his specially branded bus. The bus was shared with the Irish Alliance for Europe during its five-week tour. Preparatory research for the campaign suggested that the holding of a second referendum was not a major issue for the majority of the electorate. It was felt that on an issue of such importance, it was legitimate to go back to the people. In addition, there appeared to be a deeply rooted support for Ireland's engagement with the EU among the population. The challenge for the 'yes' campaign was thus to be visible, to take on the arguments of the 'no' campaign in a robust manner and to mobilise those who stayed at home the last time around. This they managed to do with a significant increase in turnout and in the 'yes' vote.

There are lessons from the two Nice referenda for the Convention on the Future of Europe. Output or performance legitimacy cannot on its own secure the legitimacy of a political system. There must be greater opportunity for the active participation of citizens in the politics of integration. Without the opportunity to engage politically, EU citizenship will rest on rights rather than on a shared polity.

Labour Youth and TD Jan O'Sullivan presented a giant Valentine's Day card to the Taoiseach, highlighting the dangers they said were inherent in the referendum proposal

PHOTOCALL IRELAND

Liberal triumph in abortion referendum

There was less than 1% in it, so the failure of the forces of conservatism to bring out their troops probably proved decisive to its rejection at the polls, writes **Michael Marsh**

THIS referendum was a case of déja vu all over again. It was in many respects like a re-run of the vote on divorce in 1996. One again the 'liberal' side was successful; once again it was a few thousand votes that tipped the balance; and once again it was the higher turnout where there were more 'liberal' voters that appears to have been decisive.

The overall vote margin was less than 1%, with 49.6% voting 'yes' and 50.4% voting 'no'. Voters in Dublin constituencies tended to vote 'no' by almost the same margin as they voted 'yes' in 1996: 63% to 47%. There were also 'no' majorities in other more urban areas: Wicklow, Waterford, Limerick East, Kildare, and

Cork North and South Central, with Waterford matching the national breakdown almost perfectly. Elsewhere the vote was 'yes', with the Donegal constituencies, where more than two out of every three voted 'yes', having the largest majorities.

Turnout tended to be higher where the majority voted 'no'. There turnout averaged 46%; elsewhere, only 40%. As in 1996, this difference in turnout appears to have been crucial. Of course it may be that 'no' voters were more motivated to vote, and so where there are more 'yes' voters turnout is higher.

Alternatively, it may simply be that where both 'yes' and 'no' voters were more likely to vote, it was the 'yes' side that gained more advantage.

The pattern of higher turnout in urban areas, notably in Dublin, is in line with previous referendums on all sorts of issues. As in the last divorce referendum, the weather could be blamed for the low turnout in the west, but again, the lower turnout there is not unusual. Certainly where there were majorities against the amendment in western areas, such as Galway and Cork, turnout was not higher than in neighbouring constituencies.

It is striking that the overall pattern of voting is so strongly in line with previous behaviour in 'moral issue' referendums. The pattern of voting on abortion and divorce in the 1980s, and on divorce in 1996 shows almost exactly the same profile of 'liberal' and 'conservative' constituencies, although in the 1980s the size of the respective camps were different.

This vote is almost a mirror image in 1996, and the size of the liberal and conservative camps almost identical. The people of County Westmeath, for instance, voted 'no' to divorce by 58% to 42% and 'yes' to this amendment by the same margin.

Many constituencies were within 1% or 2% of their 1996 vote. Only in Donegal was there a marked difference: in Donegal North East the 'yes' vote was more than 10% above the 'no' vote in 1996.

The consistency of this pattern suggests that this vote was very much between those who did want to restrict abortion and those who did not. The arguments of the more fundamentalist conservatives, led by Dana Rosemary Scallon, that this amendment was too liberal, does not seem to have found much of an echo.

This is in contrast to the previous referendum on the right to life in 1992, when the amendment was defeated by an alliance of fundamentalists and liberals. Voting patterns in that contest are quite unlike those in any other referendum on abortion or divorce.

This time, however, things ran true to form. That said, of course, since the final margin was so small the failure of the conservative side to marshal all their troops may have proved decisive.

The major difference between this vote and that on divorce is the turnout, down by a third in 2002.

Whether or not confusion contributed to the low turnout is another matter. Possibly some who 'did not know' came out to vote 'no' in consequence.

The level of confusion in the last polls published was remarkably high. While polls have occasionally suggested that the public think a referendum was the way to deal with the issue, such polls do not tap how strongly people felt about the matter, one way or another.

Few have ever indicated that abortion is a major election issue. For most people abortion is best left to the courts and the legislators.

Chairperson Niamh Nic Mhathúna of the Mother and Child campaign at a press conference in Buswell's Hotel PHOTOCALL IRELAND

THE ABORTION REFERENDUM: HOW IRELAND VOTED

	TURNOUT	YES VOTES	YES %	NO VOTES	NO %
Carlow-Kilkenny	42.8%	22,623	55.9%	17,887	44.2%
Cavan-Monaghan	40.4%	23,171	66.0%	11,956	34.0%
Clare	39.1%	17,498	57.8%	12,780	42.2%
Cork East	43.0%	16,897	56.0%	13,281	44.0%
Cork North west	45.5%	14,175	61.8%	8,749	38.2%
Cork South west	41.6%	11,527	53.7%	9,931	46.3%
Cork North central	41.6%	15,624	49.5%	15,943	50.5%
Cork South central	47.2%	19,979	45.8%	23,611	54.2%
Donegal North east	33.4%	13,394	70.6%	5,580	29.4%
Donegal South west	33.8%	12,084	66.8%	6,001	33.2%
Dublin Central	39.4%	10,178	41.0%	14,634	59.0%
Dublin North central	52.2%	14,070	42.0%	19,473	58.1%
Dublin North east	50.0%	10,763	35.9%	19,259	64.2%
Dublin North west	45.6%	11,064	42.0%	15,286	58.0%
Dublin South central	46.8%	12,241	39.6%	18,662	60.4%
Dublin South east	48.1%	9,414	32.5%	19,558	67.5%
Dublin North	49.5%	12,877	36.1%	22,829	63.9%
Dublin South	52.9%	17,451	35.1%	32,339	65.0%
Dublin South west	41.8%	12,369	36.1%	21,933	63.9%
Dublin West	45.4%	13,285	36.3%	23,344	63.7%
Dun Laoghaire	52.9%	14,653	31.8%	31,476	68.2%
Galway East	37.9%	16,170	63.2%	9,424	36.8%
Galway West	38.3%	15,996	49.8%	16,101	50.2%
Kerry North	36.9%	11,439	57.3%	8,537	42.7%
Kerry South	38.7%	11,392	59.5%	7,759	40.5%
Kildare North	43.8%	11,446	42.6%	15,415	57.4%
Kildare South	39.1%	10,110	49.4%	10,375	50.7%
Laois-Offaly	40.4%	23,207	61.4%	14,618	38.7%
Limerick East	42.4%	16,485	48.0%	17,890	52.0%
Limerick West	42.2%	12,543	58.8%	8,786	41.2%
Longford-Roscommon	39.0%	17,093	63.9%	9,650	36.1%
Louth	41.9%	17,025	50.3%	16,799	49.7%
Mayo	35.0%	19,797	61.6%	12,334	38.4%
Meath	40.7%	22,698	51.9%	21,012	48.1%
Sligo-Leitrim	38.4%	15,429	59.3%	10,602	40.7%
Tipperary North	41.7%	15,197	63.7%	8,647	36.3%
Tipperary South	41.6%	13,099	58.1%	9,459	41.9%
Waterford	44.2%	15,874	49.4%	16,285	50.6%
Westmeath	38.5%	11,888	58.3%	8,497	41.7%
Wexford	40.8%	19,487	51.6%	18,295	48.4%
Wicklow	47.0%	16,788	41.1%	24,032	58.9%
TOTAL	**42.7%**	**618,485**	**49.6%**	**629,041**	**50.4%**

But PJ won't be doing it: Bertie Ahern with the subsequently displaced Fianna Fáil backroom boy PJ Mara

PHOTOCALL IRELAND

FF defy the numbers to reclaim power

Michael Laver looks at the numbers and the trends of Election 2002, and spots an odd paradox

THE MOST peculiar thing about the 2002 election is how Fianna Fáil was able to get back into government with an even stronger position than before, despite the fact that fewer people voted FF than in almost any election for a very long time. This paradox came about because the election was not so much won by Fianna Fáil but lost by its traditional opponents. What is more, this "no change" election result masks what may turn out to be some very significant developments in the Irish party system.

To see 2002 in perspective we need to take ourselves back to the Haughey-Fitzgerald era, now looking very much like the last hurrah of traditional Civil War politics in Ireland. Back in the early eighties, Charlie Haughey lost elections and spent a long

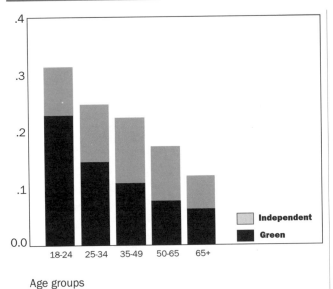

Figure 1: Age and voting for non-establishment parties

Age groups

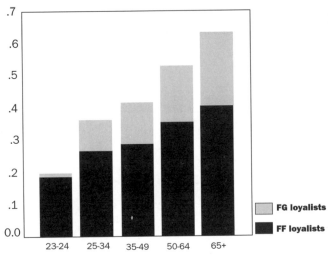

Figure 2: Age and loyalty to Civil War parties

Age groups

spell in opposition having won over 45% of the vote. Bertie Ahern won the 2002 election and gained an impregnable position in government on the basis of less than 42% of the popular vote.

This change has happened for two reasons. The first is that opposition to Fianna Fáil has become fragmented, rather than bundled together into support for Fine Gael, FF's old Civil War enemy. The second is that the "proportional" Irish electoral system, with its three-, four- and five-seat constituencies, deals unkindly with such a fragmented opposition.

To understand Irish party politics in the wake of the 2002 election, therefore, we need to understand how and why opposition to Fianna Fáil has fragmented. And we need to understand what this means for the way votes are translated into seats by the Irish version of the STV electoral system.

THE FRAGMENTING IRISH PARTY SYSTEM

Back in 1982, during those famous head-to-head contests between Charles Haughey and Garret FitzGerald, Fianna Fáil and Fine Gael between them won about 85% of the vote. If we add Labour to the mix as another party that was around at the time of the Civil War, the Big Three establishment parties won about 94% of the popular vote in 1982 – "others" won a mere 6% How different things were in 2002, when the combined FF-FG vote share was down to 64% and the total vote for the Big Three parties was less than 75% for the first time ever. In just 20 years, the proportion of Irish electors voting against the FF-FG-Labour pantheon had quadrupled.

The most obvious sign of this fragmentation is rapidly growing support for both the Greens and Sinn Féin. The RTE exit poll tells us a lot about the types of voters who turned their backs on the political establishment and voted for one of these two parties.

The most striking pattern has to do with age. Figure 1 shows the proportions of various age groups who supported either the Greens or Sinn Féin, on the one hand, or independent candidates, on the other. The age profile of Green/Sinn Féin support is particularly striking. Young voters were much more likely to vote for non-establishment parties than older voters, while it was middle-aged voters – in the 35-49 age-bracket – who were most likely to support independents.

The other side of this same coin can be seen in Figure 2, which shows the proportions of various age groups who remained loyal to Fianna Fáil or Fine Gael in both the 1997 and 2002 elections. (People who were too young to have voted in 1997 have been excluded.) Loyalty to the Civil War parties rises very rapidly with age – a pattern that is even more marked for Fine Gael than for Fianna Fáil. Really quite small numbers of younger voters voted for either Fianna Fáil or Fine Gael in two consecutive elections, a pattern that certainly opens the gate for much more fundamental change in the future.

Whether or not these patterns imply the beginning of the end of Irish politics as we know it depends upon whether these younger voters are sowing their wild oats before returning in middle age to become loyal supporters of the traditional political establishment, or are instead forming longer-term party attachments. If they're sowing their wild oats then there is a huge prize at stake as the traditional parties fight for the longer-term allegiance of the aging debutantes. If they are forming firm political attachments, then we can expect much more change in the future as this new voting generation begins to wash through the electorate while the older supporters of the

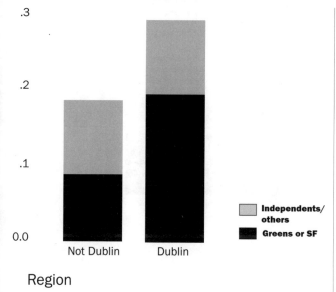

Figure 3: Dublin voters and non-establishment parties

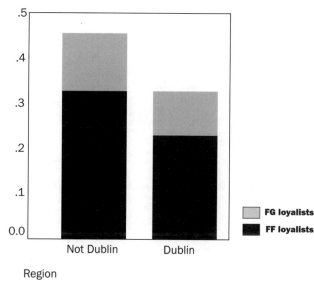

Figure 4: Dublin voters and loyalty to Civil War parties

traditional parties relentlessly die off. Either way, the patterns shown in Figure 1 imply at least the potential for considerable change in the future. The greatest challenge for the Greens and Sinn Féin is to find ways to hang on to their current crop of youthful supporters.

But age isn't the only thing that was strongly associated in 2002 with support for parties outside the traditional establishment. Figure 3 contrasts support for non-establishment parties in the greater Dublin area with that in all other parts of the country. The pattern is again quite striking. Dublin voters were very much more likely than voters elsewhere to support the Greens or Sinn Fein, though they were no more likely to support independents.

Once more the pattern for loyalty to the Civil War parties is the mirror image of this, as Figure 4 shows. The proportions of voters who supported either FF or FG in both 1997 and 2002 are much less in Dublin – a pattern that is again striking for Fine Gael.

What is significant here for long-term change is of course that it is the greater Dublin area that is growing, while the traditional heartlands of old-party loyalty are not. This implies that the trend should be towards an ever-larger group of voters less bound by traditional loyalties and more open to supporting new parties.

Finally in this context, we can see a striking contrast between the old and the new Ireland if we look at the relationship between church attendance and voting in 2002. The RTE exit poll asked people about the frequency of their church attendance and Figure 5 shows that voting for non-establishment parties was much more likely among people who went to church little or not at all. (There was no strong pattern among those voting for independents.)

Figure 6 shows that church attendance was also very strongly associated with loyalty to the traditional parties. Those who go to church once a week or more often were much more likely to remain loyal to one of the two Civil War parties for two consecutive elections – a pattern that was once again stronger for Fine Gael than for Fianna Fáil.

What all of this shows is that the 2002 election threw up a remarkable contrast between what we might think of as the "old" and the "new" Ireland. If the old Ireland in this sense is epitomised by elderly people living outside Dublin and going to church regularly, the new Ireland reflects young people living in Dublin and going to church rarely or never. New Ireland was much, much less likely to have voted loyally for a Civil War party in both 1997 and 2002 and much, much more likely to have voted for a non-establishment party such as the Greens or Sinn Fein. Loyal support for both FF and FG, and particularly for FG, seems to be much more deeply rooted in old Ireland. Demographically, of course, old Ireland is inexorably shrinking while new Ireland is growing vigorously. The most intriguing feature of these patterns the 2002 election results is thus that they may give us a glimpse into the future of Irish party politics.

INDEPENDENTS

The RTE poll gives us much less of an idea about whether the growing level of support for independent candidates is something that will continue to increase in the future. There are no strange or unusual patterns in the type of people giving their support to independent candidates – who of course, from Jackie Healy-Rae to Tony Gregory, themselves come in many different flavours. All types of voter – except perhaps the very oldest – seem open to voting for independents, whose first preferences

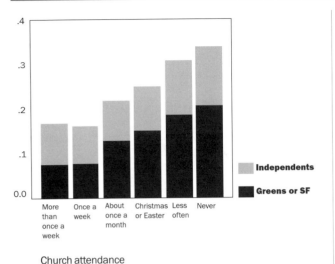

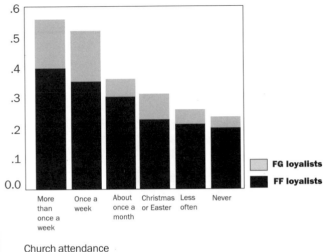

Figure 5: Church attendance and voting for non-establishment parties

Figure 6: Church attendance and loyalty to Civil War parties

are being drawn from all political parties.

There is no doubt that, holding the balance of power between 1997 and 2002 independent TDs and their little lists of demands enjoyed a great run for their money. On top of this, campaigners have now discovered that a hardworking independent candidate, win or lose, can do a huge amount to raise the profile of a local issue. Not least every independent candidate gets free postage to every voter in the constituency, courtesy of the state, to promote whatever cause they might choose. And at least local publicity is more or less guaranteed. These are hardly lessons that will be unlearned, even though coalition arithmetic means that independent TDs are in a much weaker position in the current Dáil.

If the phenomenon of independent candidates does not go away therefore, and there is no reason to suppose that it will, the main impact will be on what happens after the election when a government is being formed. At the polling booth, independents seem equally likely to damage nearly all political parties – though there is no evidence at all of voters deserting Sinn Féin for independents. After the votes have been counted, however, successful independents simply subtract from the seats available to build a government majority. The arithmetic of the 2002 result, as it happens, meant that this was not an issue and the outgoing government was easily able to sweep back into power. However, it is easy to imagine election results after which having a large number of independents could make it really difficult to form a stable government in Ireland. It is for this reason, as much as anything else, that increased levels of support for independent candidates should be of interest and concern to everyone.

AND SO?

We must of course wait and see whether the voting patterns

that showed up in 2002 will grow into something new in Irish politics. Certainly there is a group of middle class voters in Ireland who have proved very fickle in the past, switching support from Garret the Good's Fine Gael in the early eighties, to Dessie O'Malley's PDs in the late eighties and then to Dick Spring's Labour Party in the early nineties.

Two things may be different this time. The explosion of a youthful greater Dublin area, and of the new Ireland that this epitomises even in other parts of the country, has been a relentless social and economic phenomenon.

It is one that we should certainly expect to have an impact on the political system.

The early evidence is that this new group of voters is indeed thinking and behaving differently. Particularly striking is that, unlike previous middle class flirtations with novelty and change, what we are seeing now is a much more socially inclusive phenomenon.

This can be seen in the simultaneous rise of both the Greens and Sinn Féin. The RTE exit polls tells us that, while the group of "protest" voters spans all social classes, middle class voters turning their backs on the establishment are much more likely to vote for the Green Party, working class voters for Sinn Féin. For the first time, therefore, the combination of the Greens and Sinn Féin offers a full-service political menu for people of all social backgrounds who are fed up with the political parties of old Ireland.

In five years' time well will have a much better idea of whether all this is simply a flash in the pan.

But, and political scientists hate making public predictions that can easily be proved wrong by events, I have a strong feeling that what we are seeing is the beginning, not the end, of something new.

Sinn Féin President Gerry Adams and artist Tadhg McGrath take a look at his piece 'Mapping the Coastline' after Sinn Fein's General Election 2002 Manifesto launch at Chief O'Neill's Hotel in Dublin

PHOTOCALL IRELAND!

Percentage of party supporters who first mentioned issue

	FF	FG	LAB	PD	GP	SF	IND	TOTAL
Health services	14.5	16.8	19.4	4.5	8.2	12.3	24.6	15.6
Crime/law & order	13.2	14.7	12.3	14.5	7.5	12.3	10.5	12.8
Managing the economy	13.6	4.3	6.5	18.2	6.2	4.8	3.3	9.0
Honesty/integrity of politicians	3.8	15.2	9.6	9.1	15.1	7.9	9.4	8.4
Cost of living/inflation	6.8	6.4	4.5	5.5	4.8	6.6	5.1	6.1
Specific local issue	4.8	4.1	3.5	6.4	1.4	4.4	11.2	5.0
Preferred Taoiseach	6.0	2.5	0.5	0.9			0.4	3.1
Environment/pollution	0.9	0.9	1.5	0.9	34.9	2.6	2.9	3.0
Housing/house prices	1.7	1.5	5.3		2.1	5.3	3.3	2.5
Drugs	2.0	2.1	1.3	2.7	0.7	7.5	1.1	2.2
Taxation	2.0	0.5	1.5	7.3		2.2	1.1	1.7
Northern Ireland	0.5		0.3		0.7	8.8	0.7	0.9

Source: RTE/Lansdowne exit poll

THE CONTRIBUTORS

Michael Marsh is Associate Professor of Political Science at Trinity College Dublin. He has written extensively on Irish electoral politics in newspapers, books and academic journals, co-edited *How Ireland Voted 1997* (1999) and *How Ireland Voted 2002* to be published in 2003 by Palgrave. He is currently co-directing the first academic survey of voting behaviour in an Irish election.

Michael Clifford is a *Sunday Tribune* journalist who has reported on the workings of the tribunals for several years.

Shane Coleman is political correspondent of *The Sunday Tribune.*

Stephen Collins is political editor of *The Sunday Tribune* and the author of several books on Irish politics including *The Power Game: Ireland under Fianna Fáil* (Dublin, 2001); *The Cosgrave Legacy* (Dublin, 1996) and *Spring and the Labour Story* (Dublin, 1993).

Matt Cooper was editor of *The Sunday Tribune* from September 1996 to November 2002, and is a frequent contributor to current affairs programmes on radio and television.

Michael Laver is Professor of Political Science at Trinity College Dublin and the author of more than a dozen books on politics including most recently *Making and Breaking Governments* (1996), *Private Desires, Political Actions* (1997) and *Playing Politics: The Nightmare Continues* (1997) and has edited several others including *How Ireland Voted 1987* (1988) and *How Ireland Voted 1992* (1993).

Bridgid Laffan is Jean Monnet Professor of European Politics at University College Dublin and Director of the Dublin European Institute, UCD She is the author of many books about the politics of the European Union including *Integration and co-operation in Europe* (1992); *The finances of the European Union* (Macmillan, 1997) and *Europe's experimental union: rethinking integration* (1999). She edited *Constitution-building in the European Union* (Institute of European Affairs, 1996) and played a leading role in the second Nice referendum campaign.

Joe Lee is director of Glucksman Ireland House at New York University and was a regular *Sunday Tribune* columnist from 1996 to 2002. His books include the best-selling *Ireland 1912-1985: Politics and Society* (1989); *The Age of de Valera* (1984); *Ireland, 1945-70* (1979) and *The Shifting Balance of Power – Exploring the 20th Century* (The Sunday Tribune, 2000).